50,000,000 PEARLS FANS
CAN'T BE WRONG

823

Other *Pearls Before Swine* Collections

The Saturday Evening Pearls
Macho Macho Animals
The Sopratos
Da Brudderhood of Zeeba Zeeba Eata
The Ratvolution Will Not Be Televised
Nighthogs
This Little Piggy Stayed Home
BLTs Taste So Darn Good

Treasuries

Pearls Sells Out
The Crass Menagerie
Lions and Tigers and Crocs, Oh My!
Sgt. Piggy's Lonely Hearts Club Comic

Gift Book

Da Crockydile Book o' Frendsheep

50,000,000 PEARLS FANS CAN'T BE WRONG

A *Pearls Before Swine* Collection

by Stephan Pastis

Andrews McMeel
Publishing, LLC
Kansas City • Sydney • London

Pearls Before Swine is distributed internationally by United Feature Syndicate.

50,000,000 Pearls Fans Can't Be Wrong copyright © 2010 by Stephan Pastis. All rights reserved. Printed in the United States of America. No part of this book may be used or reproduced in any manner whatsoever without written permission except in the case of reprints in the context of reviews. For information, write Andrews McMeel Publishing, LLC, an Andrews McMeel Universal company, 1130 Walnut Street, Kansas City, Missouri 64106.

10 11 12 13 14 RR2 10 9 8 7 6 5 4 3 2 1

ISBN-13: 978-0-7407-9141-3
ISBN-10: 0-7407-9141-9

Library of Congress Control Number: 2009939467

www.andrewsmcmeel.com

Pearls Before Swine can be viewed on the Internet at
www.comics.com/pearls_before_swine

These strips appeared in newspapers from February 17, 2008, to November 16, 2008.

─── **ATTENTION: SCHOOLS AND BUSINESSES** ───

Andrews McMeel books are available at quantity discounts with bulk purchase for educational, business, or sales promotional use. For information, please write to: Special Sales Department, Andrews McMeel Publishing, LLC, 1130 Walnut Street, Kansas City, Missouri 64106.

INTRODUCTION

I do not like to leave my bedroom.

I do not like to leave my bedroom because all the bad things that happen in my life seem to happen after I leave that bedroom. For one thing, people are on the other side of that door. People who want things. People who talk. People who block entire grocery aisles with their shopping carts.

I see nothing wrong with staying in that bedroom. The world would be a lot better place if everybody stayed in their bedroom.

Mind you, it's not the bedroom I sleep in. It's a spare bedroom downstairs. It's got my drawing desk and my computer and my books. If I could just drag the toilet and refrigerator in there, I could hermetically seal the door.

So it's for reasons I can't explain that I accepted an invitation last September to go on a USO tour of military hospitals.

For those who don't know, USO stands for United Service Organizations. They're a nonprofit organization whose mission is, in their words, to "support the troops by providing morale, welfare and recreation-type services to our men and women in uniform." Most people know the USO from the big shows that Bob Hope used to put together for them.

Nowadays, they still put together shows for the troops that include all sorts of big-name entertainers, from Bruce Willis to Kid Rock. Plus, they seem to have a lot of hot women, from Scarlett Johansson to the Dallas Cowboys Cheerleaders.

Oh, and then there are the cartoonists. I don't want to rip my entire profession by saying we're about ten rungs below rock stars and cheerleaders on the desirability scale, but let me just say this: If I were a soldier who had just had Scarlett Johansson sitting on my bed, and I saw a middle-aged, balding fat guy coming to draw funny pictures for me, I'd call security.

And yet somehow that didn't happen.

What did happen was Chris Frost.

I met Chris at the Walter Reed Army Medical Center in Washington, D.C.

We, the middle-aged-balding-fat-guys-come-to-draw-funny-pictures, were informally lined up to enter the gym where the injured soldiers do their rehab.

I was the last guy to enter the room.

As I did, I heard the other cartoonists talking to a soldier in a wheelchair by the door. And all I heard the soldier say was, "I'm just waiting for the creator of my favorite strip, *Pearls Before Swine.*"

I was surprised. The soldiers we had met that day all seemed to be very into their PlayStations or iPods. Very few were fans of the comics. And even fewer had heard of *Pearls*.

So I wanted to meet this guy who either couldn't afford an iPod or simply had too much time on his hands.

Chris was a Weapons Intelligence Team Leader in Iraq. His job was to go to sites where there had been an explosion of an improvised explosive device (or IED, as they are more commonly known) and do a post-blast investigation. Sometimes he would arrive there before the explosive had detonated. In short, not a job for which people clamor.

On May 18, 2008, during a trip to do an investigation in Samarra (seventy-five miles north of Baghdad), Chris's truck hit an IED. Chris lost his right leg below the knee and had severe injuries to his left. The others in his truck were less fortunate.

If you're like I was and have never visited soldiers in a military hospital, you feel a little awkward at first. At least I did. Should you talk about the injury? Not talk about the injury? Talk about the war? Not talk about the war?

Chris put all that to rest.

"I found an IED the easy way," he explained. "I ran over it."

Bye-bye, awkwardness.

For the next half-hour or so, Chris and I talked about everything. The war. Where he was from. His job before the war. His injury. And all his surgeries (forty and counting).

It was like we had been friends for years.

We also talked a lot about the strip. We talked about past *Pearls* books (Chris had a couple on his lap). We talked about the next *Pearls* book that had not yet been released (Chris already knew the title). We talked about some past *Pearls* strips (he could quote them).

I have been lucky enough to hear some kind words from *Pearls* readers before, but never did they mean so much.

Yet the thing that stands out the most for me from that day was the look on Chris's face.

He was always smiling.

Here I was, a guy whose day can be ruined by a dry cleaner who creases the collar of his shirt (probably ticked that very day because the hotel I was staying in only had powdered cream and not the liquid kind for my coffee). And here was Chris—one leg missing and another that didn't work—and he was the one doing the smiling.

That is the strange and wonderful thing about visiting the soldiers in those hospitals. In theory, you're the one who's supposed to be giving *them* something. And yet it's they who do the giving.

They teach you to stop complaining. They teach you to appreciate the ease with which you go through your day. They teach you to appreciate your home. They teach you what it means to have your health.

And they teach you a lot about courage.

An odd thing, courage. Often mistaken for something loud and brash, big and bold. Something that looks like Rambo and shouts like John Wayne.

But that's not my definition.

My definition of courage is smiling after sleeping four months in a hospital. It's enduring forty surgeries and wanting to discuss a comic strip. It's a man whose job it is to help locate buried mines saying after losing his leg to one of those mines: "I found an IED the easy way."

My definition is Chris.

Glad I left my bedroom.

Stephan Pastis
March 2010

For Chris Frost

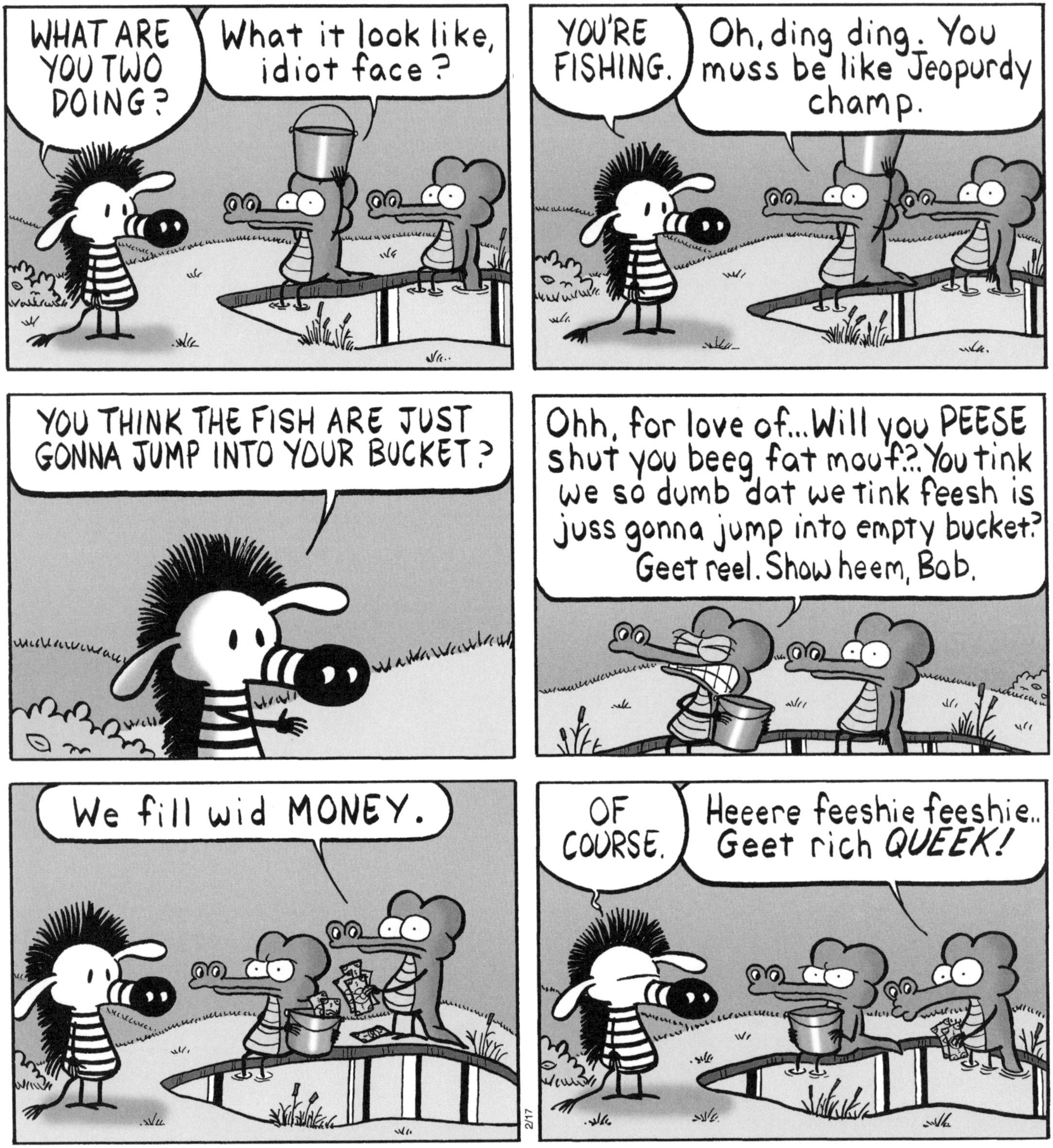
WHAT ARE YOU TWO DOING?
What it look like, idiot face?
YOU'RE FISHING.
Oh, ding ding. You muss be like Jeopurdy champ.
YOU THINK THE FISH ARE JUST GONNA JUMP INTO YOUR BUCKET?
Ohh, for love of... Will you PEESE shut you beeg fat mouf?? You tink we so dumb dat we tink feesh is juss gonna jump into empty bucket? Geet reel. Show heem, Bob.
We fill wid MONEY.
2/17
OF COURSE.
Heeere feeshie feeshie.. Geet rich QUEEK!

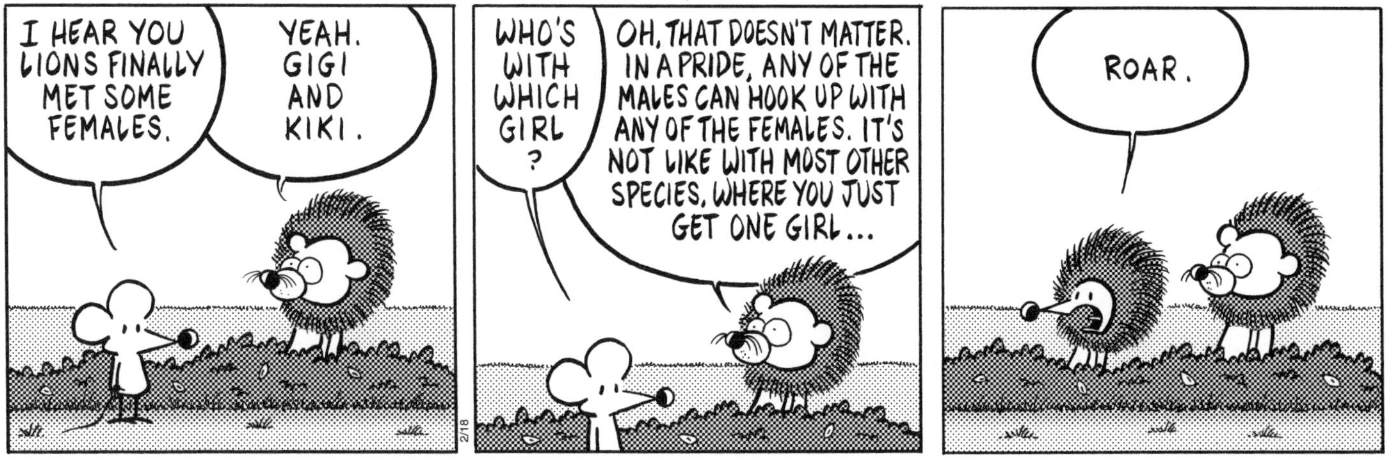
I HEAR YOU LIONS FINALLY MET SOME FEMALES.
YEAH. GIGI AND KIKI.
2/18
WHO'S WITH WHICH GIRL?
OH, THAT DOESN'T MATTER. IN A PRIDE, ANY OF THE MALES CAN HOOK UP WITH ANY OF THE FEMALES. IT'S NOT LIKE WITH MOST OTHER SPECIES, WHERE YOU JUST GET ONE GIRL...
ROAR.

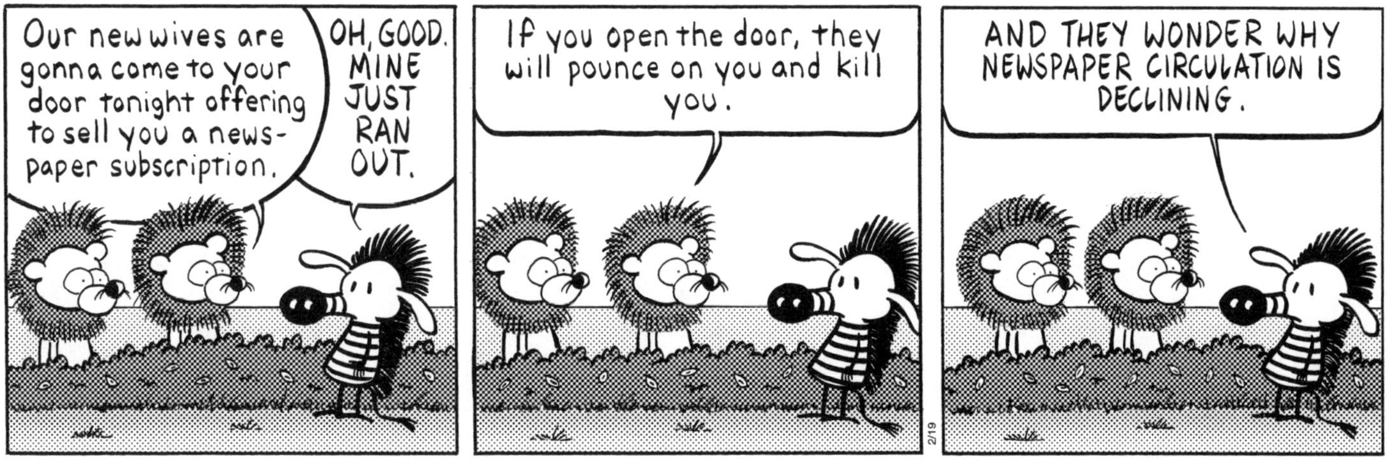
Our new wives are gonna come to your door tonight offering to sell you a news-paper subscription.
OH, GOOD. MINE JUST RAN OUT.
If you open the door, they will pounce on you and kill you.
2/19
AND THEY WONDER WHY NEWSPAPER CIRCULATION IS DECLINING.

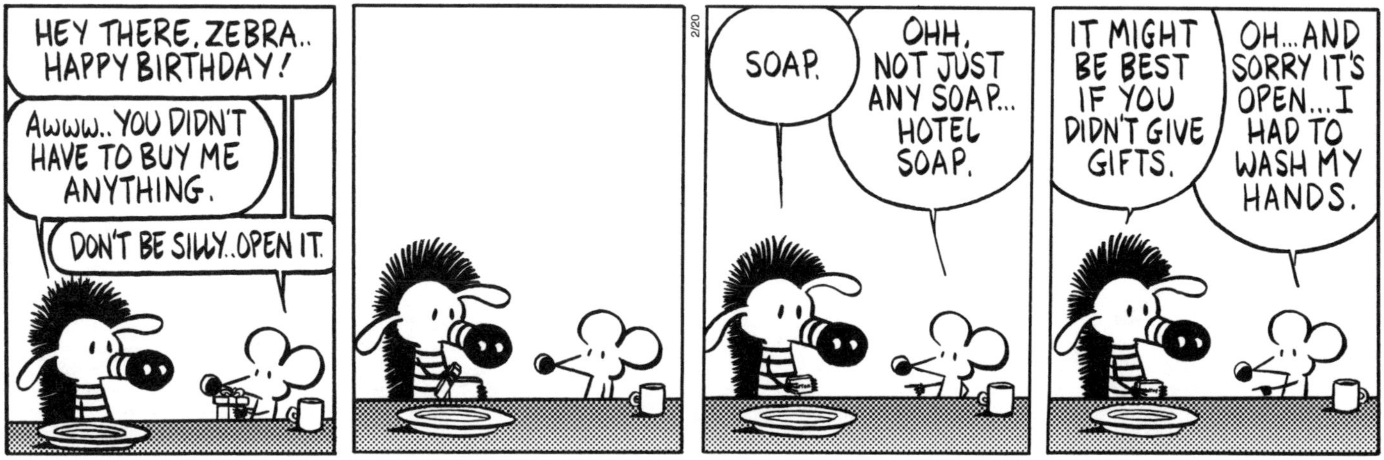
HEY THERE, ZEBRA.. HAPPY BIRTHDAY!
Awww.. YOU DIDN'T HAVE TO BUY ME ANYTHING.
DON'T BE SILLY.. OPEN IT.
2/20
SOAP.
OHH, NOT JUST ANY SOAP... HOTEL SOAP.
IT MIGHT BE BEST IF YOU DIDN'T GIVE GIFTS.
OH... AND SORRY IT'S OPEN... I HAD TO WASH MY HANDS.

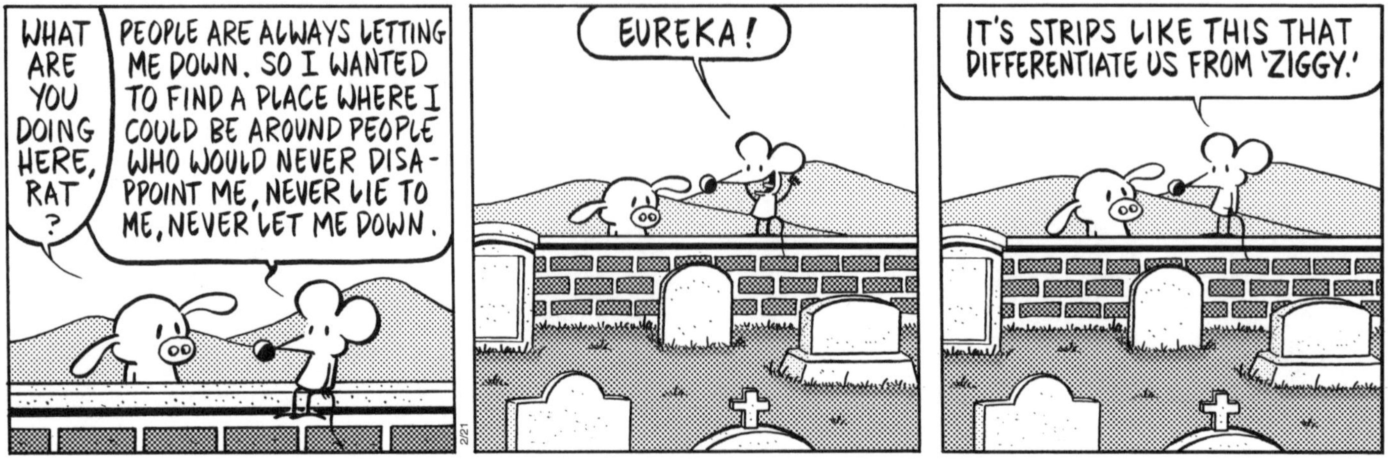
WHAT ARE YOU DOING HERE, RAT?
PEOPLE ARE ALWAYS LETTING ME DOWN. SO I WANTED TO FIND A PLACE WHERE I COULD BE AROUND PEOPLE WHO WOULD NEVER DISAPPOINT ME, NEVER LIE TO ME, NEVER LET ME DOWN.
2/21
EUREKA!
IT'S STRIPS LIKE THIS THAT DIFFERENTIATE US FROM 'ZIGGY.'

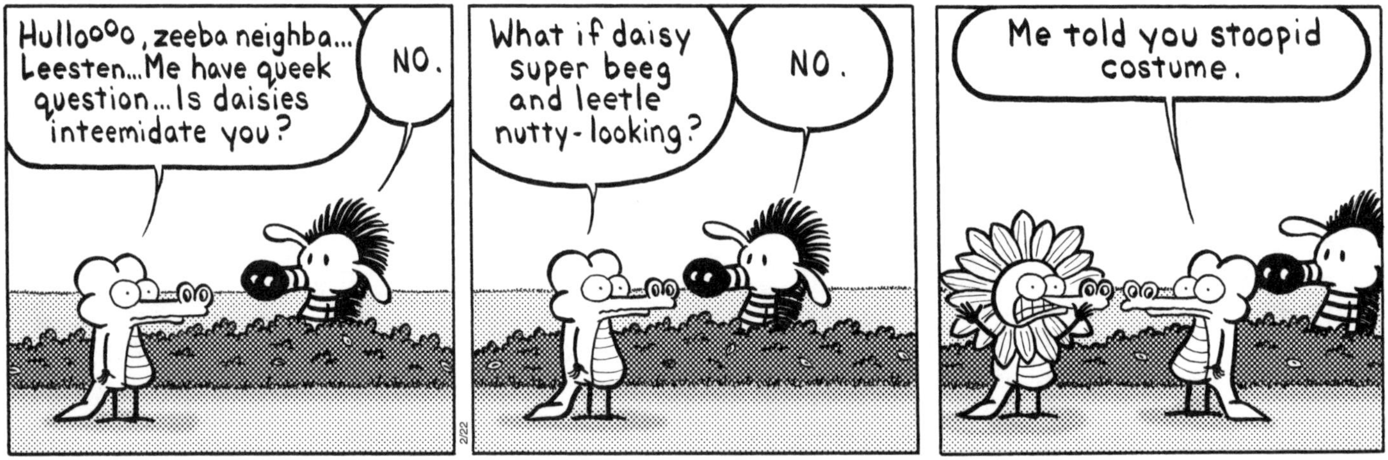
Hulloooo, zeeba neighba... Leesten...Me have queek question...Is daisies inteemidate you?
NO.
2/22
What if daisy super beeg and leetle nutty-looking?
NO.
Me told you stoopid costume.

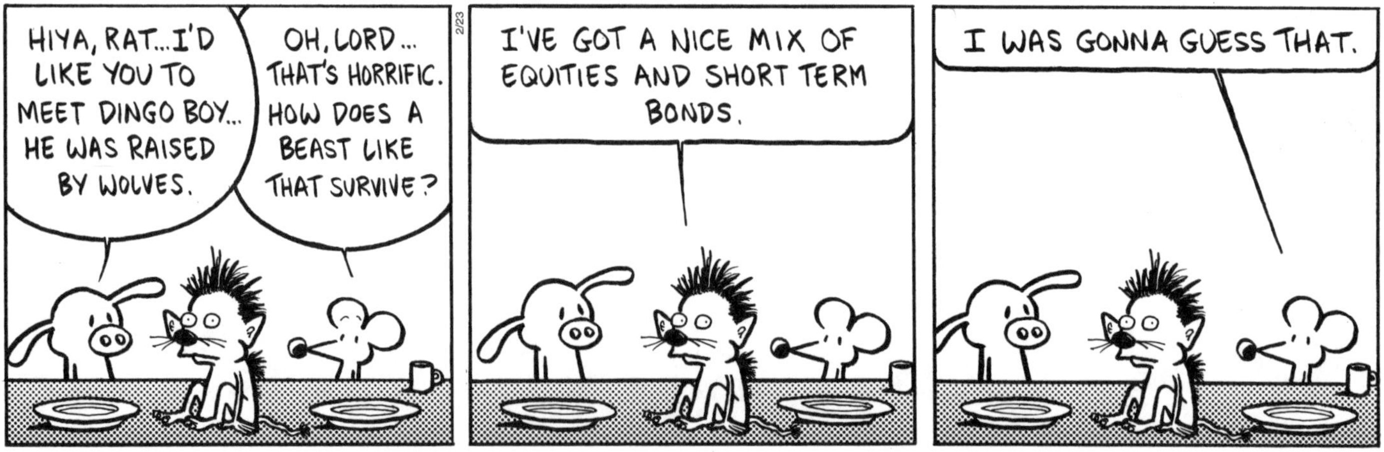
HIYA, RAT...I'D LIKE YOU TO MEET DINGO BOY... HE WAS RAISED BY WOLVES.
OH, LORD... THAT'S HORRIFIC. HOW DOES A BEAST LIKE THAT SURVIVE?
2/23
I'VE GOT A NICE MIX OF EQUITIES AND SHORT TERM BONDS.
I WAS GONNA GUESS THAT.

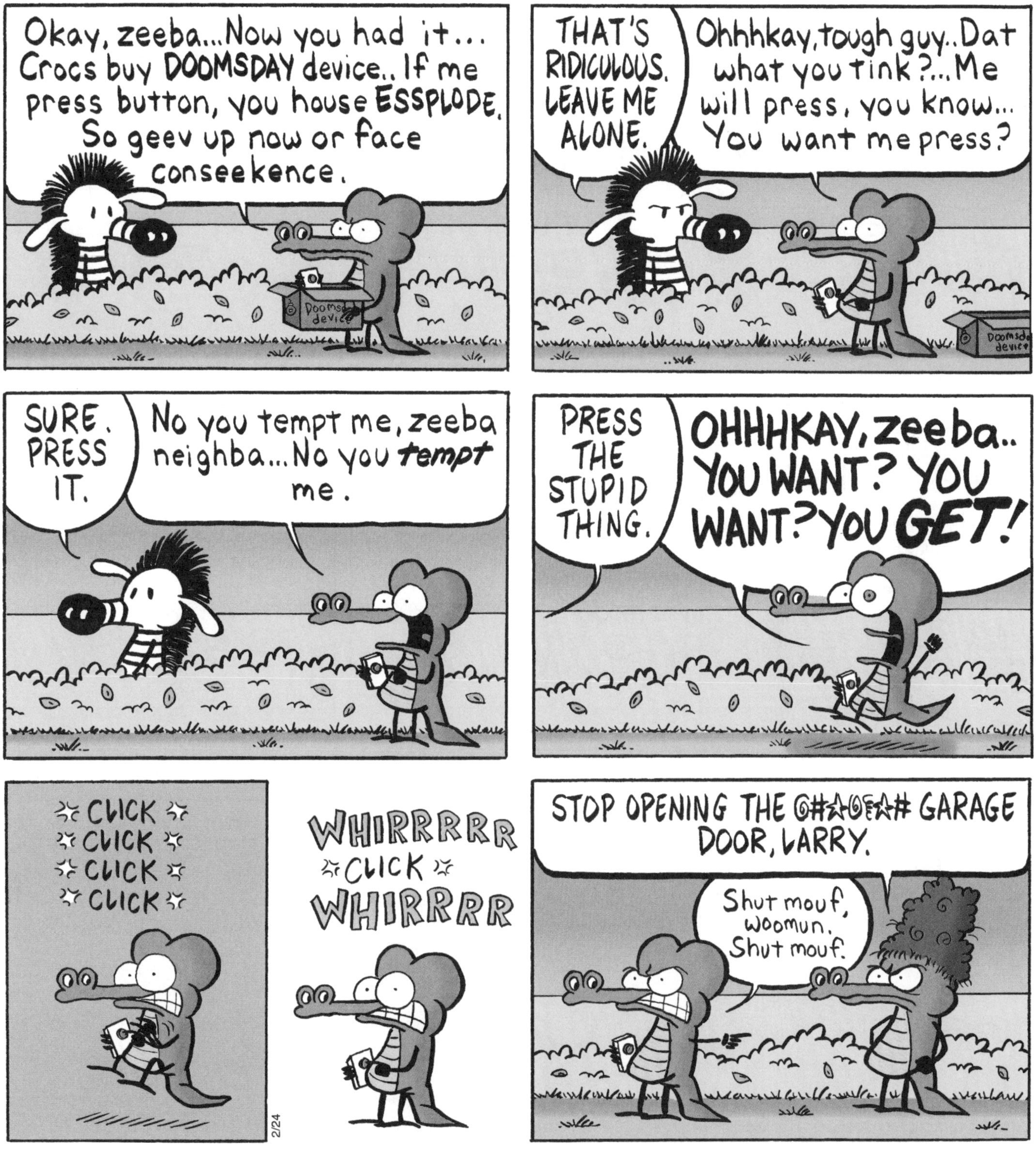

Okay, zeeba...Now you had it... Crocs buy DOOMSDAY device.. If me press button, you house ESSPLODE. So geev up now or face conseekence.
THAT'S RIDICULOUS. LEAVE ME ALONE.
Ohhhkay, tough guy..Dat what you tink?...Me will press, you know... You want me press?
SURE. PRESS IT.
No you tempt me, zeeba neighba...No you *tempt* me.
PRESS THE STUPID THING.
OHHHKAY, zeeba.. YOU WANT? YOU WANT? YOU GET!
CLICK CLICK CLICK CLICK
2/24
WHIRRRRR CLICK WHIRRRR
STOP OPENING THE @#☆@☆# GARAGE DOOR, LARRY.
Shut mouf, woomun. Shut mouf.

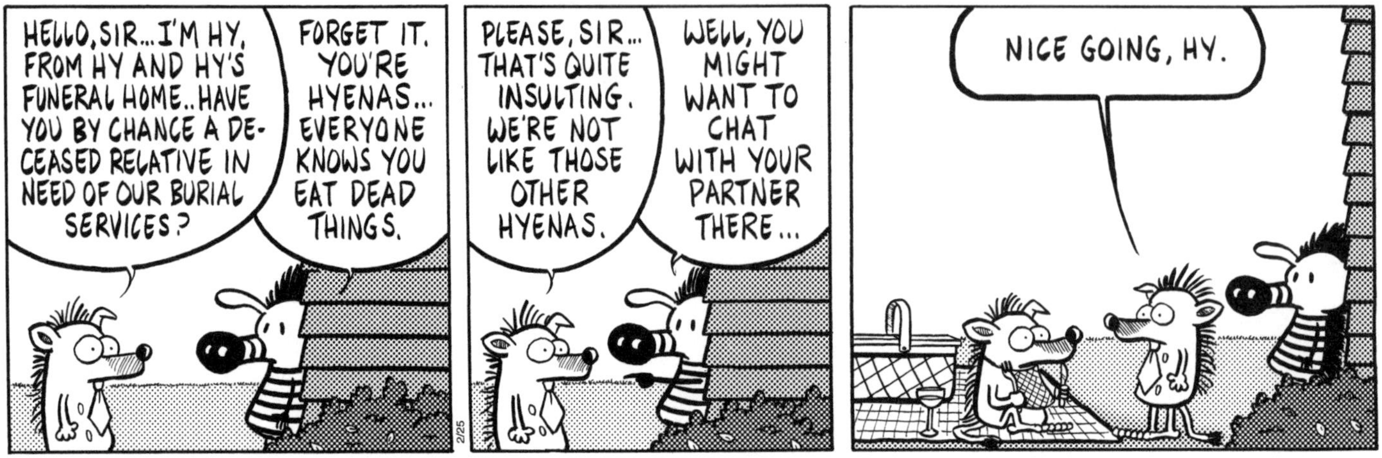
HELLO, SIR... I'M HY, FROM HY AND HY'S FUNERAL HOME.. HAVE YOU BY CHANCE A DECEASED RELATIVE IN NEED OF OUR BURIAL SERVICES?
FORGET IT. YOU'RE HYENAS... EVERYONE KNOWS YOU EAT DEAD THINGS.
PLEASE, SIR... THAT'S QUITE INSULTING. WE'RE NOT LIKE THOSE OTHER HYENAS.
WELL, YOU MIGHT WANT TO CHAT WITH YOUR PARTNER THERE...
2/25
NICE GOING, HY.

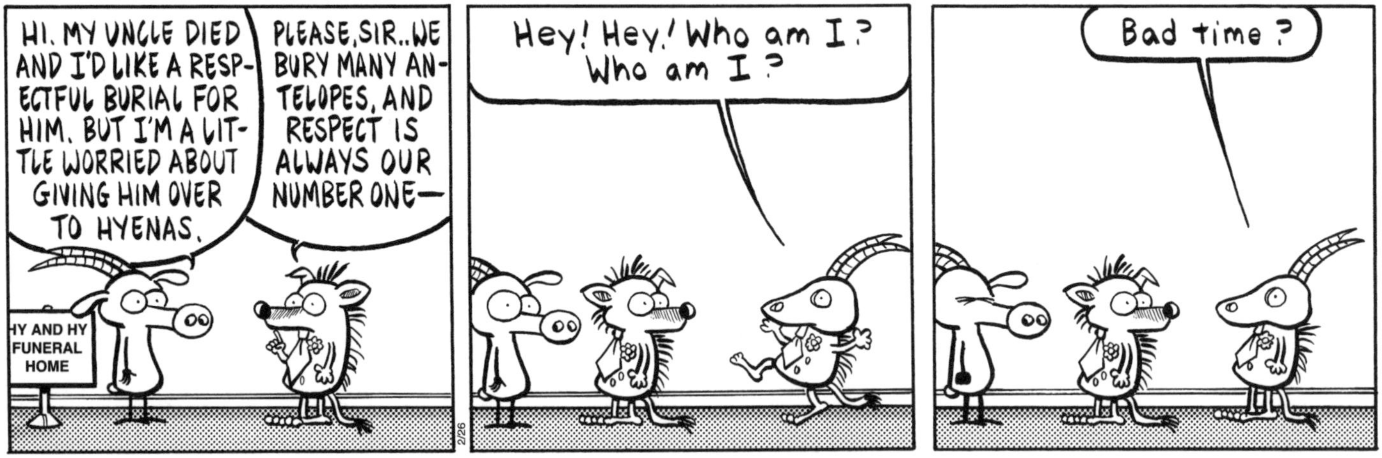
HI. MY UNCLE DIED AND I'D LIKE A RESPECTFUL BURIAL FOR HIM. BUT I'M A LITTLE WORRIED ABOUT GIVING HIM OVER TO HYENAS.
PLEASE, SIR.. WE BURY MANY ANTELOPES, AND RESPECT IS ALWAYS OUR NUMBER ONE—
HY AND HY FUNERAL HOME
2/26
Hey! Hey! Who am I? Who am I?
Bad time?

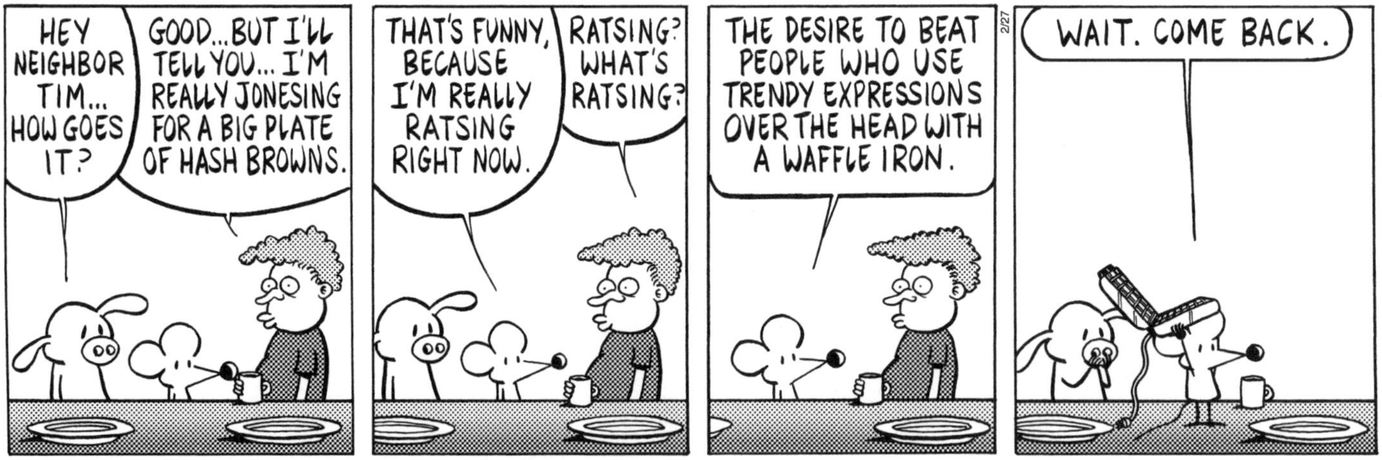
HEY NEIGHBOR TIM... HOW GOES IT?
GOOD... BUT I'LL TELL YOU... I'M REALLY JONESING FOR A BIG PLATE OF HASH BROWNS.
THAT'S FUNNY, BECAUSE I'M REALLY RATSING RIGHT NOW.
RATSING? WHAT'S RATSING?
THE DESIRE TO BEAT PEOPLE WHO USE TRENDY EXPRESSIONS OVER THE HEAD WITH A WAFFLE IRON.
2/27
WAIT. COME BACK.

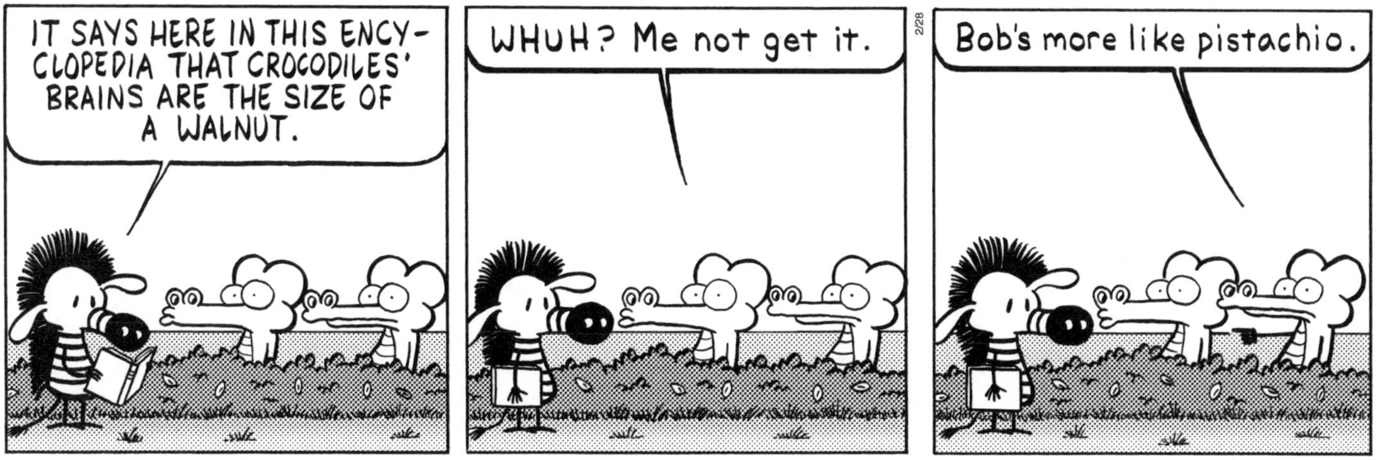
IT SAYS HERE IN THIS ENCYCLOPEDIA THAT CROCODILES' BRAINS ARE THE SIZE OF A WALNUT.
WHUH? Me not get it.
2/28
Bob's more like pistachio.

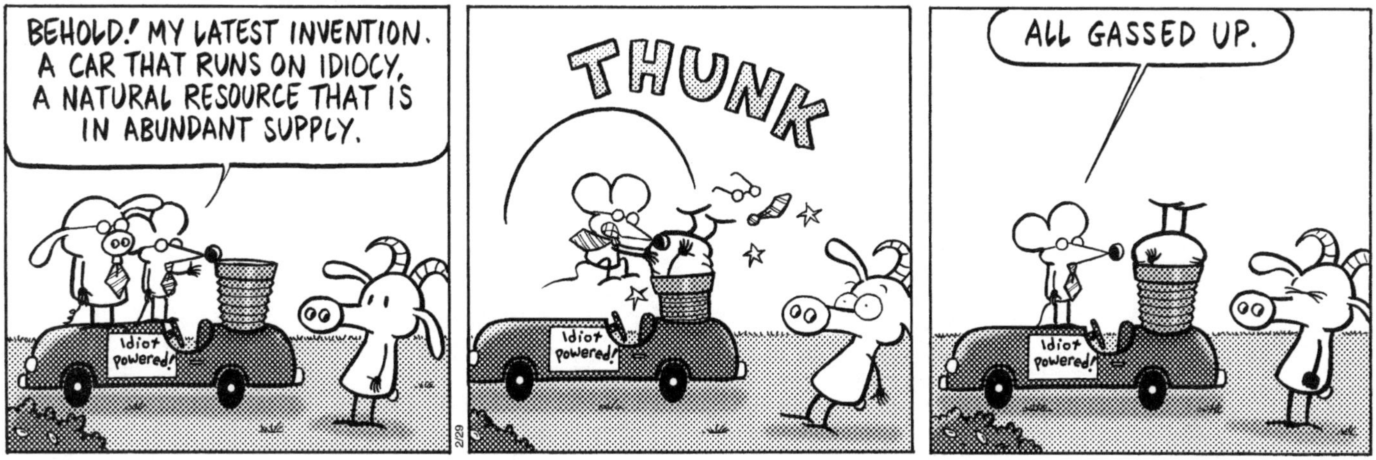
BEHOLD! MY LATEST INVENTION. A CAR THAT RUNS ON IDIOCY, A NATURAL RESOURCE THAT IS IN ABUNDANT SUPPLY.
Idiot powered!
2/29
THUNK
ALL GASSED UP.

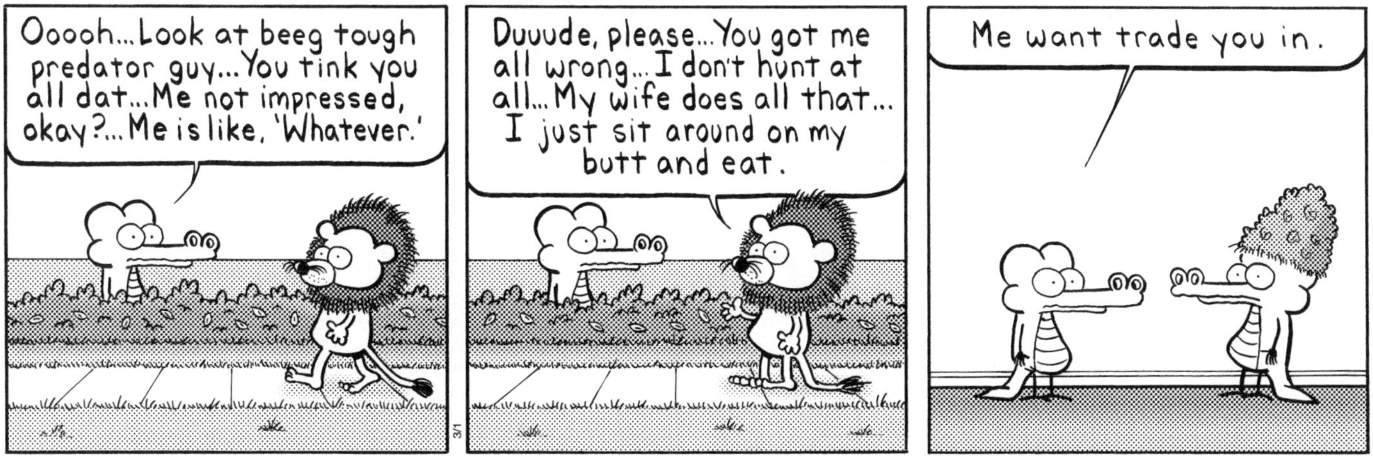
Ooooh...Look at beeg tough predator guy...You tink you all dat...Me not impressed, okay?...Me is like, 'Whatever.'
3/1
Duuude, please...You got me all wrong...I don't hunt at all...My wife does all that... I just sit around on my butt and eat.
Me want trade you in.

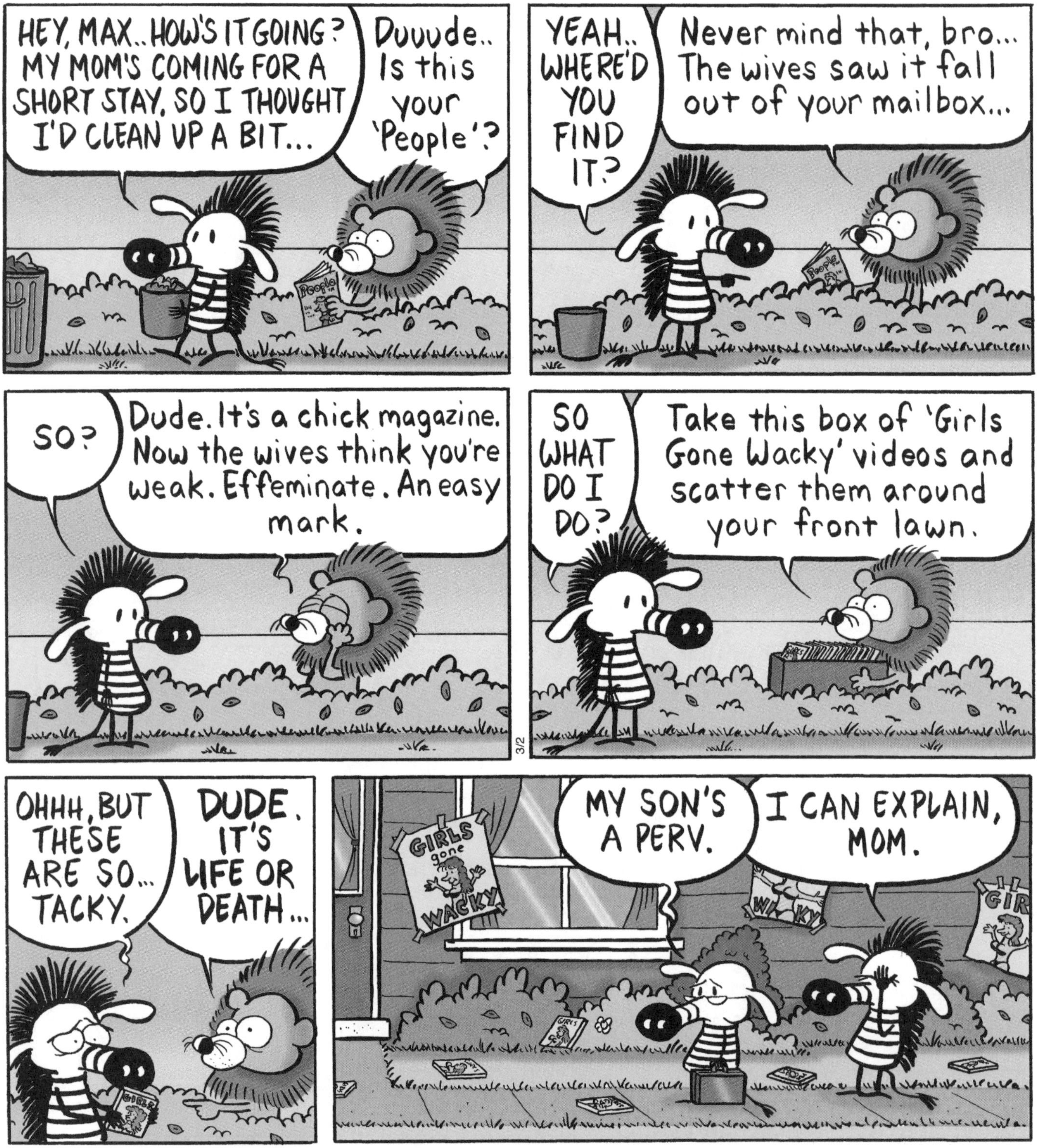
HEY, MAX.. HOW'S IT GOING? MY MOM'S COMING FOR A SHORT STAY, SO I THOUGHT I'D CLEAN UP A BIT...
Duuude.. Is this your 'People'?
People
YEAH.. WHERE'D YOU FIND IT?
Never mind that, bro... The wives saw it fall out of your mailbox...
SO?
Dude. It's a chick magazine. Now the wives think you're weak. Effeminate. An easy mark.
SO WHAT DO I DO?
Take this box of 'Girls Gone Wacky' videos and scatter them around your front lawn.
3/2
OHHH, BUT THESE ARE SO... TACKY.
DUDE. IT'S LIFE OR DEATH...
GIRLS gone WACKY
MY SON'S A PERV.
I CAN EXPLAIN, MOM.

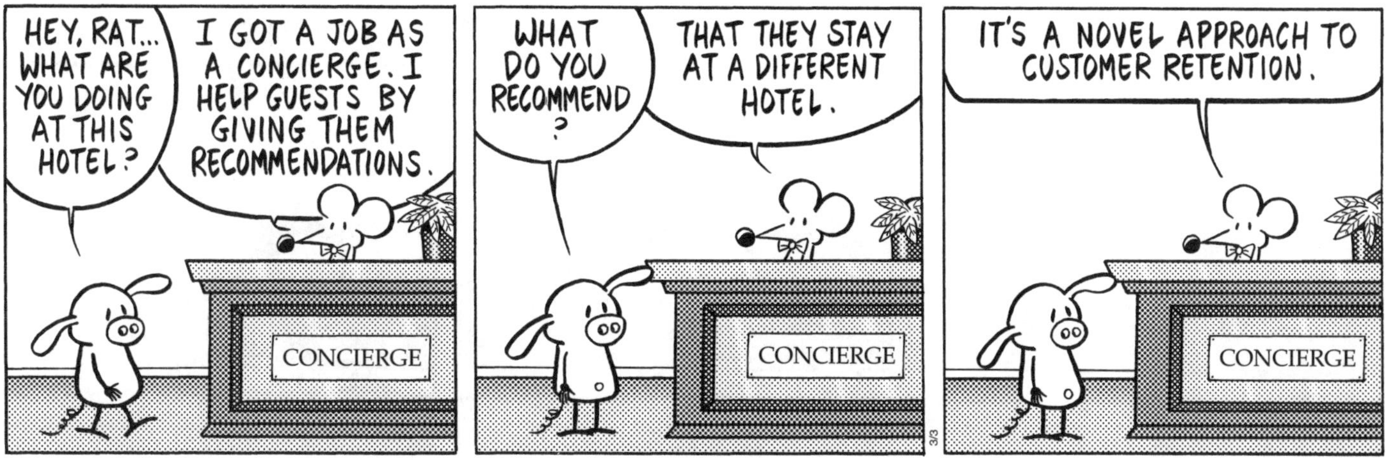
HEY, RAT... WHAT ARE YOU DOING AT THIS HOTEL?
I GOT A JOB AS A CONCIERGE. I HELP GUESTS BY GIVING THEM RECOMMENDATIONS.
CONCIERGE
WHAT DO YOU RECOMMEND?
THAT THEY STAY AT A DIFFERENT HOTEL.
CONCIERGE
3/3
IT'S A NOVEL APPROACH TO CUSTOMER RETENTION.
CONCIERGE

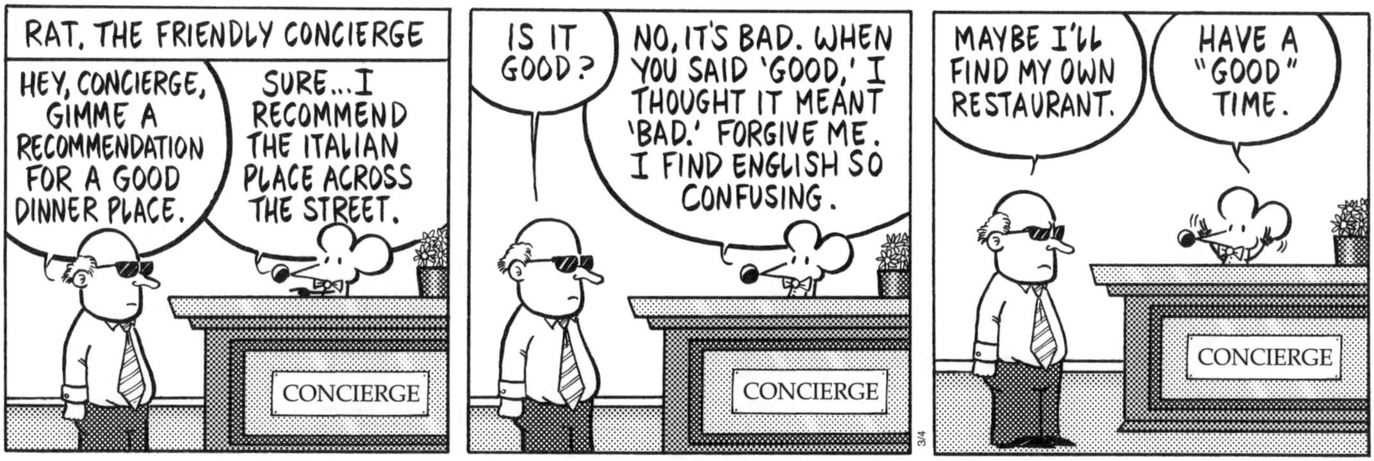
RAT, THE FRIENDLY CONCIERGE
HEY, CONCIERGE, GIMME A RECOMMENDATION FOR A GOOD DINNER PLACE.
SURE...I RECOMMEND THE ITALIAN PLACE ACROSS THE STREET.
CONCIERGE
IS IT GOOD?
NO, IT'S BAD. WHEN YOU SAID 'GOOD,' I THOUGHT IT MEANT 'BAD.' FORGIVE ME. I FIND ENGLISH SO CONFUSING.
CONCIERGE
3/4
MAYBE I'LL FIND MY OWN RESTAURANT.
HAVE A "GOOD" TIME.
CONCIERGE

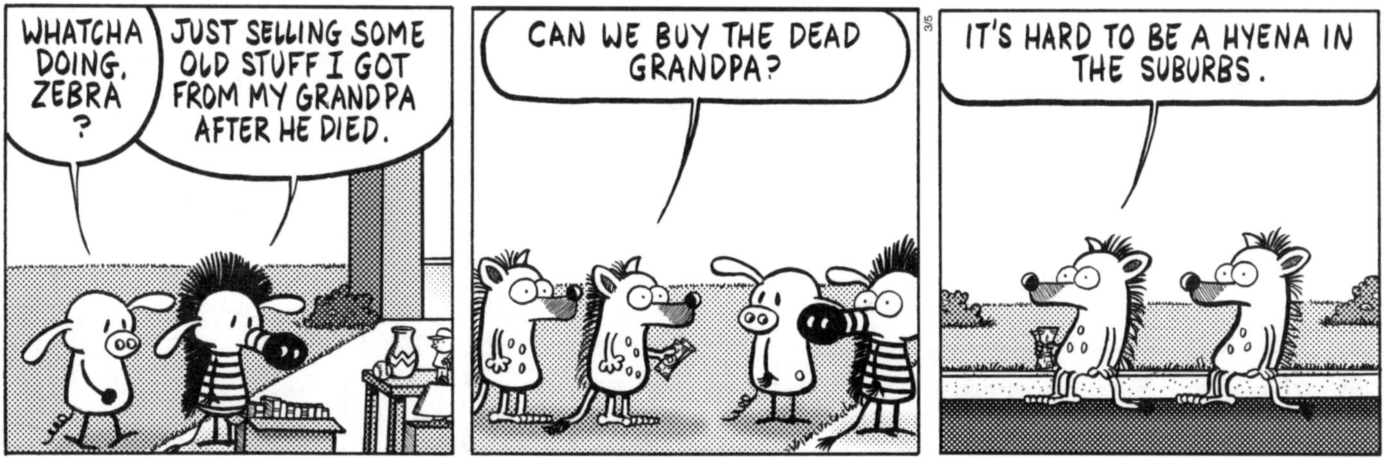
WHATCHA DOING, ZEBRA?
JUST SELLING SOME OLD STUFF I GOT FROM MY GRANDPA AFTER HE DIED.
3/5
CAN WE BUY THE DEAD GRANDPA?
IT'S HARD TO BE A HYENA IN THE SUBURBS.

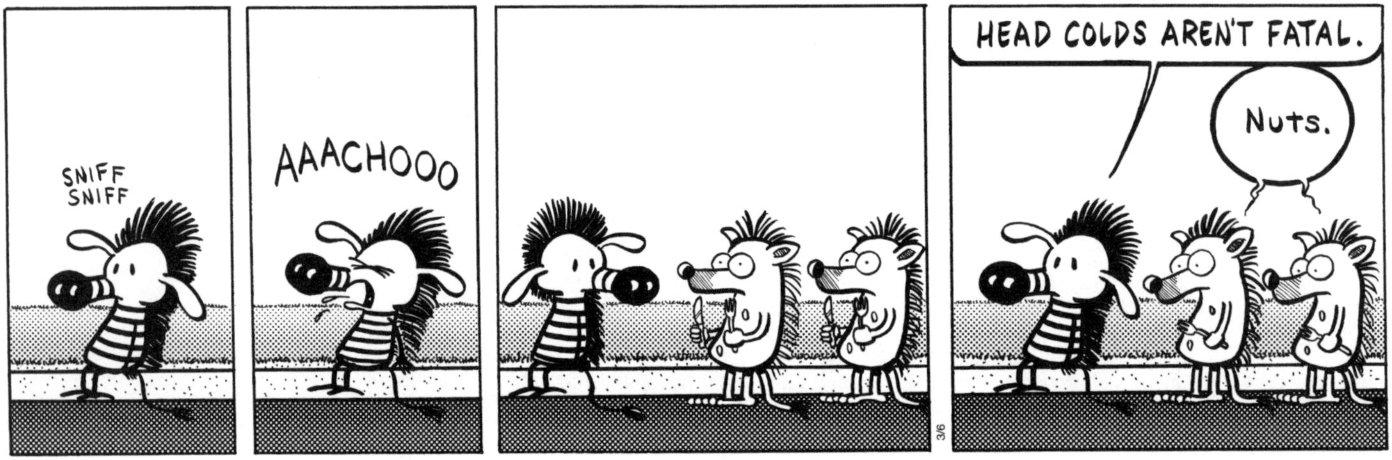
SNIFF SNIFF
AAACHOOO
HEAD COLDS AREN'T FATAL.
Nuts.
3/6

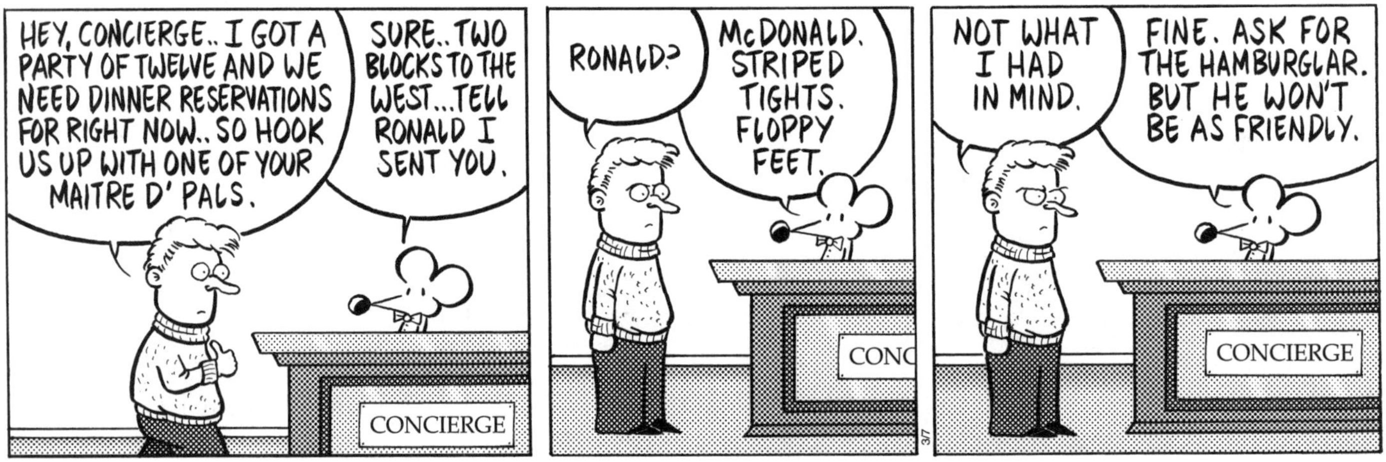
HEY, CONCIERGE.. I GOT A PARTY OF TWELVE AND WE NEED DINNER RESERVATIONS FOR RIGHT NOW.. SO HOOK US UP WITH ONE OF YOUR MAITRE D' PALS.
SURE.. TWO BLOCKS TO THE WEST...TELL RONALD I SENT YOU.
CONCIERGE
RONALD?
McDONALD. STRIPED TIGHTS. FLOPPY FEET.
NOT WHAT I HAD IN MIND.
FINE. ASK FOR THE HAMBURGLAR. BUT HE WON'T BE AS FRIENDLY.
CONCIERGE
3/7

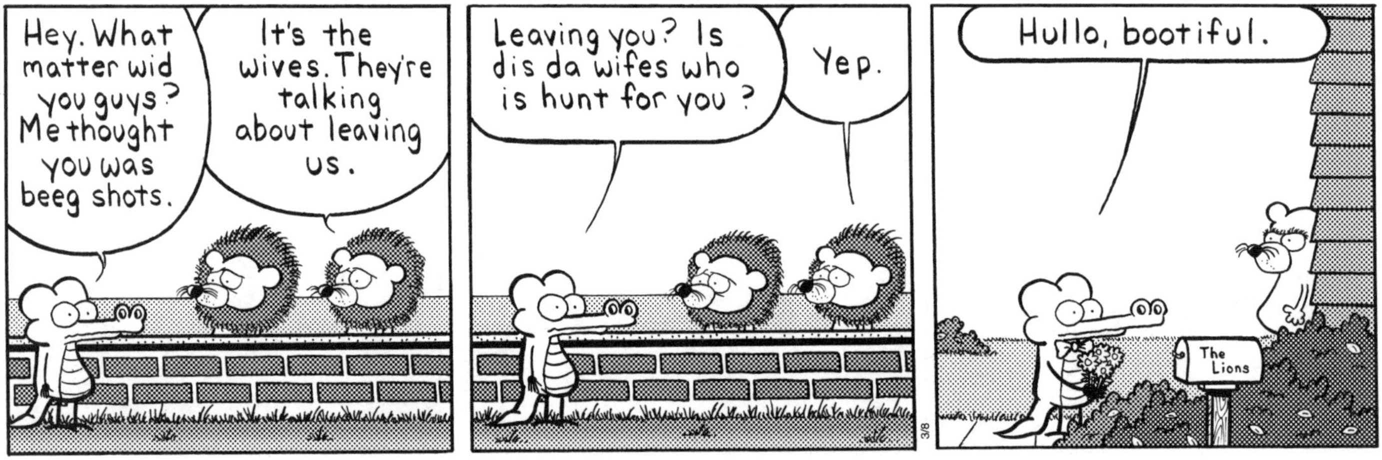
Hey. What matter wid you guys? Me thought you was beeg shots.
It's the wives. They're talking about leaving us.
Leaving you? Is dis da wifes who is hunt for you?
Yep.
Hullo, bootiful.
The Lions
3/8

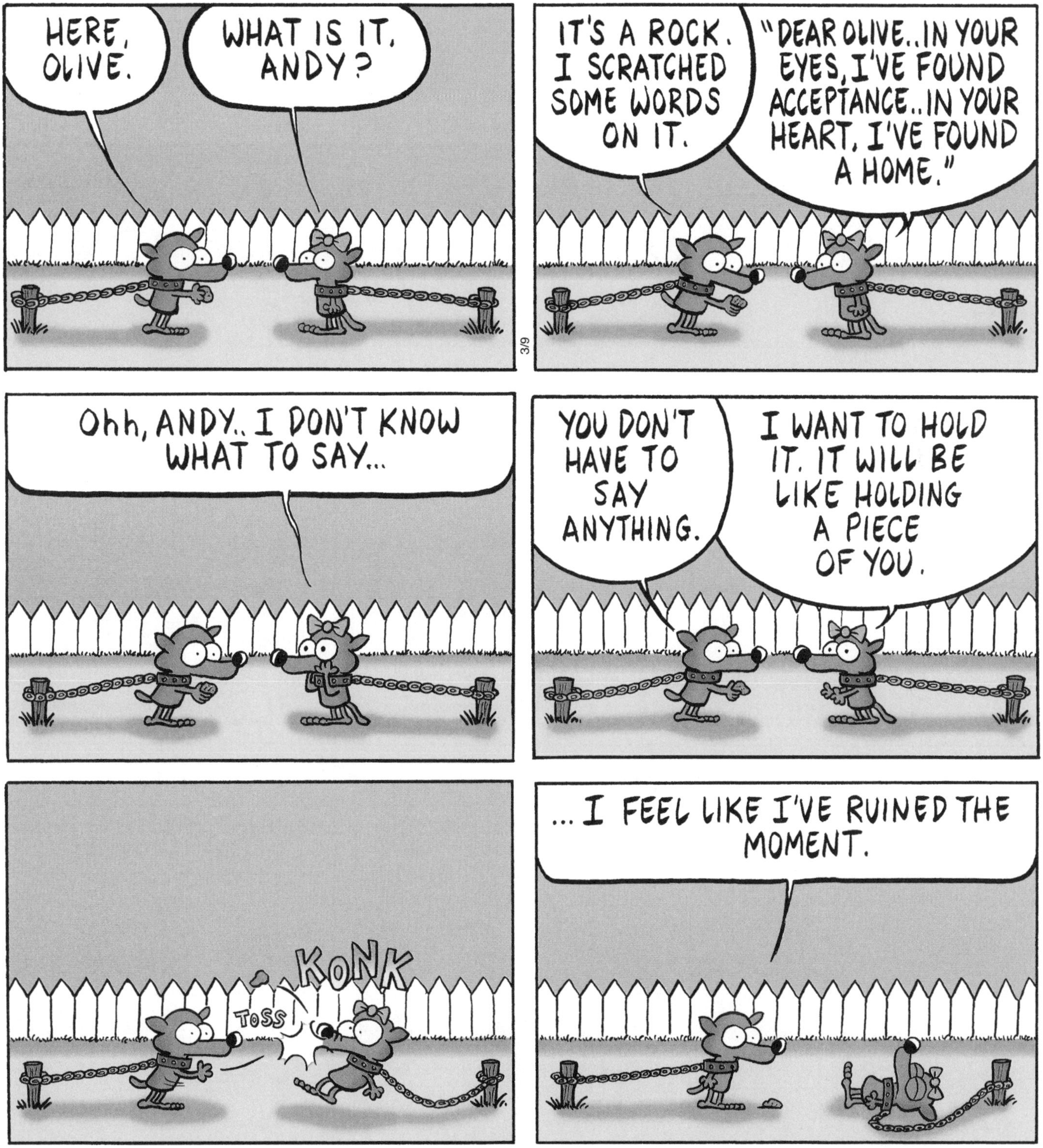
HERE, OLIVE.
WHAT IS IT, ANDY?
3/9
IT'S A ROCK. I SCRATCHED SOME WORDS ON IT.
"DEAR OLIVE.. IN YOUR EYES, I'VE FOUND ACCEPTANCE.. IN YOUR HEART, I'VE FOUND A HOME."
Ohh, ANDY.. I DON'T KNOW WHAT TO SAY...
YOU DON'T HAVE TO SAY ANYTHING.
I WANT TO HOLD IT. IT WILL BE LIKE HOLDING A PIECE OF YOU.
TOSS
KONK
... I FEEL LIKE I'VE RUINED THE MOMENT.

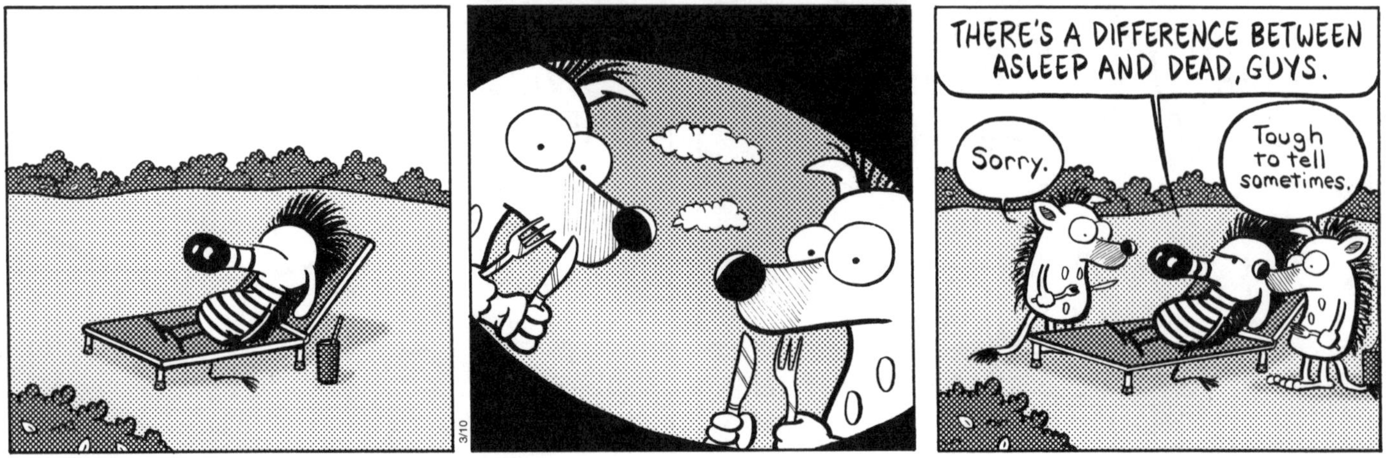
3/10
THERE'S A DIFFERENCE BETWEEN ASLEEP AND DEAD, GUYS.
Sorry.
Tough to tell sometimes.

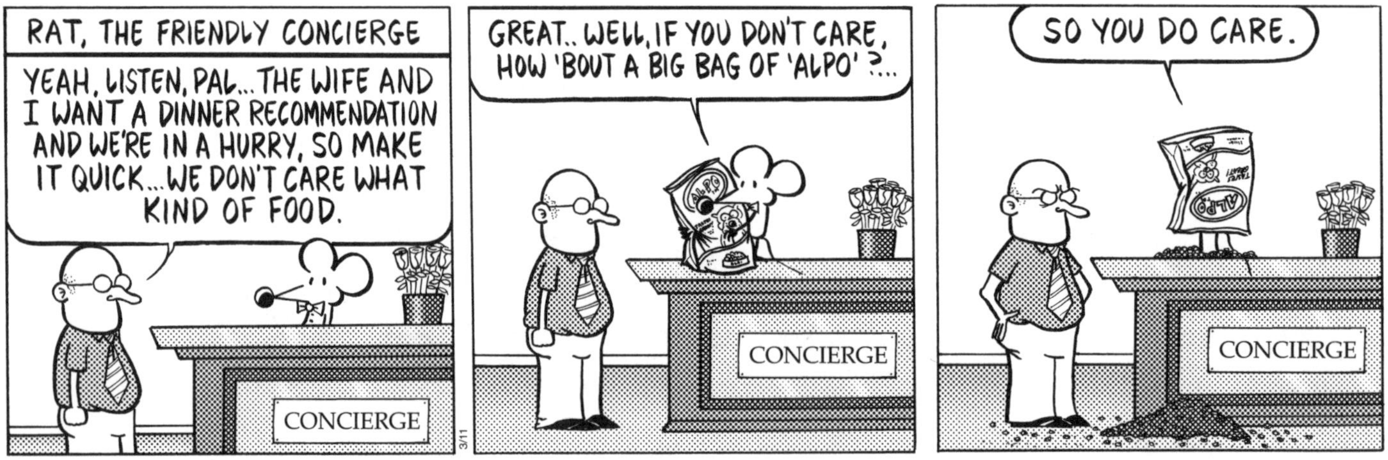
RAT, THE FRIENDLY CONCIERGE
YEAH, LISTEN, PAL... THE WIFE AND I WANT A DINNER RECOMMENDATION AND WE'RE IN A HURRY, SO MAKE IT QUICK... WE DON'T CARE WHAT KIND OF FOOD.
CONCIERGE
3/11
GREAT.. WELL, IF YOU DON'T CARE, HOW 'BOUT A BIG BAG OF 'ALPO'?...
CONCIERGE
SO YOU DO CARE.
CONCIERGE

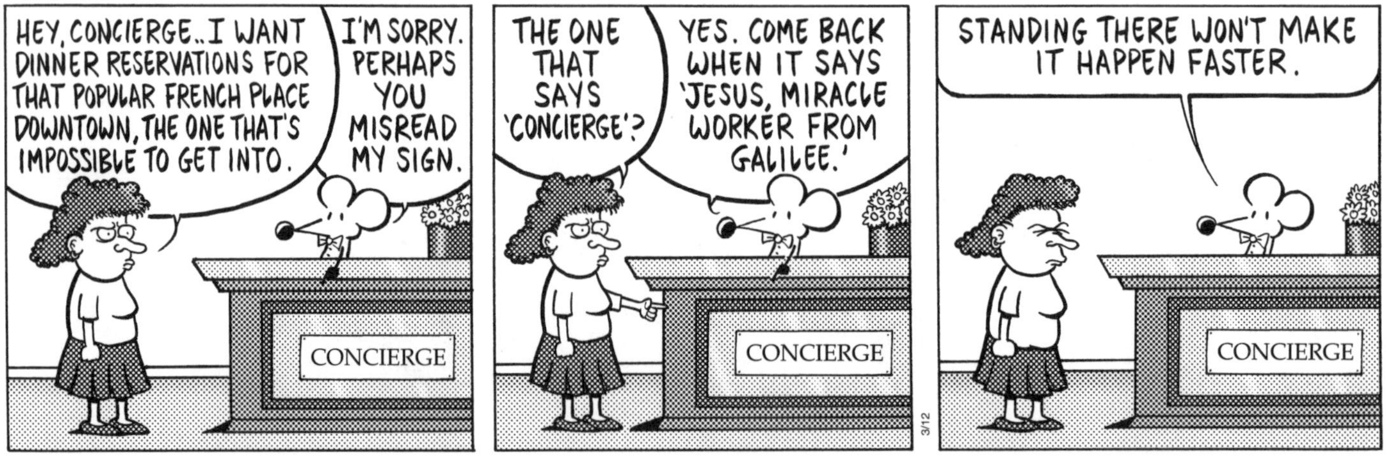
HEY, CONCIERGE.. I WANT DINNER RESERVATIONS FOR THAT POPULAR FRENCH PLACE DOWNTOWN, THE ONE THAT'S IMPOSSIBLE TO GET INTO.
I'M SORRY. PERHAPS YOU MISREAD MY SIGN.
CONCIERGE
THE ONE THAT SAYS 'CONCIERGE'?
YES. COME BACK WHEN IT SAYS 'JESUS, MIRACLE WORKER FROM GALILEE.'
CONCIERGE
3/12
STANDING THERE WON'T MAKE IT HAPPEN FASTER.
CONCIERGE

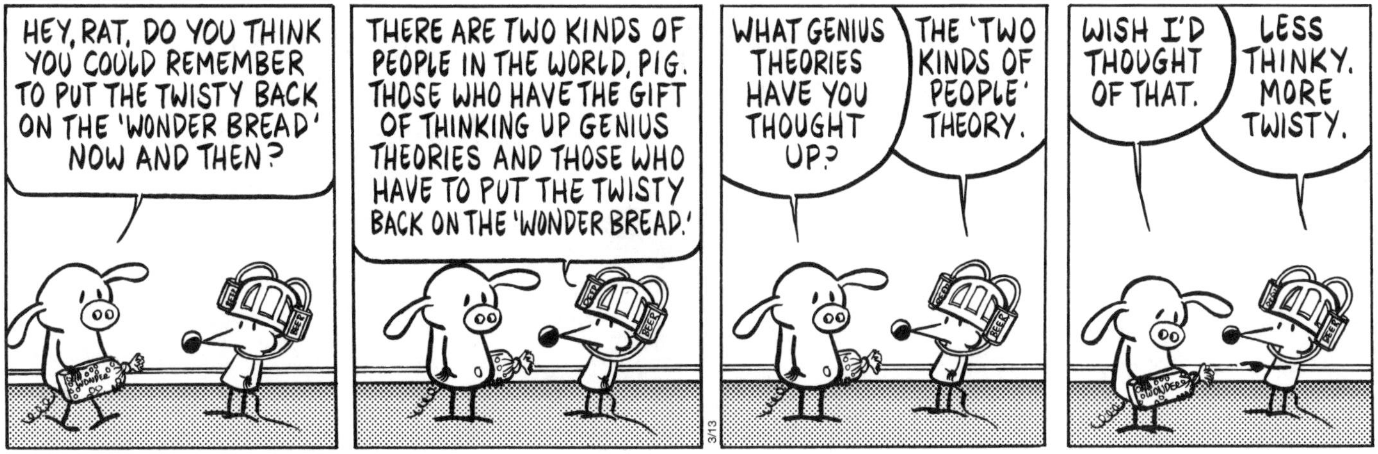
HEY, RAT, DO YOU THINK YOU COULD REMEMBER TO PUT THE TWISTY BACK ON THE 'WONDER BREAD' NOW AND THEN?
THERE ARE TWO KINDS OF PEOPLE IN THE WORLD, PIG. THOSE WHO HAVE THE GIFT OF THINKING UP GENIUS THEORIES AND THOSE WHO HAVE TO PUT THE TWISTY BACK ON THE 'WONDER BREAD.'
WHAT GENIUS THEORIES HAVE YOU THOUGHT UP?
THE 'TWO KINDS OF PEOPLE' THEORY.
WISH I'D THOUGHT OF THAT.
LESS THINKY. MORE TWISTY.
3/13

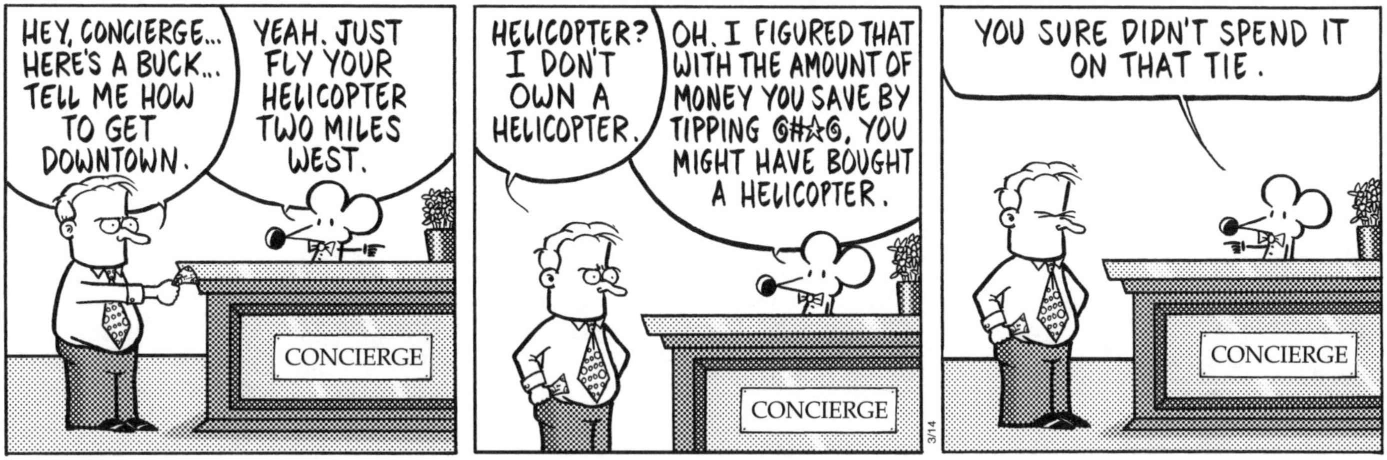
HEY, CONCIERGE... HERE'S A BUCK... TELL ME HOW TO GET DOWNTOWN.
YEAH. JUST FLY YOUR HELICOPTER TWO MILES WEST.
CONCIERGE
HELICOPTER? I DON'T OWN A HELICOPTER.
OH. I FIGURED THAT WITH THE AMOUNT OF MONEY YOU SAVE BY TIPPING @#☆@, YOU MIGHT HAVE BOUGHT A HELICOPTER.
CONCIERGE
3/14
YOU SURE DIDN'T SPEND IT ON THAT TIE.
CONCIERGE

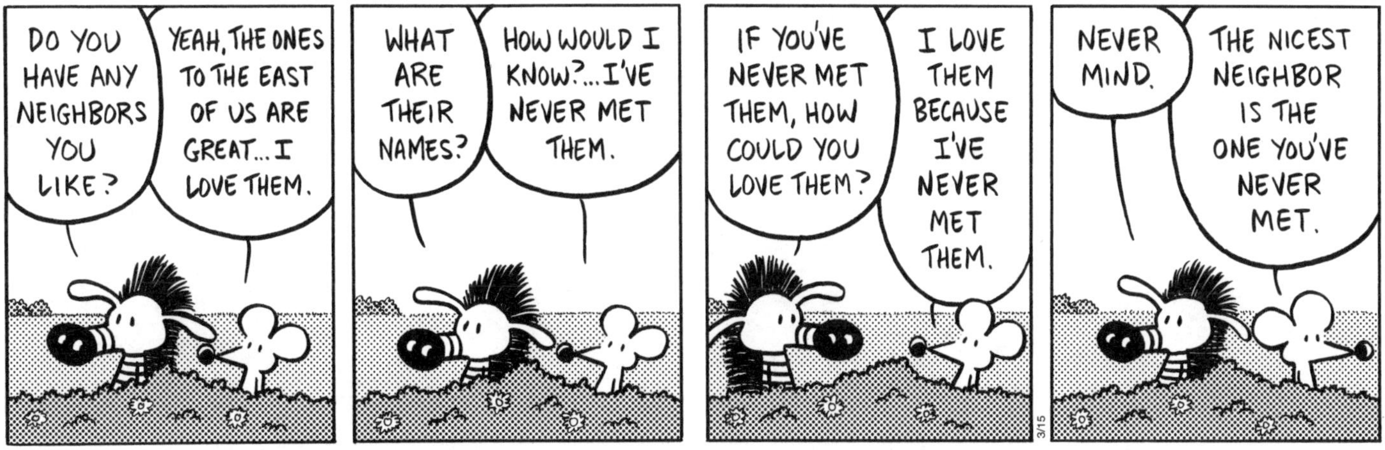
DO YOU HAVE ANY NEIGHBORS YOU LIKE?
YEAH, THE ONES TO THE EAST OF US ARE GREAT... I LOVE THEM.
WHAT ARE THEIR NAMES?
HOW WOULD I KNOW?... I'VE NEVER MET THEM.
IF YOU'VE NEVER MET THEM, HOW COULD YOU LOVE THEM?
I LOVE THEM BECAUSE I'VE NEVER MET THEM.
3/15
NEVER MIND.
THE NICEST NEIGHBOR IS THE ONE YOU'VE NEVER MET.

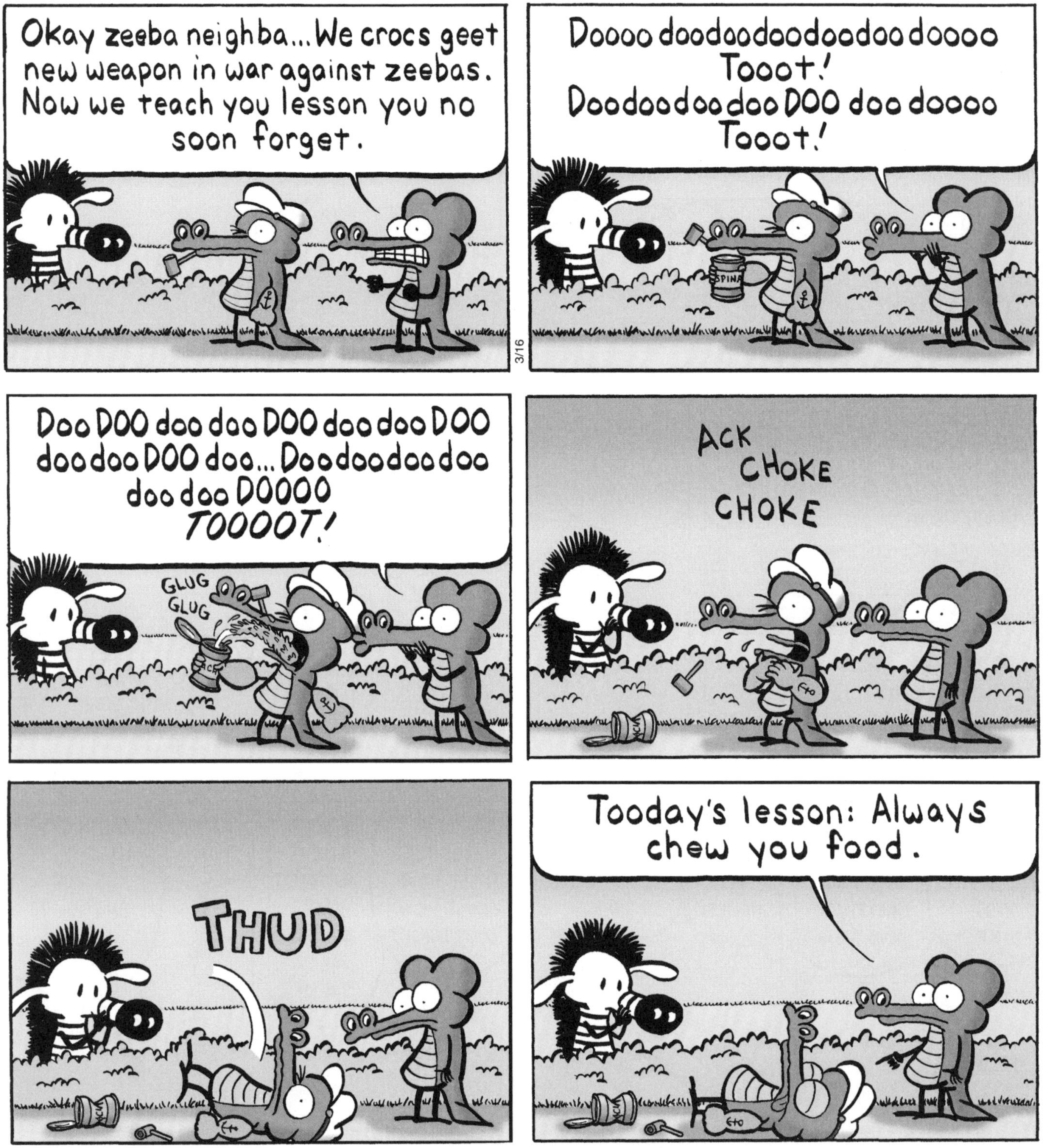
Okay zeeba neighba... We crocs geet new weapon in war against zeebas. Now we teach you lesson you no soon forget.
3/16
Doooo doodoodoodoodoo doooo Tooot! Doodoodoodoo DOO doo doooo Tooot!
SPINA
Doo DOO doo doo DOO doo doo DOO doo doo DOO doo... Doodoodoodoo doo doo DOOOO TOOOOT!
GLUG GLUG
ACK CHOKE CHOKE
THUD
Tooday's lesson: Always chew you food.

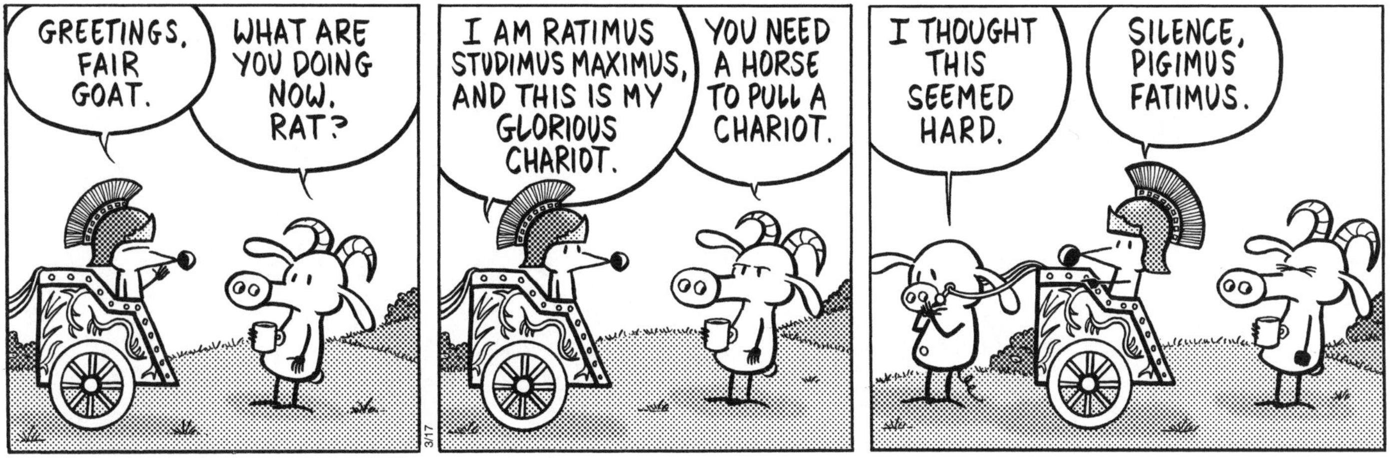
GREETINGS, FAIR GOAT.
WHAT ARE YOU DOING NOW, RAT?
I AM RATIMUS STUDIMUS MAXIMUS, AND THIS IS MY GLORIOUS CHARIOT.
YOU NEED A HORSE TO PULL A CHARIOT.
I THOUGHT THIS SEEMED HARD.
SILENCE, PIGIMUS FATIMUS.
3/17

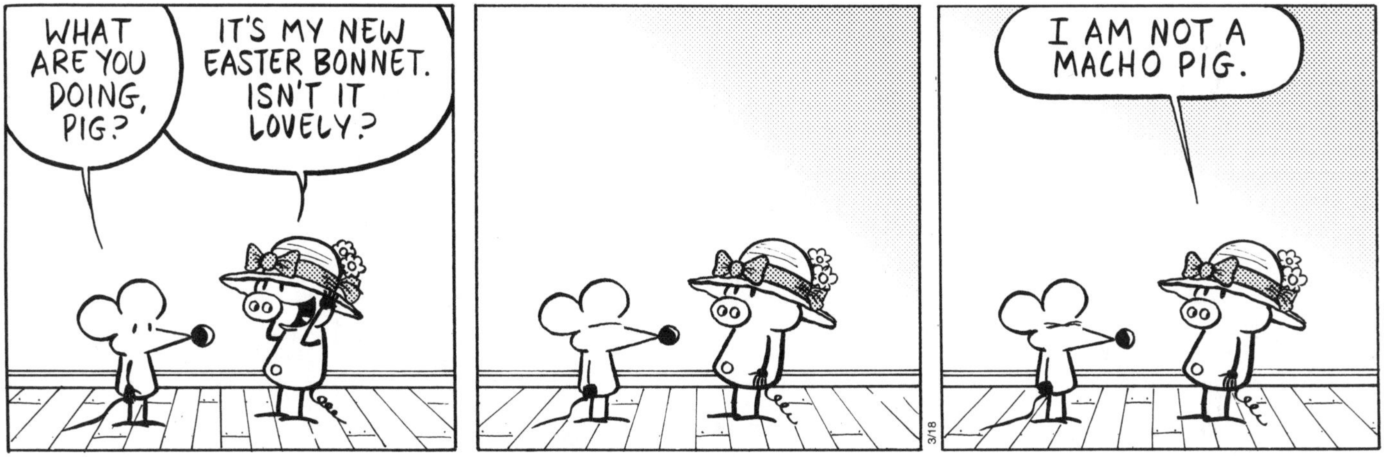
WHAT ARE YOU DOING, PIG?
IT'S MY NEW EASTER BONNET. ISN'T IT LOVELY?
I AM NOT A MACHO PIG.
3/18

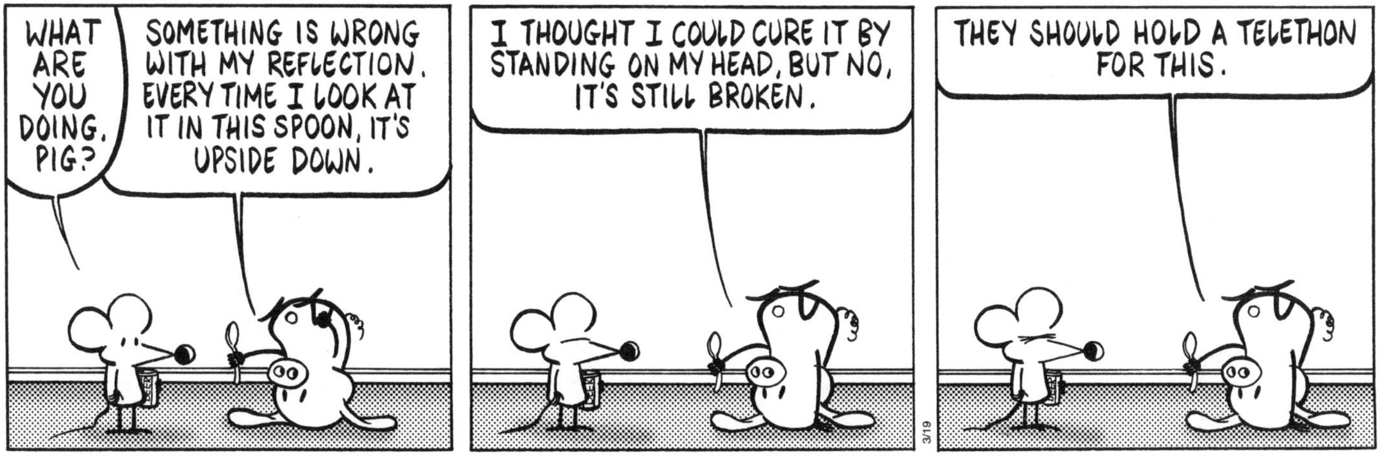
WHAT ARE YOU DOING, PIG?
SOMETHING IS WRONG WITH MY REFLECTION. EVERY TIME I LOOK AT IT IN THIS SPOON, IT'S UPSIDE DOWN.
I THOUGHT I COULD CURE IT BY STANDING ON MY HEAD, BUT NO, IT'S STILL BROKEN.
THEY SHOULD HOLD A TELETHON FOR THIS.
3/19

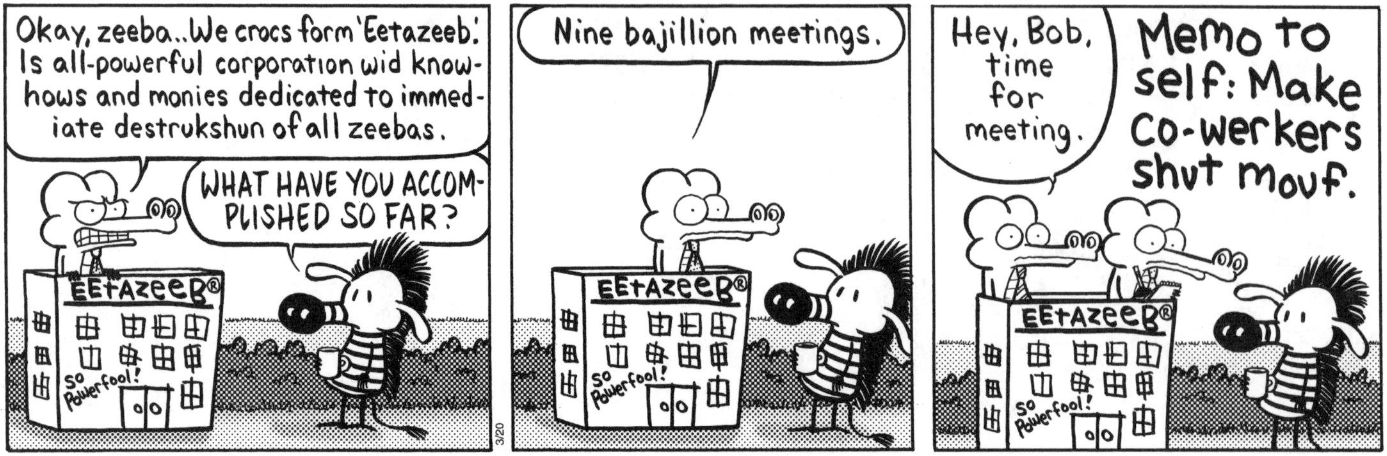
Okay, zeeba...We crocs form 'Eetazeeb.' Is all-powerful corporation wid know-hows and monies dedicated to immediate destrukshun of all zeebas.
WHAT HAVE YOU ACCOMPLISHED SO FAR?
EEtAzeeB®
So Powerfool!
Nine bajillion meetings.
Hey, Bob, time for meeting.
Memo to self: Make co-werkers shut mouf.
3/20

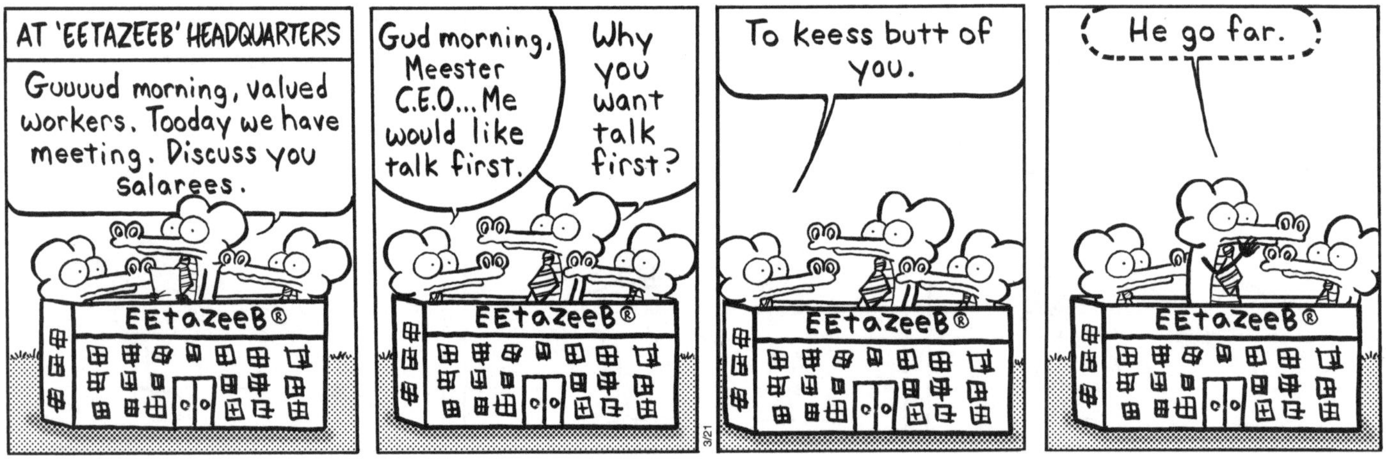
AT 'EETAZEEB' HEADQUARTERS
Guuuud morning, valued workers. Tooday we have meeting. Discuss you salarees.
EEtazeeB®
Gud morning, Meester C.E.O... Me would like talk first.
Why you want talk first?
To keess butt of you.
He go far.
3/21

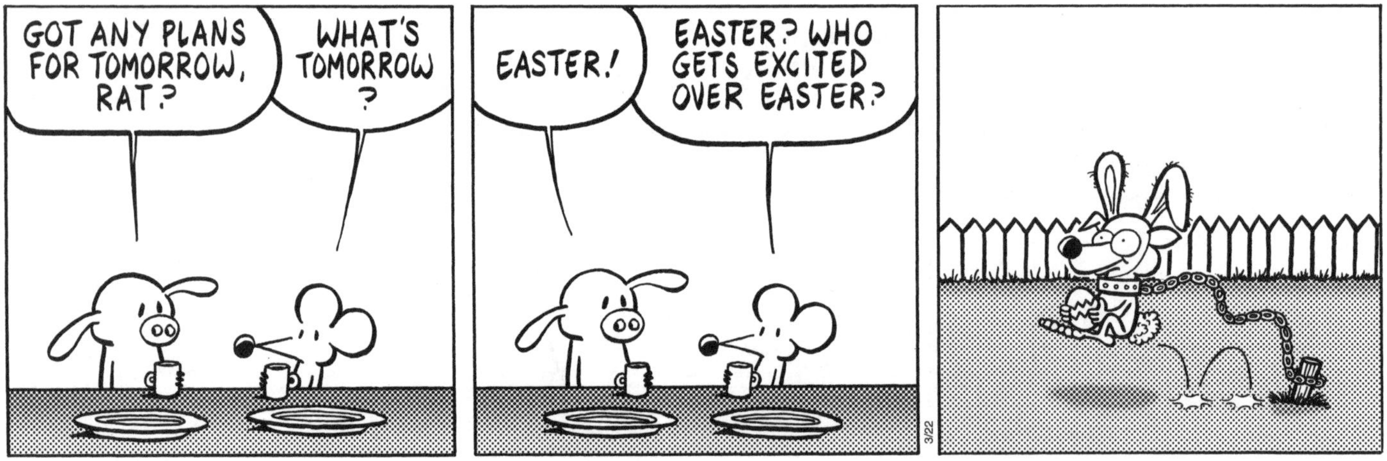
GOT ANY PLANS FOR TOMORROW, RAT?
WHAT'S TOMORROW?
EASTER!
EASTER? WHO GETS EXCITED OVER EASTER?
3/22

STORY UPDATE:
The crocs have formed 'Eetazeeb,' a corporation dedicated to the killing of all zebras. We join their annual Salary Review Meeting, already in progress.

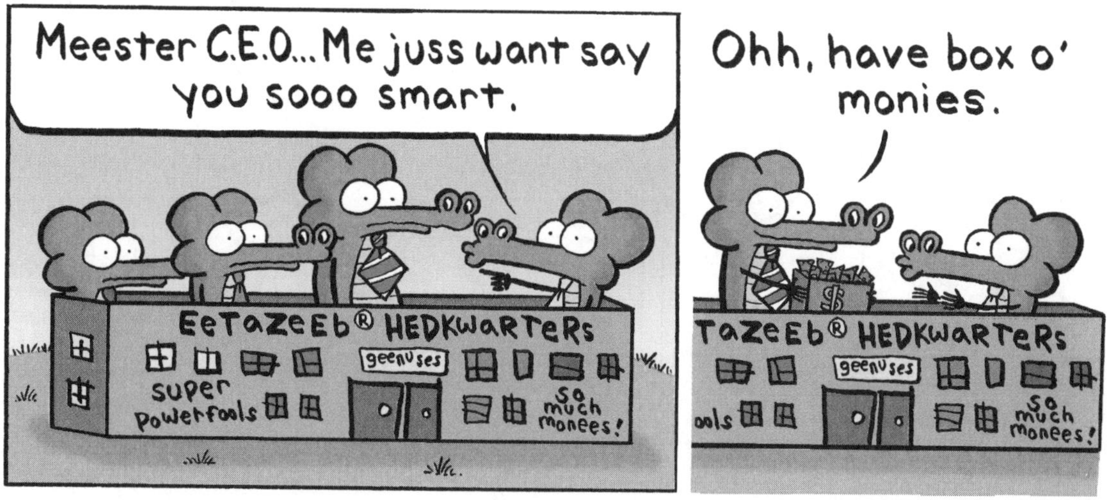

Meester C.E.O... Me juss want say you sooo smart.
EeTazeEb® HEDKWaRTeRs
geenuses
super Powerfools
so much monees!
Ohh, have box o' monies.

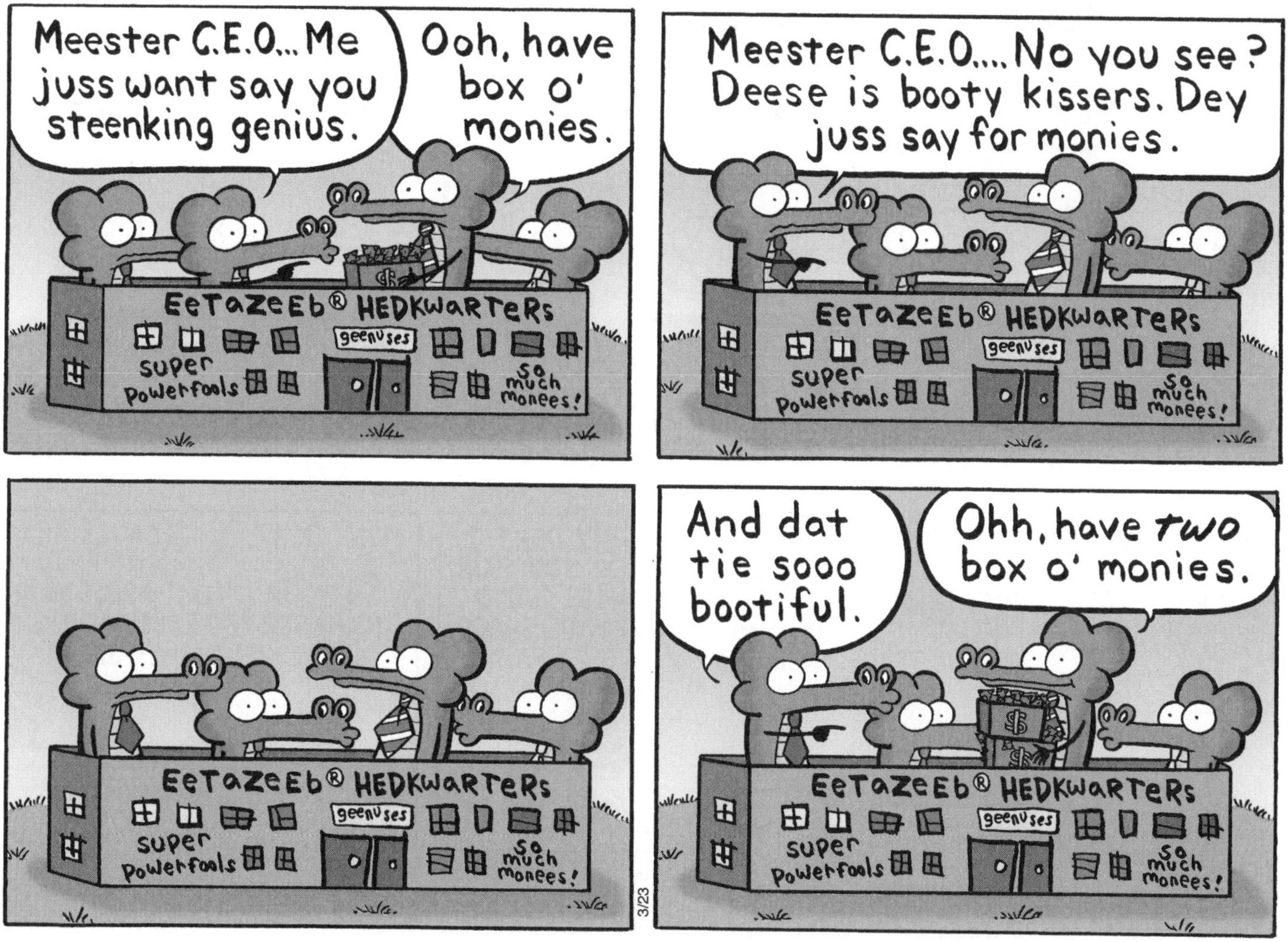

Meester C.E.O... Me juss want say you steenking genius.
Ooh, have box o' monies.
Meester C.E.O.... No you see? Deese is booty kissers. Dey juss say for monies.
EeTazeEb® HEDKWaRTeRs
geenuses
super Powerfools
so much monees!
3/23
And dat tie sooo bootiful.
Ohh, have *two* box o' monies.

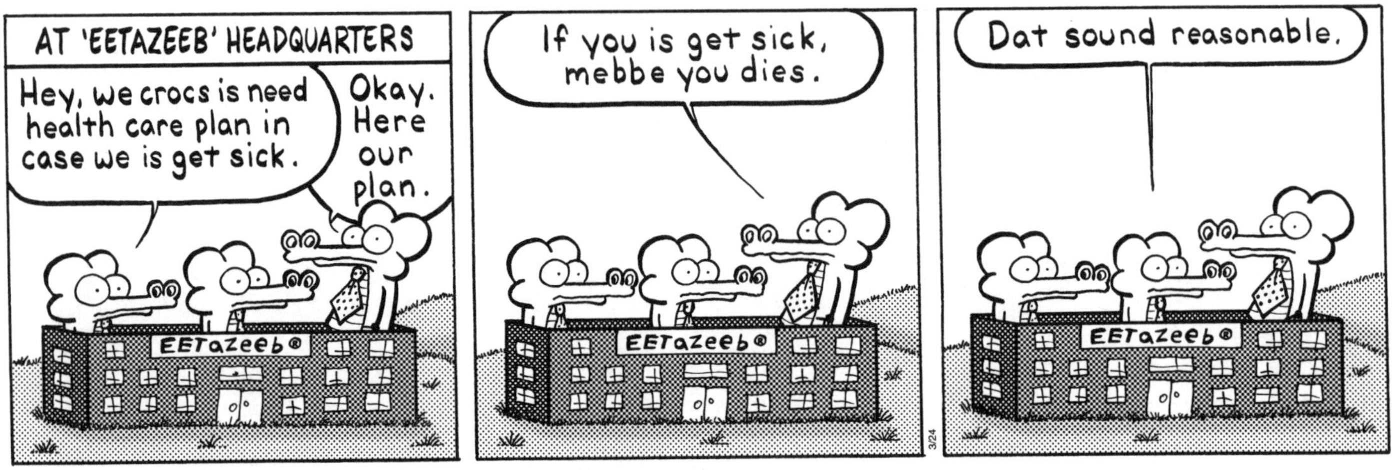
AT 'EETAZEEB' HEADQUARTERS
Hey, we crocs is need health care plan in case we is get sick.
Okay. Here our plan.
EETazeeb®
If you is get sick, mebbe you dies.
EETazeeb®
Dat sound reasonable.
EETazeeb®
3/24

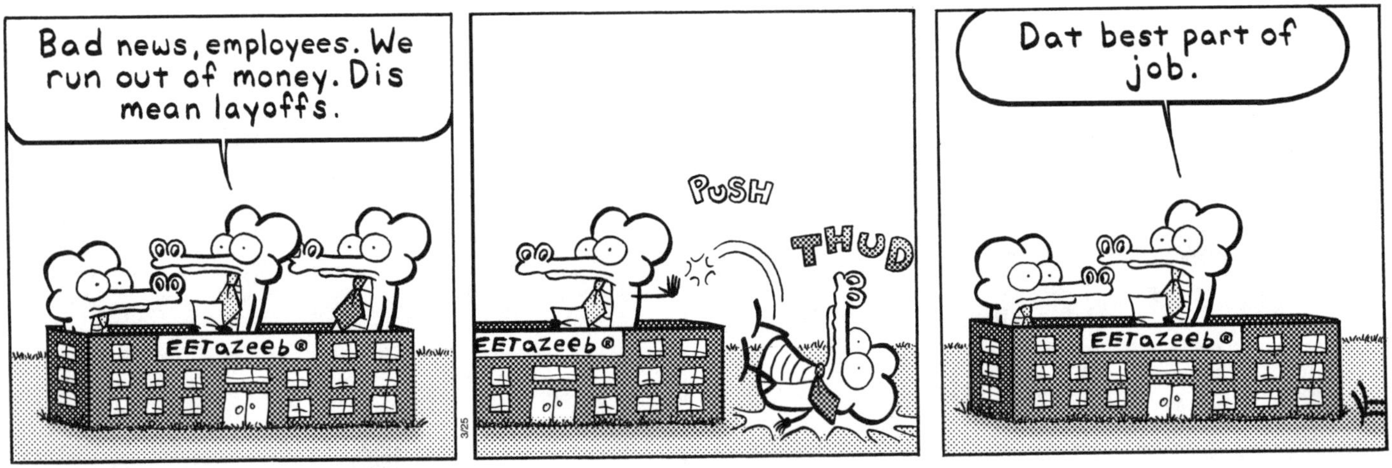
Bad news, employees. We run out of money. Dis mean layoffs.
EETazeeb®
3/25
PUSH
THUD
EETazeeb®
Dat best part of job.
EETazeeb®

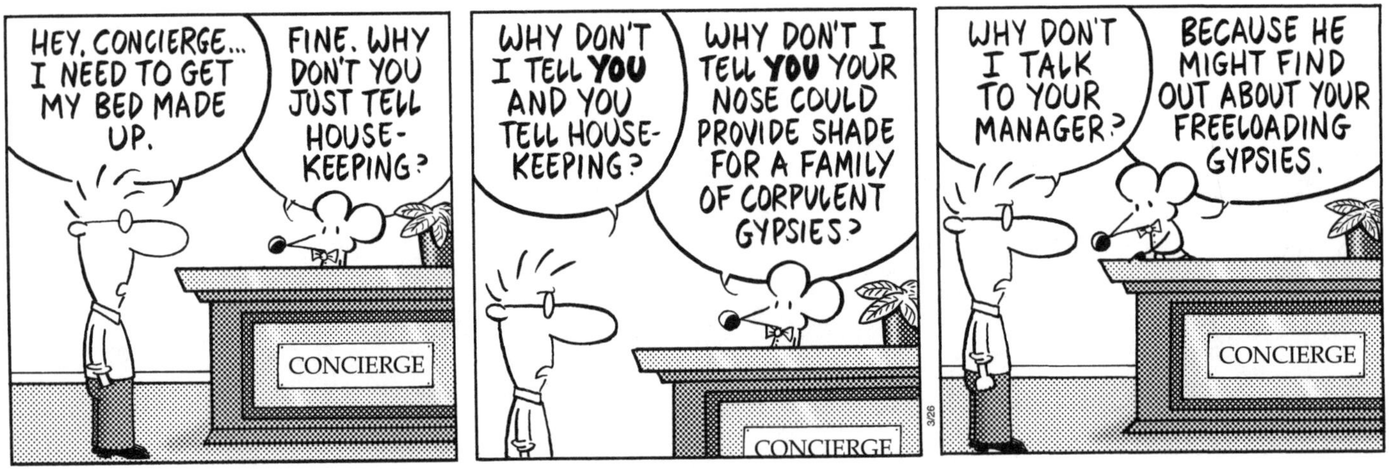
HEY, CONCIERGE... I NEED TO GET MY BED MADE UP.
FINE. WHY DON'T YOU JUST TELL HOUSE-KEEPING?
CONCIERGE
WHY DON'T I TELL **YOU** AND YOU TELL HOUSE-KEEPING?
WHY DON'T I TELL **YOU** YOUR NOSE COULD PROVIDE SHADE FOR A FAMILY OF CORPULENT GYPSIES?
CONCIERGE
3/26
WHY DON'T I TALK TO YOUR MANAGER?
BECAUSE HE MIGHT FIND OUT ABOUT YOUR FREELOADING GYPSIES.
CONCIERGE

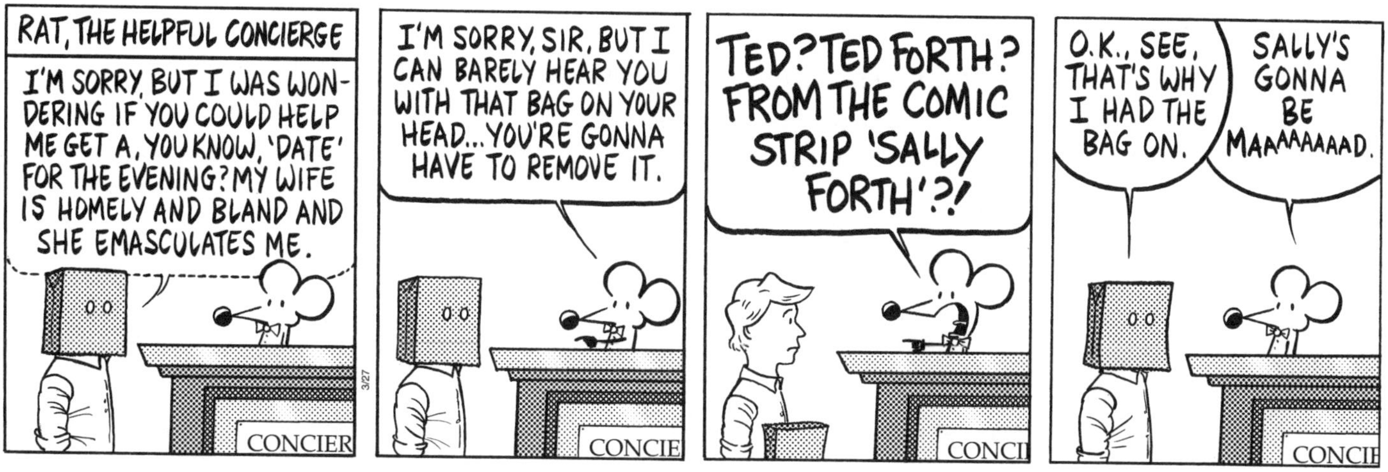
RAT, THE HELPFUL CONCIERGE
I'M SORRY, BUT I WAS WONDERING IF YOU COULD HELP ME GET A, YOU KNOW, 'DATE' FOR THE EVENING? MY WIFE IS HOMELY AND BLAND AND SHE EMASCULATES ME.
CONCIER
3/27
I'M SORRY, SIR, BUT I CAN BARELY HEAR YOU WITH THAT BAG ON YOUR HEAD... YOU'RE GONNA HAVE TO REMOVE IT.
CONCIE
TED? TED FORTH? FROM THE COMIC STRIP 'SALLY FORTH'?!
CONCI
O.K., SEE, THAT'S WHY I HAD THE BAG ON.
SALLY'S GONNA BE MAAAAAAAD.
CONCIE

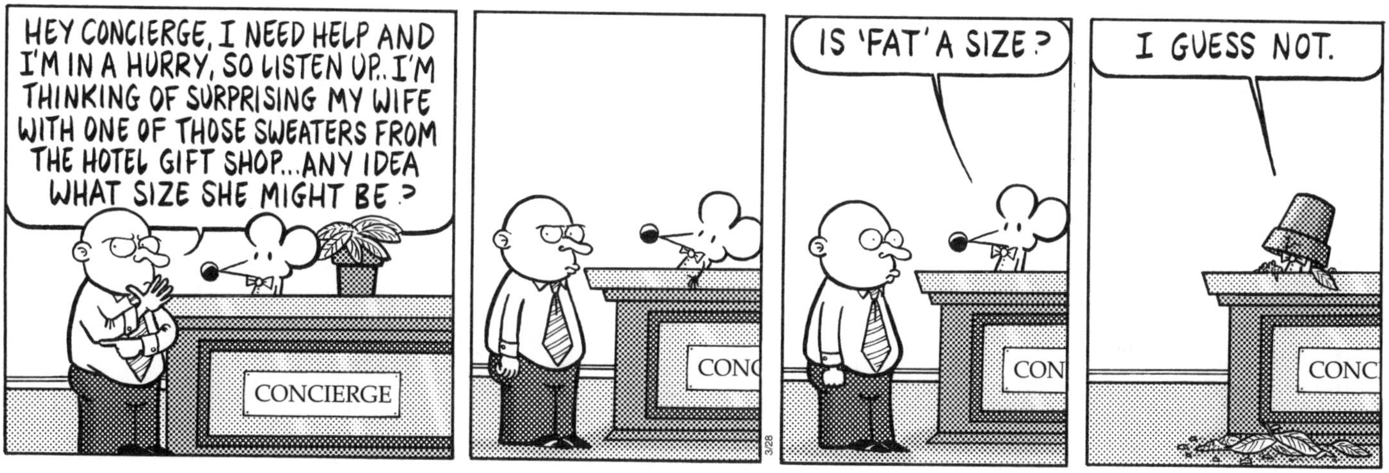
HEY CONCIERGE, I NEED HELP AND I'M IN A HURRY, SO LISTEN UP.. I'M THINKING OF SURPRISING MY WIFE WITH ONE OF THOSE SWEATERS FROM THE HOTEL GIFT SHOP... ANY IDEA WHAT SIZE SHE MIGHT BE?
CONCIERGE
CONC
3/28
IS 'FAT' A SIZE?
CON
I GUESS NOT.
CONC

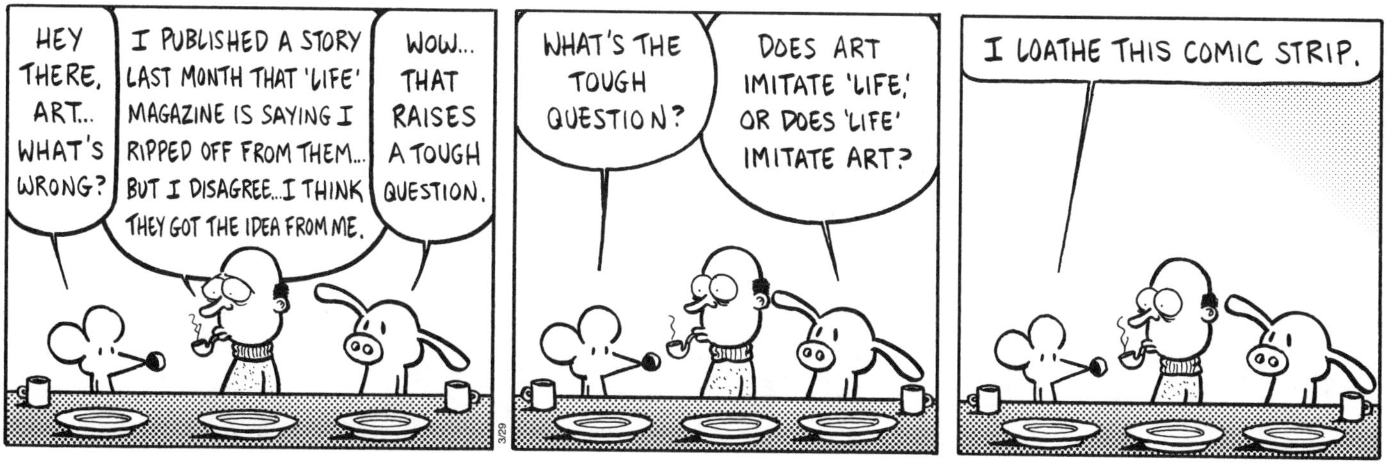
HEY THERE, ART... WHAT'S WRONG?
I PUBLISHED A STORY LAST MONTH THAT 'LIFE' MAGAZINE IS SAYING I RIPPED OFF FROM THEM... BUT I DISAGREE... I THINK THEY GOT THE IDEA FROM ME.
WOW... THAT RAISES A TOUGH QUESTION.
3/29
WHAT'S THE TOUGH QUESTION?
DOES ART IMITATE 'LIFE,' OR DOES 'LIFE' IMITATE ART?
I LOATHE THIS COMIC STRIP.

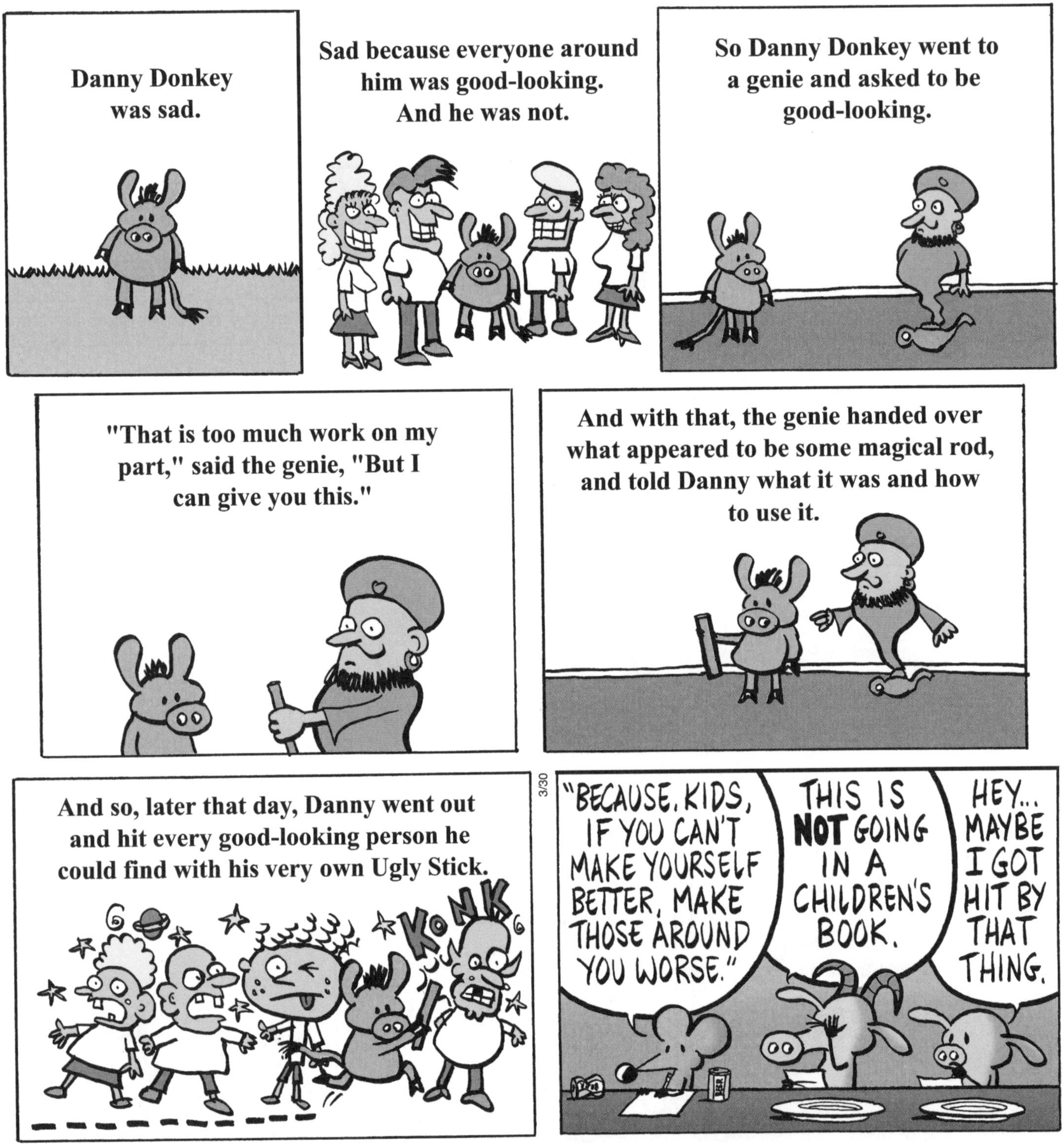
Danny Donkey was sad.
Sad because everyone around him was good-looking. And he was not.
So Danny Donkey went to a genie and asked to be good-looking.
"That is too much work on my part," said the genie, "But I can give you this."
And with that, the genie handed over what appeared to be some magical rod, and told Danny what it was and how to use it.
And so, later that day, Danny went out and hit every good-looking person he could find with his very own Ugly Stick.
KONK
3/30
"BECAUSE, KIDS, IF YOU CAN'T MAKE YOURSELF BETTER, MAKE THOSE AROUND YOU WORSE."
THIS IS NOT GOING IN A CHILDREN'S BOOK.
HEY... MAYBE I GOT HIT BY THAT THING.

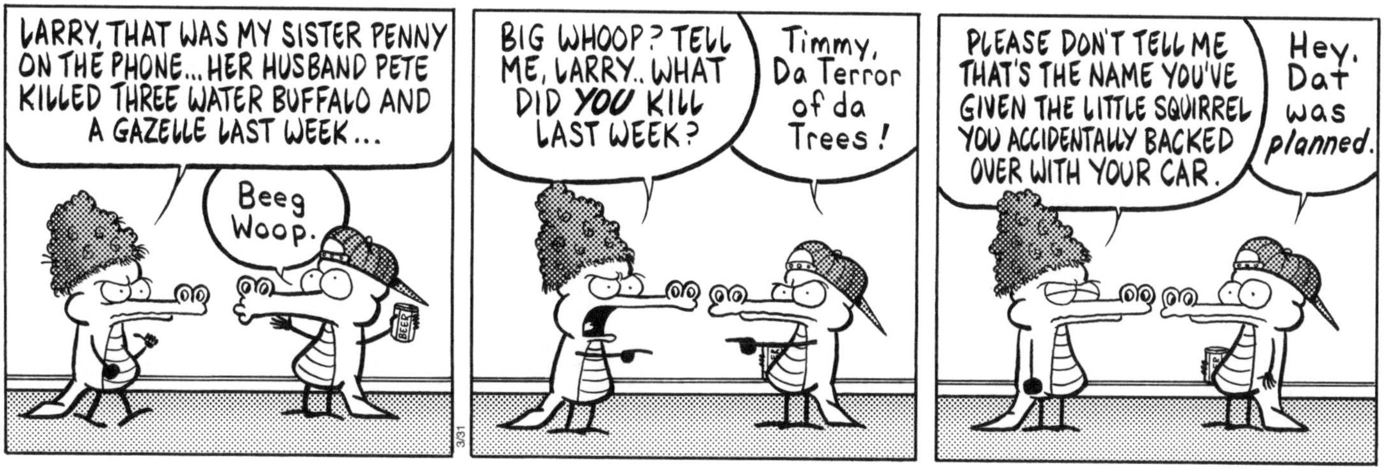
LARRY, THAT WAS MY SISTER PENNY ON THE PHONE... HER HUSBAND PETE KILLED THREE WATER BUFFALO AND A GAZELLE LAST WEEK...
Beeg Woop.
BIG WHOOP? TELL ME, LARRY.. WHAT DID *YOU* KILL LAST WEEK?
Timmy, Da Terror of da Trees!
PLEASE DON'T TELL ME THAT'S THE NAME YOU'VE GIVEN THE LITTLE SQUIRREL YOU ACCIDENTALLY BACKED OVER WITH YOUR CAR.
Hey. Dat was *planned*.
3/31

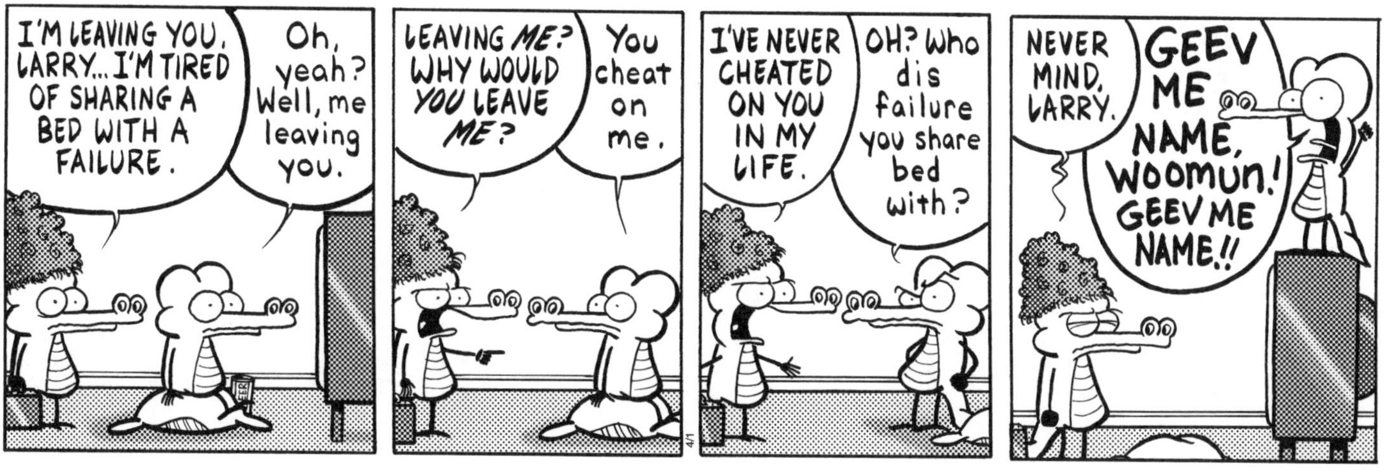
I'M LEAVING YOU, LARRY... I'M TIRED OF SHARING A BED WITH A FAILURE.
Oh, yeah? Well, me leaving you.
LEAVING *ME*? WHY WOULD *YOU* LEAVE *ME*?
You cheat on me.
I'VE NEVER CHEATED ON YOU IN MY LIFE.
OH? Who dis failure you share bed with?
NEVER MIND, LARRY.
GEEV ME NAME, WOOMUN! GEEV ME NAME!!
4/1

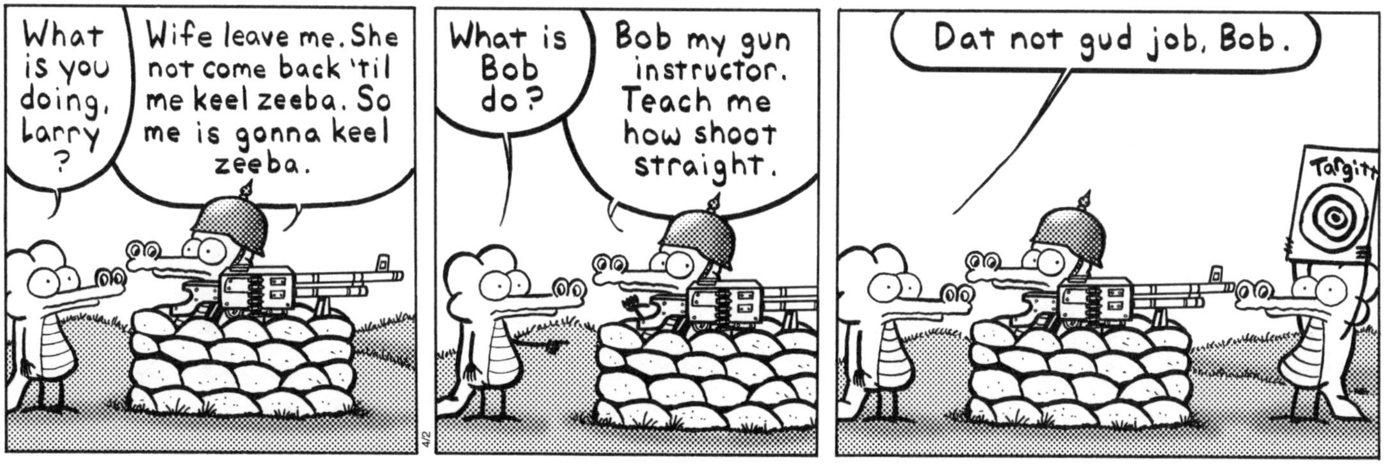
What is you doing, Larry?
Wife leave me. She not come back 'til me keel zeeba. So me is gonna keel zeeba.
What is Bob do?
Bob my gun instructor. Teach me how shoot straight.
Dat not gud job, Bob.
4/2

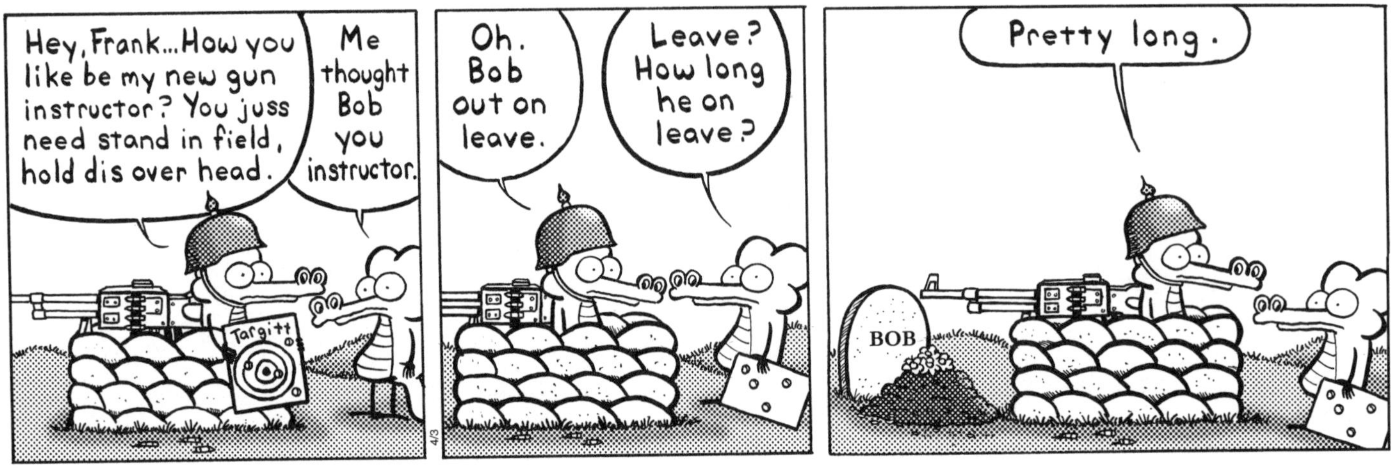
Hey, Frank...How you like be my new gun instructor? You juss need stand in field, hold dis over head.
Me thought Bob you instructor.
Targitt
4/3
Oh. Bob out on leave.
Leave? How long he on leave?
Pretty long.
BOB

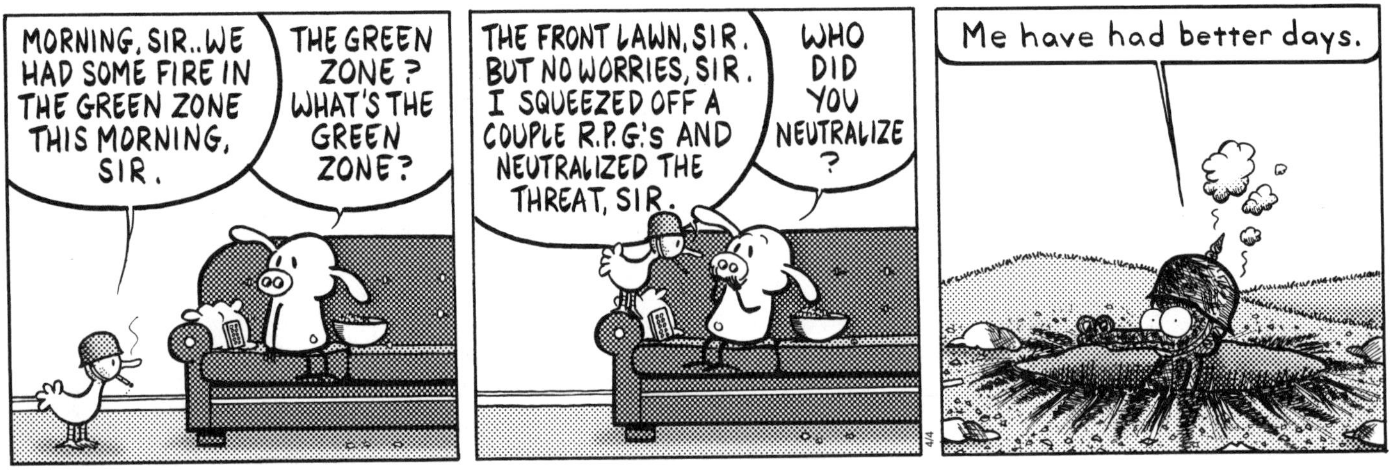
MORNING, SIR..WE HAD SOME FIRE IN THE GREEN ZONE THIS MORNING, SIR.
THE GREEN ZONE? WHAT'S THE GREEN ZONE?
THE FRONT LAWN, SIR. BUT NO WORRIES, SIR. I SQUEEZED OFF A COUPLE R.P.G.'S AND NEUTRALIZED THE THREAT, SIR.
WHO DID YOU NEUTRALIZE?
Me have had better days.
4/4

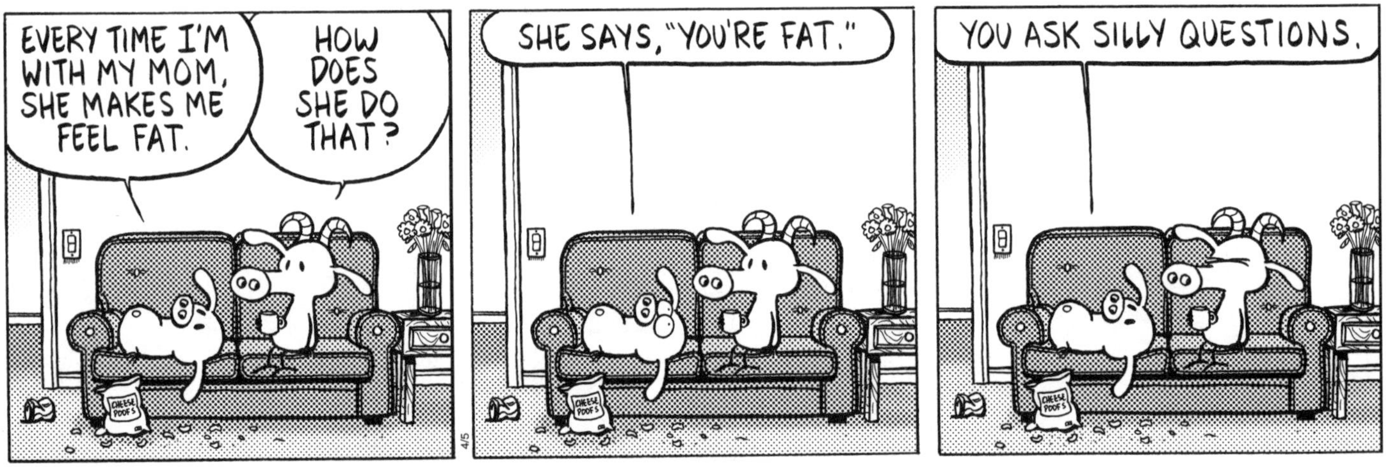
EVERY TIME I'M WITH MY MOM, SHE MAKES ME FEEL FAT.
HOW DOES SHE DO THAT?
CHEESE POOFS
4/5
SHE SAYS, "YOU'RE FAT."
YOU ASK SILLY QUESTIONS.

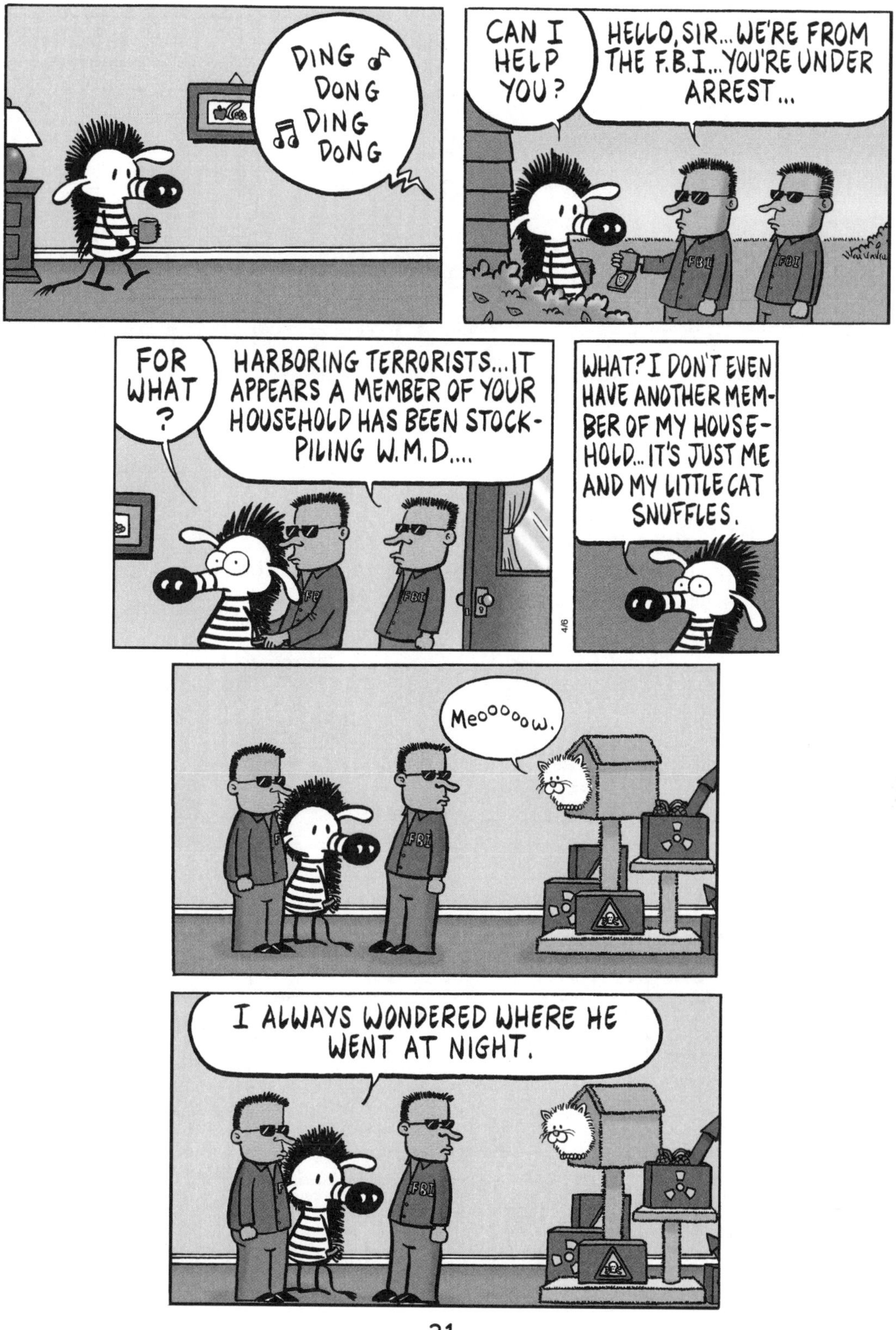
DING DONG DING DONG
CAN I HELP YOU?
HELLO, SIR... WE'RE FROM THE F.B.I... YOU'RE UNDER ARREST...
FOR WHAT?
HARBORING TERRORISTS... IT APPEARS A MEMBER OF YOUR HOUSEHOLD HAS BEEN STOCK-PILING W.M.D....
WHAT? I DON'T EVEN HAVE ANOTHER MEM-BER OF MY HOUSE-HOLD... IT'S JUST ME AND MY LITTLE CAT SNUFFLES.
Meooooow.
I ALWAYS WONDERED WHERE HE WENT AT NIGHT.

I CAN'T BELIEVE YOU'RE IN JAIL, ZEBRA.

I CAN'T EITHER, PIG...TO THINK THAT MY L'IL CAT, SNUFFLES, HAS BEEN STOCKPILING W.M.D... SOME OF THE STUFF HE'S HAD FOR FIVE YEARS.

FIVE YEARS? WHERE'D HE EVEN GET IT?

HIDE THESE.

OKAY, SNUFFLES, THE F.B.I. RELEASED ME FROM PRISON ON THE CONDITION THAT I GET A CONFESSION FROM YOU AS TO ALL YOUR MYSTERIOUS NIGHTTIME ACTIVITIES...

NOW I KNOW ABOUT THE ARMS YOU SOLD TO THE SYRIANS AND THE PAKISTANIS, BUT YOU DON'T HAVE ANY OTHER INVOLVEMENT WITH THESE GUYS, DO YOU?

Meow.

WHAT DO YOU MEAN YOU MADE A VIDEO YOU NOW SORT OF REGRET?

كافر الله زيبرا

Meow to you, great Satan.

Hullo. My wife leave me... Say she come back if me get job keeling zeeba...Peese geev job.

Okay. But first we is ask question...Is you qualeefied?

EETazeeb®

Whoa. Me no expekk pop quiz.

Mebbe answer no.

EETazeeb®

32

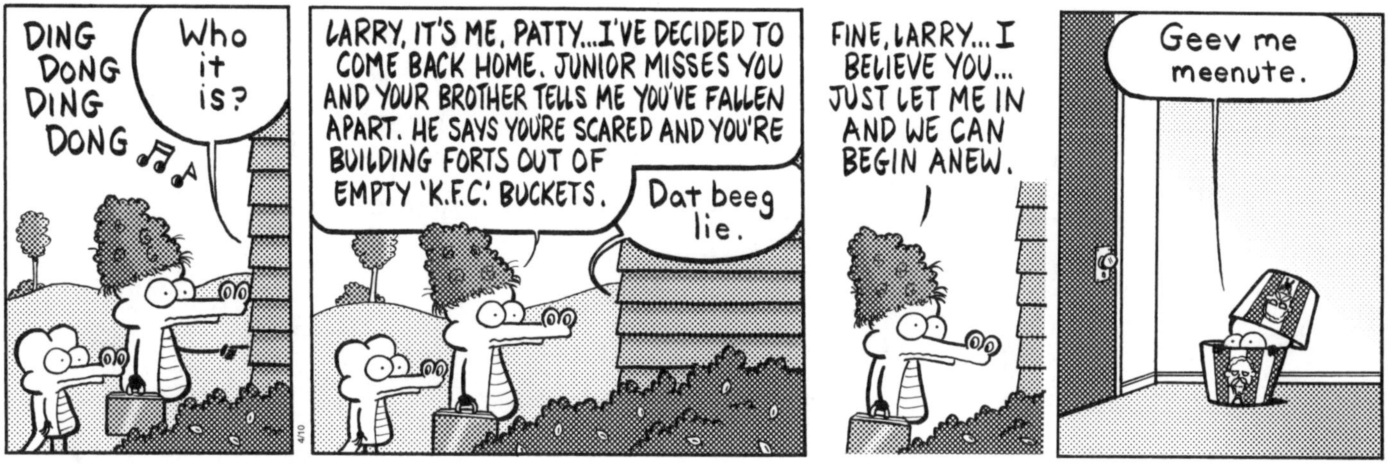
DING DONG DING DONG
Who it is?
LARRY, IT'S ME, PATTY...I'VE DECIDED TO COME BACK HOME. JUNIOR MISSES YOU AND YOUR BROTHER TELLS ME YOU'VE FALLEN APART. HE SAYS YOU'RE SCARED AND YOU'RE BUILDING FORTS OUT OF EMPTY 'K.F.C.' BUCKETS.
Dat beeg lie.
FINE, LARRY... I BELIEVE YOU... JUST LET ME IN AND WE CAN BEGIN ANEW.
Geev me meenute.

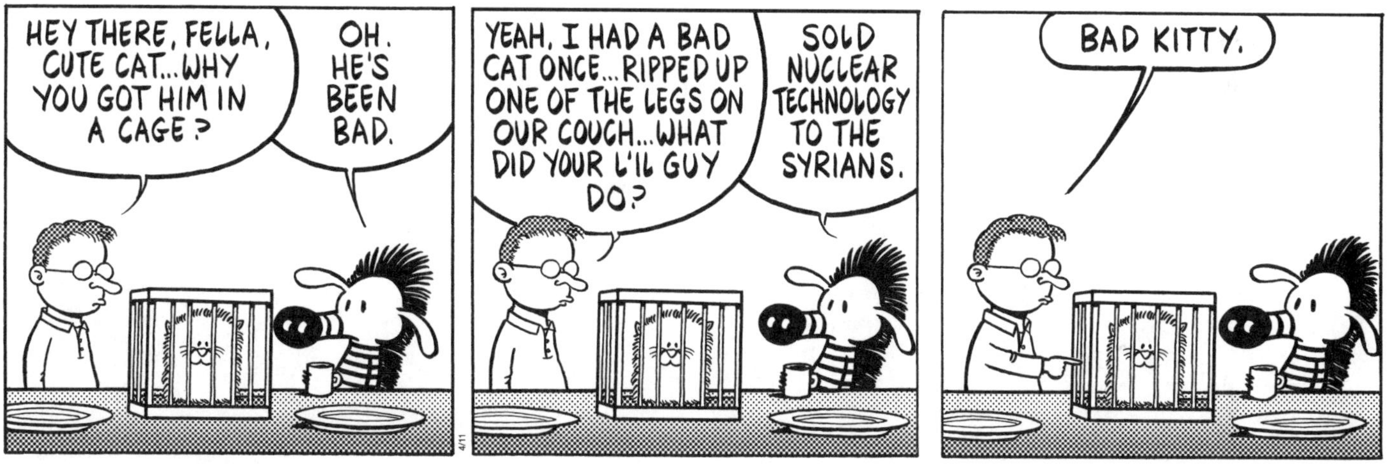
HEY THERE, FELLA, CUTE CAT...WHY YOU GOT HIM IN A CAGE?
OH. HE'S BEEN BAD.
YEAH. I HAD A BAD CAT ONCE...RIPPED UP ONE OF THE LEGS ON OUR COUCH...WHAT DID YOUR L'IL GUY DO?
SOLD NUCLEAR TECHNOLOGY TO THE SYRIANS.
BAD KITTY.

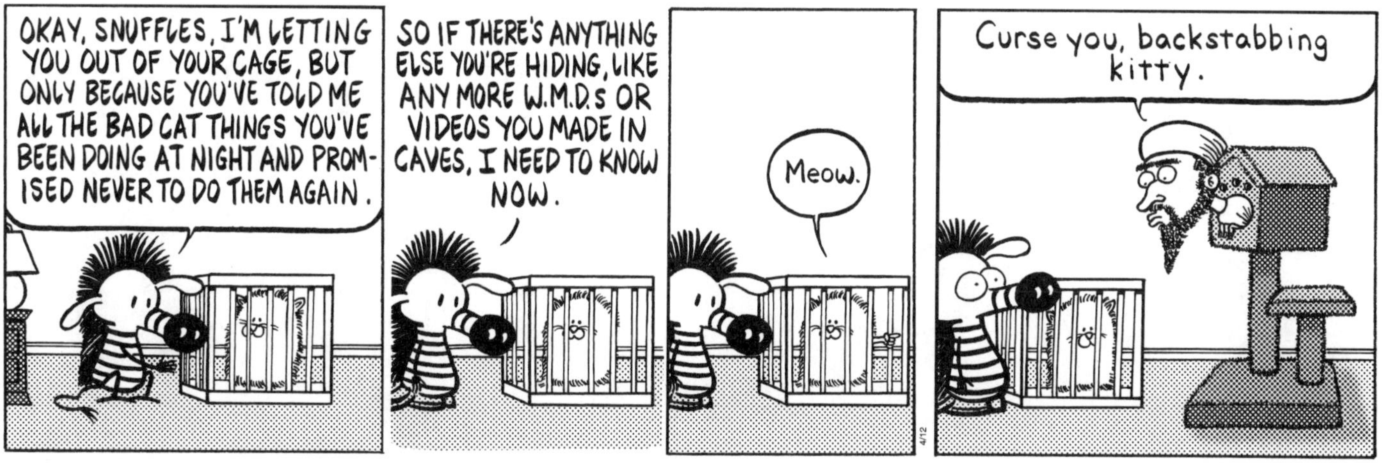
OKAY, SNUFFLES, I'M LETTING YOU OUT OF YOUR CAGE, BUT ONLY BECAUSE YOU'VE TOLD ME ALL THE BAD CAT THINGS YOU'VE BEEN DOING AT NIGHT AND PROMISED NEVER TO DO THEM AGAIN.
SO IF THERE'S ANYTHING ELSE YOU'RE HIDING, LIKE ANY MORE W.M.D.s OR VIDEOS YOU MADE IN CAVES, I NEED TO KNOW NOW.
Meow.
Curse you, backstabbing kitty.

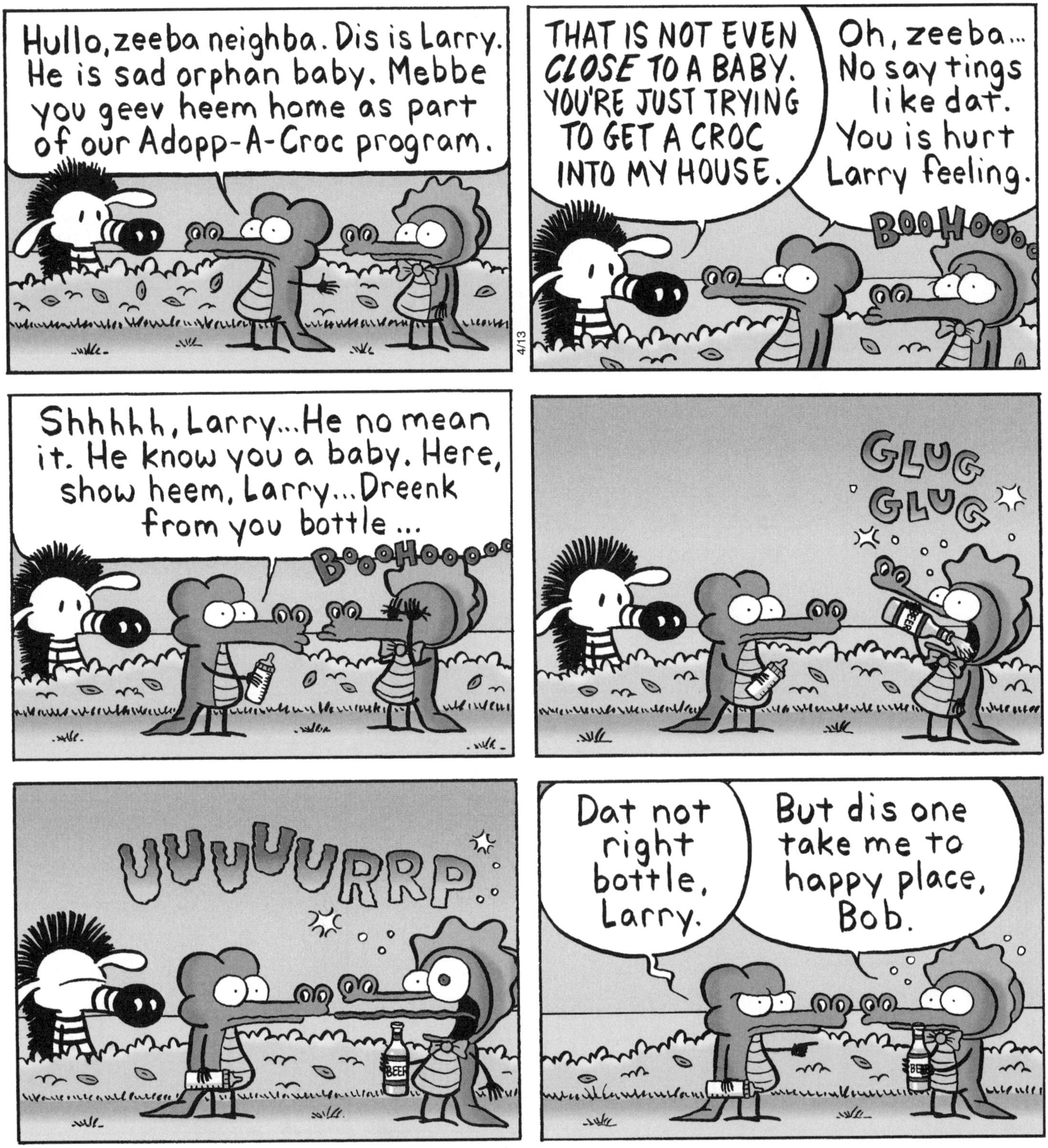
Hullo, zeeba neighba. Dis is Larry. He is sad orphan baby. Mebbe you geev heem home as part of our Adopp-A-Croc program.
4/13
THAT IS NOT EVEN *CLOSE* TO A BABY. YOU'RE JUST TRYING TO GET A CROC INTO MY HOUSE.
Oh, zeeba... No say tings like dat. You is hurt Larry feeling.
BOOHOOOOO
Shhhhh, Larry... He no mean it. He know you a baby. Here, show heem, Larry... Dreenk from you bottle...
BOOHOOOOOO
GLUG GLUG
BEER
UUUUURRP
BEER
Dat not right bottle, Larry.
But dis one take me to happy place, Bob.
BEER

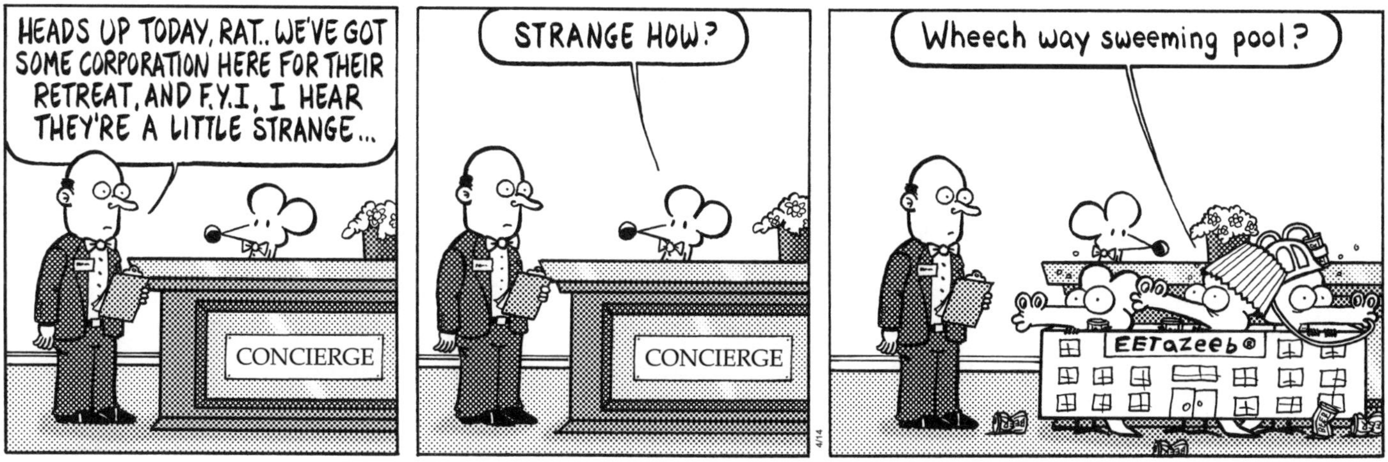
HEADS UP TODAY, RAT.. WE'VE GOT SOME CORPORATION HERE FOR THEIR RETREAT, AND F.Y.I., I HEAR THEY'RE A LITTLE STRANGE...
CONCIERGE
STRANGE HOW?
CONCIERGE
4/14
Wheech way sweeming pool?
EETazeeb®

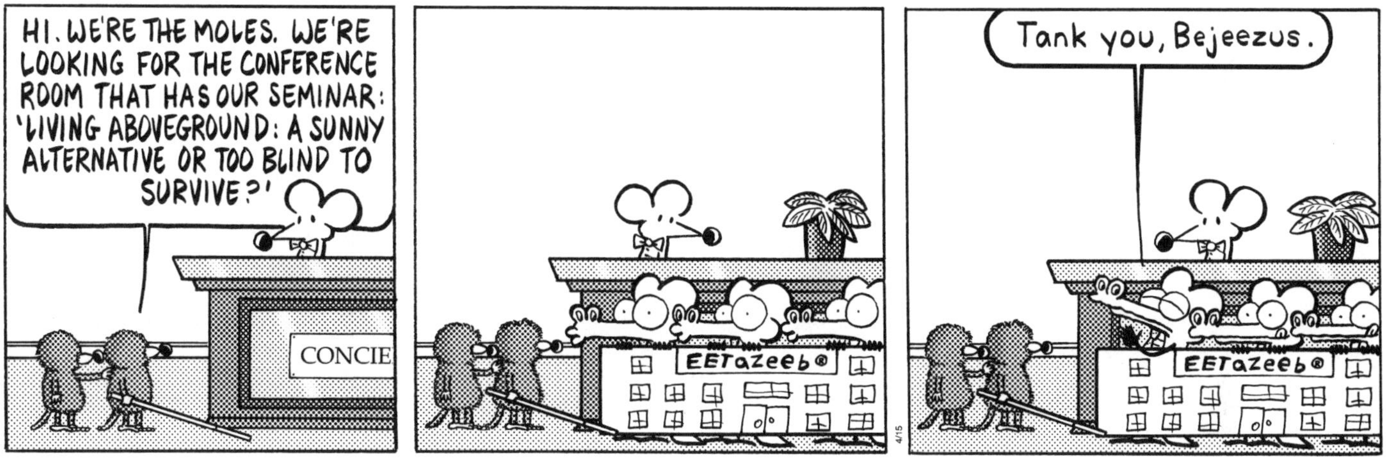
HI. WE'RE THE MOLES. WE'RE LOOKING FOR THE CONFERENCE ROOM THAT HAS OUR SEMINAR: 'LIVING ABOVEGROUND: A SUNNY ALTERNATIVE OR TOO BLIND TO SURVIVE?'
CONCIE
EETazeeb®
4/15
Tank you, Bejeezus.
EETazeeb®

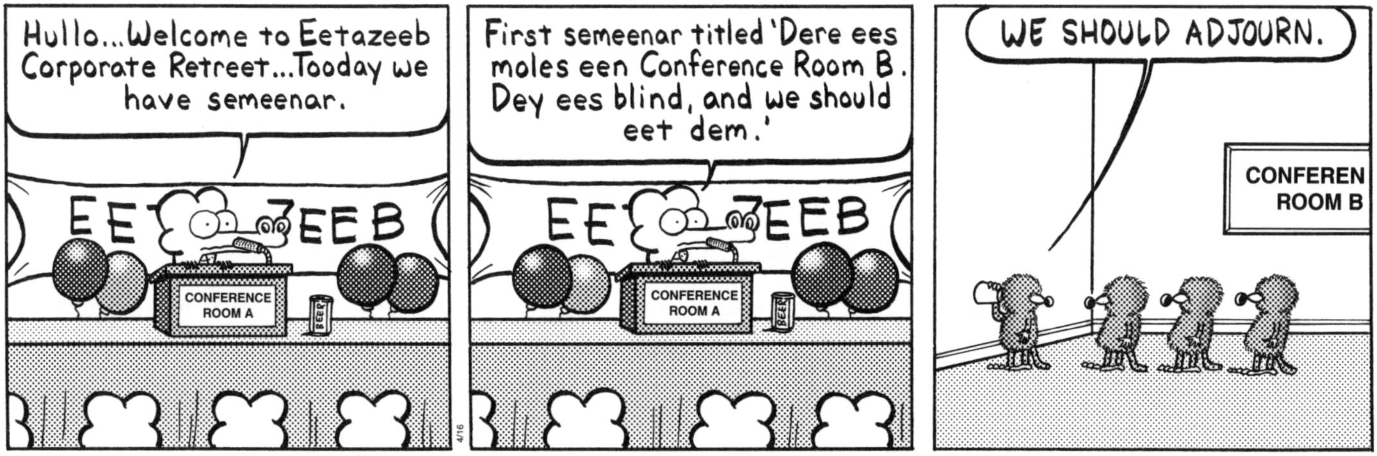
Hullo...Welcome to Eetazeeb Corporate Retreet...Tooday we have semeenar.
CONFERENCE ROOM A
BEER
4/16
First semeenar titled 'Dere ees moles een Conference Room B. Dey ees blind, and we should eet dem.'
CONFERENCE ROOM A
BEER
WE SHOULD ADJOURN.
CONFEREN
ROOM B

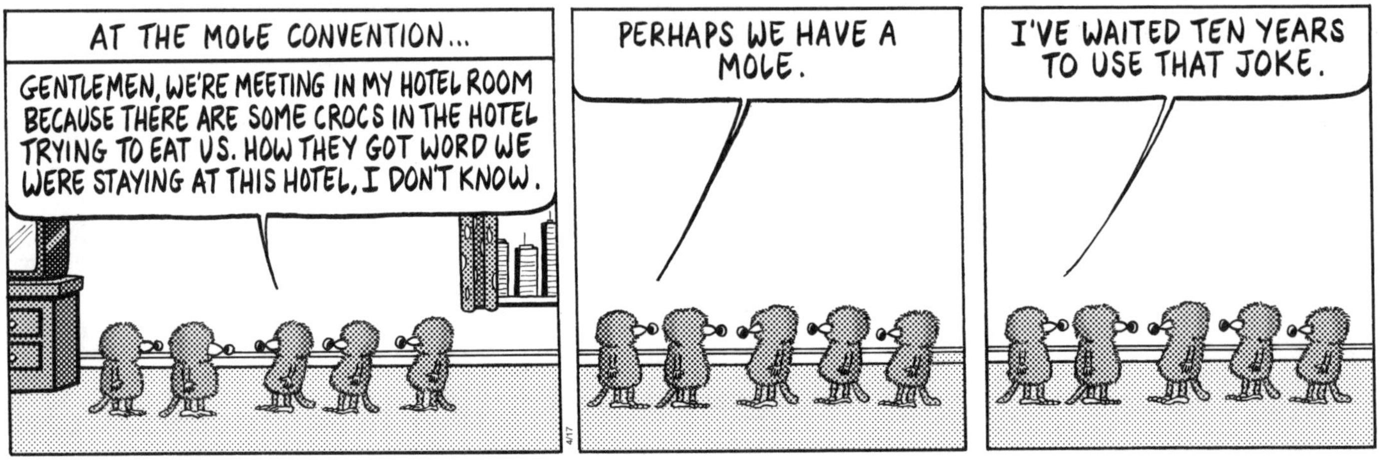
AT THE MOLE CONVENTION...
GENTLEMEN, WE'RE MEETING IN MY HOTEL ROOM BECAUSE THERE ARE SOME CROCS IN THE HOTEL TRYING TO EAT US. HOW THEY GOT WORD WE WERE STAYING AT THIS HOTEL, I DON'T KNOW.
4/17
PERHAPS WE HAVE A MOLE.
I'VE WAITED TEN YEARS TO USE THAT JOKE.

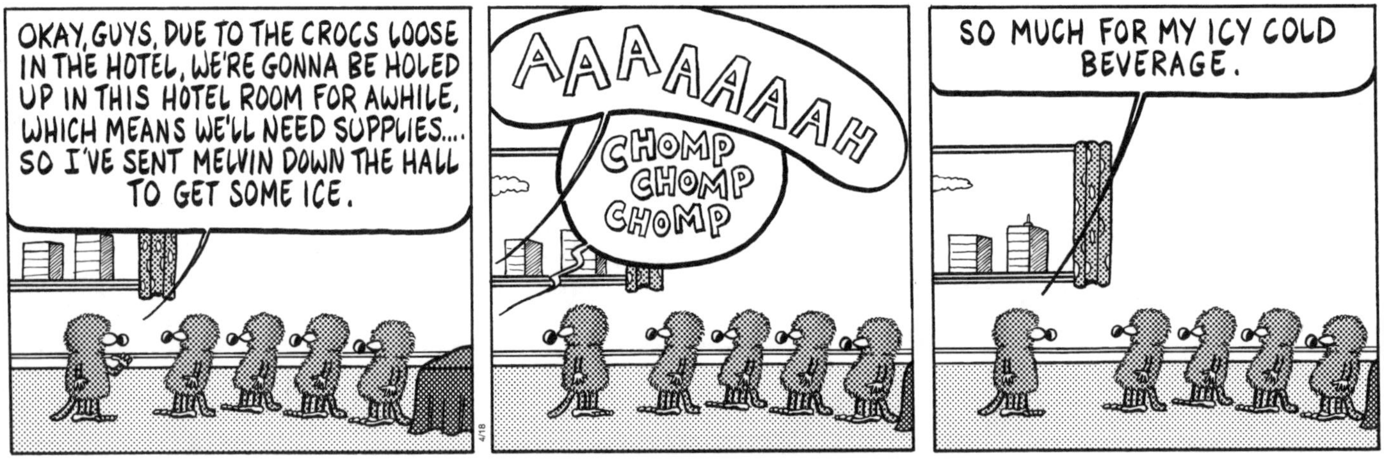
OKAY, GUYS, DUE TO THE CROCS LOOSE IN THE HOTEL, WE'RE GONNA BE HOLED UP IN THIS HOTEL ROOM FOR AWHILE, WHICH MEANS WE'LL NEED SUPPLIES.... SO I'VE SENT MELVIN DOWN THE HALL TO GET SOME ICE.
4/18
AAAAAAAAH
CHOMP CHOMP CHOMP
SO MUCH FOR MY ICY COLD BEVERAGE.

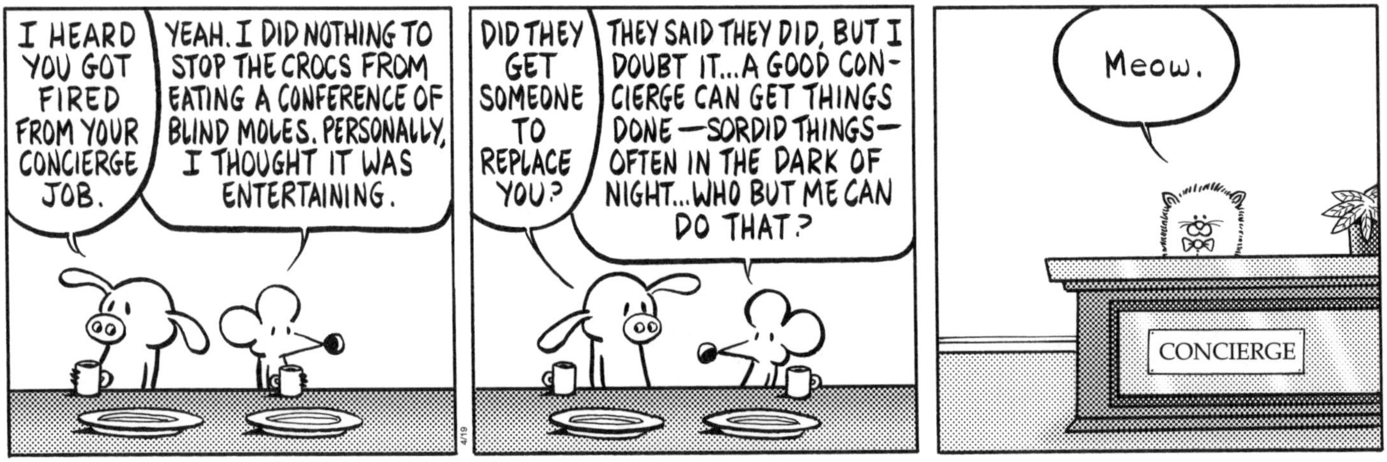
I HEARD YOU GOT FIRED FROM YOUR CONCIERGE JOB.
YEAH. I DID NOTHING TO STOP THE CROCS FROM EATING A CONFERENCE OF BLIND MOLES. PERSONALLY, I THOUGHT IT WAS ENTERTAINING.
4/19
DID THEY GET SOMEONE TO REPLACE YOU?
THEY SAID THEY DID, BUT I DOUBT IT...A GOOD CONCIERGE CAN GET THINGS DONE—SORDID THINGS—OFTEN IN THE DARK OF NIGHT...WHO BUT ME CAN DO THAT?
Meow.
CONCIERGE

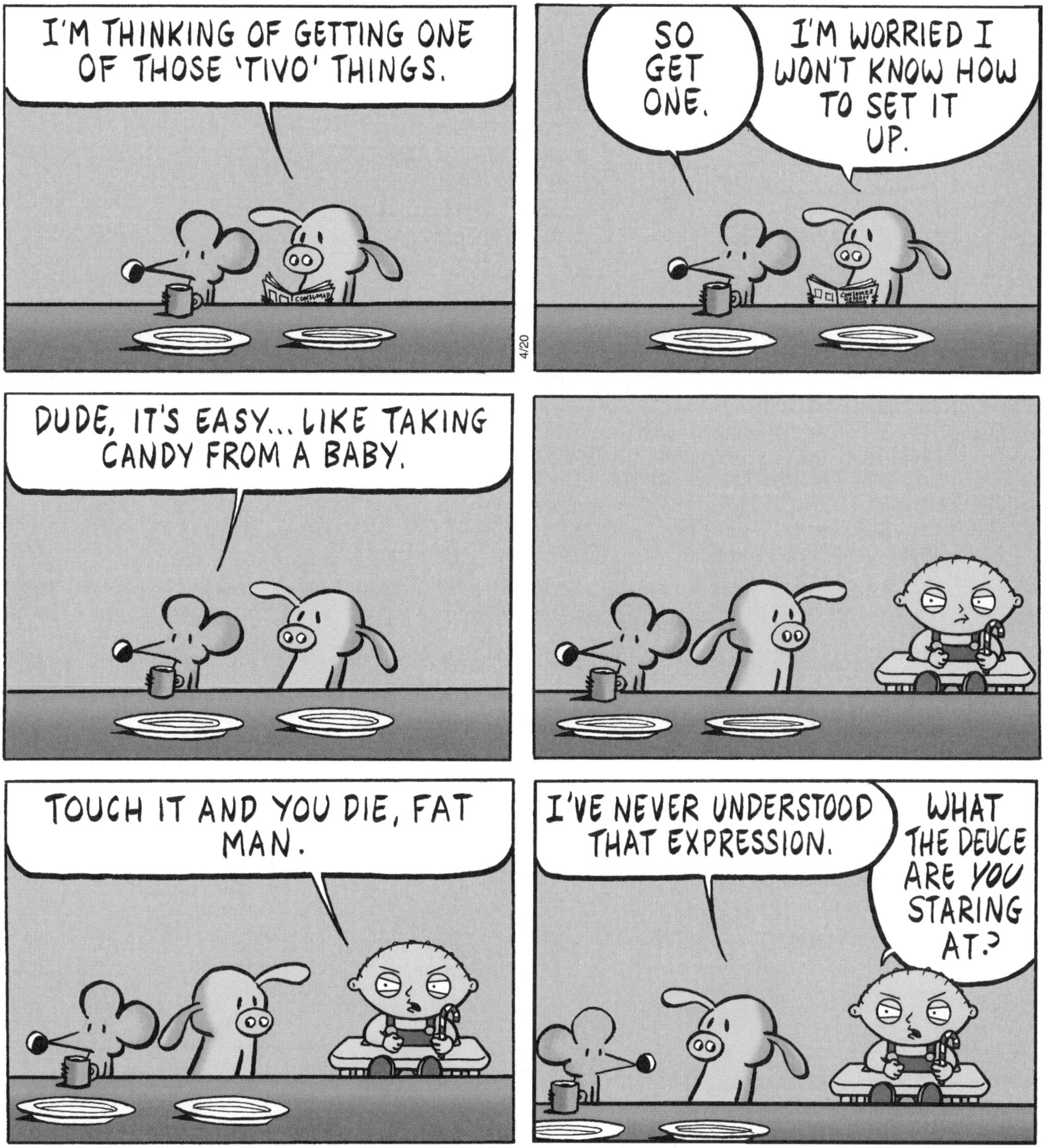
I'M THINKING OF GETTING ONE OF THOSE 'TIVO' THINGS.
4/20
SO GET ONE.
I'M WORRIED I WON'T KNOW HOW TO SET IT UP.
DUDE, IT'S EASY... LIKE TAKING CANDY FROM A BABY.
TOUCH IT AND YOU DIE, FAT MAN.
I'VE NEVER UNDERSTOOD THAT EXPRESSION.
WHAT THE DEUCE ARE *YOU* STARING AT?

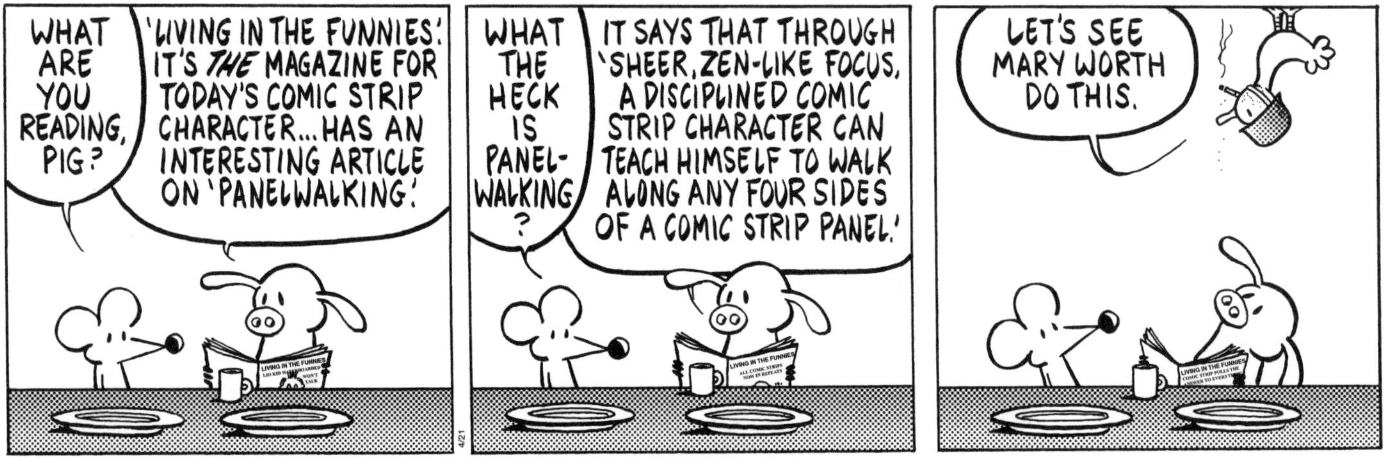
WHAT ARE YOU READING, PIG?
'LIVING IN THE FUNNIES.' IT'S *THE* MAGAZINE FOR TODAY'S COMIC STRIP CHARACTER... HAS AN INTERESTING ARTICLE ON 'PANELWALKING.'
WHAT THE HECK IS PANEL-WALKING?
IT SAYS THAT THROUGH 'SHEER, ZEN-LIKE FOCUS, A DISCIPLINED COMIC STRIP CHARACTER CAN TEACH HIMSELF TO WALK ALONG ANY FOUR SIDES OF A COMIC STRIP PANEL.'
LET'S SEE MARY WORTH DO THIS.

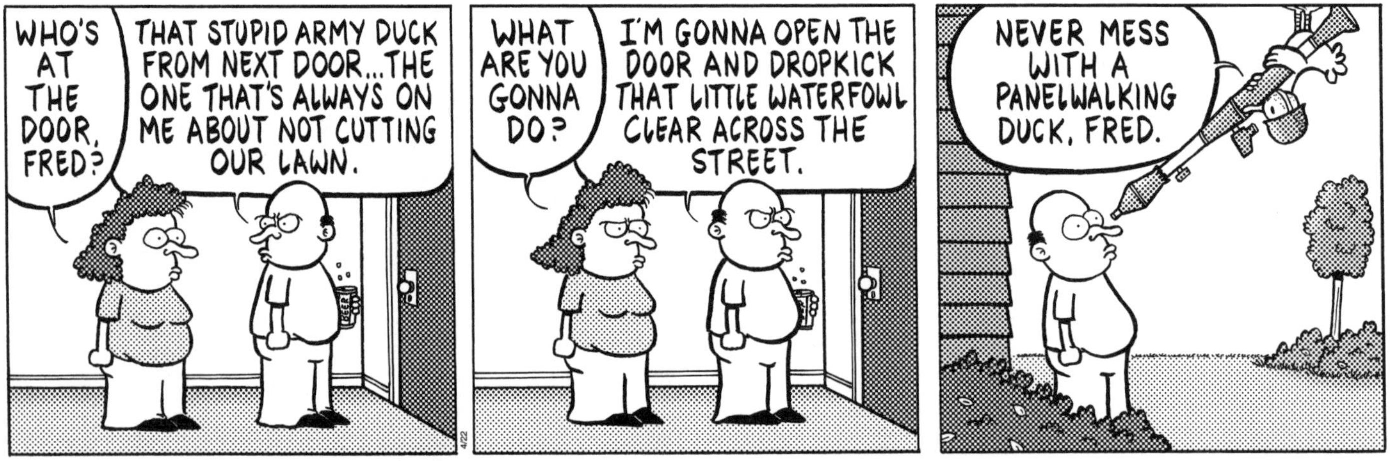
WHO'S AT THE DOOR, FRED?
THAT STUPID ARMY DUCK FROM NEXT DOOR... THE ONE THAT'S ALWAYS ON ME ABOUT NOT CUTTING OUR LAWN.
WHAT ARE YOU GONNA DO?
I'M GONNA OPEN THE DOOR AND DROPKICK THAT LITTLE WATERFOWL CLEAR ACROSS THE STREET.
NEVER MESS WITH A PANELWALKING DUCK, FRED.

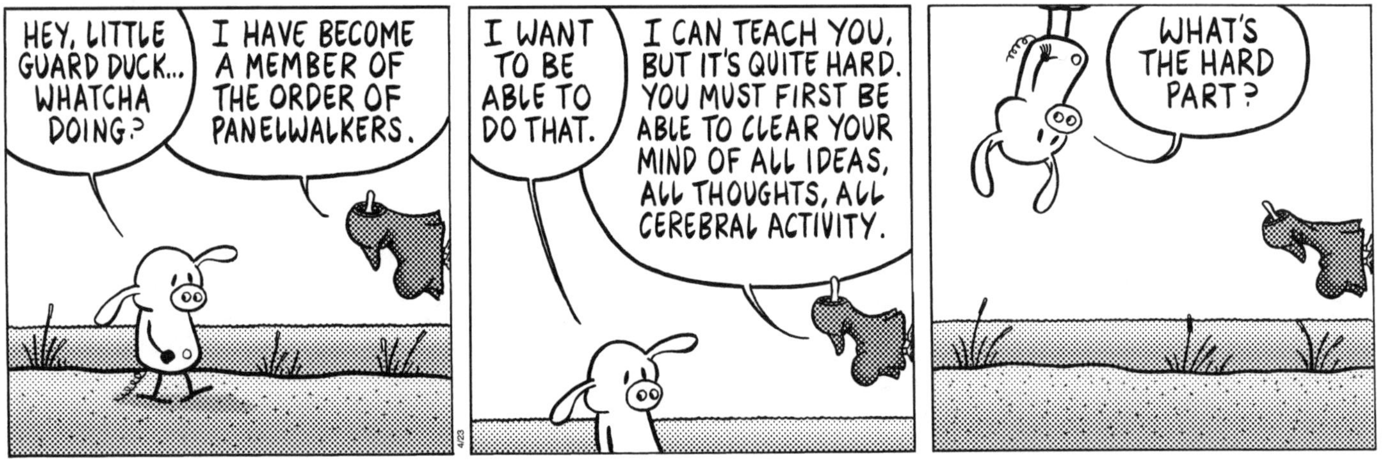
HEY, LITTLE GUARD DUCK... WHATCHA DOING?
I HAVE BECOME A MEMBER OF THE ORDER OF PANELWALKERS.
I WANT TO BE ABLE TO DO THAT.
I CAN TEACH YOU, BUT IT'S QUITE HARD. YOU MUST FIRST BE ABLE TO CLEAR YOUR MIND OF ALL IDEAS, ALL THOUGHTS, ALL CEREBRAL ACTIVITY.
WHAT'S THE HARD PART?

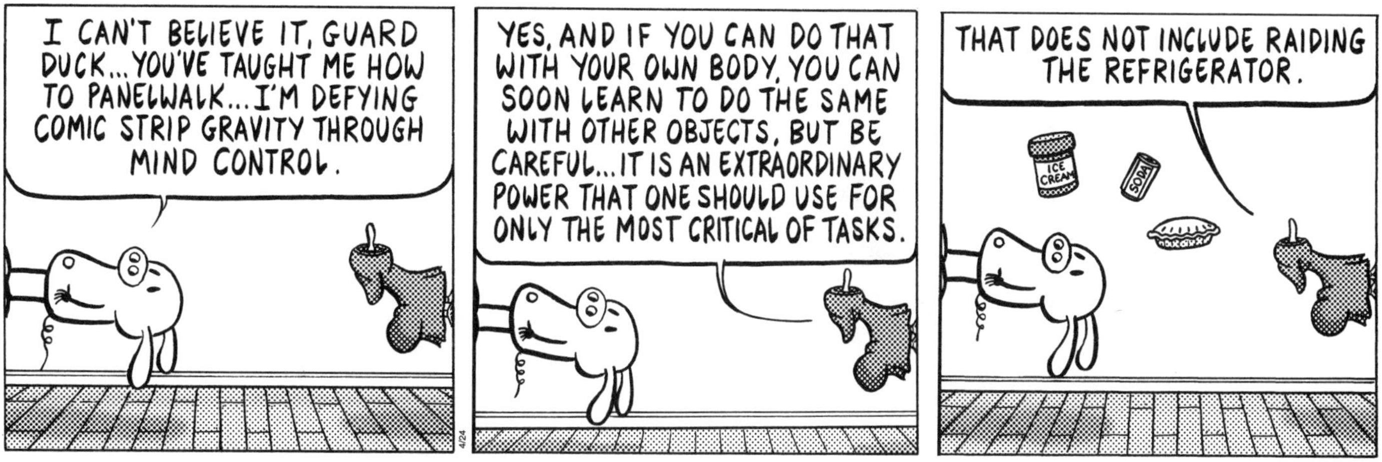
I CAN'T BELIEVE IT, GUARD DUCK... YOU'VE TAUGHT ME HOW TO PANELWALK... I'M DEFYING COMIC STRIP GRAVITY THROUGH MIND CONTROL.
YES, AND IF YOU CAN DO THAT WITH YOUR OWN BODY, YOU CAN SOON LEARN TO DO THE SAME WITH OTHER OBJECTS. BUT BE CAREFUL... IT IS AN EXTRAORDINARY POWER THAT ONE SHOULD USE FOR ONLY THE MOST CRITICAL OF TASKS.
THAT DOES NOT INCLUDE RAIDING THE REFRIGERATOR.
ICE CREAM
SODA

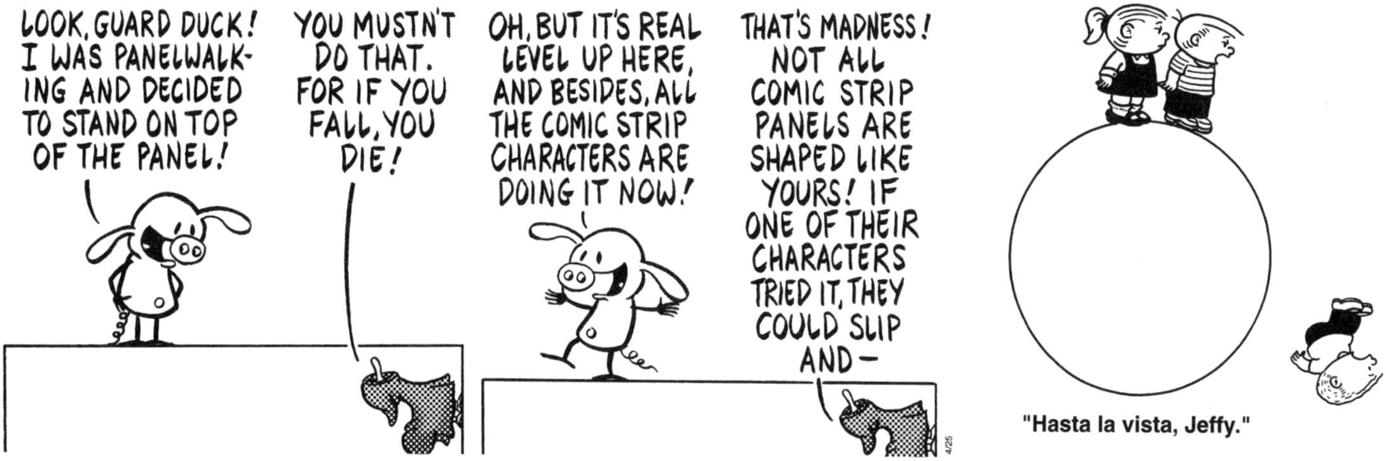
LOOK, GUARD DUCK! I WAS PANELWALKING AND DECIDED TO STAND ON TOP OF THE PANEL!
YOU MUSTN'T DO THAT. FOR IF YOU FALL, YOU DIE!
OH, BUT IT'S REAL LEVEL UP HERE, AND BESIDES, ALL THE COMIC STRIP CHARACTERS ARE DOING IT NOW!
THAT'S MADNESS! NOT ALL COMIC STRIP PANELS ARE SHAPED LIKE YOURS! IF ONE OF THEIR CHARACTERS TRIED IT, THEY COULD SLIP AND—
"Hasta la vista, Jeffy."

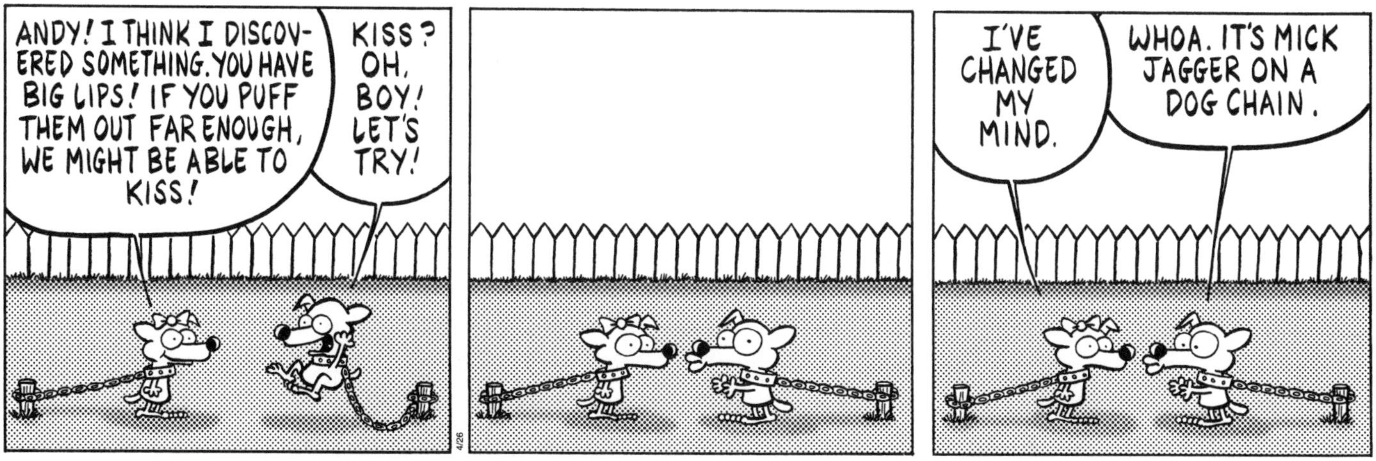
ANDY! I THINK I DISCOVERED SOMETHING. YOU HAVE BIG LIPS! IF YOU PUFF THEM OUT FAR ENOUGH, WE MIGHT BE ABLE TO KISS!
KISS? OH, BOY! LET'S TRY!
I'VE CHANGED MY MIND.
WHOA. IT'S MICK JAGGER ON A DOG CHAIN.

Yawn

OH, BOY... WHAT A MORNING.

ARE YOU UP YET, OLIVE?

Dear Andy,
My chain broke during the night. I don't know how it happened. It just snapped.

Please don't hate me for not waking you. I knew it was my one chance to be free and I couldn't bear to see you cry.

My only consolation is in knowing that you can be so happy even while attached to a chain... I love you.

4/27

40

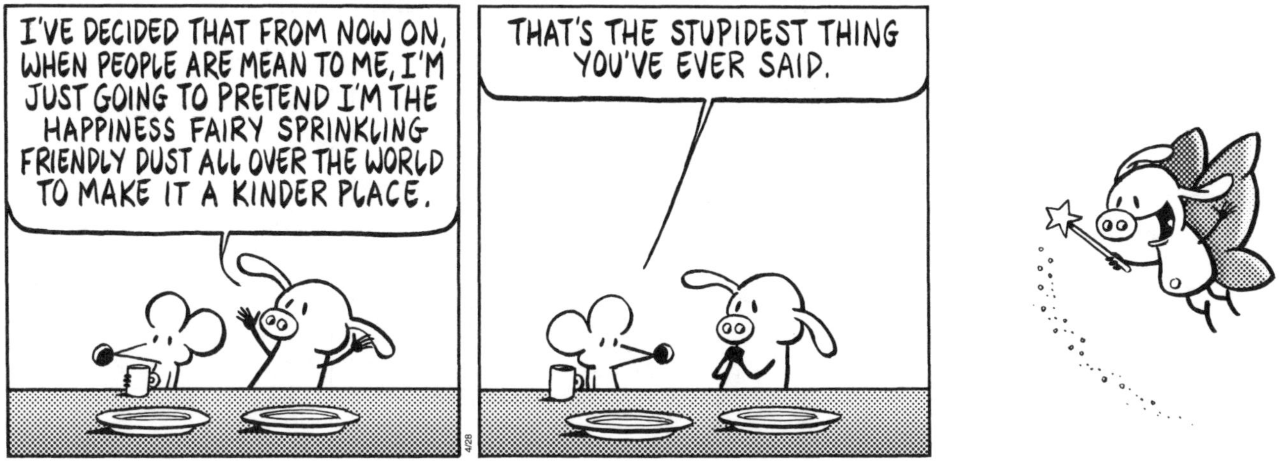
I'VE DECIDED THAT FROM NOW ON, WHEN PEOPLE ARE MEAN TO ME, I'M JUST GOING TO PRETEND I'M THE HAPPINESS FAIRY SPRINKLING FRIENDLY DUST ALL OVER THE WORLD TO MAKE IT A KINDER PLACE.
4/28
THAT'S THE STUPIDEST THING YOU'VE EVER SAID.

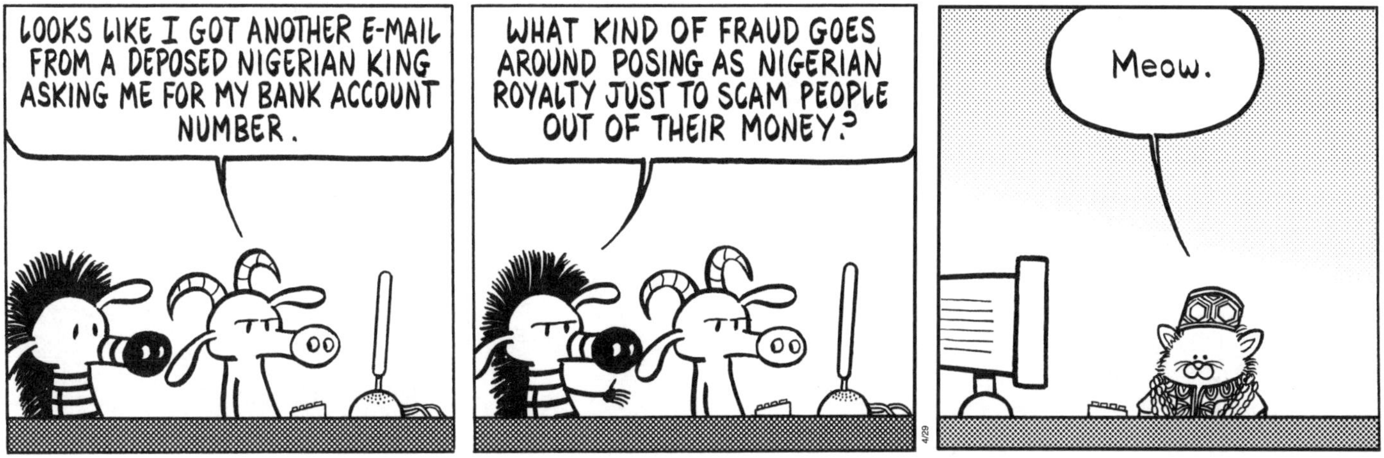
LOOKS LIKE I GOT ANOTHER E-MAIL FROM A DEPOSED NIGERIAN KING ASKING ME FOR MY BANK ACCOUNT NUMBER.
WHAT KIND OF FRAUD GOES AROUND POSING AS NIGERIAN ROYALTY JUST TO SCAM PEOPLE OUT OF THEIR MONEY?
4/29
Meow.

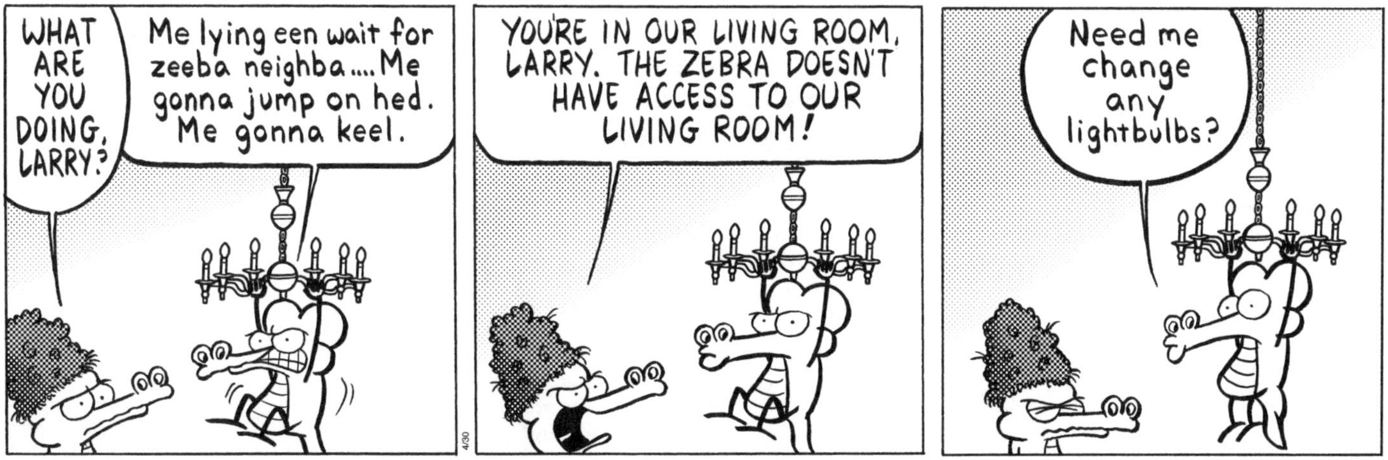
WHAT ARE YOU DOING, LARRY?
Me lying een wait for zeeba neighba.... Me gonna jump on hed. Me gonna keel.
4/30
YOU'RE IN OUR LIVING ROOM, LARRY. THE ZEBRA DOESN'T HAVE ACCESS TO OUR LIVING ROOM!
Need me change any lightbulbs?

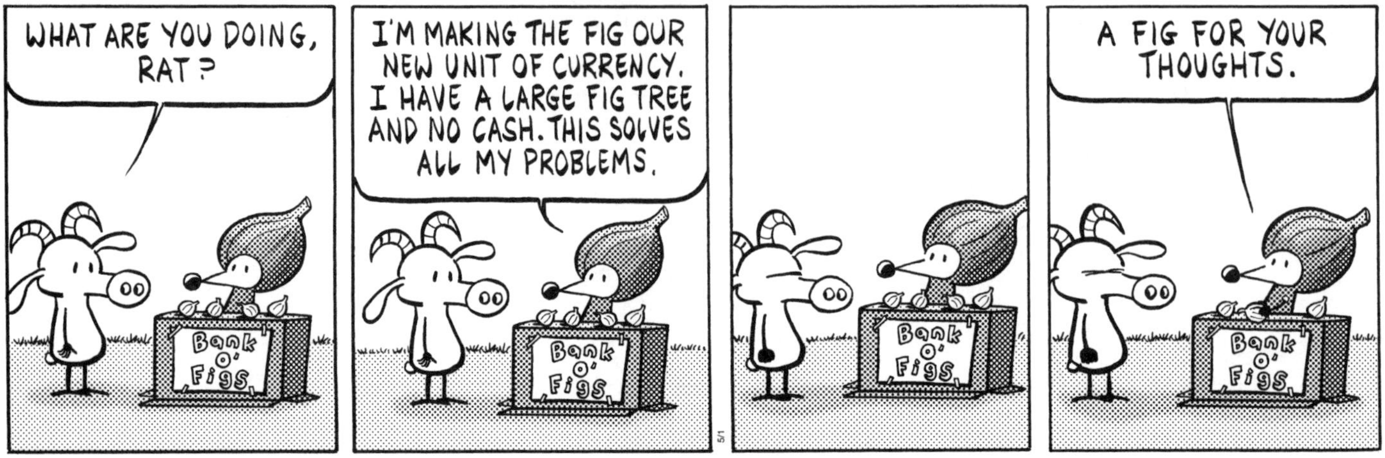
WHAT ARE YOU DOING, RAT?
I'M MAKING THE FIG OUR NEW UNIT OF CURRENCY. I HAVE A LARGE FIG TREE AND NO CASH. THIS SOLVES ALL MY PROBLEMS.
Bank o' Figs
A FIG FOR YOUR THOUGHTS.

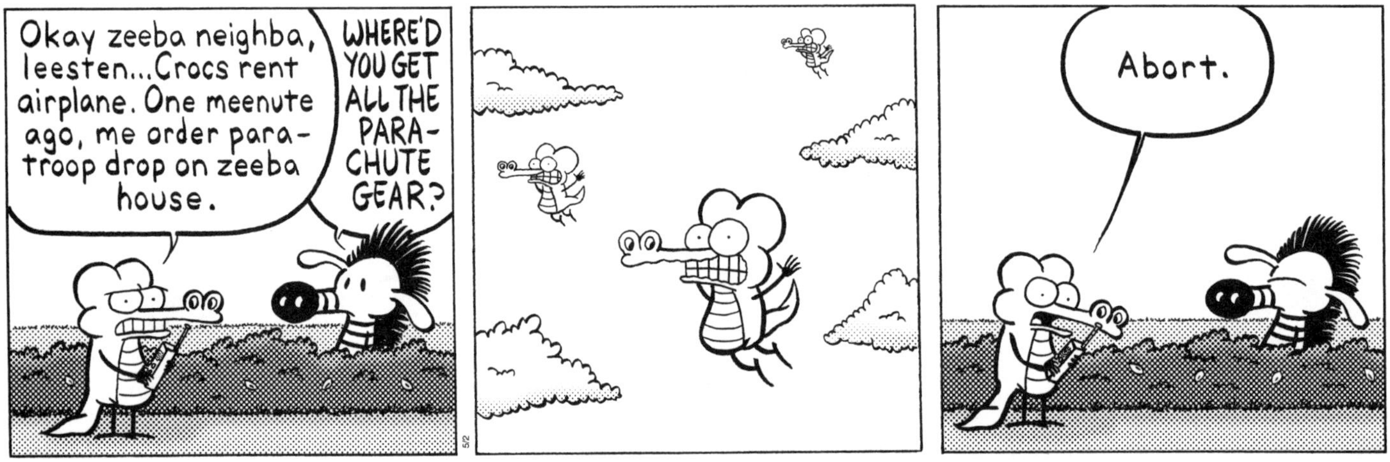
Okay zeeba neighba, leesten...Crocs rent airplane. One meenute ago, me order para-troop drop on zeeba house.
WHERE'D YOU GET ALL THE PARA-CHUTE GEAR?
Abort.

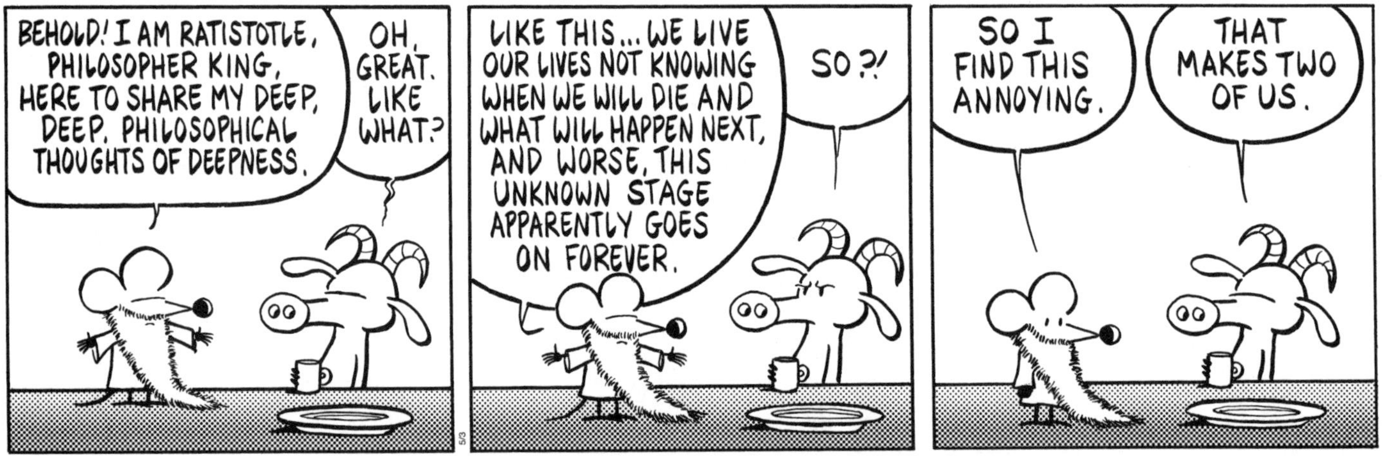
BEHOLD! I AM RATISTOTLE, PHILOSOPHER KING, HERE TO SHARE MY DEEP, DEEP, PHILOSOPHICAL THOUGHTS OF DEEPNESS.
OH, GREAT. LIKE WHAT?
LIKE THIS... WE LIVE OUR LIVES NOT KNOWING WHEN WE WILL DIE AND WHAT WILL HAPPEN NEXT, AND WORSE, THIS UNKNOWN STAGE APPARENTLY GOES ON FOREVER.
SO?!
SO I FIND THIS ANNOYING.
THAT MAKES TWO OF US.

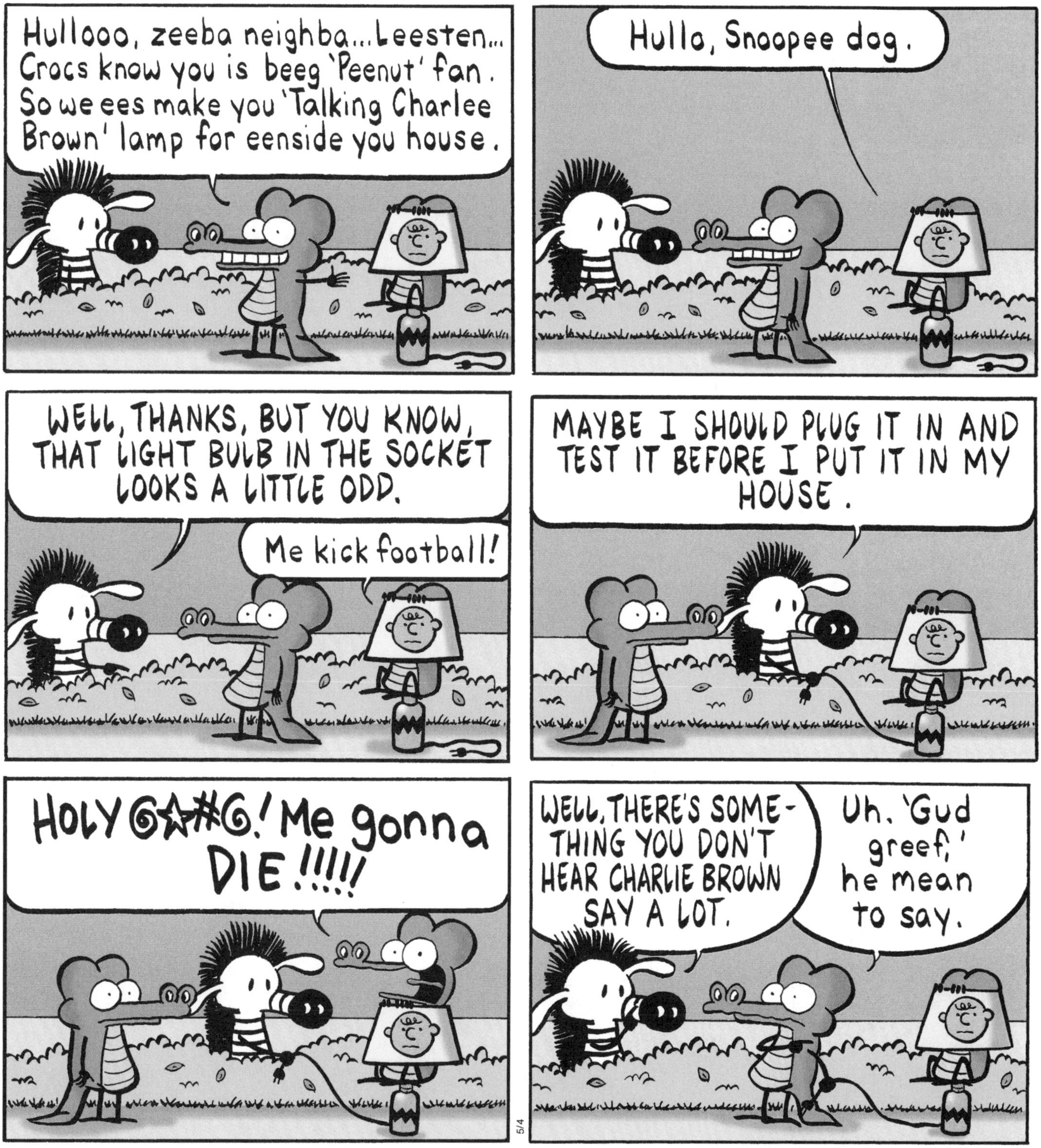
Hullooo, zeeba neighba...Leesten... Crocs know you is beeg 'Peenut' fan. So we ees make you 'Talking Charlee Brown' lamp for eenside you house.
Hullo, Snoopee dog.
WELL, THANKS, BUT YOU KNOW, THAT LIGHT BULB IN THE SOCKET LOOKS A LITTLE ODD.
Me kick football!
MAYBE I SHOULD PLUG IT IN AND TEST IT BEFORE I PUT IT IN MY HOUSE.
HOLY @☆#@! Me gonna DIE!!!!!
WELL, THERE'S SOME-THING YOU DON'T HEAR CHARLIE BROWN SAY A LOT.
Uh. 'Gud greef,' he mean to say.
5/4

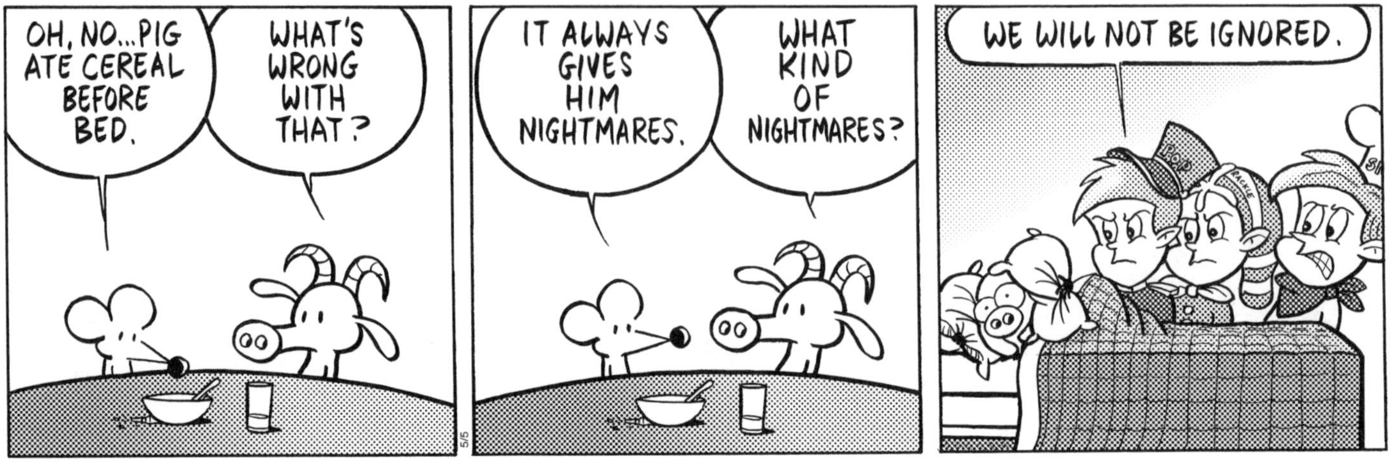
OH, NO...PIG ATE CEREAL BEFORE BED.
WHAT'S WRONG WITH THAT?
IT ALWAYS GIVES HIM NIGHTMARES.
WHAT KIND OF NIGHTMARES?
WE WILL NOT BE IGNORED.
POP
5/5

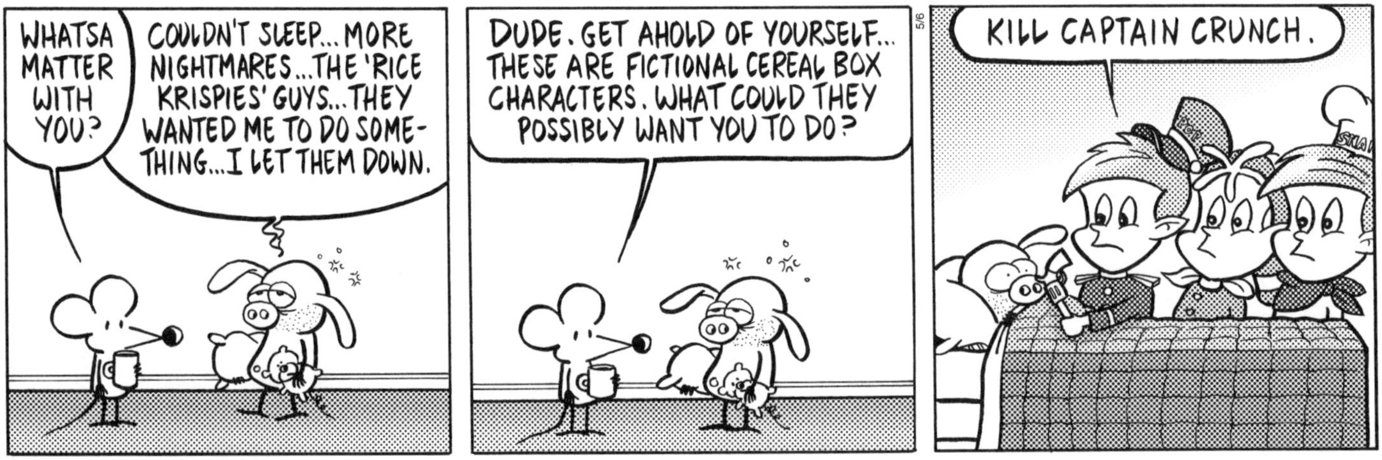
WHATSA MATTER WITH YOU?
COULDN'T SLEEP... MORE NIGHTMARES...THE 'RICE KRISPIES' GUYS...THEY WANTED ME TO DO SOMETHING...I LET THEM DOWN.
DUDE. GET AHOLD OF YOURSELF... THESE ARE FICTIONAL CEREAL BOX CHARACTERS. WHAT COULD THEY POSSIBLY WANT YOU TO DO?
KILL CAPTAIN CRUNCH.
POP
5/6

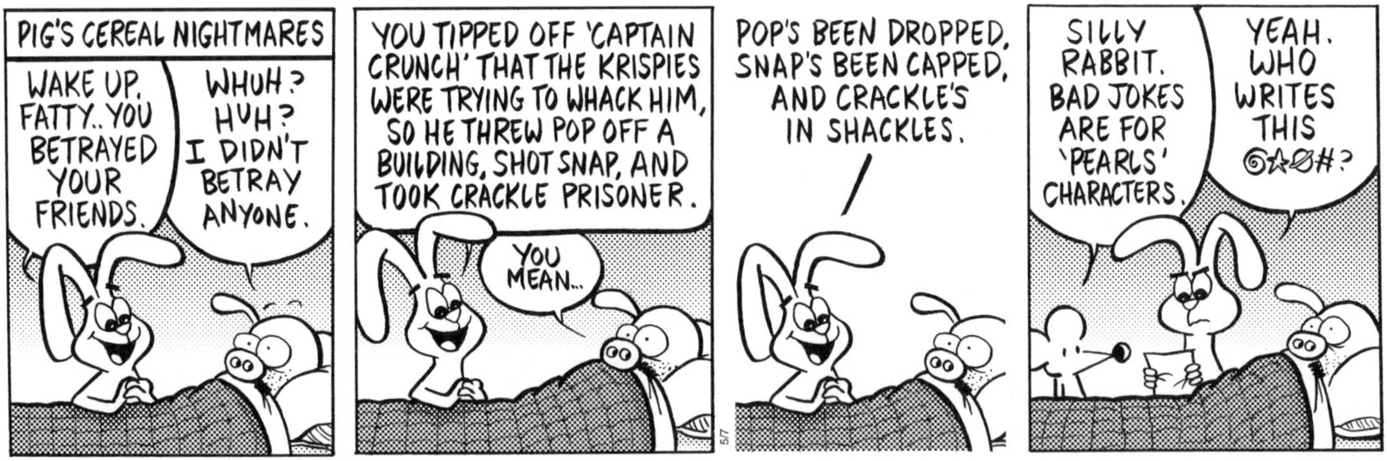
PIG'S CEREAL NIGHTMARES
WAKE UP, FATTY.. YOU BETRAYED YOUR FRIENDS.
WHUH? HUH? I DIDN'T BETRAY ANYONE.
YOU TIPPED OFF 'CAPTAIN CRUNCH' THAT THE KRISPIES WERE TRYING TO WHACK HIM, SO HE THREW POP OFF A BUILDING, SHOT SNAP, AND TOOK CRACKLE PRISONER.
YOU MEAN...
POP'S BEEN DROPPED, SNAP'S BEEN CAPPED, AND CRACKLE'S IN SHACKLES.
SILLY RABBIT. BAD JOKES ARE FOR 'PEARLS' CHARACTERS.
YEAH. WHO WRITES THIS @☆@#?
5/7

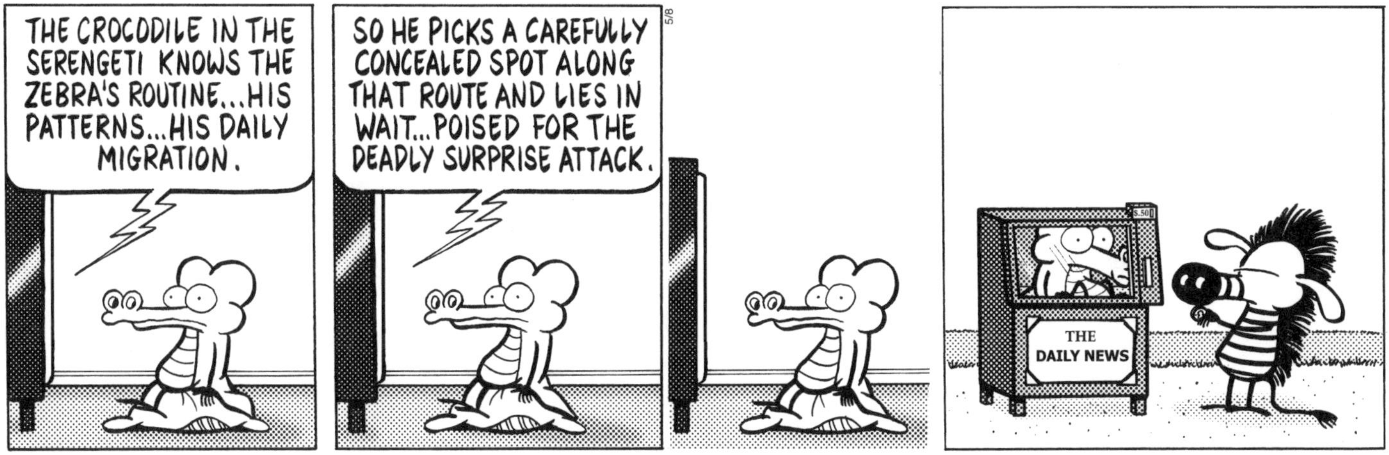
THE CROCODILE IN THE SERENGETI KNOWS THE ZEBRA'S ROUTINE...HIS PATTERNS...HIS DAILY MIGRATION.
SO HE PICKS A CAREFULLY CONCEALED SPOT ALONG THAT ROUTE AND LIES IN WAIT...POISED FOR THE DEADLY SURPRISE ATTACK.
5/8
THE DAILY NEWS

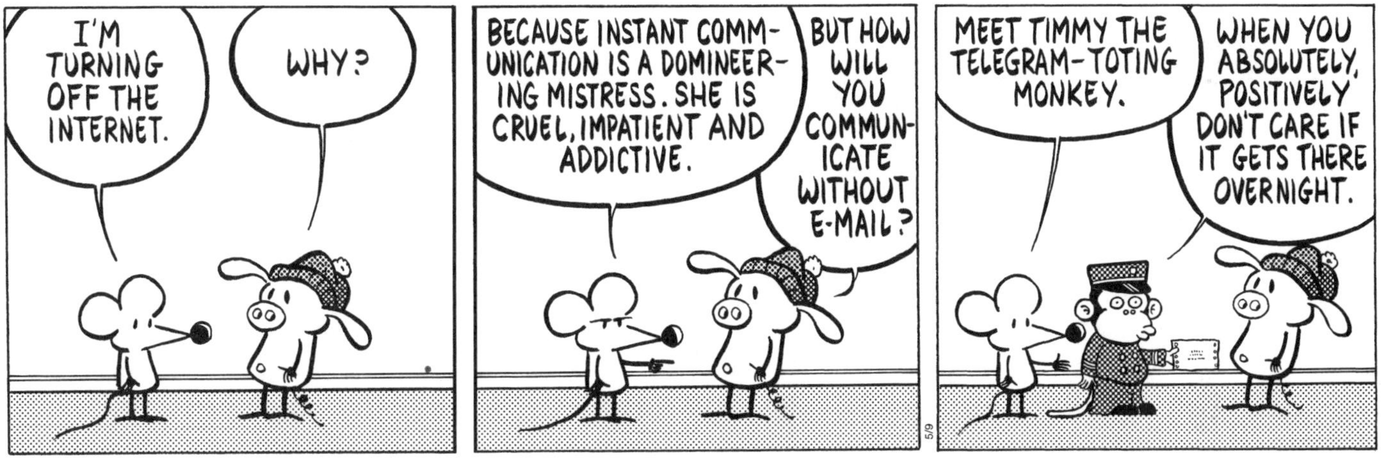
I'M TURNING OFF THE INTERNET.
WHY?
BECAUSE INSTANT COMMUNICATION IS A DOMINEERING MISTRESS. SHE IS CRUEL, IMPATIENT AND ADDICTIVE.
BUT HOW WILL YOU COMMUNICATE WITHOUT E-MAIL?
MEET TIMMY THE TELEGRAM-TOTING MONKEY.
WHEN YOU ABSOLUTELY, POSITIVELY DON'T CARE IF IT GETS THERE OVERNIGHT.
5/9

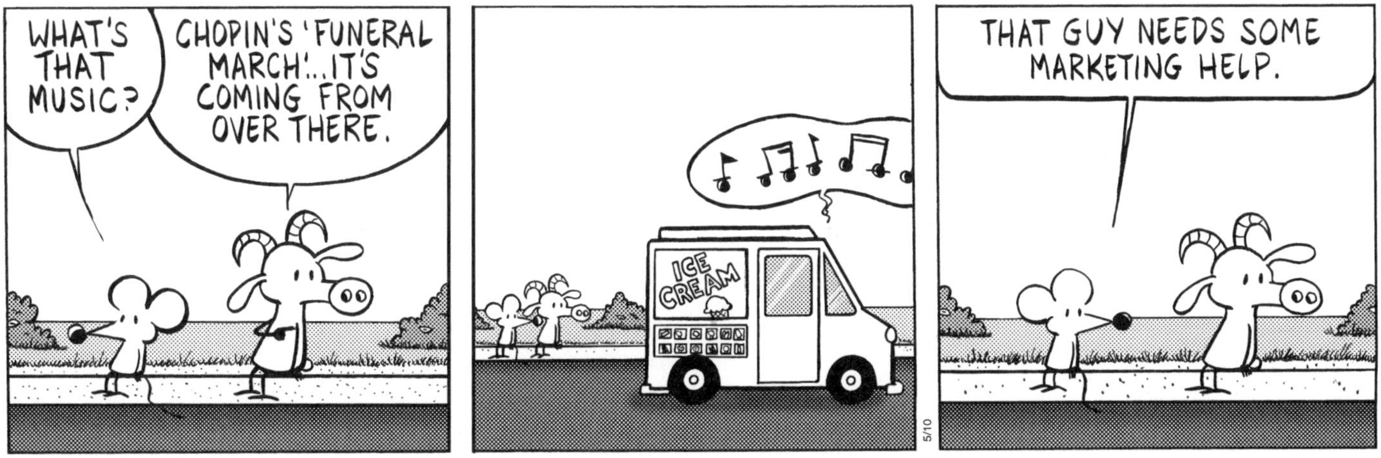
WHAT'S THAT MUSIC?
CHOPIN'S 'FUNERAL MARCH'...IT'S COMING FROM OVER THERE.
ICE CREAM
THAT GUY NEEDS SOME MARKETING HELP.
5/10

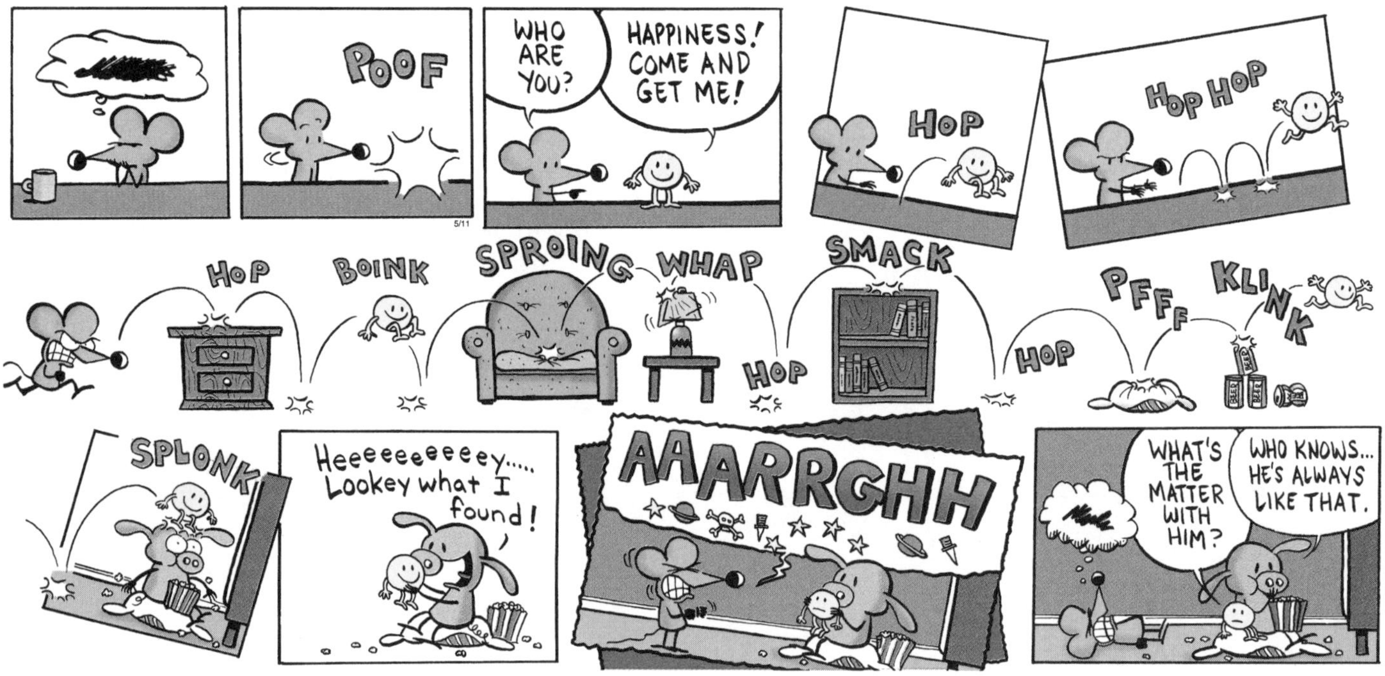
POOF
5/11
WHO ARE YOU?
HAPPINESS! COME AND GET ME!
HOP
HOP HOP
HOP
BOINK
SPROING
WHAP
HOP
SMACK
HOP
PFFF
KLINK
SPLONK
Heeeeeeeeeey..... Lookey what I found!
AAARRGHH
WHAT'S THE MATTER WITH HIM?
WHO KNOWS... HE'S ALWAYS LIKE THAT.

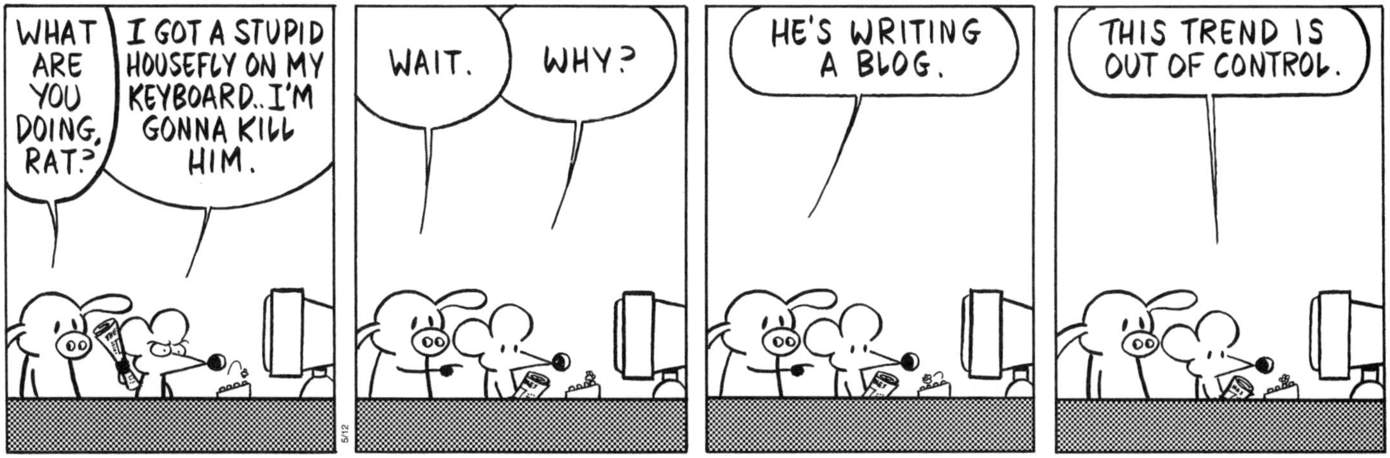
WHAT ARE YOU DOING, RAT?
I GOT A STUPID HOUSEFLY ON MY KEYBOARD.. I'M GONNA KILL HIM.
5/12
WAIT.
WHY?
HE'S WRITING A BLOG.
THIS TREND IS OUT OF CONTROL.

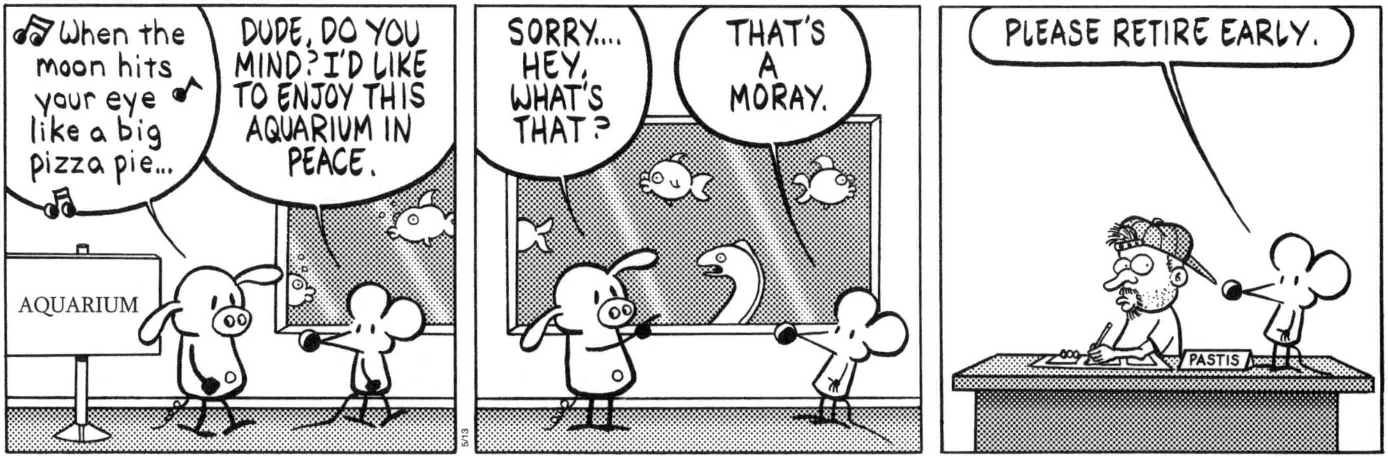
When the moon hits your eye like a big pizza pie...
DUDE, DO YOU MIND? I'D LIKE TO ENJOY THIS AQUARIUM IN PEACE.
AQUARIUM
5/13
SORRY.... HEY, WHAT'S THAT?
THAT'S A MORAY.
PLEASE RETIRE EARLY.
PASTIS

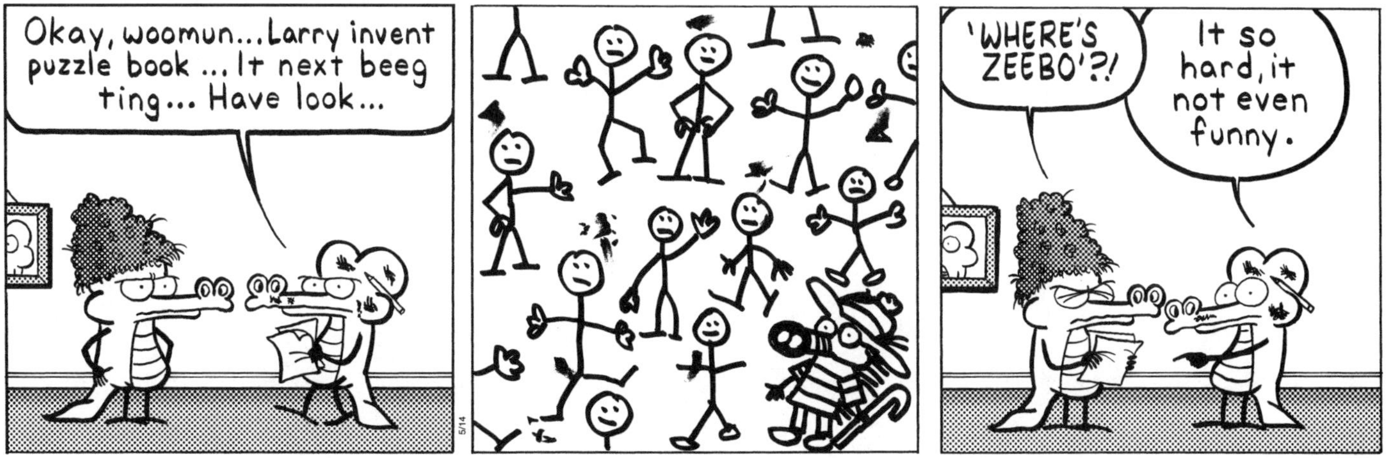
Okay, woomun... Larry invent puzzle book ... It next beeg ting... Have look...
5/14
'WHERE'S ZEEBO'?!
It so hard, it not even funny.

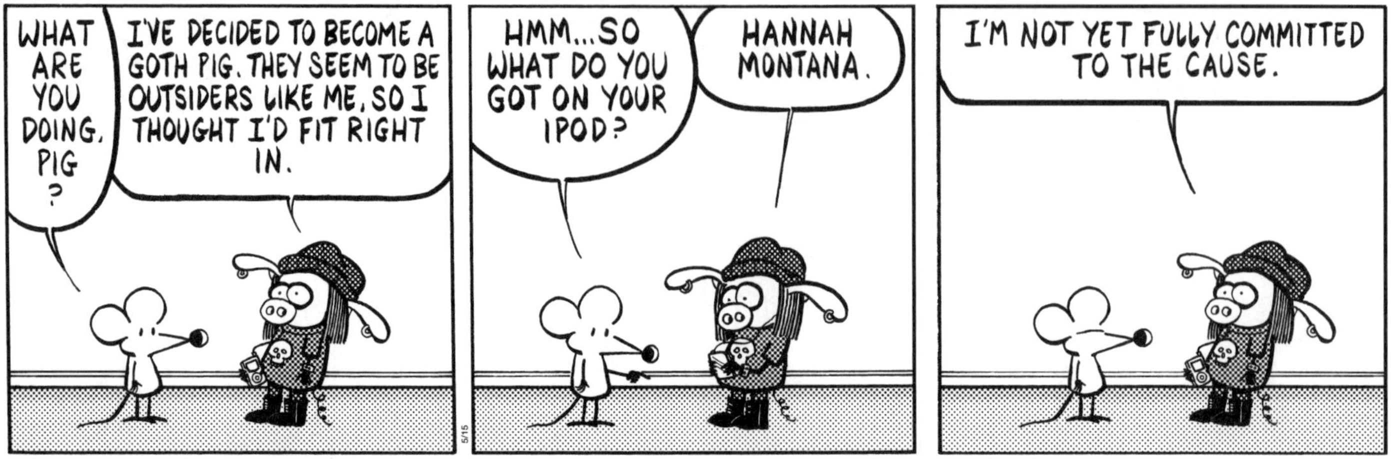
WHAT ARE YOU DOING, PIG?
I'VE DECIDED TO BECOME A GOTH PIG. THEY SEEM TO BE OUTSIDERS LIKE ME, SO I THOUGHT I'D FIT RIGHT IN.
HMM...SO WHAT DO YOU GOT ON YOUR IPOD?
HANNAH MONTANA.
I'M NOT YET FULLY COMMITTED TO THE CAUSE.

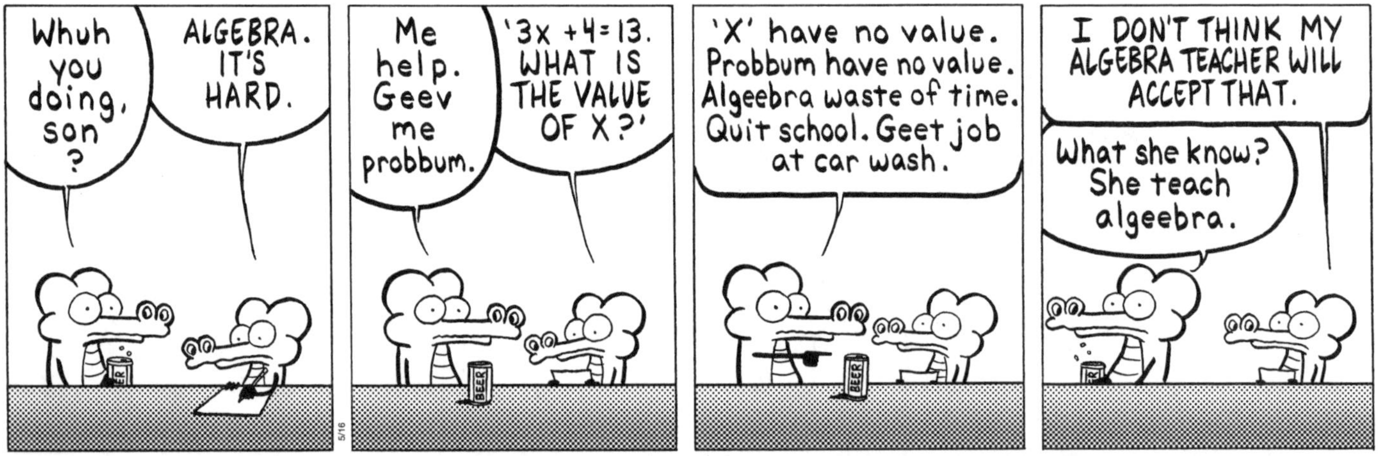
Whuh you doing, son?
ALGEBRA. IT'S HARD.
Me help. Geev me probbum.
'3X + 4 = 13. WHAT IS THE VALUE OF X?'
'X' have no value. Probbum have no value. Algeebra waste of time. Quit school. Geet job at car wash.
I DON'T THINK MY ALGEBRA TEACHER WILL ACCEPT THAT.
What she know? She teach algeebra.

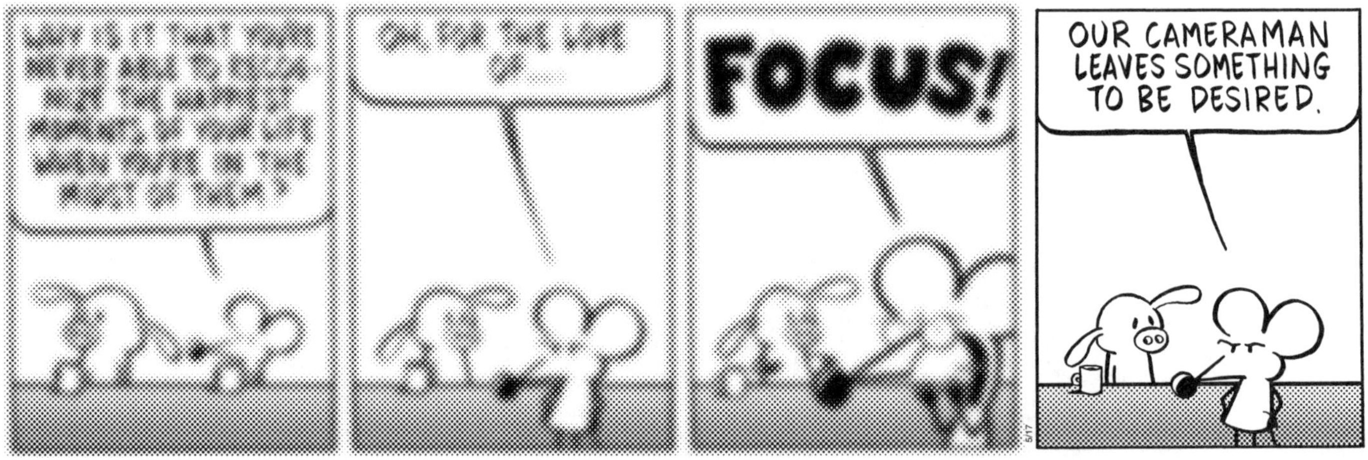
FOCUS!
OUR CAMERAMAN LEAVES SOMETHING TO BE DESIRED.

Dear Werld Wyldlife Funnd, We hear you does gud stuff sayving aneemals like zeebas. Gud for you.

But me and Bob have better plan.

KEEL DEM

We not care how. Sticks. Stones. Brake dere bones. Just keel dem all and ship to us.

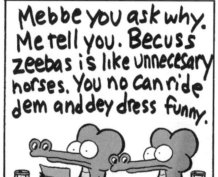

Mebbe you ask why. Me tell you. Becuss zeebas is like unnecesary horses. You no can ride dem and dey dress funny.

You know, Larry... Some people say you no can keel zeebas like dat becuss you disrupt vital link in food chain.

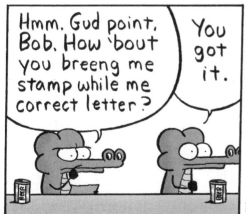

Hmm. Gud point, Bob. How 'bout you breeng me stamp while me correct letter?

You got it.

P.S. Peese keel Bob too.

5/18

49

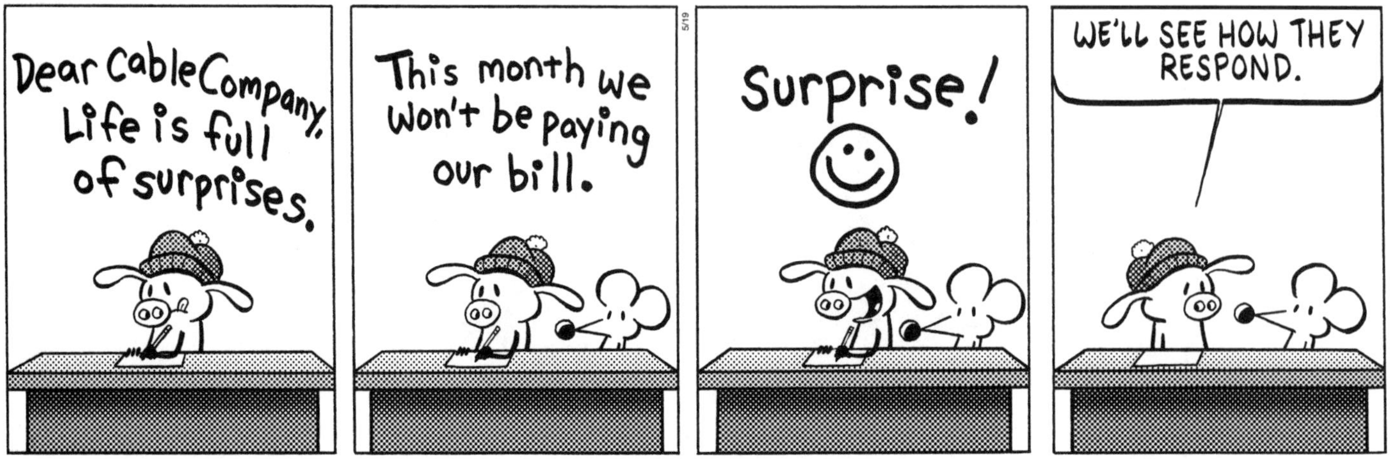
Dear Cable Company, Life is full of surprises.
This month we won't be paying our bill.
Surprise!
WE'LL SEE HOW THEY RESPOND.

5/19

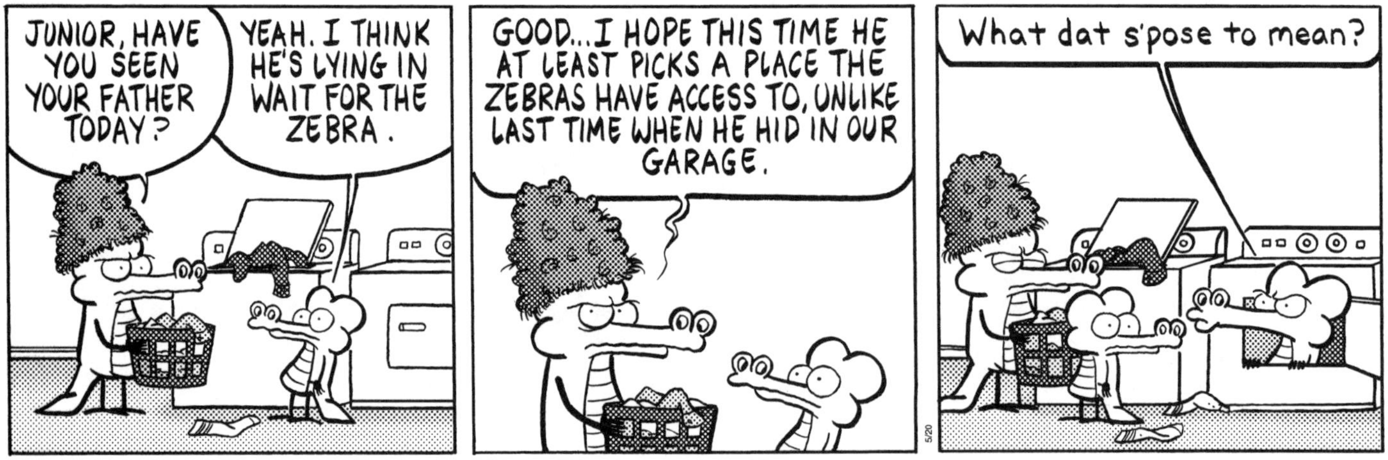
JUNIOR, HAVE YOU SEEN YOUR FATHER TODAY?
YEAH. I THINK HE'S LYING IN WAIT FOR THE ZEBRA.
GOOD...I HOPE THIS TIME HE AT LEAST PICKS A PLACE THE ZEBRAS HAVE ACCESS TO, UNLIKE LAST TIME WHEN HE HID IN OUR GARAGE.
What dat s'pose to mean?

5/20

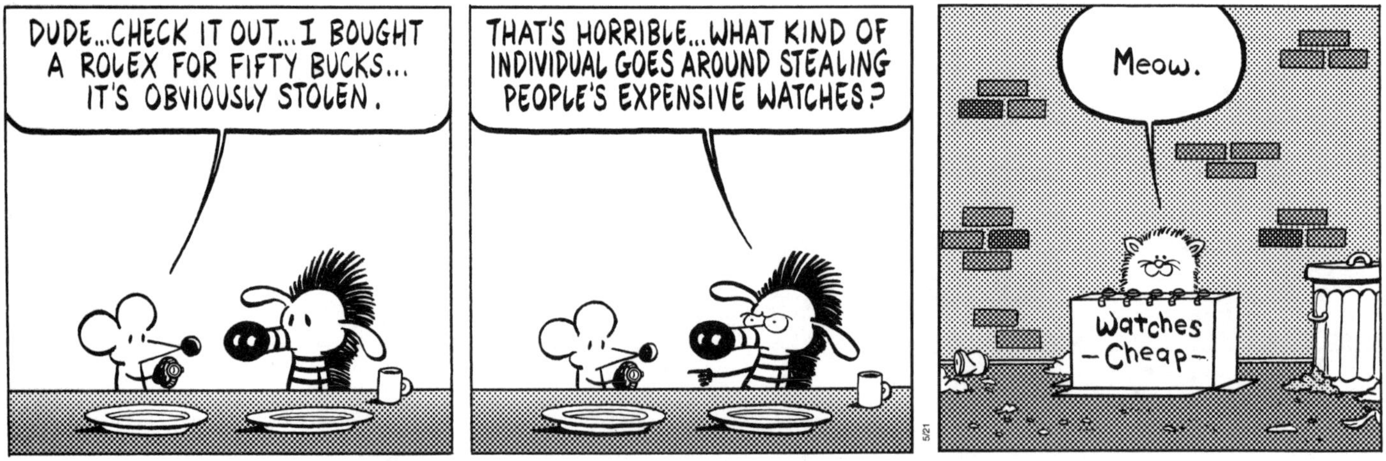
DUDE...CHECK IT OUT...I BOUGHT A ROLEX FOR FIFTY BUCKS... IT'S OBVIOUSLY STOLEN.
THAT'S HORRIBLE...WHAT KIND OF INDIVIDUAL GOES AROUND STEALING PEOPLE'S EXPENSIVE WATCHES?
Meow.
Watches -Cheap-

5/21

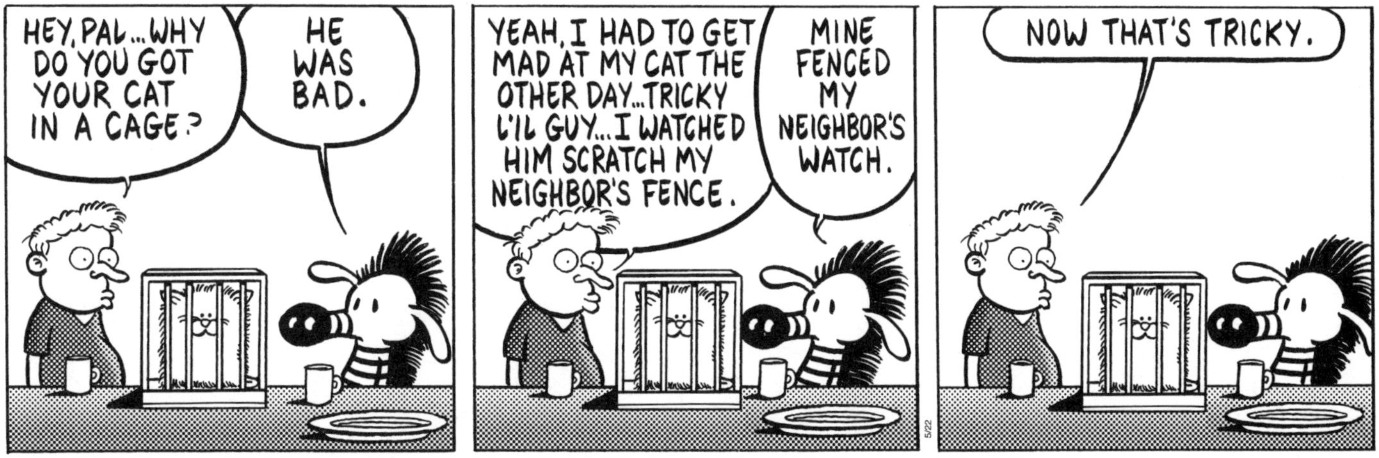
HEY, PAL...WHY DO YOU GOT YOUR CAT IN A CAGE?
HE WAS BAD.
YEAH, I HAD TO GET MAD AT MY CAT THE OTHER DAY...TRICKY L'IL GUY...I WATCHED HIM SCRATCH MY NEIGHBOR'S FENCE.
MINE FENCED MY NEIGHBOR'S WATCH.
5/22
NOW THAT'S TRICKY.

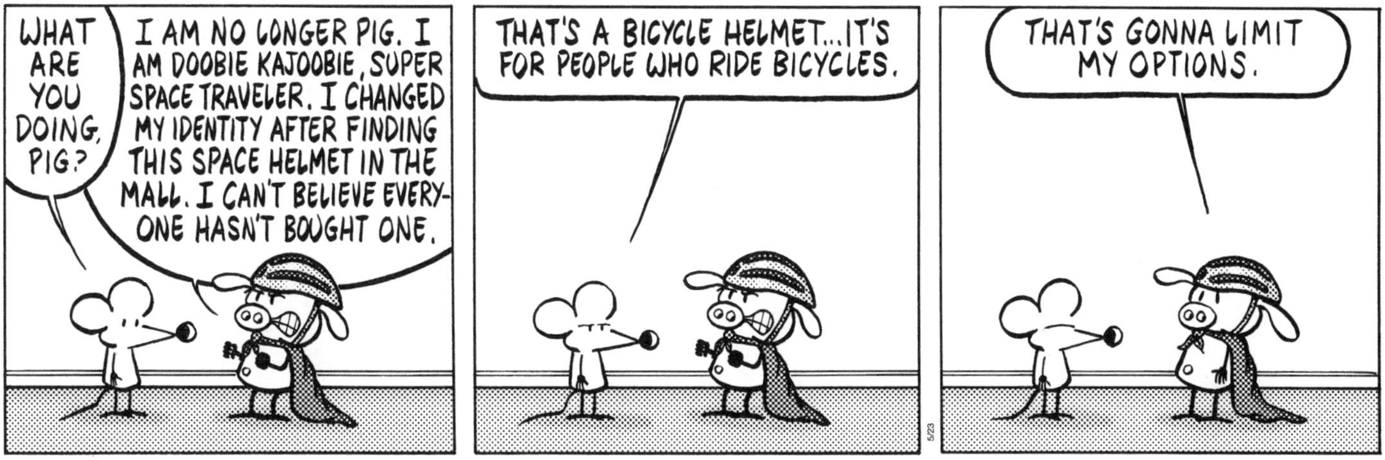
WHAT ARE YOU DOING, PIG?
I AM NO LONGER PIG. I AM DOOBIE KAJOOBIE, SUPER SPACE TRAVELER. I CHANGED MY IDENTITY AFTER FINDING THIS SPACE HELMET IN THE MALL. I CAN'T BELIEVE EVERY-ONE HASN'T BOUGHT ONE.
THAT'S A BICYCLE HELMET...IT'S FOR PEOPLE WHO RIDE BICYCLES.
5/23
THAT'S GONNA LIMIT MY OPTIONS.

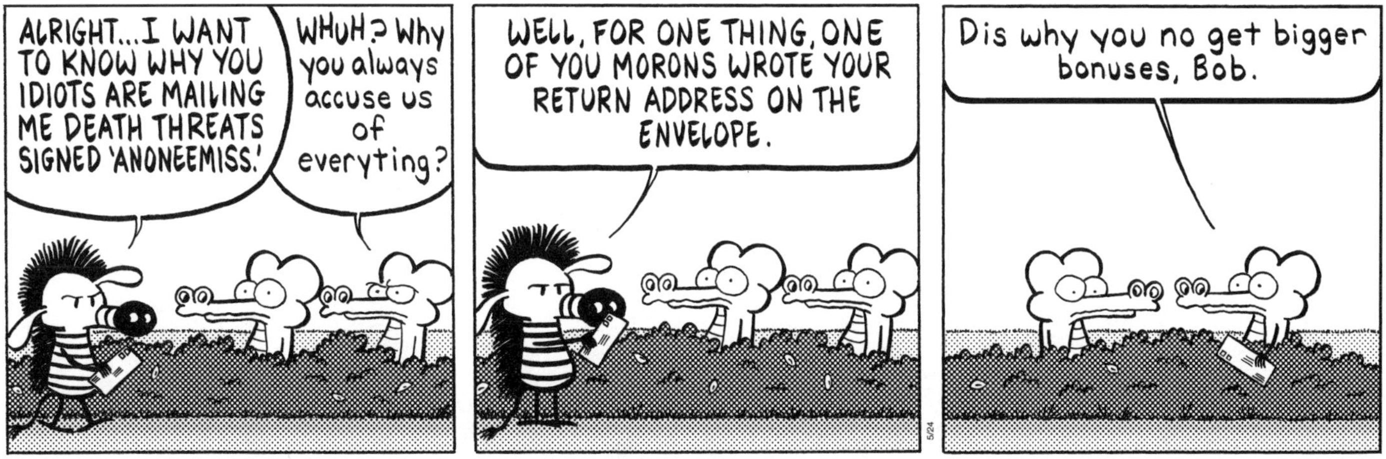
ALRIGHT...I WANT TO KNOW WHY YOU IDIOTS ARE MAILING ME DEATH THREATS SIGNED 'ANONEEMISS.'
WHUH? Why you always accuse us of everyting?
WELL, FOR ONE THING, ONE OF YOU MORONS WROTE YOUR RETURN ADDRESS ON THE ENVELOPE.
5/24
Dis why you no get bigger bonuses, Bob.

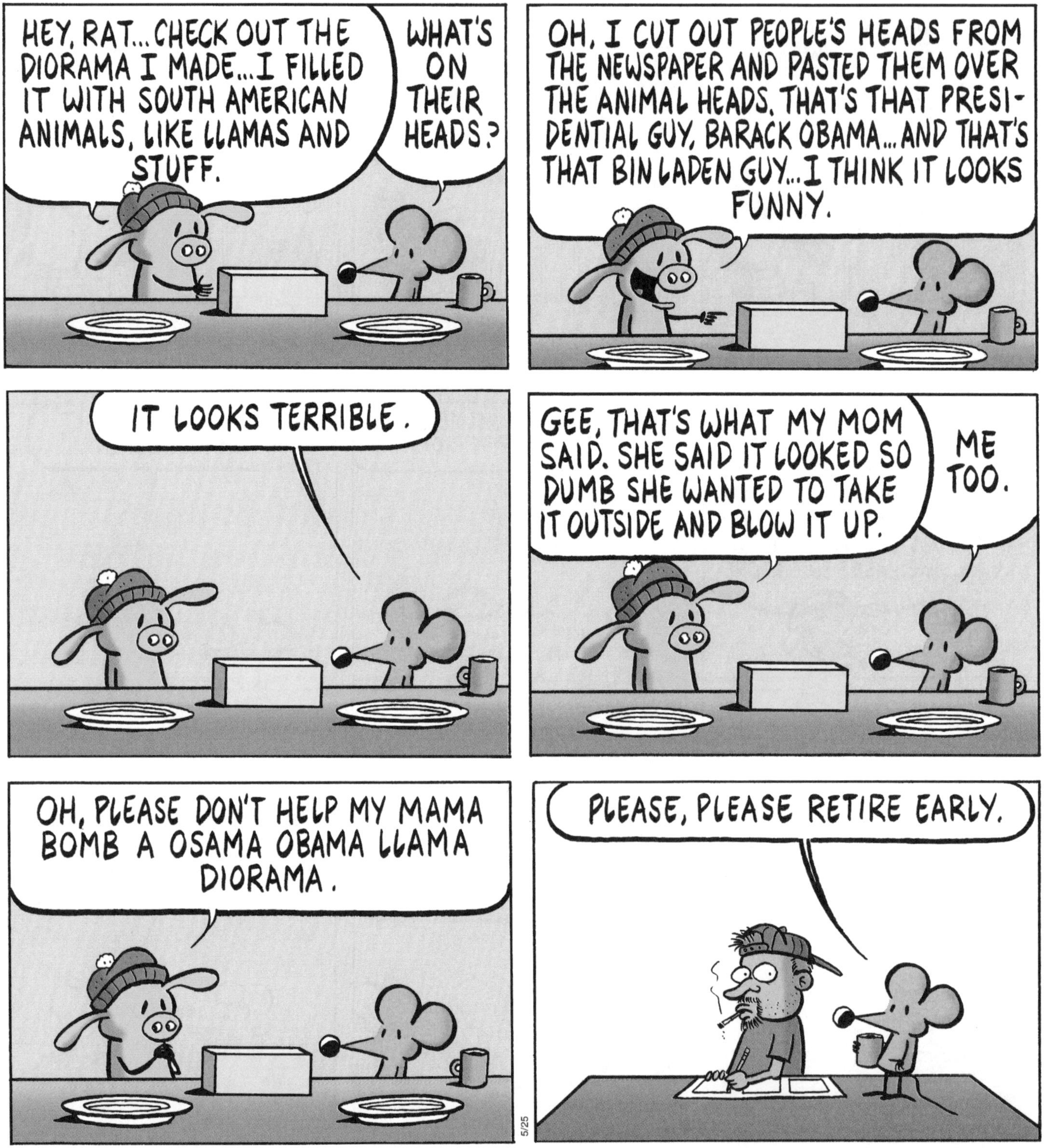
HEY, RAT...CHECK OUT THE DIORAMA I MADE...I FILLED IT WITH SOUTH AMERICAN ANIMALS, LIKE LLAMAS AND STUFF.
WHAT'S ON THEIR HEADS?
OH, I CUT OUT PEOPLE'S HEADS FROM THE NEWSPAPER AND PASTED THEM OVER THE ANIMAL HEADS. THAT'S THAT PRESI-DENTIAL GUY, BARACK OBAMA...AND THAT'S THAT BIN LADEN GUY...I THINK IT LOOKS FUNNY.
IT LOOKS TERRIBLE.
GEE, THAT'S WHAT MY MOM SAID. SHE SAID IT LOOKED SO DUMB SHE WANTED TO TAKE IT OUTSIDE AND BLOW IT UP.
ME TOO.
OH, PLEASE DON'T HELP MY MAMA BOMB A OSAMA OBAMA LLAMA DIORAMA.
5/25
PLEASE, PLEASE RETIRE EARLY.

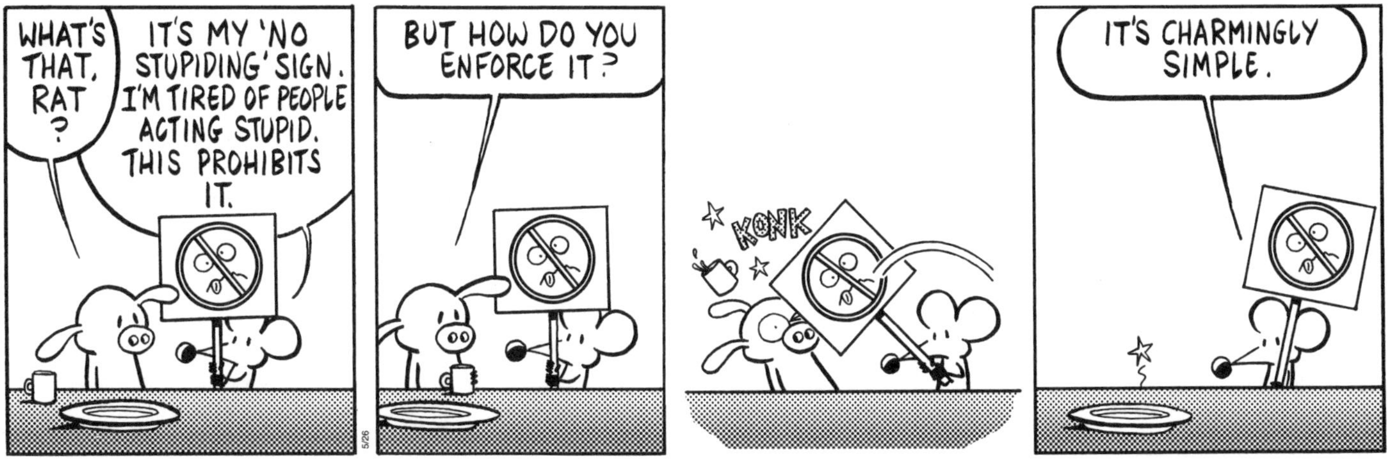
WHAT'S THAT, RAT?
IT'S MY 'NO STUPIDING' SIGN. I'M TIRED OF PEOPLE ACTING STUPID. THIS PROHIBITS IT.
5/26
BUT HOW DO YOU ENFORCE IT?
KONK
IT'S CHARMINGLY SIMPLE.

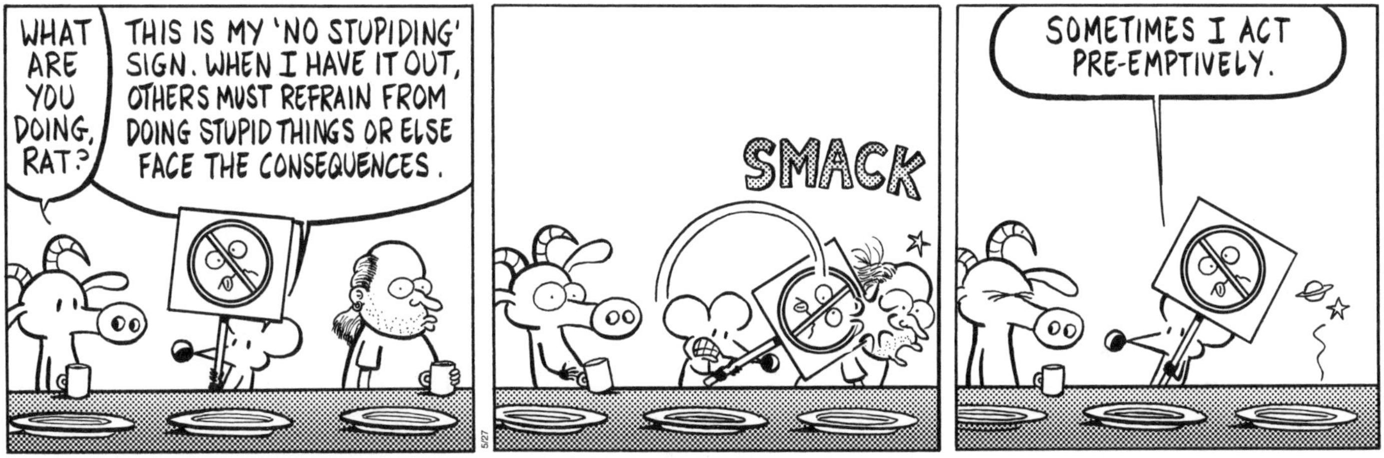
WHAT ARE YOU DOING, RAT?
THIS IS MY 'NO STUPIDING' SIGN. WHEN I HAVE IT OUT, OTHERS MUST REFRAIN FROM DOING STUPID THINGS OR ELSE FACE THE CONSEQUENCES.
5/27
SMACK
SOMETIMES I ACT PRE-EMPTIVELY.

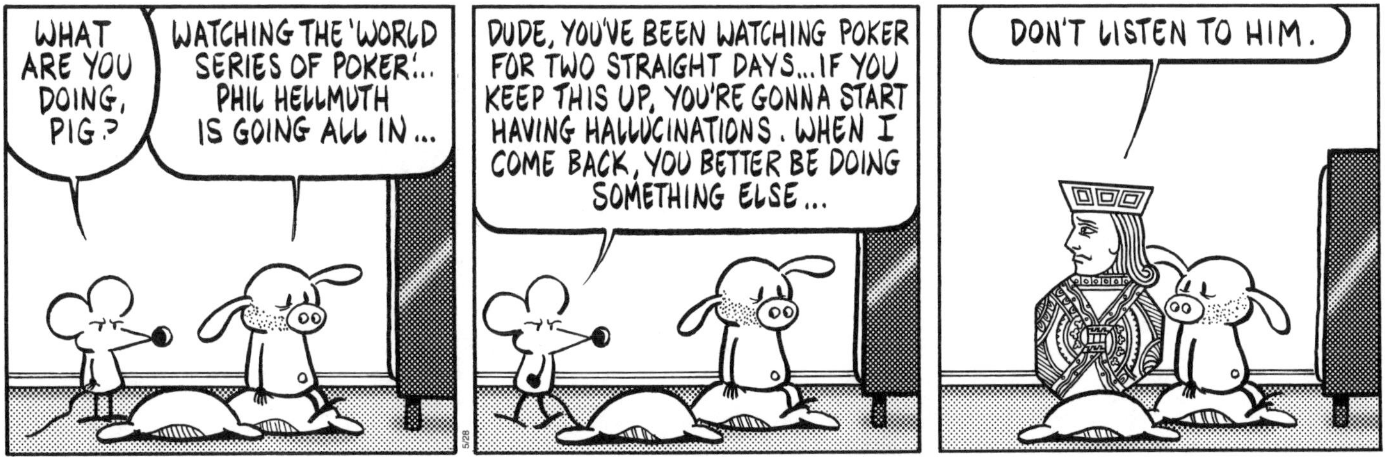
WHAT ARE YOU DOING, PIG?
WATCHING THE 'WORLD SERIES OF POKER'... PHIL HELLMUTH IS GOING ALL IN...
5/28
DUDE, YOU'VE BEEN WATCHING POKER FOR TWO STRAIGHT DAYS... IF YOU KEEP THIS UP, YOU'RE GONNA START HAVING HALLUCINATIONS. WHEN I COME BACK, YOU BETTER BE DOING SOMETHING ELSE...
DON'T LISTEN TO HIM.

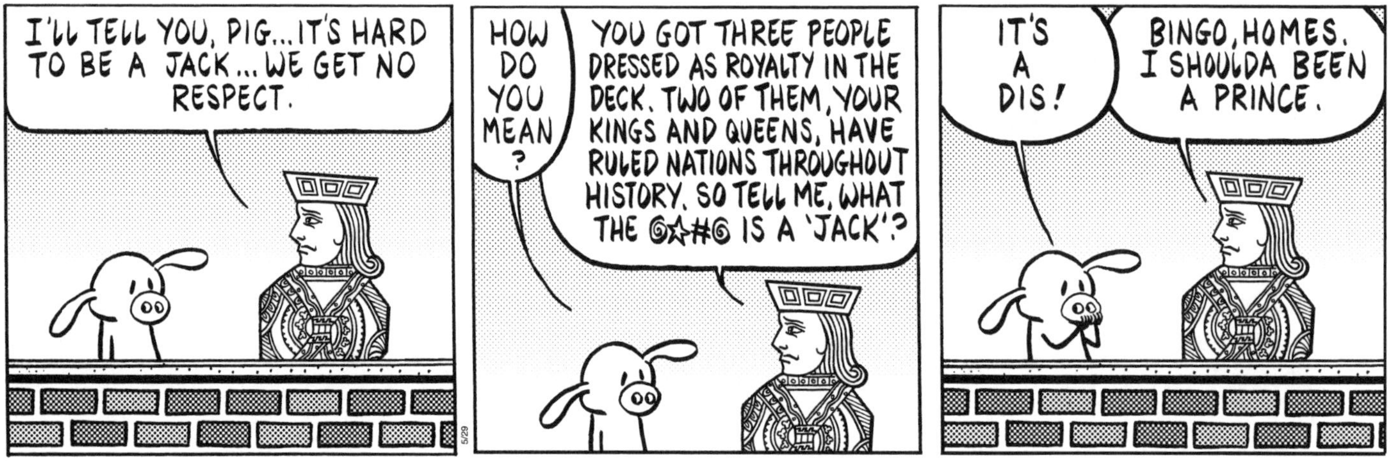
I'LL TELL YOU, PIG... IT'S HARD TO BE A JACK... WE GET NO RESPECT.
5/29
HOW DO YOU MEAN?
YOU GOT THREE PEOPLE DRESSED AS ROYALTY IN THE DECK. TWO OF THEM, YOUR KINGS AND QUEENS, HAVE RULED NATIONS THROUGHOUT HISTORY. SO TELL ME, WHAT THE @☆#@ IS A 'JACK'?
IT'S A DIS!
BINGO, HOMES. I SHOULDA BEEN A PRINCE.

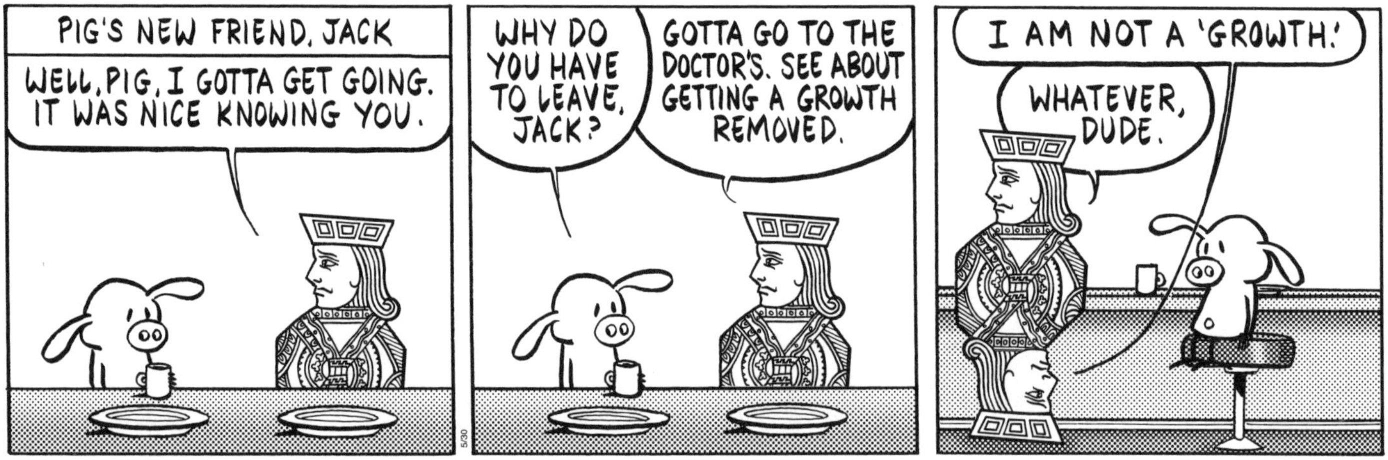
PIG'S NEW FRIEND, JACK
WELL, PIG, I GOTTA GET GOING. IT WAS NICE KNOWING YOU.
5/30
WHY DO YOU HAVE TO LEAVE, JACK?
GOTTA GO TO THE DOCTOR'S. SEE ABOUT GETTING A GROWTH REMOVED.
I AM NOT A 'GROWTH.'
WHATEVER, DUDE.

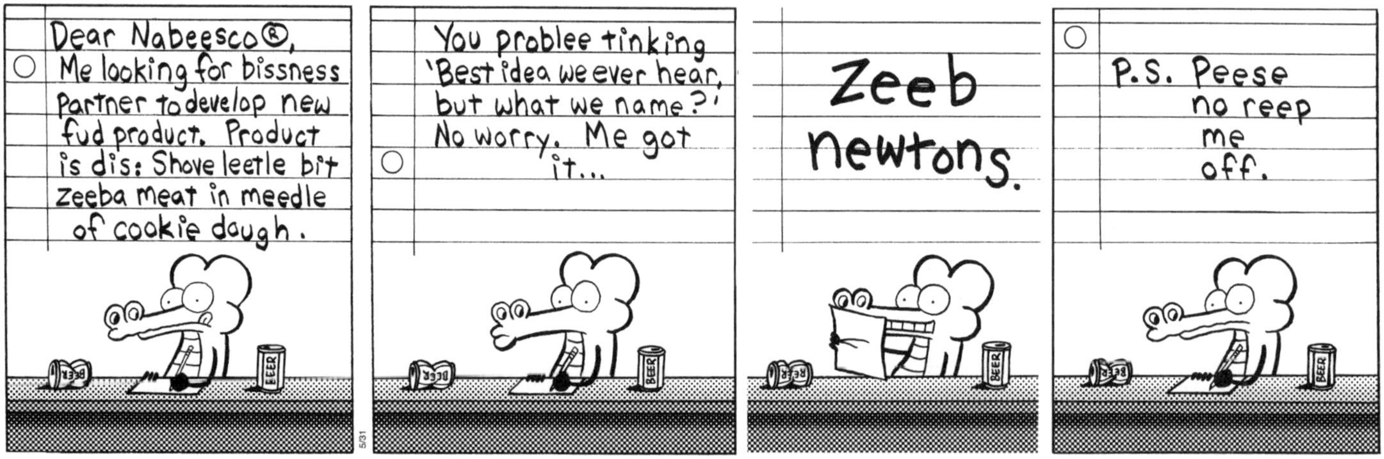
Dear Nabeesco®, Me looking for bissness partner to develop new fud product. Product is dis: Shove leetle bit zeeba meat in meedle of cookie dough.
BEER
BEER
5/31
You problee tinking 'Best idea we ever hear, but what we name?' No worry. Me got it...
BEER
Zeeb newtons.
BEER
P.S. Peese no reep me off.
BEER

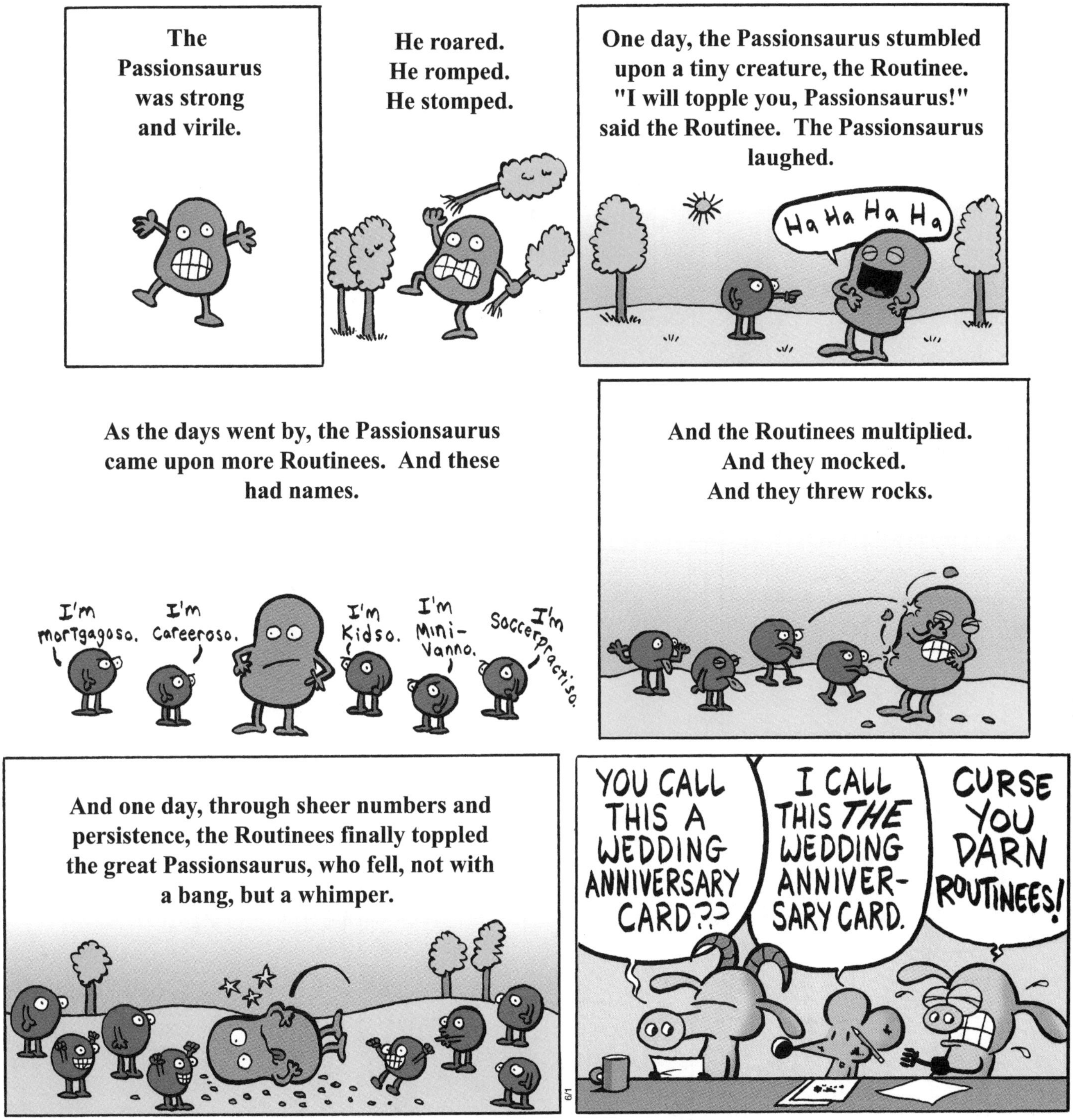
The Passionsaurus was strong and virile.
He roared. He romped. He stomped.
One day, the Passionsaurus stumbled upon a tiny creature, the Routinee. "I will topple you, Passionsaurus!" said the Routinee. The Passionsaurus laughed.
Ha Ha Ha Ha
As the days went by, the Passionsaurus came upon more Routinees. And these had names.
I'm Mortgagoso.
I'm Careeroso.
I'm Kidso.
I'm Mini-Vanno.
I'm Soccerpractiso.
And the Routinees multiplied. And they mocked. And they threw rocks.
And one day, through sheer numbers and persistence, the Routinees finally toppled the great Passionsaurus, who fell, not with a bang, but a whimper.
YOU CALL THIS A WEDDING ANNIVERSARY CARD?
I CALL THIS *THE* WEDDING ANNIVERSARY CARD.
CURSE YOU DARN ROUTINEES!

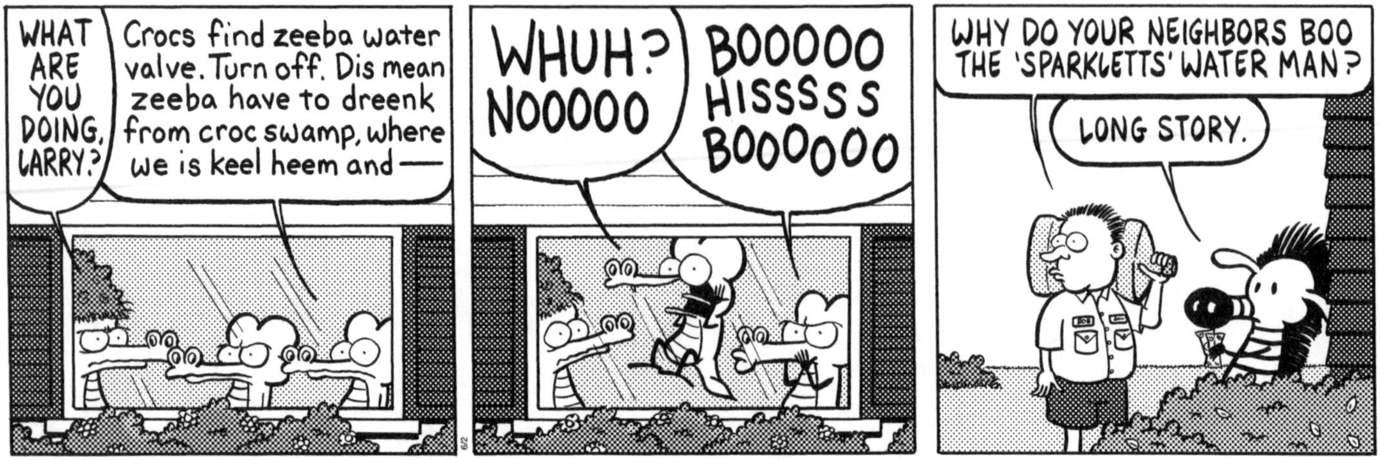
WHAT ARE YOU DOING, LARRY?
Crocs find zeeba water valve. Turn off. Dis mean zeeba have to dreenk from croc swamp, where we is keel heem and—
WHUH? NOOOOO
BOOOOO HISSSSS BOOOOOO
WHY DO YOUR NEIGHBORS BOO THE 'SPARKLETTS' WATER MAN?
LONG STORY.

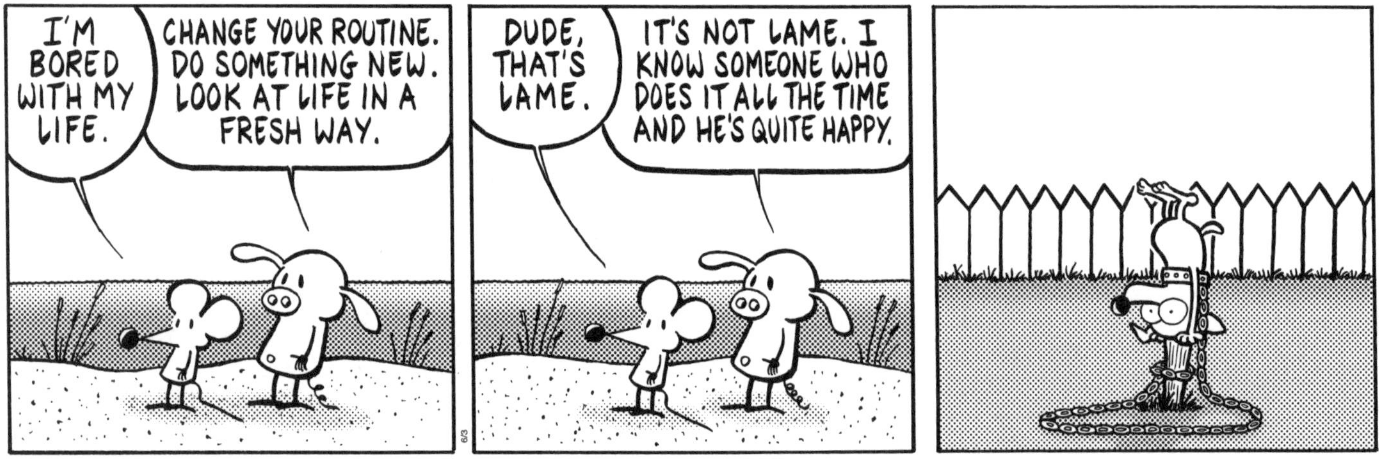
I'M BORED WITH MY LIFE.
CHANGE YOUR ROUTINE. DO SOMETHING NEW. LOOK AT LIFE IN A FRESH WAY.
DUDE, THAT'S LAME.
IT'S NOT LAME. I KNOW SOMEONE WHO DOES IT ALL THE TIME AND HE'S QUITE HAPPY.

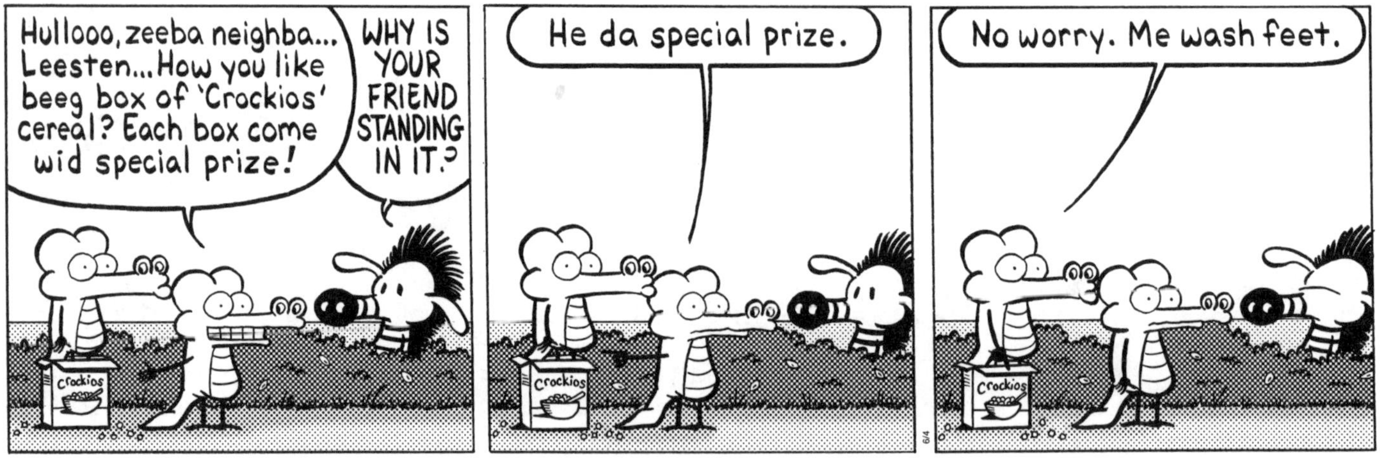
Hullooo, zeeba neighba... Leesten... How you like beeg box of 'Crockios' cereal? Each box come wid special prize!
WHY IS YOUR FRIEND STANDING IN IT?
He da special prize.
No worry. Me wash feet.
Crockios

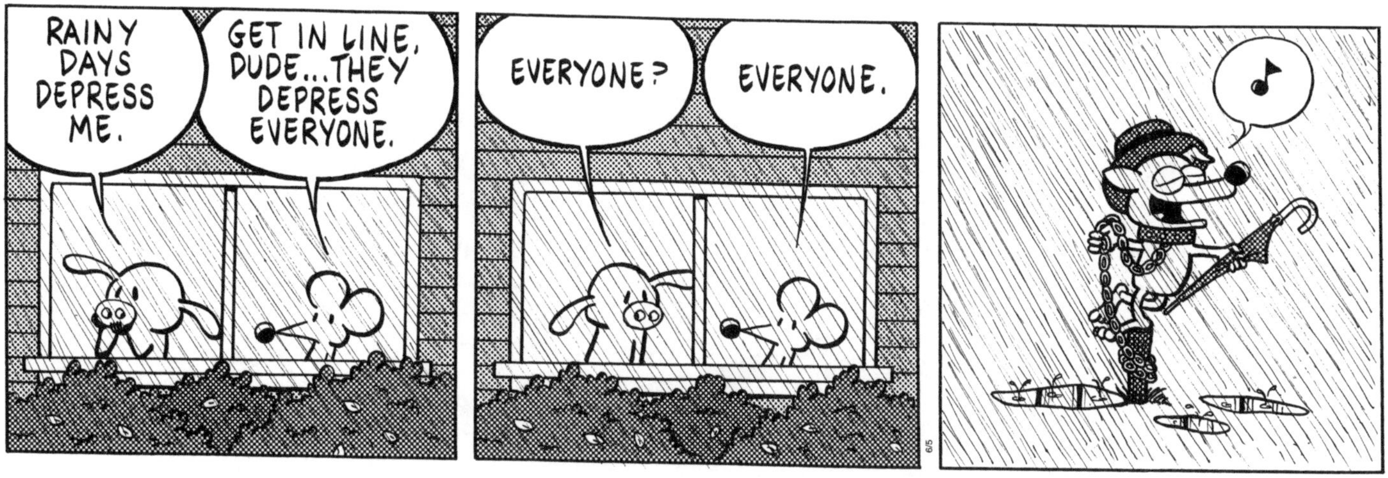
RAINY DAYS DEPRESS ME.
GET IN LINE, DUDE...THEY DEPRESS EVERYONE.
EVERYONE?
EVERYONE.
♪
6/5

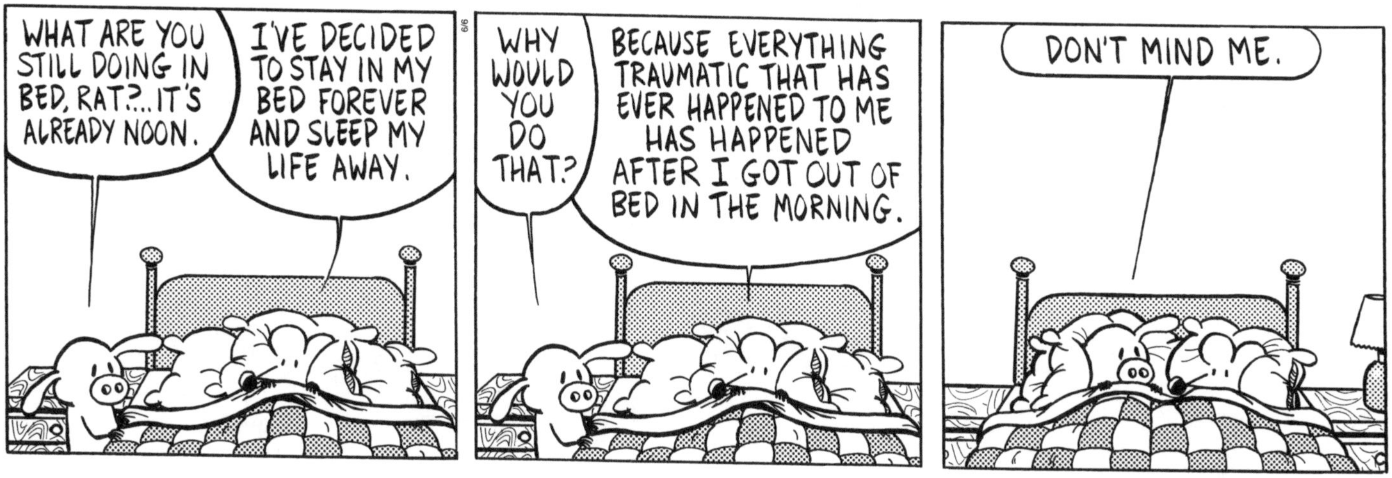
WHAT ARE YOU STILL DOING IN BED, RAT?...IT'S ALREADY NOON.
I'VE DECIDED TO STAY IN MY BED FOREVER AND SLEEP MY LIFE AWAY.
6/6
WHY WOULD YOU DO THAT?
BECAUSE EVERYTHING TRAUMATIC THAT HAS EVER HAPPENED TO ME HAS HAPPENED AFTER I GOT OUT OF BED IN THE MORNING.
DON'T MIND ME.

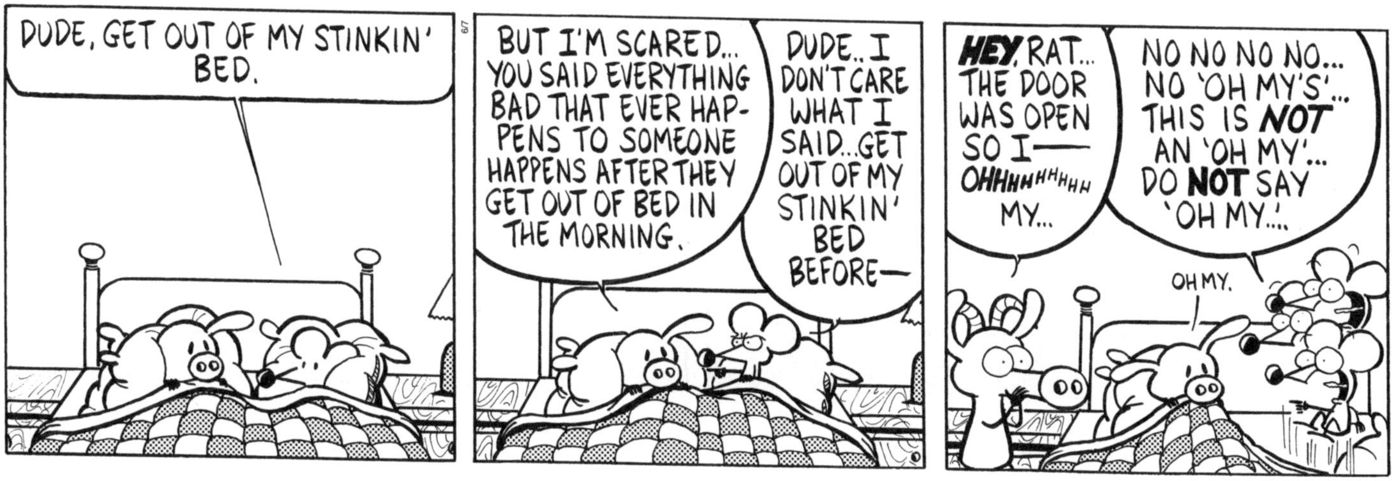
DUDE, GET OUT OF MY STINKIN' BED.
6/7
BUT I'M SCARED... YOU SAID EVERYTHING BAD THAT EVER HAPPENS TO SOMEONE HAPPENS AFTER THEY GET OUT OF BED IN THE MORNING.
DUDE.. I DON'T CARE WHAT I SAID...GET OUT OF MY STINKIN' BED BEFORE—
HEY, RAT... THE DOOR WAS OPEN SO I— OHHHHHHHHH MY...
NO NO NO NO... NO 'OH MY'S'... THIS IS NOT AN 'OH MY'... DO NOT SAY 'OH MY.'...
OH MY.

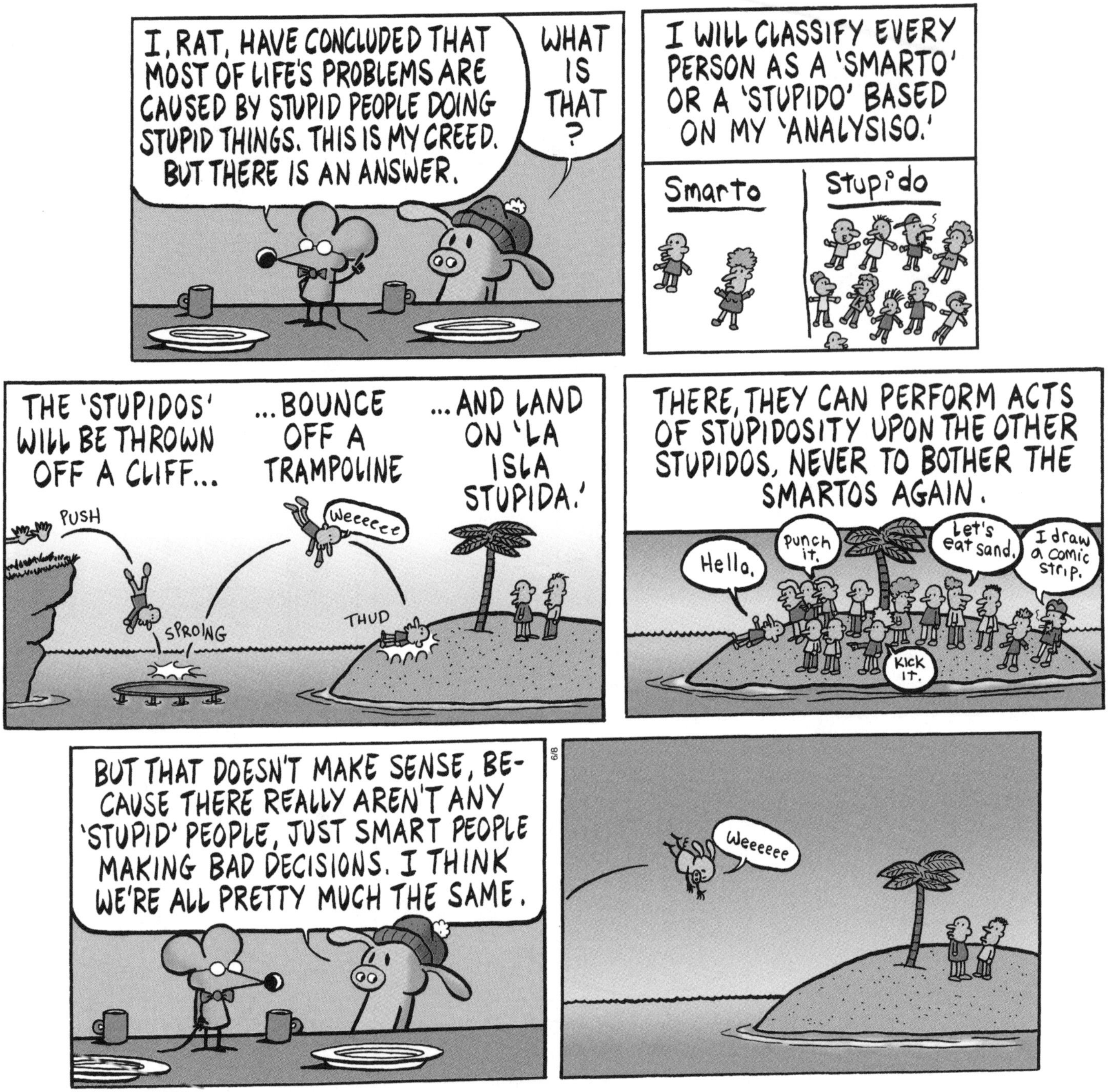
I, RAT, HAVE CONCLUDED THAT MOST OF LIFE'S PROBLEMS ARE CAUSED BY STUPID PEOPLE DOING STUPID THINGS. THIS IS MY CREED. BUT THERE IS AN ANSWER.
WHAT IS THAT?
I WILL CLASSIFY EVERY PERSON AS A 'SMARTO' OR A 'STUPIDO' BASED ON MY 'ANALYSISO.'
Smarto
Stupido
THE 'STUPIDOS' WILL BE THROWN OFF A CLIFF...
PUSH
SPROING
...BOUNCE OFF A TRAMPOLINE
Weeeeeee
...AND LAND ON 'LA ISLA STUPIDA.'
THUD
THERE, THEY CAN PERFORM ACTS OF STUPIDOSITY UPON THE OTHER STUPIDOS, NEVER TO BOTHER THE SMARTOS AGAIN.
Hello.
Punch it.
Let's eat sand.
I draw a comic strip.
Kick it.
BUT THAT DOESN'T MAKE SENSE, BECAUSE THERE REALLY AREN'T ANY 'STUPID' PEOPLE, JUST SMART PEOPLE MAKING BAD DECISIONS. I THINK WE'RE ALL PRETTY MUCH THE SAME.
6/8
Weeeeee

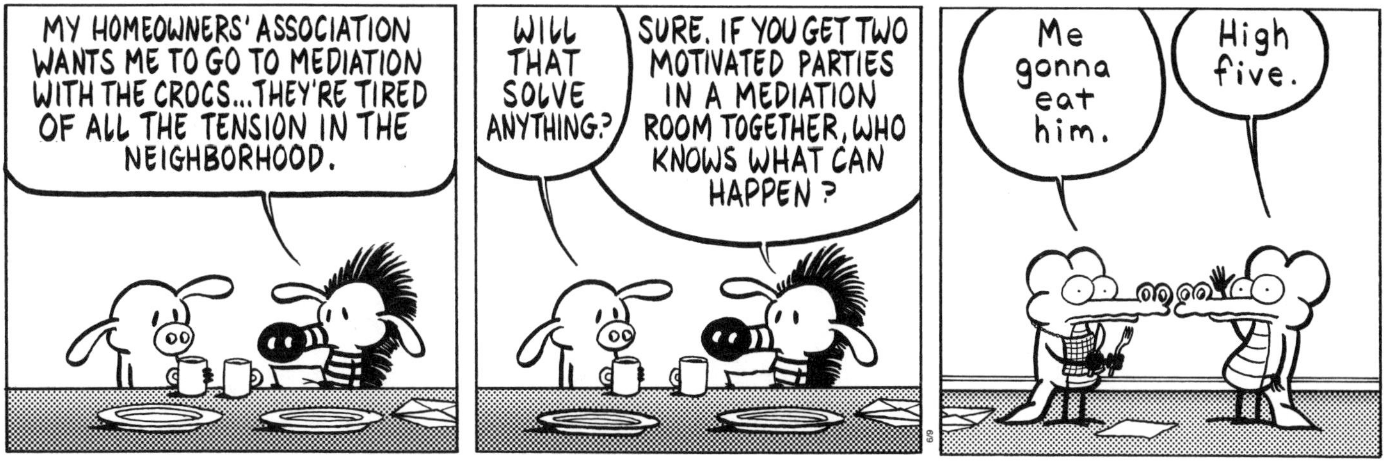
MY HOMEOWNERS' ASSOCIATION WANTS ME TO GO TO MEDIATION WITH THE CROCS...THEY'RE TIRED OF ALL THE TENSION IN THE NEIGHBORHOOD.
WILL THAT SOLVE ANYTHING?
SURE. IF YOU GET TWO MOTIVATED PARTIES IN A MEDIATION ROOM TOGETHER, WHO KNOWS WHAT CAN HAPPEN?
Me gonna eat him.
High five.

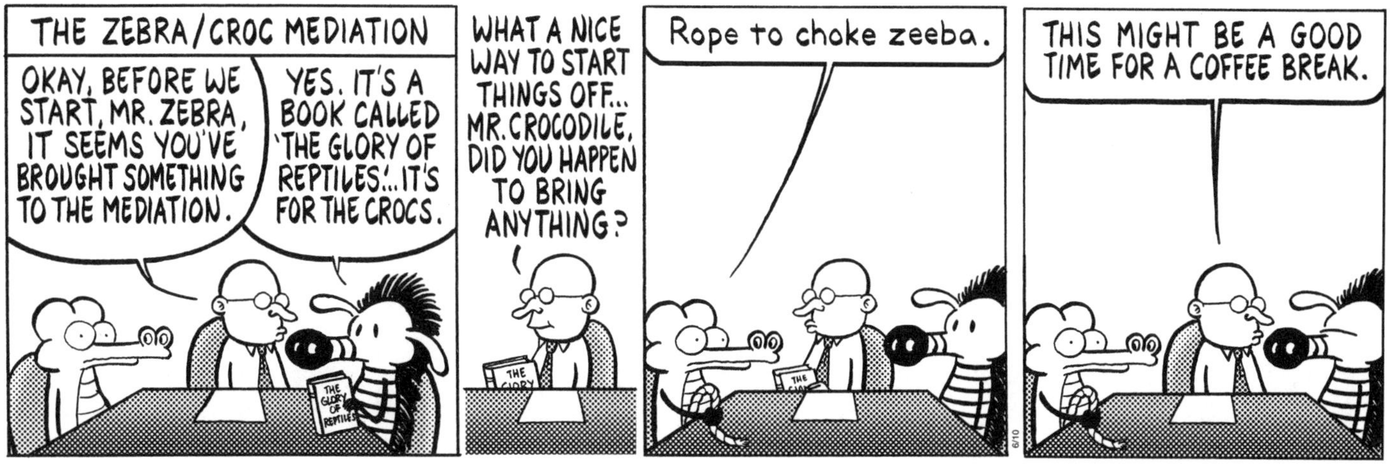
THE ZEBRA/CROC MEDIATION
OKAY, BEFORE WE START, MR. ZEBRA, IT SEEMS YOU'VE BROUGHT SOMETHING TO THE MEDIATION.
YES. IT'S A BOOK CALLED 'THE GLORY OF REPTILES.'...IT'S FOR THE CROCS.
THE GLORY OF REPTILES
WHAT A NICE WAY TO START THINGS OFF... MR. CROCODILE, DID YOU HAPPEN TO BRING ANYTHING?
Rope to choke zeeba.
THIS MIGHT BE A GOOD TIME FOR A COFFEE BREAK.

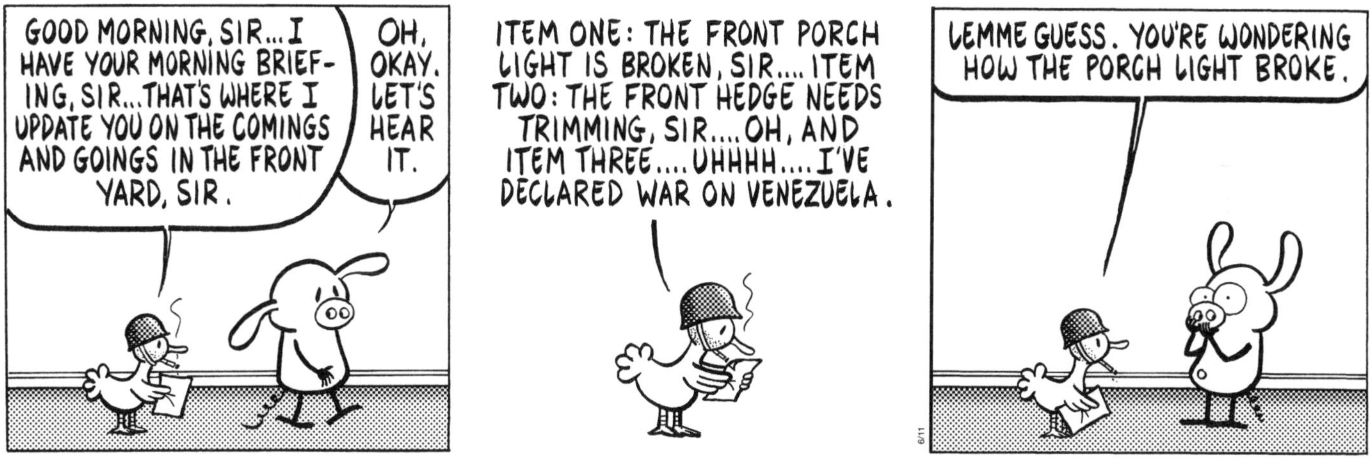
GOOD MORNING, SIR...I HAVE YOUR MORNING BRIEFING, SIR...THAT'S WHERE I UPDATE YOU ON THE COMINGS AND GOINGS IN THE FRONT YARD, SIR.
OH, OKAY. LET'S HEAR IT.
ITEM ONE: THE FRONT PORCH LIGHT IS BROKEN, SIR.... ITEM TWO: THE FRONT HEDGE NEEDS TRIMMING, SIR.... OH, AND ITEM THREE.... UHHHH.... I'VE DECLARED WAR ON VENEZUELA.
LEMME GUESS. YOU'RE WONDERING HOW THE PORCH LIGHT BROKE.

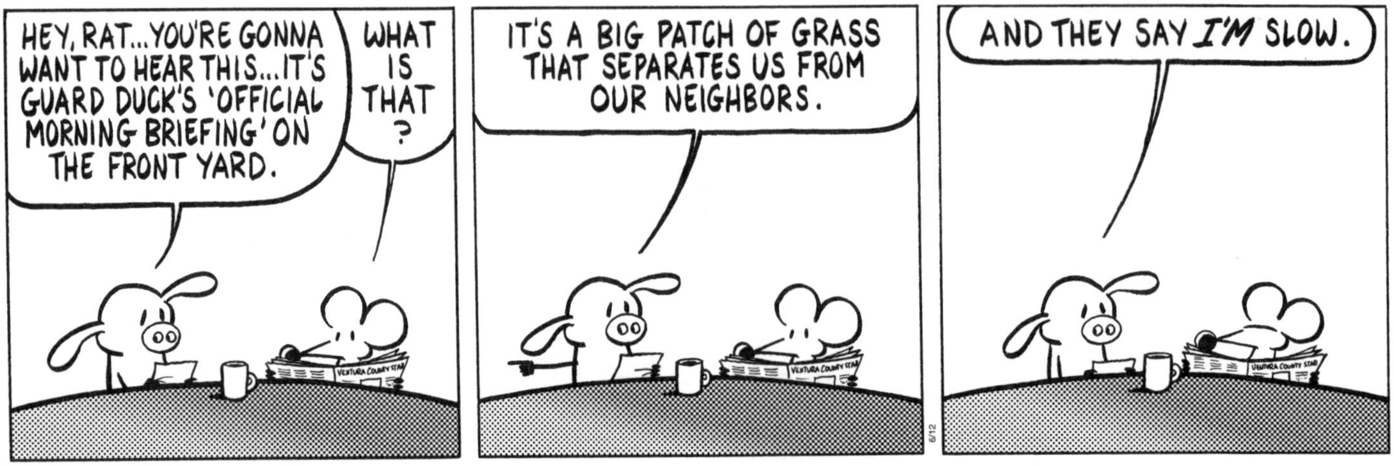
HEY, RAT...YOU'RE GONNA WANT TO HEAR THIS...IT'S GUARD DUCK'S 'OFFICIAL MORNING BRIEFING' ON THE FRONT YARD.
WHAT IS THAT ?
IT'S A BIG PATCH OF GRASS THAT SEPARATES US FROM OUR NEIGHBORS.
AND THEY SAY *I'M* SLOW.
6/12

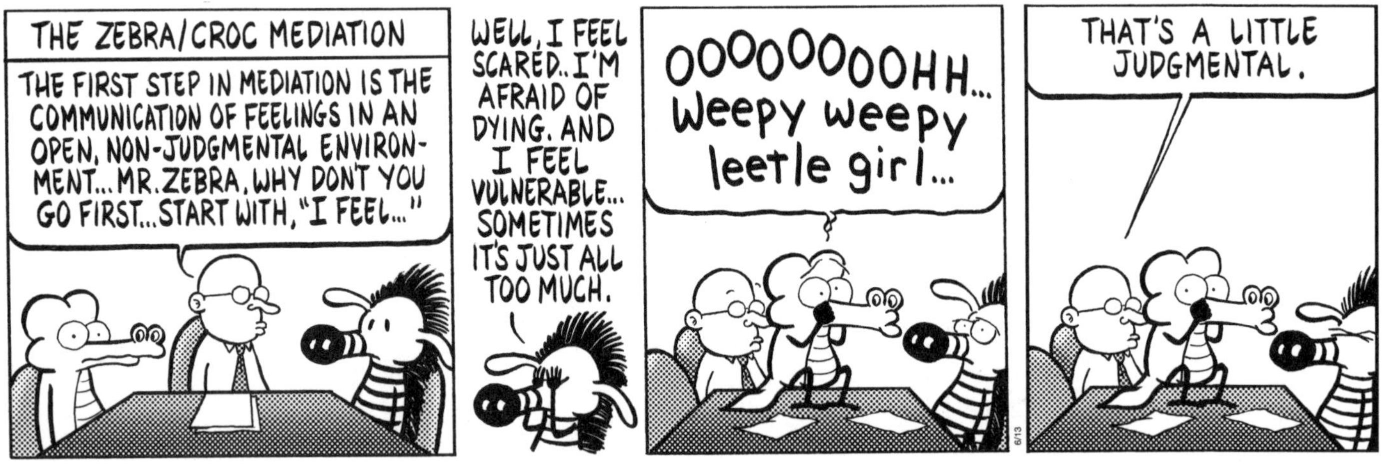
THE ZEBRA/CROC MEDIATION
THE FIRST STEP IN MEDIATION IS THE COMMUNICATION OF FEELINGS IN AN OPEN, NON-JUDGMENTAL ENVIRONMENT... MR. ZEBRA, WHY DON'T YOU GO FIRST...START WITH, "I FEEL..."
WELL, I FEEL SCARED.. I'M AFRAID OF DYING. AND I FEEL VULNERABLE... SOMETIMES IT'S JUST ALL TOO MUCH.
OOOOOOOOOHH... Weepy weepy leetle girl...
THAT'S A LITTLE JUDGMENTAL.
6/13

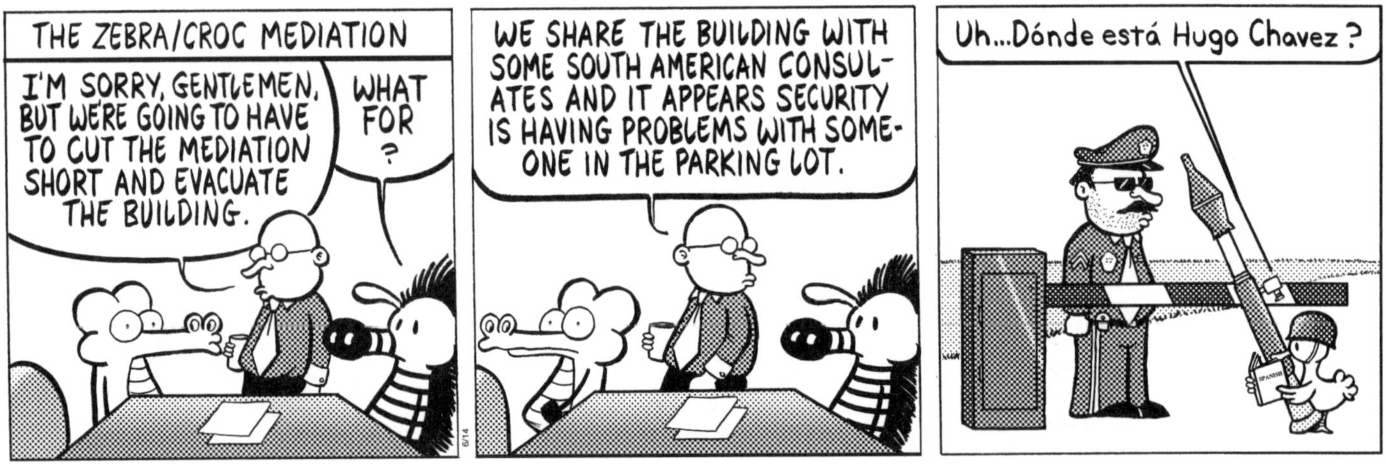
THE ZEBRA/CROC MEDIATION
I'M SORRY, GENTLEMEN, BUT WE'RE GOING TO HAVE TO CUT THE MEDIATION SHORT AND EVACUATE THE BUILDING.
WHAT FOR ?
WE SHARE THE BUILDING WITH SOME SOUTH AMERICAN CONSULATES AND IT APPEARS SECURITY IS HAVING PROBLEMS WITH SOMEONE IN THE PARKING LOT.
Uh...Dónde está Hugo Chavez ?
6/14

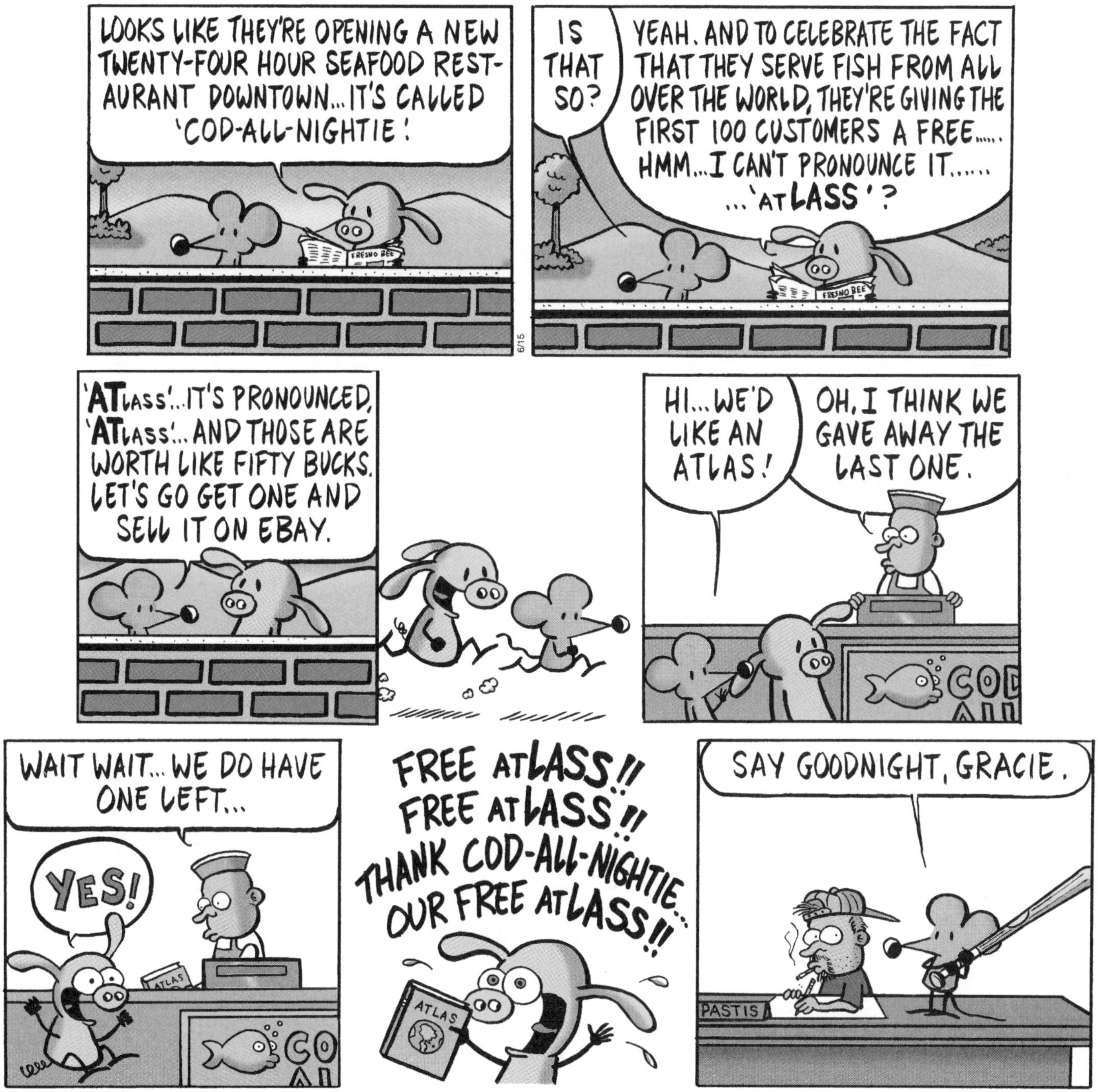
LOOKS LIKE THEY'RE OPENING A NEW TWENTY-FOUR HOUR SEAFOOD REST-AURANT DOWNTOWN... IT'S CALLED 'COD-ALL-NIGHTIE'.
FRESNO BEE
IS THAT SO?
YEAH. AND TO CELEBRATE THE FACT THAT THEY SERVE FISH FROM ALL OVER THE WORLD, THEY'RE GIVING THE FIRST 100 CUSTOMERS A FREE...... HMM... I CAN'T PRONOUNCE IT...... ...'ATLASS'?
FRESNO BEE
6/15
'ATLASS'... IT'S PRONOUNCED, 'ATLASS'... AND THOSE ARE WORTH LIKE FIFTY BUCKS. LET'S GO GET ONE AND SELL IT ON EBAY.
HI... WE'D LIKE AN ATLAS!
OH, I THINK WE GAVE AWAY THE LAST ONE.
COD
WAIT WAIT... WE DO HAVE ONE LEFT...
YES!
ATLAS
CO
FREE ATLASS!! FREE ATLASS!! THANK COD-ALL-NIGHTIE... OUR FREE ATLASS!!
ATLAS
SAY GOODNIGHT, GRACIE.
PASTIS

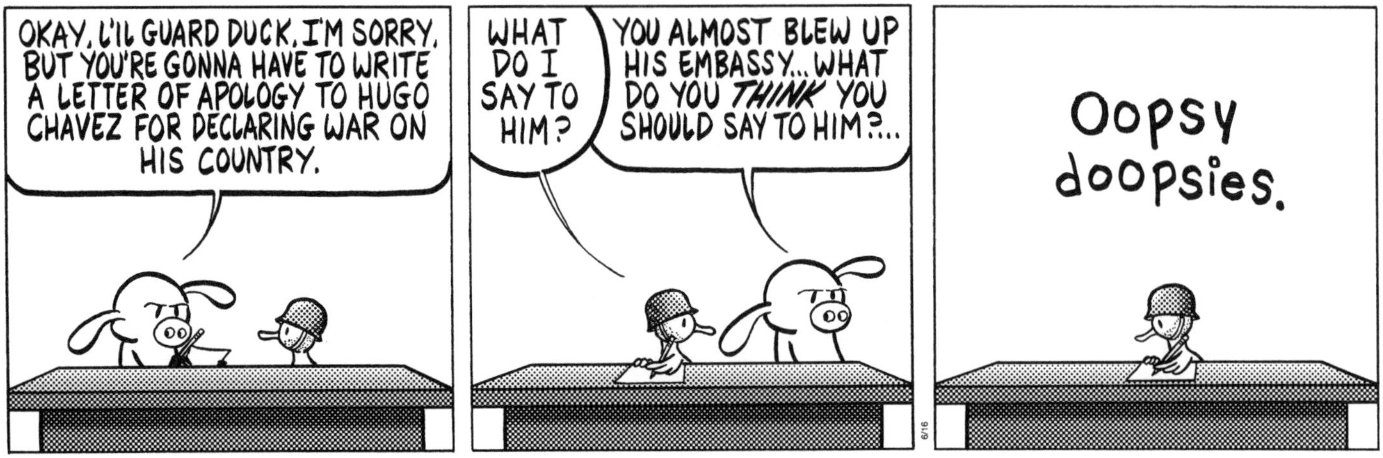
OKAY, L'IL GUARD DUCK, I'M SORRY, BUT YOU'RE GONNA HAVE TO WRITE A LETTER OF APOLOGY TO HUGO CHAVEZ FOR DECLARING WAR ON HIS COUNTRY.
WHAT DO I SAY TO HIM?
YOU ALMOST BLEW UP HIS EMBASSY... WHAT DO YOU *THINK* YOU SHOULD SAY TO HIM?...
6/16
Oopsy doopsies.

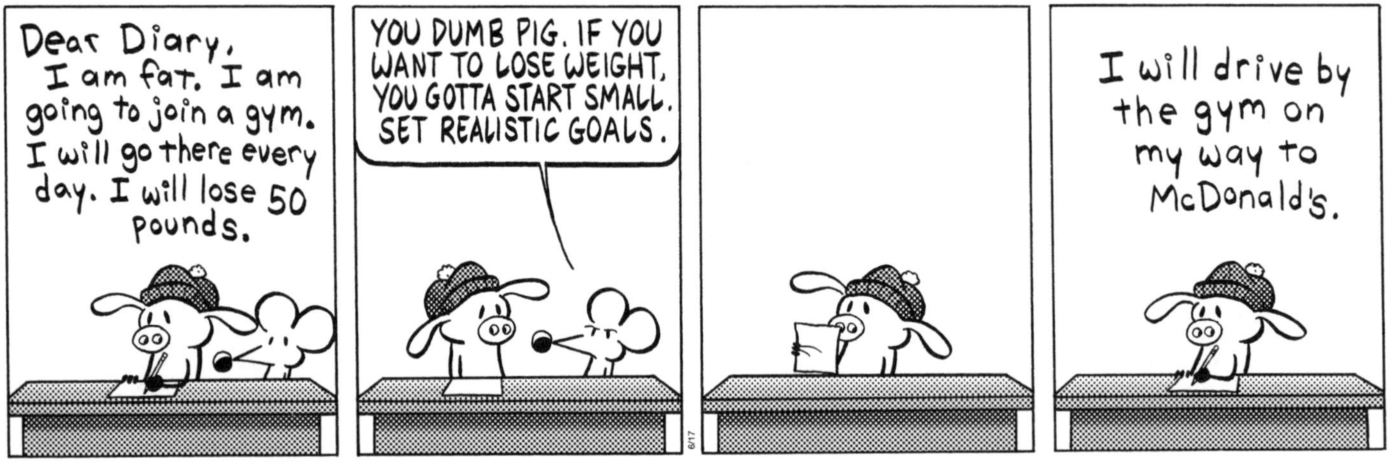
Dear Diary,
I am fat. I am going to join a gym. I will go there every day. I will lose 50 pounds.
YOU DUMB PIG. IF YOU WANT TO LOSE WEIGHT, YOU GOTTA START SMALL. SET REALISTIC GOALS.
6/17
I will drive by the gym on my way to McDonald's.

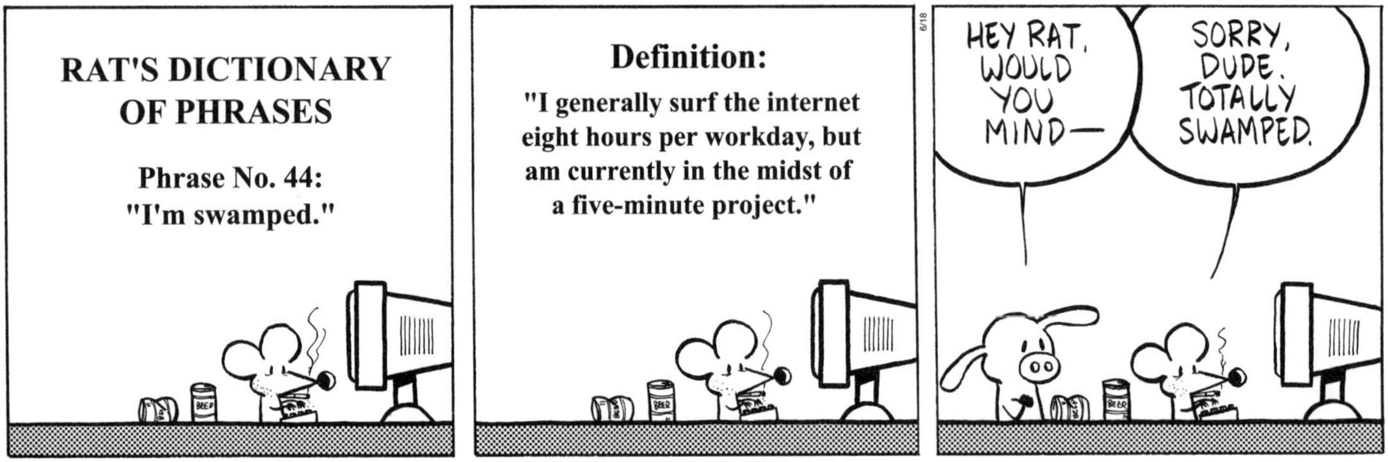
RAT'S DICTIONARY OF PHRASES
Phrase No. 44:
"I'm swamped."
BEER
Definition:
"I generally surf the internet eight hours per workday, but am currently in the midst of a five-minute project."
6/18
HEY RAT, WOULD YOU MIND—
SORRY, DUDE. TOTALLY SWAMPED.

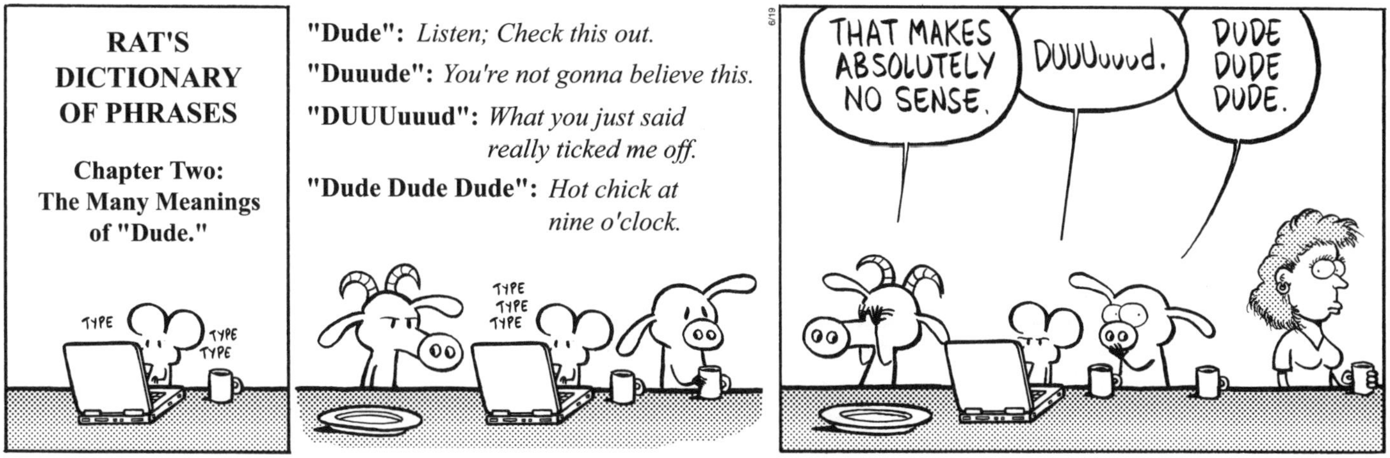
RAT'S DICTIONARY OF PHRASES
Chapter Two: The Many Meanings of "Dude."
TYPE
TYPE TYPE
"Dude": Listen; Check this out.
"Duuude": You're not gonna believe this.
"DUUUuuud": What you just said really ticked me off.
"Dude Dude Dude": Hot chick at nine o'clock.
TYPE TYPE TYPE
6/19
THAT MAKES ABSOLUTELY NO SENSE.
DUUUuuud.
DUDE DUDE DUDE.

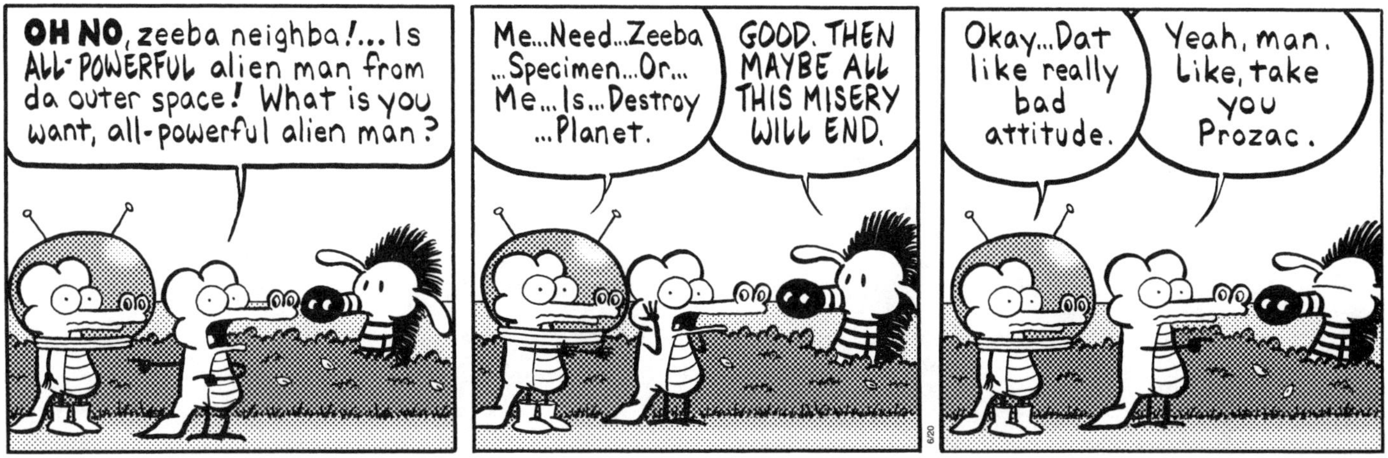
OH NO, zeeba neighba!... Is ALL-POWERFUL alien man from da outer space! What is you want, all-powerful alien man?
Me...Need...Zeeba ...Specimen...Or... Me...Is...Destroy ...Planet.
GOOD. THEN MAYBE ALL THIS MISERY WILL END.
Okay...Dat like really bad attitude.
Yeah, man. Like, take you Prozac.
6/20

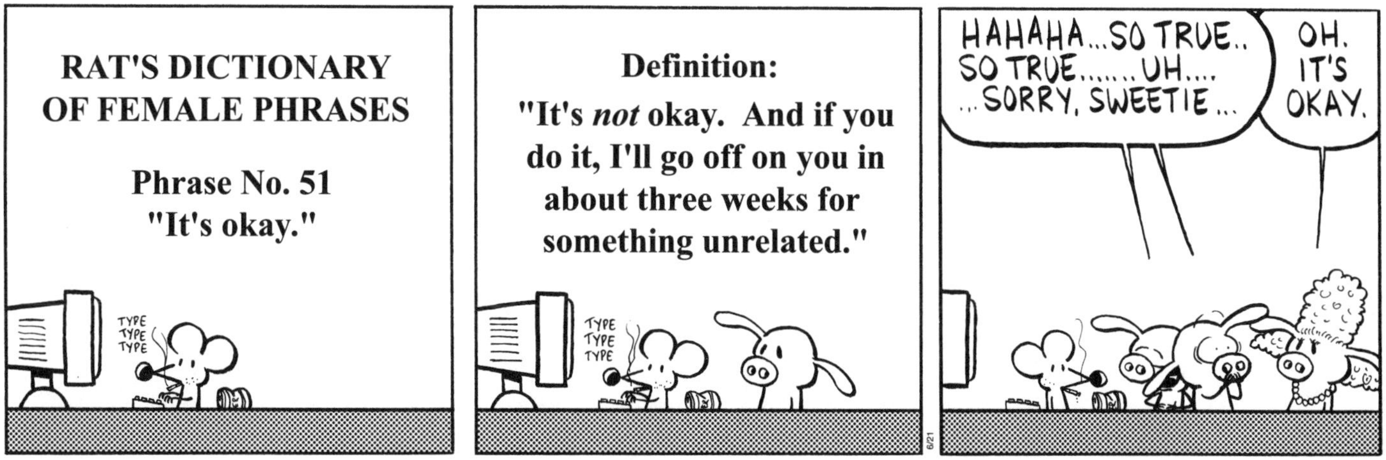
RAT'S DICTIONARY OF FEMALE PHRASES
Phrase No. 51
"It's okay."
TYPE TYPE TYPE
Definition:
"It's not okay. And if you do it, I'll go off on you in about three weeks for something unrelated."
TYPE TYPE TYPE
6/21
HAHAHA...SO TRUE.. SO TRUE.......UH.... ...SORRY, SWEETIE...
OH. IT'S OKAY.

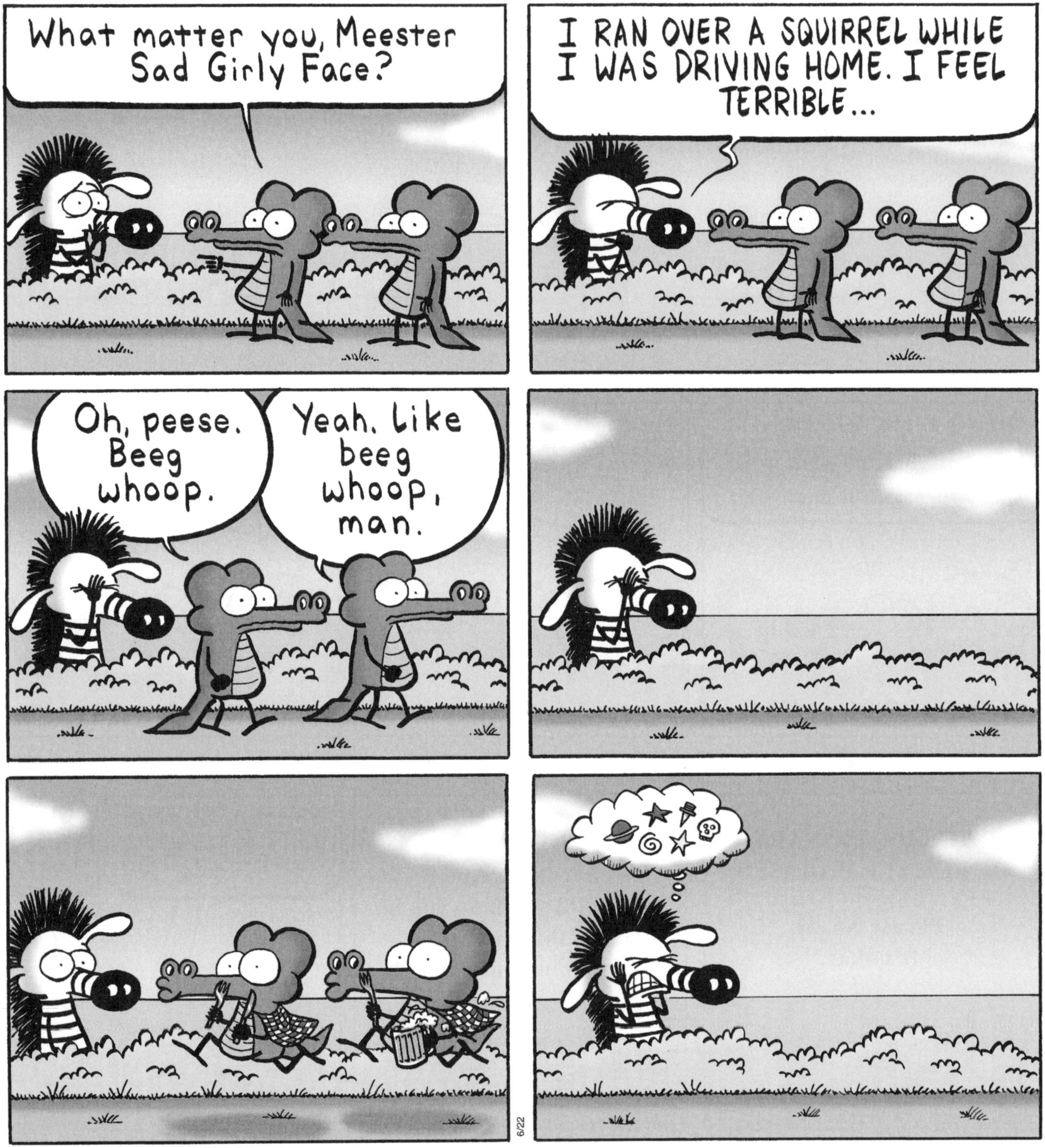
What matter you, Meester Sad Girly Face?
I RAN OVER A SQUIRREL WHILE I WAS DRIVING HOME. I FEEL TERRIBLE...
Oh, peese. Beeg whoop.
Yeah. Like beeg whoop, man.
6/22

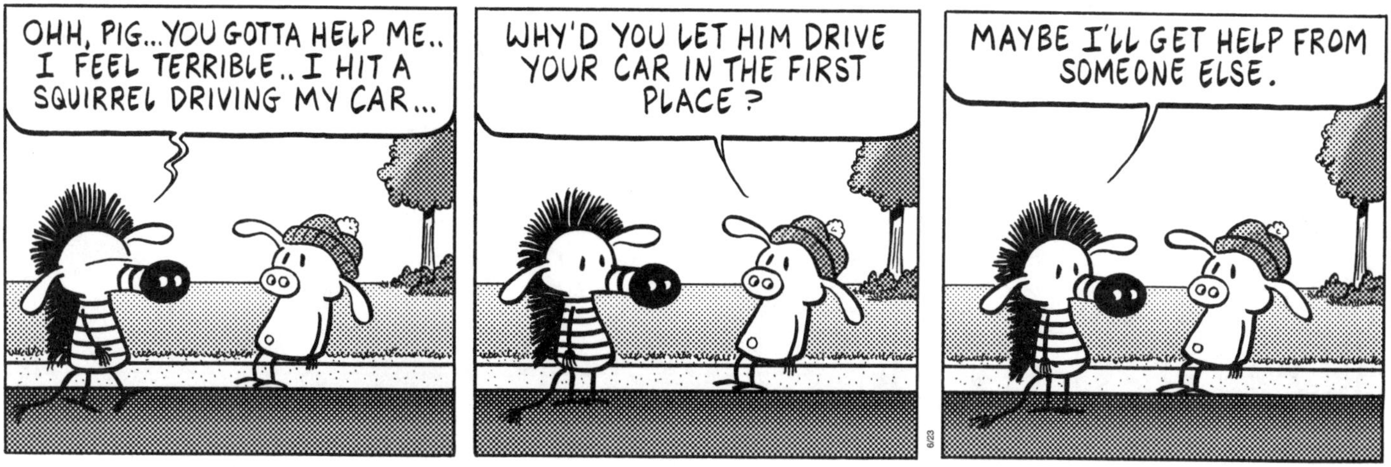
OHH, PIG...YOU GOTTA HELP ME.. I FEEL TERRIBLE.. I HIT A SQUIRREL DRIVING MY CAR...
WHY'D YOU LET HIM DRIVE YOUR CAR IN THE FIRST PLACE ?
MAYBE I'LL GET HELP FROM SOMEONE ELSE.
6/23

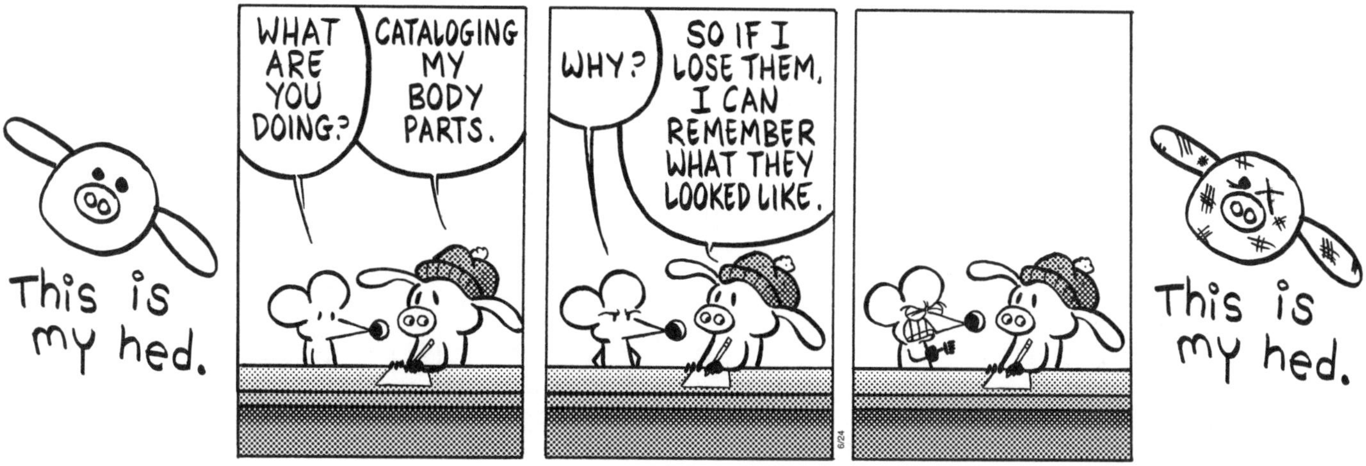
This is my hed.
WHAT ARE YOU DOING?
CATALOGING MY BODY PARTS.
WHY?
SO IF I LOSE THEM, I CAN REMEMBER WHAT THEY LOOKED LIKE.
This is my hed.
6/24

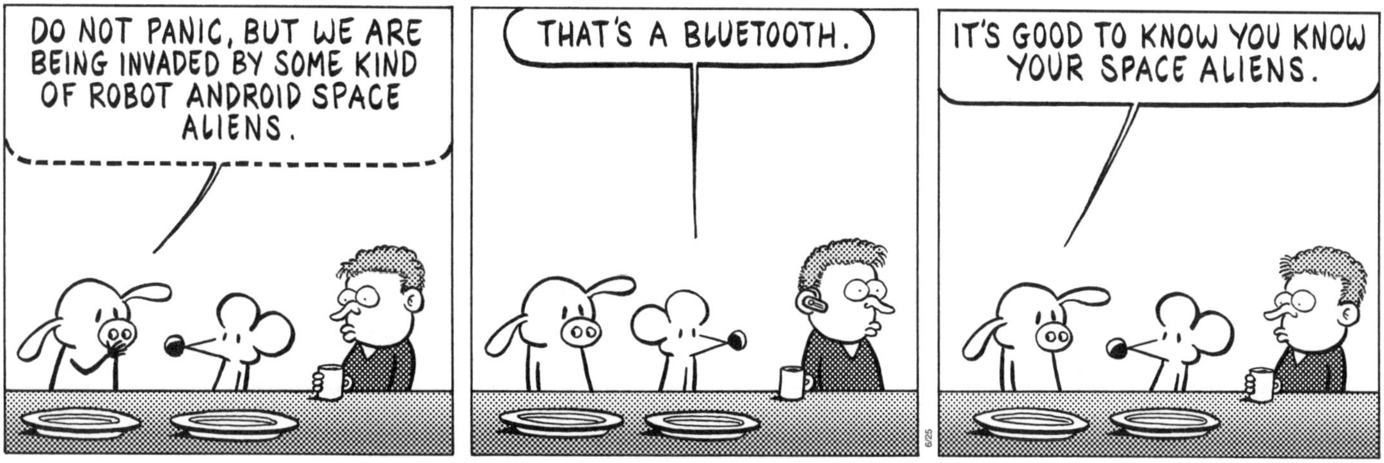
DO NOT PANIC, BUT WE ARE BEING INVADED BY SOME KIND OF ROBOT ANDROID SPACE ALIENS.
THAT'S A BLUETOOTH.
IT'S GOOD TO KNOW YOU KNOW YOUR SPACE ALIENS.
6/25

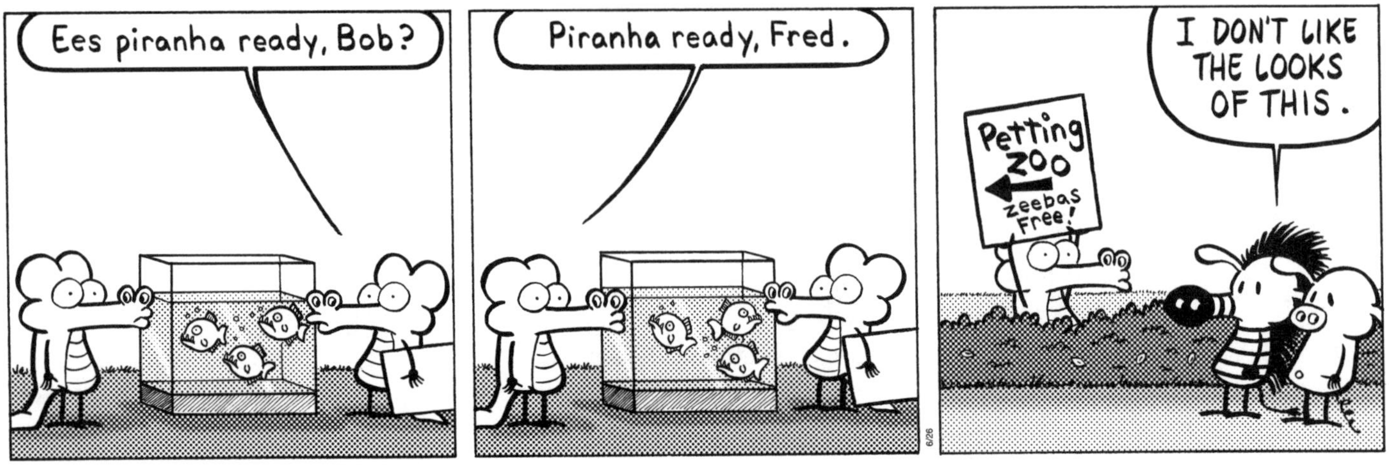
Ees piranha ready, Bob?
Piranha ready, Fred.
Petting Zoo zeebas Free!
I DON'T LIKE THE LOOKS OF THIS.
6/26

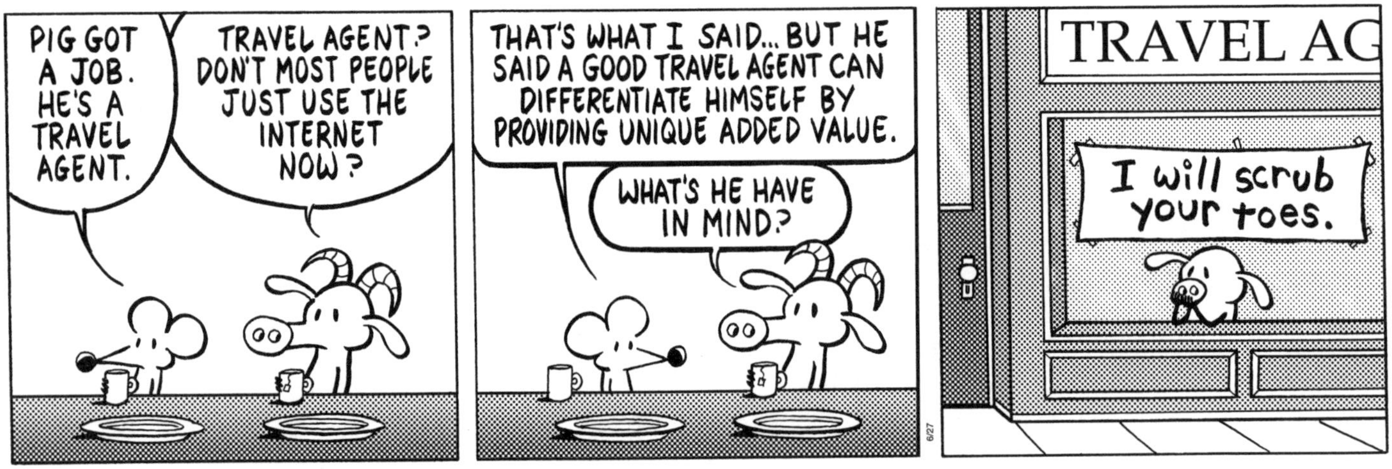
PIG GOT A JOB. HE'S A TRAVEL AGENT.
TRAVEL AGENT? DON'T MOST PEOPLE JUST USE THE INTERNET NOW?
THAT'S WHAT I SAID... BUT HE SAID A GOOD TRAVEL AGENT CAN DIFFERENTIATE HIMSELF BY PROVIDING UNIQUE ADDED VALUE.
WHAT'S HE HAVE IN MIND?
TRAVEL AG
I will scrub your toes.
6/27

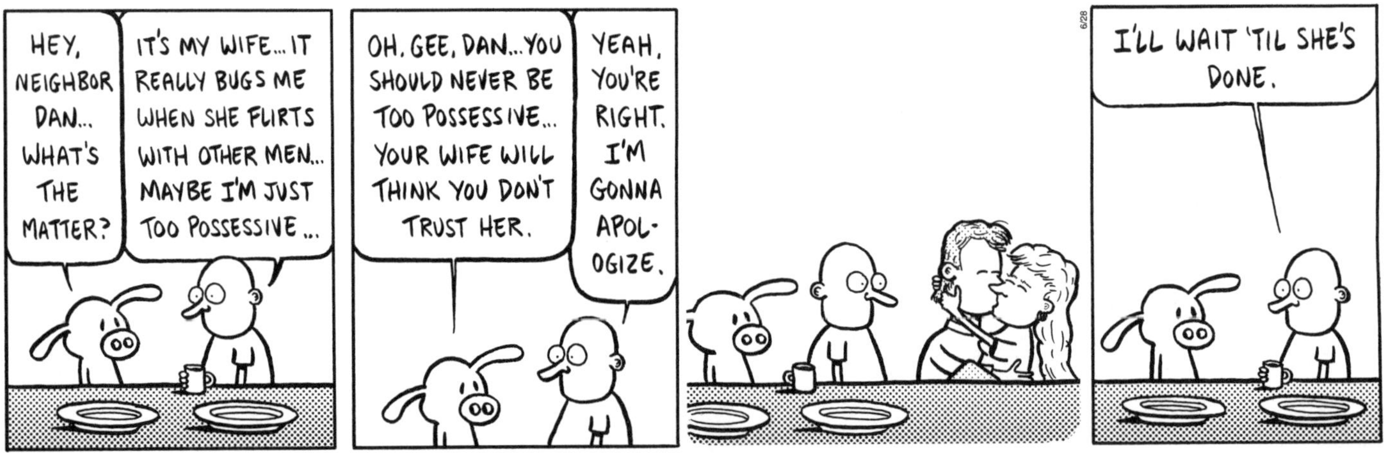
HEY, NEIGHBOR DAN... WHAT'S THE MATTER?
IT'S MY WIFE... IT REALLY BUGS ME WHEN SHE FLIRTS WITH OTHER MEN... MAYBE I'M JUST TOO POSSESSIVE...
OH, GEE, DAN... YOU SHOULD NEVER BE TOO POSSESSIVE... YOUR WIFE WILL THINK YOU DON'T TRUST HER.
YEAH, YOU'RE RIGHT. I'M GONNA APOL-OGIZE.
I'LL WAIT 'TIL SHE'S DONE.
6/28

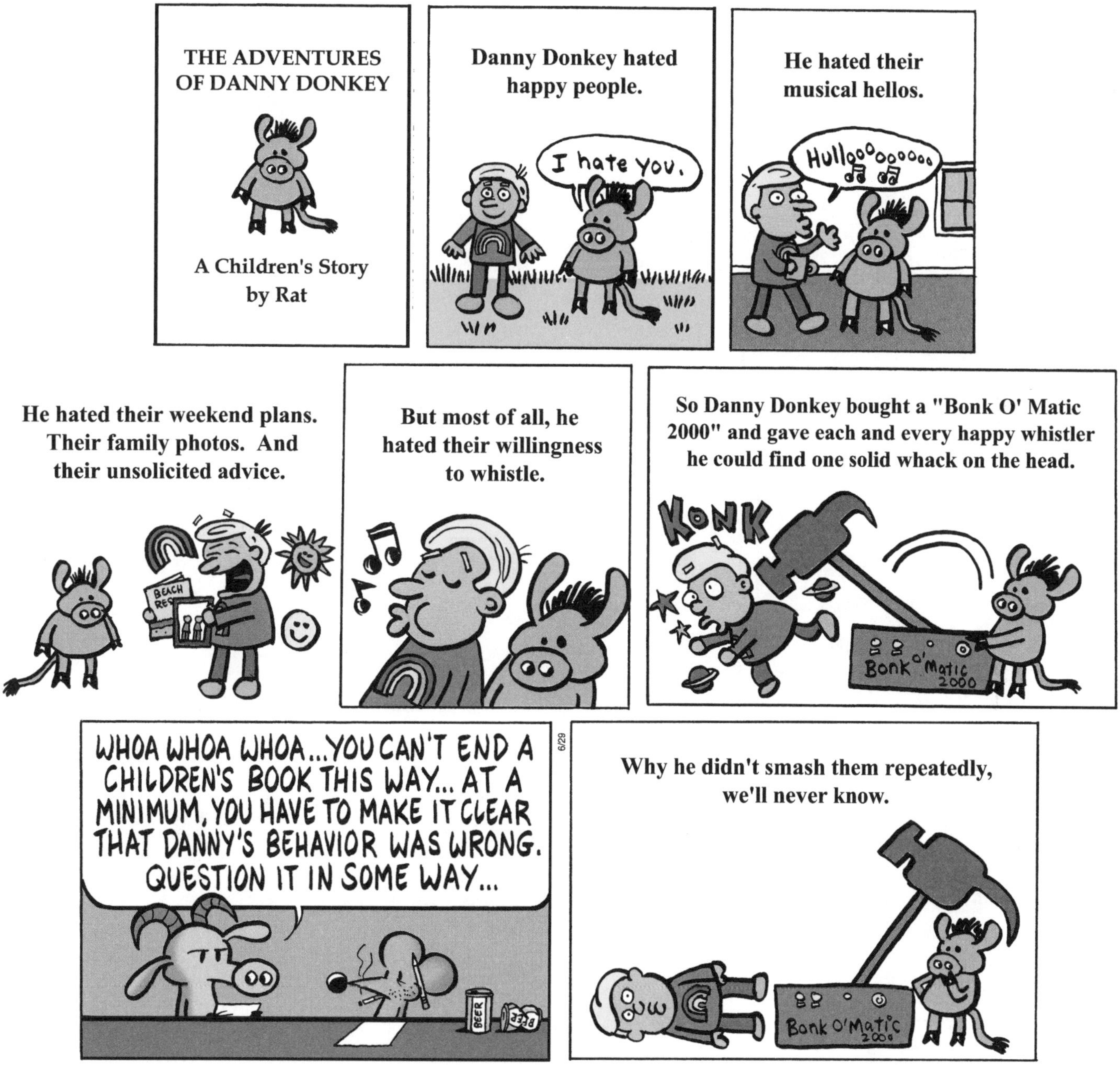
THE ADVENTURES OF DANNY DONKEY
A Children's Story by Rat
Danny Donkey hated happy people.
I hate you.
He hated their musical hellos.
Hulloooooooooo
He hated their weekend plans. Their family photos. And their unsolicited advice.
BEACH RES
But most of all, he hated their willingness to whistle.
So Danny Donkey bought a "Bonk O' Matic 2000" and gave each and every happy whistler he could find one solid whack on the head.
KONK
Bonk O' Matic 2000
WHOA WHOA WHOA...YOU CAN'T END A CHILDREN'S BOOK THIS WAY... AT A MINIMUM, YOU HAVE TO MAKE IT CLEAR THAT DANNY'S BEHAVIOR WAS WRONG. QUESTION IT IN SOME WAY...
BEER
BEER
6/29
Why he didn't smash them repeatedly, we'll never know.
Bonk O'Matic 2000

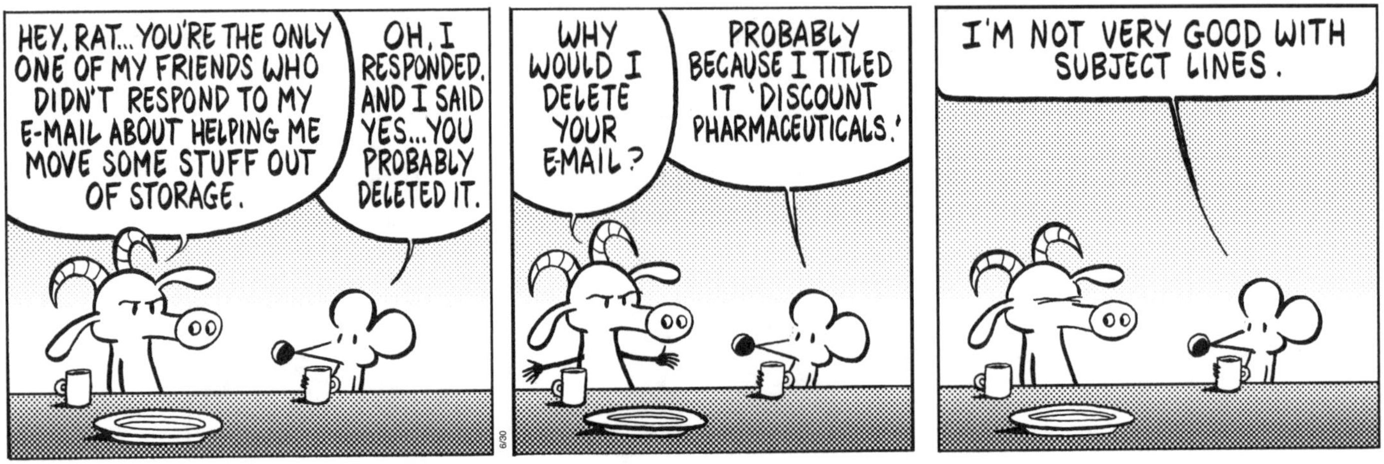
HEY, RAT... YOU'RE THE ONLY ONE OF MY FRIENDS WHO DIDN'T RESPOND TO MY E-MAIL ABOUT HELPING ME MOVE SOME STUFF OUT OF STORAGE.
OH, I RESPONDED, AND I SAID YES... YOU PROBABLY DELETED IT.
WHY WOULD I DELETE YOUR E-MAIL?
PROBABLY BECAUSE I TITLED IT 'DISCOUNT PHARMACEUTICALS.'
I'M NOT VERY GOOD WITH SUBJECT LINES.

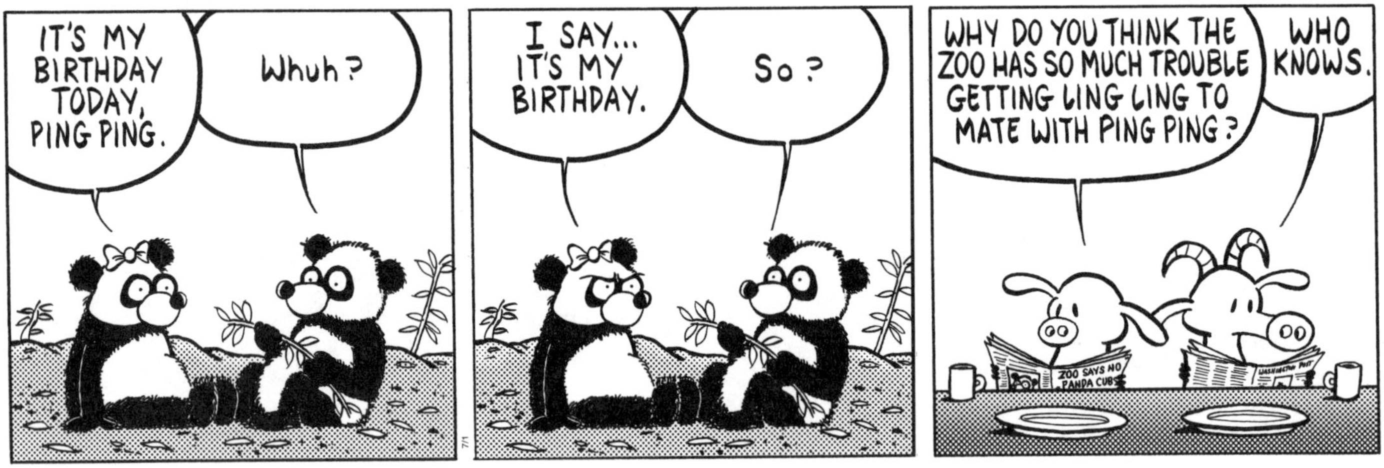
IT'S MY BIRTHDAY TODAY, PING PING.
Whuh?
I SAY... IT'S MY BIRTHDAY.
So?
WHY DO YOU THINK THE ZOO HAS SO MUCH TROUBLE GETTING LING LING TO MATE WITH PING PING?
WHO KNOWS.
ZOO SAYS NO PANDA CUBS

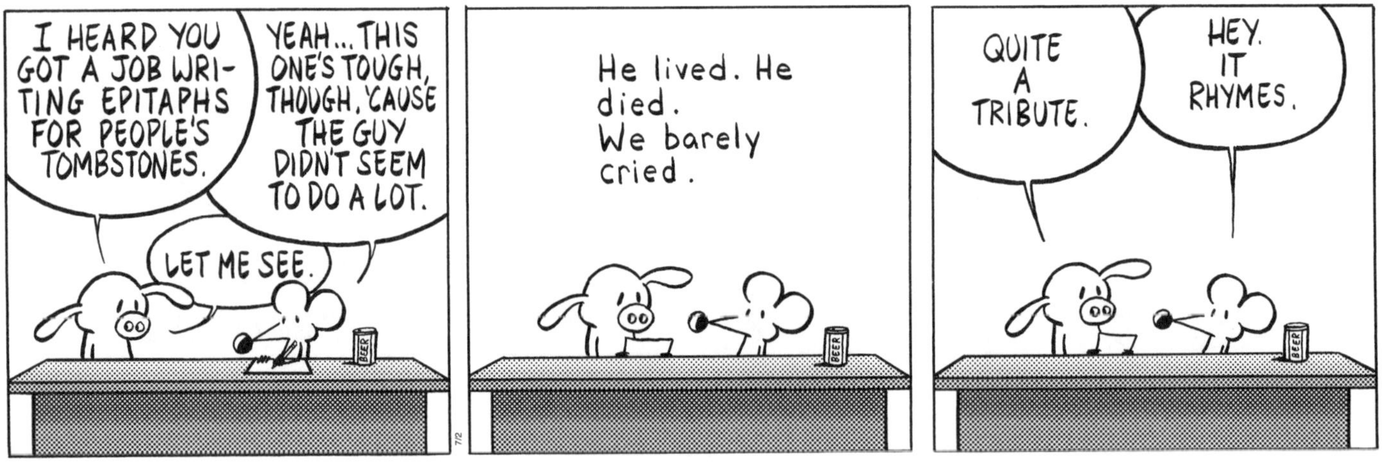
I HEARD YOU GOT A JOB WRITING EPITAPHS FOR PEOPLE'S TOMBSTONES.
YEAH... THIS ONE'S TOUGH, THOUGH, 'CAUSE THE GUY DIDN'T SEEM TO DO A LOT.
LET ME SEE.
He lived. He died. We barely cried.
QUITE A TRIBUTE.
HEY. IT RHYMES.

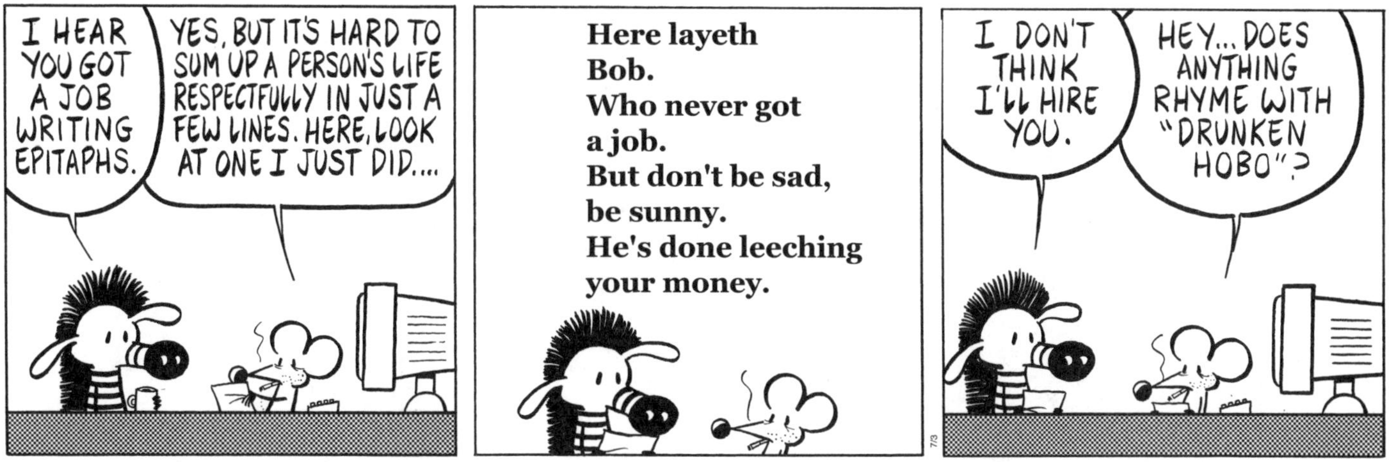
I HEAR YOU GOT A JOB WRITING EPITAPHS.
YES, BUT IT'S HARD TO SUM UP A PERSON'S LIFE RESPECTFULLY IN JUST A FEW LINES. HERE, LOOK AT ONE I JUST DID....
Here layeth Bob.
Who never got a job.
But don't be sad, be sunny.
He's done leeching your money.
I DON'T THINK I'LL HIRE YOU.
HEY... DOES ANYTHING RHYME WITH "DRUNKEN HOBO"?

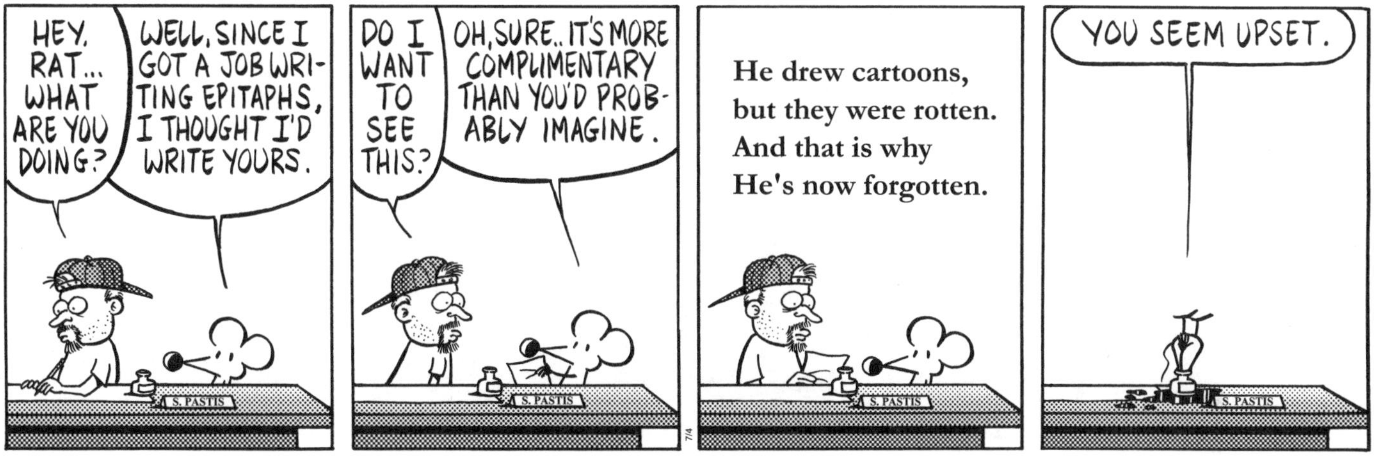
HEY, RAT... WHAT ARE YOU DOING?
WELL, SINCE I GOT A JOB WRITING EPITAPHS, I THOUGHT I'D WRITE YOURS.
S. PASTIS
DO I WANT TO SEE THIS?
OH, SURE.. IT'S MORE COMPLIMENTARY THAN YOU'D PROBABLY IMAGINE.
He drew cartoons,
but they were rotten.
And that is why
He's now forgotten.
YOU SEEM UPSET.

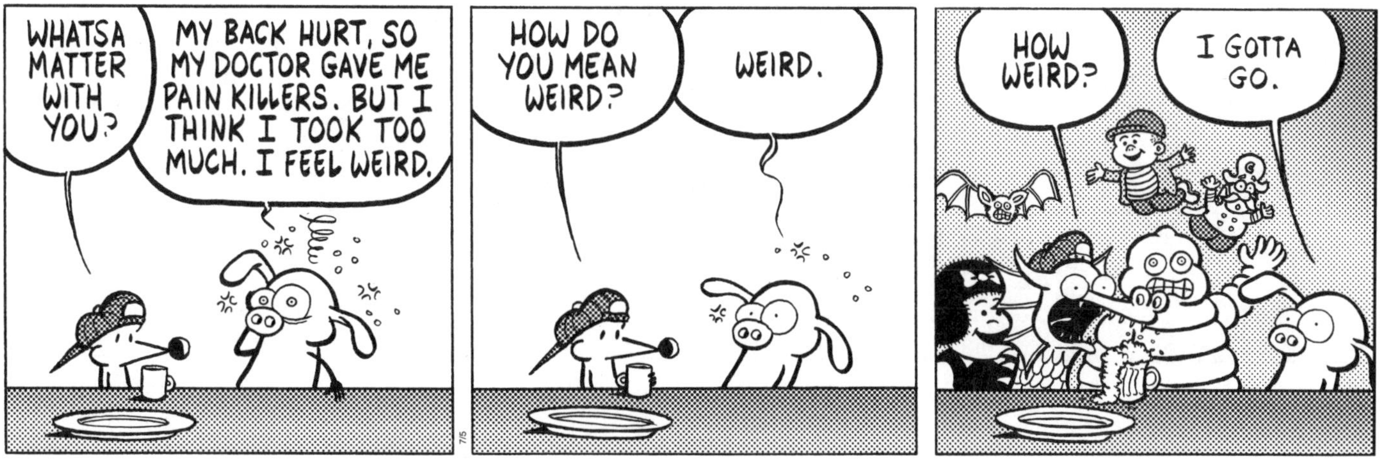
WHATSA MATTER WITH YOU?
MY BACK HURT, SO MY DOCTOR GAVE ME PAIN KILLERS. BUT I THINK I TOOK TOO MUCH. I FEEL WEIRD.
HOW DO YOU MEAN WEIRD?
WEIRD.
HOW WEIRD?
I GOTTA GO.

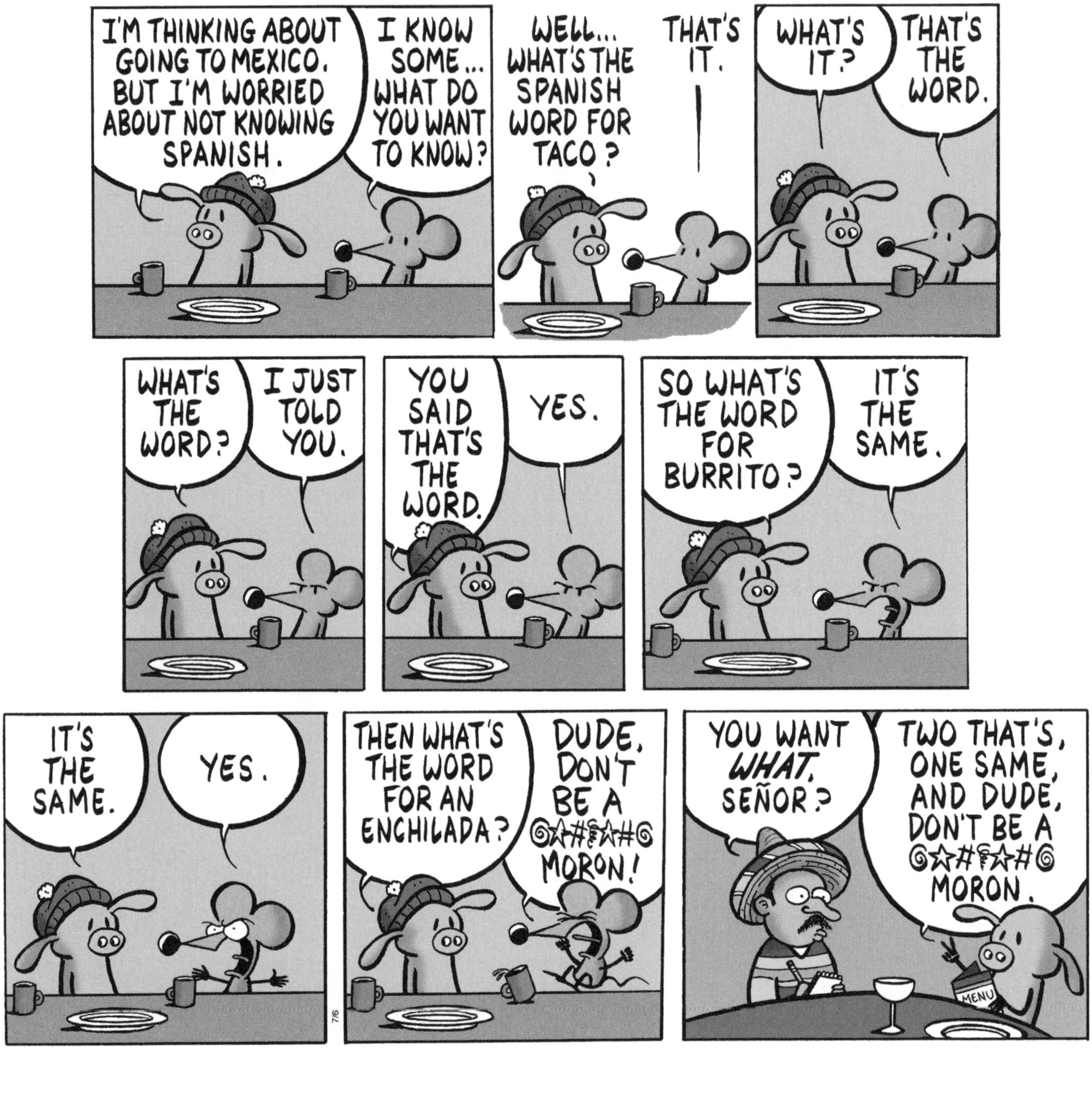
I'M THINKING ABOUT GOING TO MEXICO. BUT I'M WORRIED ABOUT NOT KNOWING SPANISH.
I KNOW SOME... WHAT DO YOU WANT TO KNOW?
WELL... WHAT'S THE SPANISH WORD FOR TACO?
THAT'S IT.
WHAT'S IT?
THAT'S THE WORD.
WHAT'S THE WORD?
I JUST TOLD YOU.
YOU SAID THAT'S THE WORD.
YES.
SO WHAT'S THE WORD FOR BURRITO?
IT'S THE SAME.
IT'S THE SAME.
YES.
THEN WHAT'S THE WORD FOR AN ENCHILADA?
DUDE, DON'T BE A MORON!
YOU WANT *WHAT*, SEÑOR?
TWO THAT'S, ONE SAME, AND DUDE, DON'T BE A MORON.
MENU

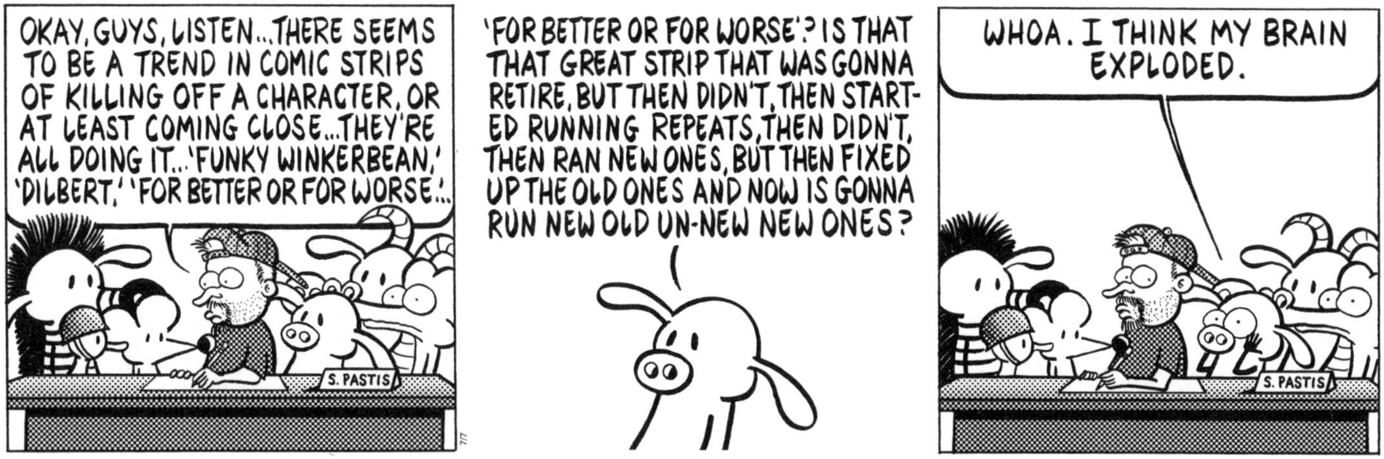
OKAY, GUYS, LISTEN...THERE SEEMS TO BE A TREND IN COMIC STRIPS OF KILLING OFF A CHARACTER, OR AT LEAST COMING CLOSE...THEY'RE ALL DOING IT...'FUNKY WINKERBEAN,' 'DILBERT,' 'FOR BETTER OR FOR WORSE'...
S. PASTIS
'FOR BETTER OR FOR WORSE'? IS THAT THAT GREAT STRIP THAT WAS GONNA RETIRE, BUT THEN DIDN'T, THEN STARTED RUNNING REPEATS, THEN DIDN'T, THEN RAN NEW ONES, BUT THEN FIXED UP THE OLD ONES AND NOW IS GONNA RUN NEW OLD UN-NEW NEW ONES?
WHOA. I THINK MY BRAIN EXPLODED.
S. PASTIS

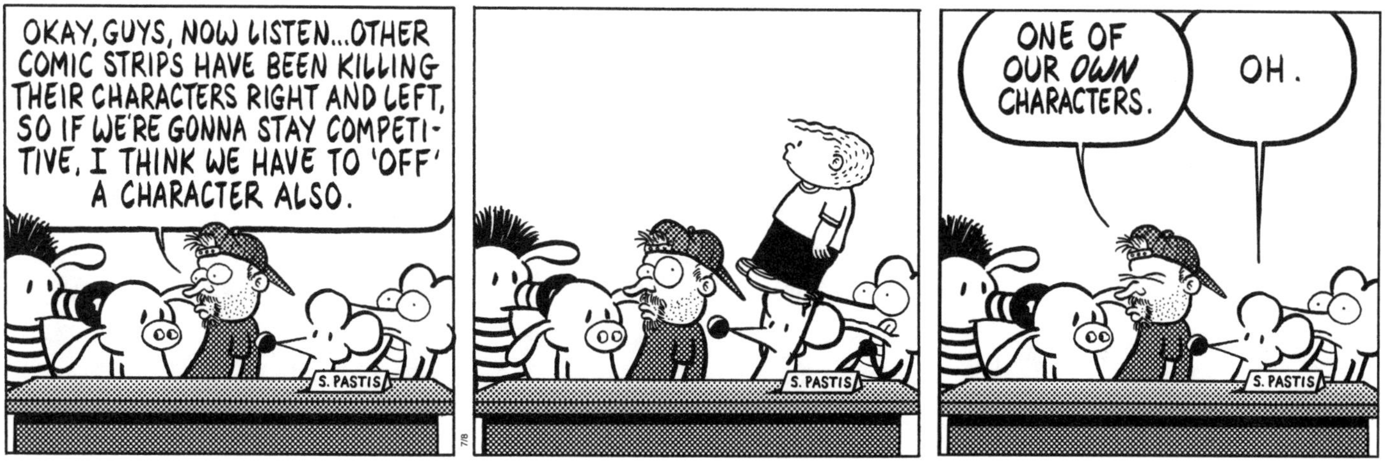
OKAY, GUYS, NOW LISTEN...OTHER COMIC STRIPS HAVE BEEN KILLING THEIR CHARACTERS RIGHT AND LEFT, SO IF WE'RE GONNA STAY COMPETITIVE, I THINK WE HAVE TO 'OFF' A CHARACTER ALSO.
S. PASTIS
S. PASTIS
ONE OF OUR *OWN* CHARACTERS.
OH.
S. PASTIS

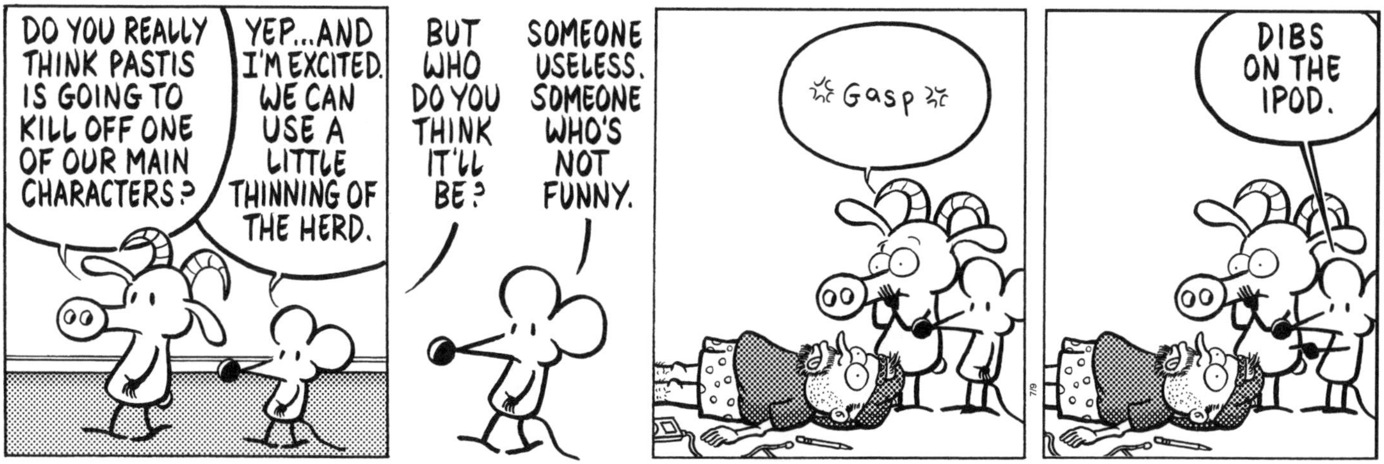
DO YOU REALLY THINK PASTIS IS GOING TO KILL OFF ONE OF OUR MAIN CHARACTERS?
YEP...AND I'M EXCITED. WE CAN USE A LITTLE THINNING OF THE HERD.
BUT WHO DO YOU THINK IT'LL BE?
SOMEONE USELESS. SOMEONE WHO'S NOT FUNNY.
Gasp
DIBS ON THE IPOD.

Row 1

OHMYGAWD! I CAN'T BELIEVE IT! OUR OWN CREATOR DIED.. IT'S SO SAD!

SAD? DUDE, IT *ROCKS*.. HE SAID A CHARACTER HAD TO DIE THIS WEEK, AND IT'S NOT US! WOOHOO!

DID HE SAY IT WAS ONLY ONE?

WELL, NO, BUT I— ✻ACK✻

THUD

I SUPPOSE IT WOULD LOOK BAD TO JUMP UP AND CHEER.

Row 2

WHOA. DUDE. I DIED IN MY OWN STRIP. THIS IS SO MESSED UP.

YOU? WHO CARES ABOUT YOU? *I* DIED! ME. THE STAR! AND I'M STUCK IN ETERNITY WITH YOU!

WELL, WHERE DO WE GO NOW?

HOW DO I KNOW? DON'T WE GET SOME SORT OF ANGEL ESCORT OR SOMETHING?

THAT'S ONE HOMELY ANGEL.

Row 3

WELL, HERE WE ARE, THE CREATOR AND STAR OF THIS STUPID STRIP, DEAD AND STUCK SOME- WHERE IN THE—WHUH?

Steeeephan... It's me, Lisa Klem Wilson, the head of your syndicaaate... Behold... You and Rat cannot diiiie... There's too much money to be maaade.. the books, the calendars, the stuffed animaaaals...

THANKS TO MIKHAELA REID FOR THE GIANT LISA HEAD DRAWING

WHOA. THAT'S AMAZING.

YOU MEAN HOW THE HEAD OF OUR SYNDICATE TRANSFORMED HERSELF INTO A GIANT HEAD IN THE SKY?

NO...HOW SHE SLIPPED IN ALL THOSE PLUGS.

THAT WAS IMPRESSIVE.

I'm gooooood.

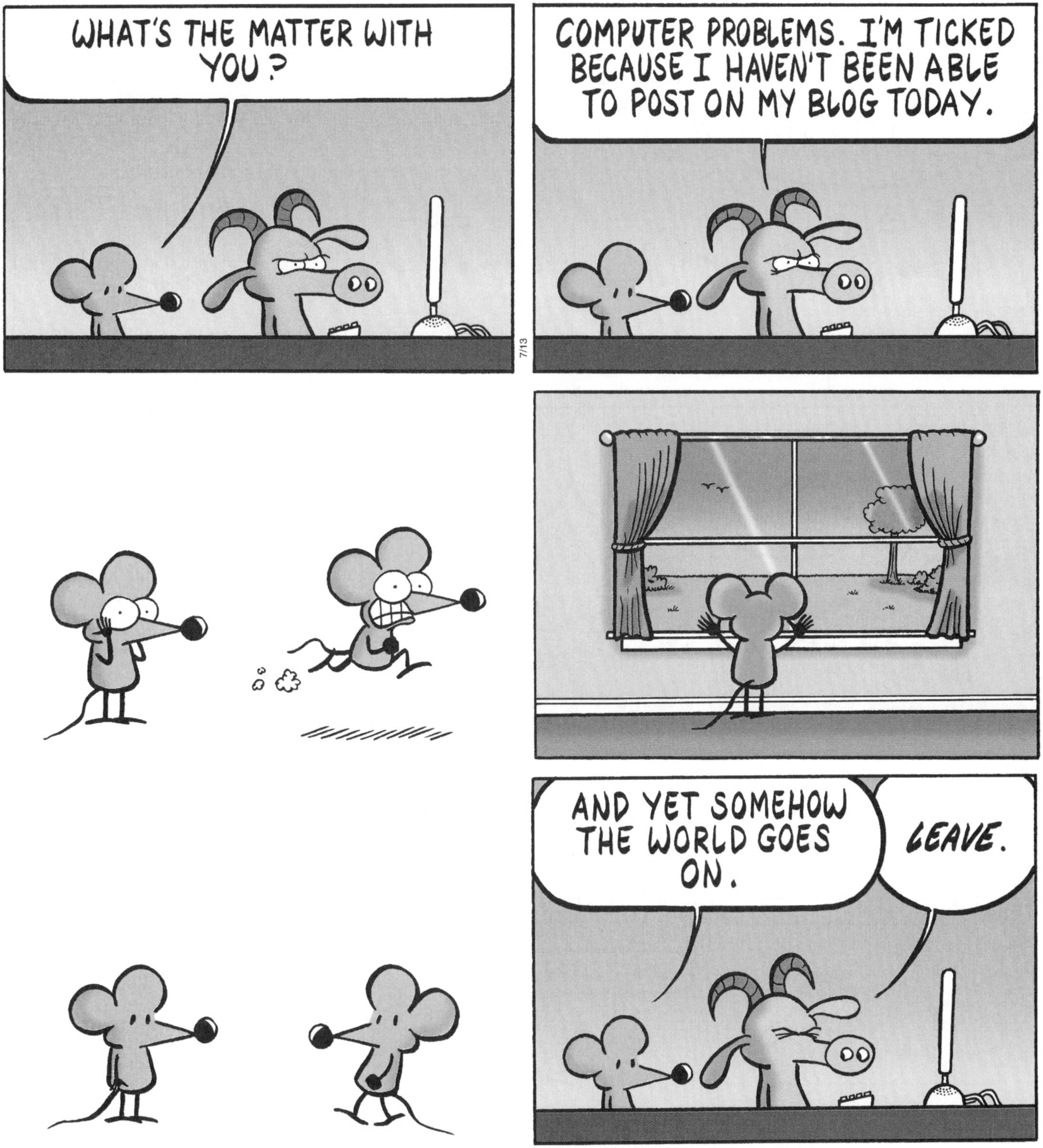
WHAT'S THE MATTER WITH YOU?
7/13
COMPUTER PROBLEMS. I'M TICKED BECAUSE I HAVEN'T BEEN ABLE TO POST ON MY BLOG TODAY.
AND YET SOMEHOW THE WORLD GOES ON.
LEAVE.

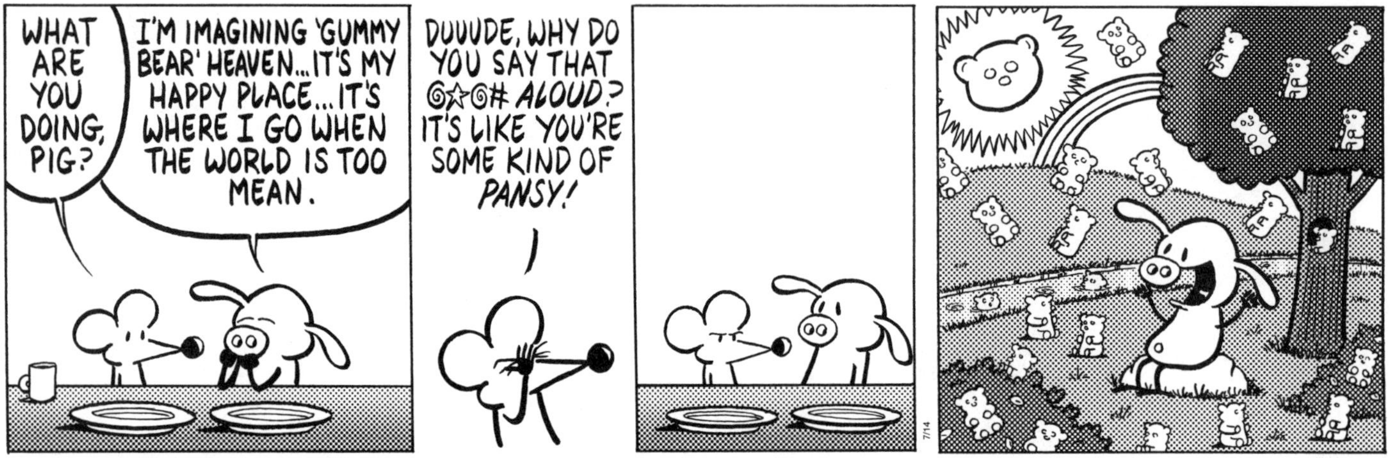
WHAT ARE YOU DOING, PIG?
I'M IMAGINING 'GUMMY BEAR' HEAVEN... IT'S MY HAPPY PLACE... IT'S WHERE I GO WHEN THE WORLD IS TOO MEAN.
DUUUDE, WHY DO YOU SAY THAT @☆@# ALOUD? IT'S LIKE YOU'RE SOME KIND OF PANSY!
7/14

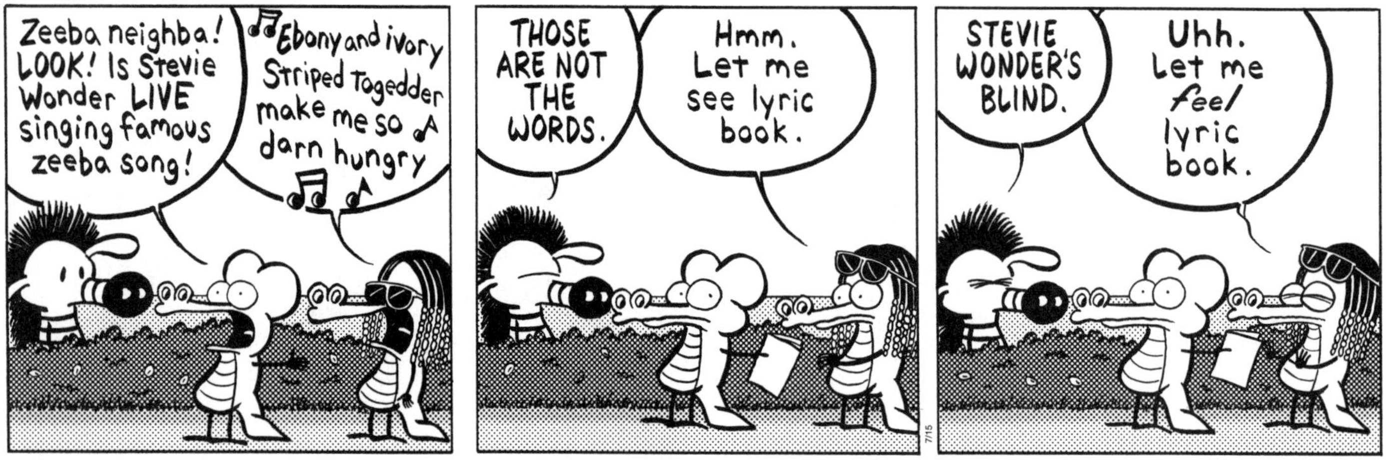
Zeeba neighba! LOOK! Is Stevie Wonder LIVE singing famous zeeba song!
Ebony and ivory Striped Togedder make me so darn hungry
THOSE ARE NOT THE WORDS.
Hmm. Let me see lyric book.
STEVIE WONDER'S BLIND.
Uhh. Let me feel lyric book.
7/15

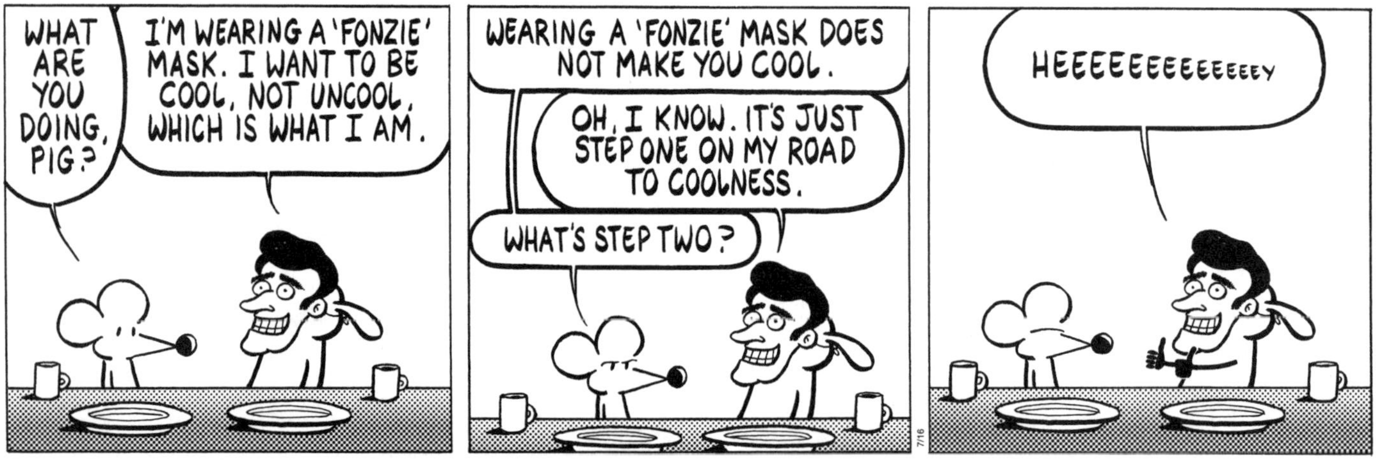
WHAT ARE YOU DOING, PIG?
I'M WEARING A 'FONZIE' MASK. I WANT TO BE COOL, NOT UNCOOL, WHICH IS WHAT I AM.
WEARING A 'FONZIE' MASK DOES NOT MAKE YOU COOL.
OH, I KNOW. IT'S JUST STEP ONE ON MY ROAD TO COOLNESS.
WHAT'S STEP TWO?
HEEEEEEEEEEEEEY
7/16

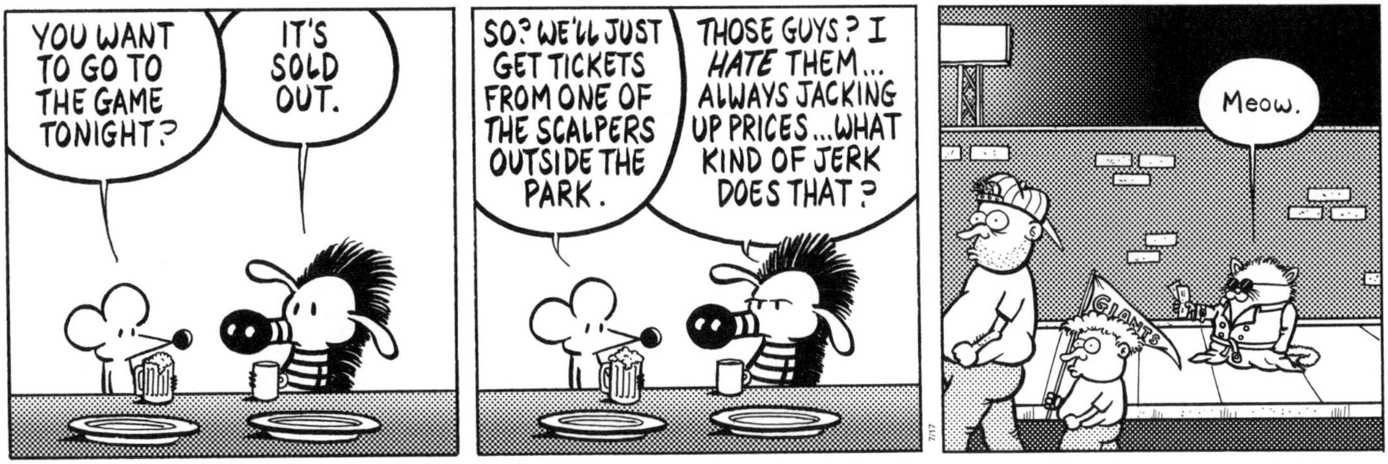
YOU WANT TO GO TO THE GAME TONIGHT?
IT'S SOLD OUT.
SO? WE'LL JUST GET TICKETS FROM ONE OF THE SCALPERS OUTSIDE THE PARK.
THOSE GUYS? I *HATE* THEM... ALWAYS JACKING UP PRICES... WHAT KIND OF JERK DOES THAT?
GIANTS
Meow.
7/17

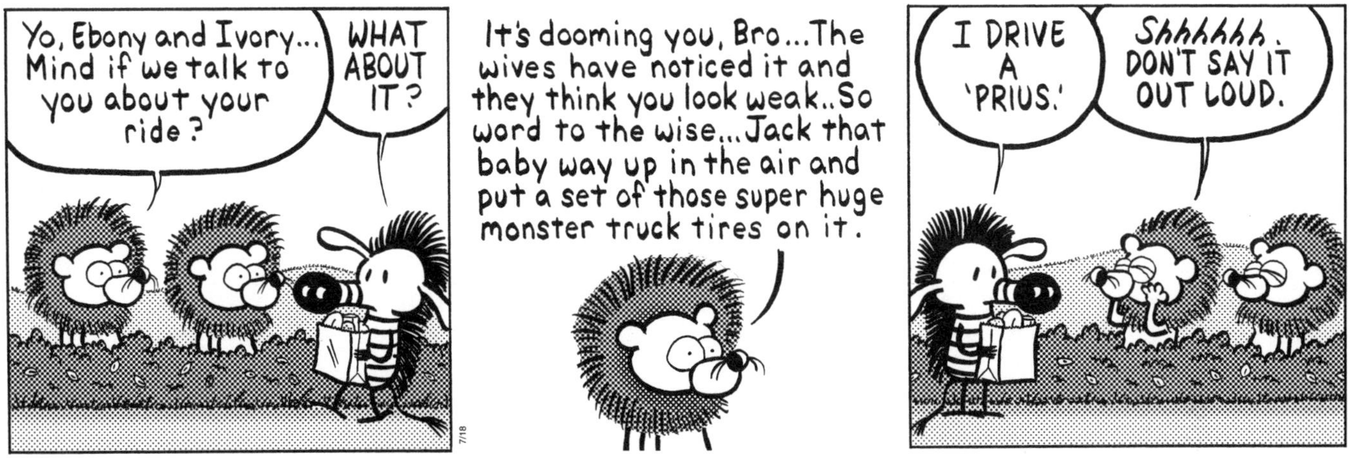
Yo, Ebony and Ivory... Mind if we talk to you about your ride?
WHAT ABOUT IT?
It's dooming you, Bro... The wives have noticed it and they think you look weak.. So word to the wise... Jack that baby way up in the air and put a set of those super huge monster truck tires on it.
7/18
I DRIVE A 'PRIUS.'
Shhhhhh. DON'T SAY IT OUT LOUD.

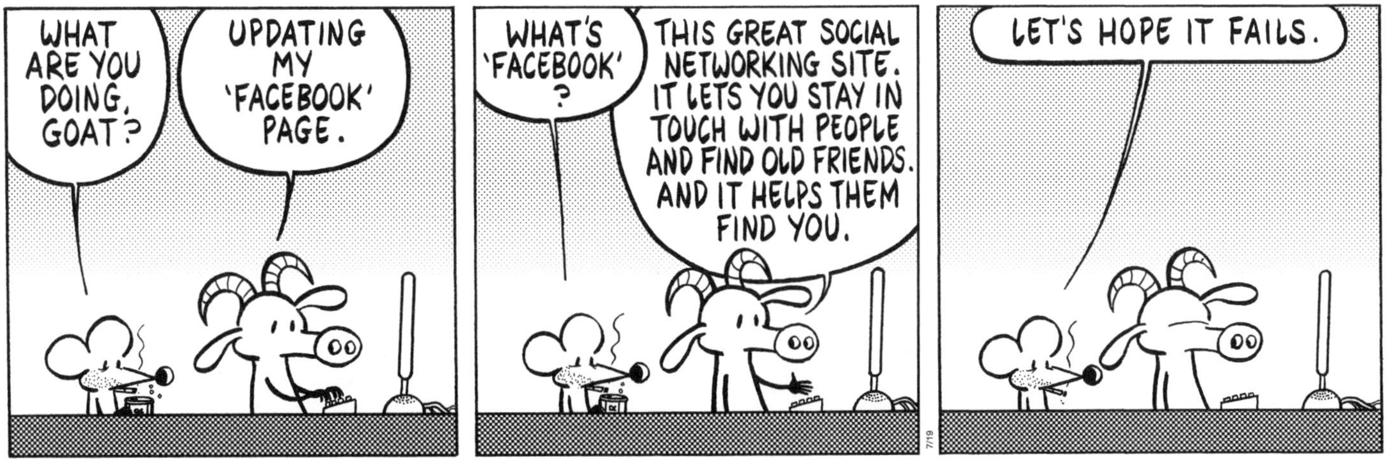
WHAT ARE YOU DOING, GOAT?
UPDATING MY 'FACEBOOK' PAGE.
WHAT'S 'FACEBOOK'?
THIS GREAT SOCIAL NETWORKING SITE. IT LETS YOU STAY IN TOUCH WITH PEOPLE AND FIND OLD FRIENDS. AND IT HELPS THEM FIND YOU.
7/19
LET'S HOPE IT FAILS.

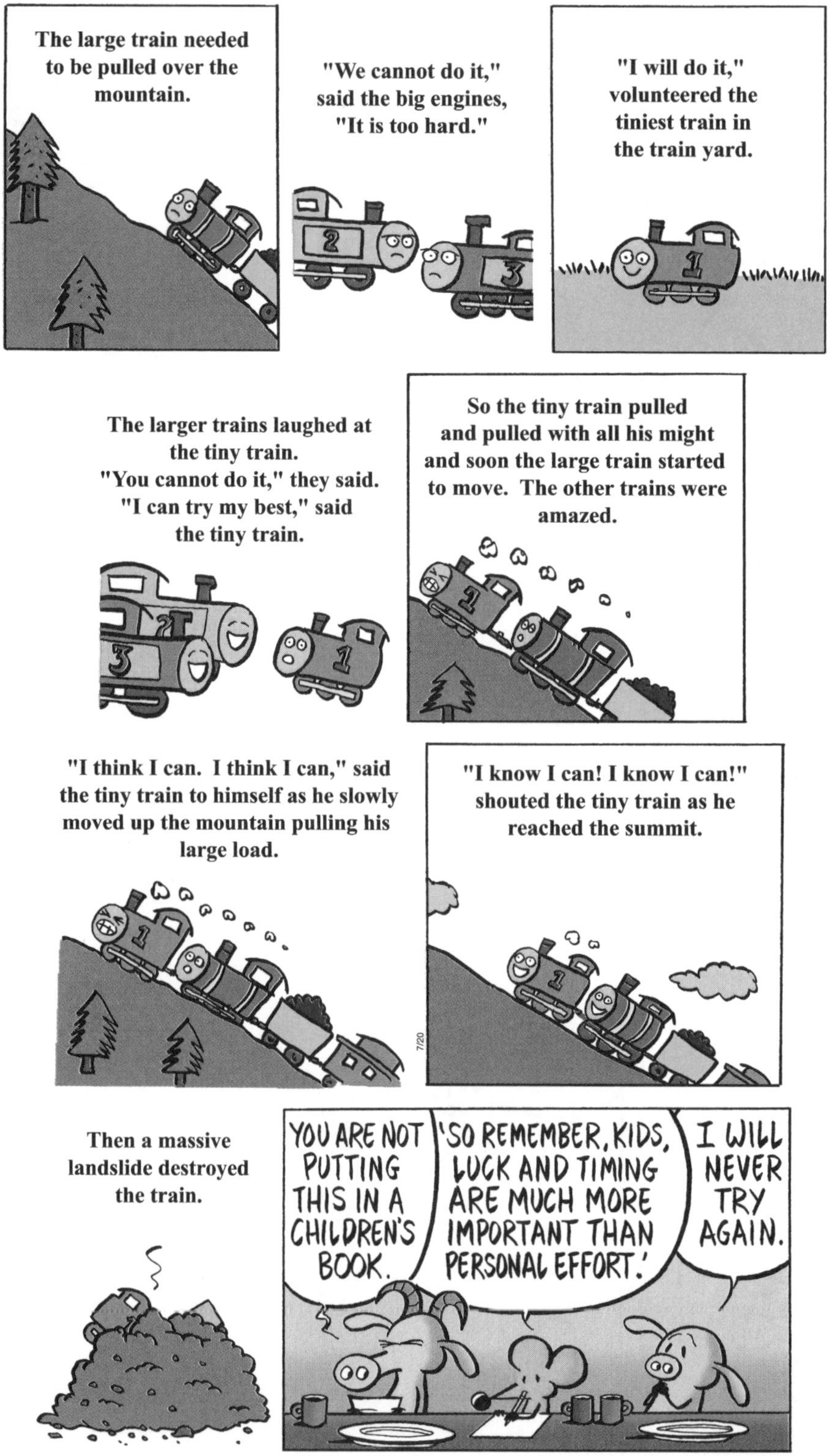

The large train needed to be pulled over the mountain.
"We cannot do it," said the big engines, "It is too hard."
"I will do it," volunteered the tiniest train in the train yard.
The larger trains laughed at the tiny train. "You cannot do it," they said. "I can try my best," said the tiny train.
So the tiny train pulled and pulled with all his might and soon the large train started to move. The other trains were amazed.
"I think I can. I think I can," said the tiny train to himself as he slowly moved up the mountain pulling his large load.
7/20
"I know I can! I know I can!" shouted the tiny train as he reached the summit.
Then a massive landslide destroyed the train.
YOU ARE NOT PUTTING THIS IN A CHILDREN'S BOOK.
'SO REMEMBER, KIDS, LUCK AND TIMING ARE MUCH MORE IMPORTANT THAN PERSONAL EFFORT.'
I WILL NEVER TRY AGAIN.

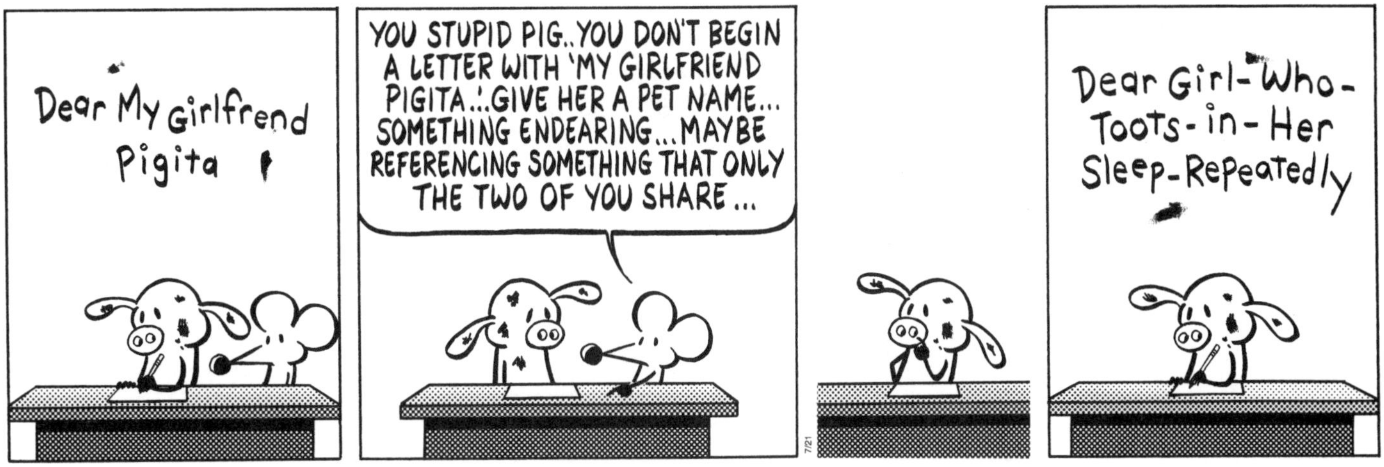
Dear My Girlfriend Pigita
YOU STUPID PIG..YOU DON'T BEGIN A LETTER WITH 'MY GIRLFRIEND PIGITA.'..GIVE HER A PET NAME... SOMETHING ENDEARING...MAYBE REFERENCING SOMETHING THAT ONLY THE TWO OF YOU SHARE...
7/21
Dear Girl-Who-Toots-in-Her Sleep-Repeatedly

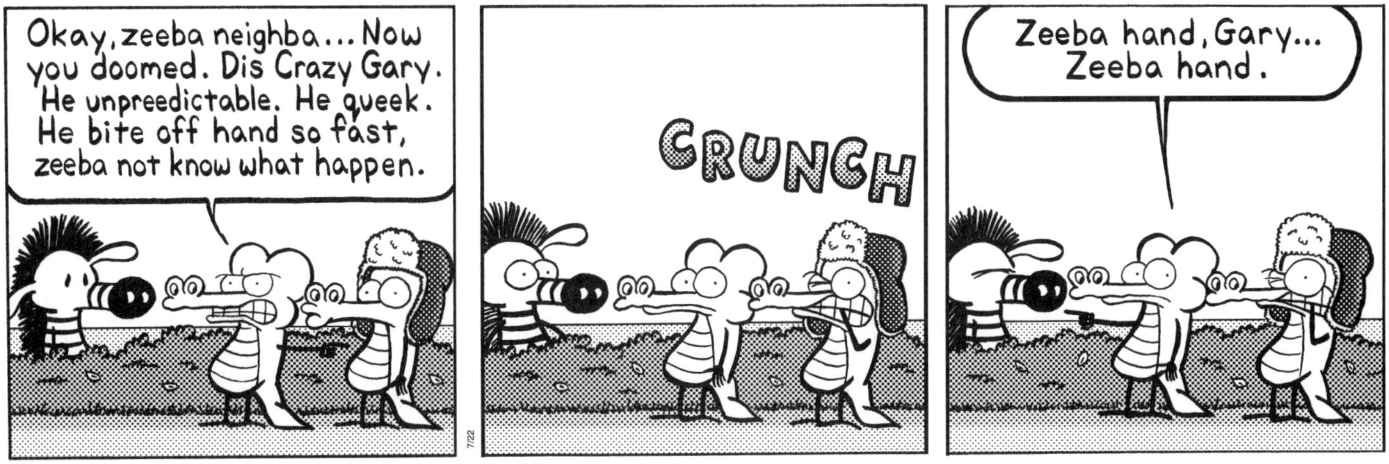
Okay, zeeba neighba... Now you doomed. Dis Crazy Gary. He unpreedictable. He queek. He bite off hand so fast, zeeba not know what happen.
7/22
CRUNCH
Zeeba hand, Gary... Zeeba hand.

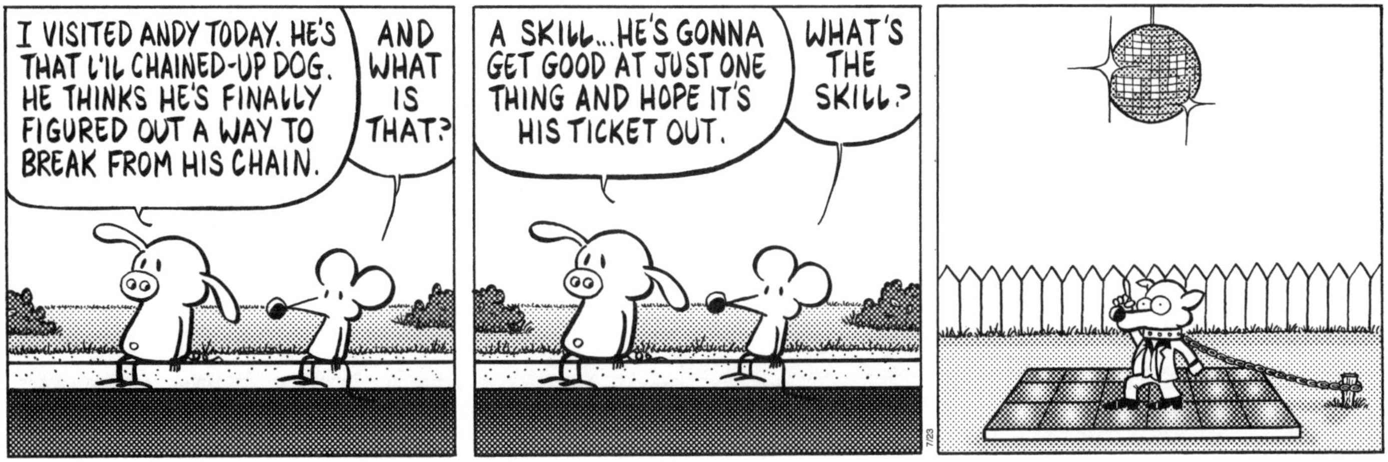
I VISITED ANDY TODAY. HE'S THAT L'IL CHAINED-UP DOG. HE THINKS HE'S FINALLY FIGURED OUT A WAY TO BREAK FROM HIS CHAIN.
AND WHAT IS THAT?
A SKILL...HE'S GONNA GET GOOD AT JUST ONE THING AND HOPE IT'S HIS TICKET OUT.
WHAT'S THE SKILL?
7/23

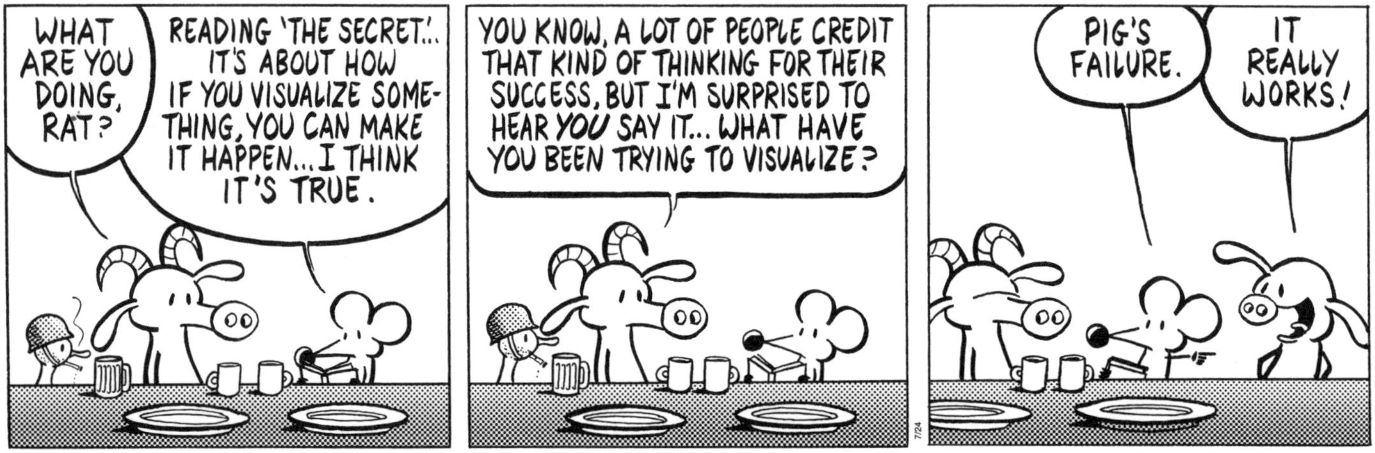
WHAT ARE YOU DOING, RAT?
READING 'THE SECRET'... IT'S ABOUT HOW IF YOU VISUALIZE SOMETHING, YOU CAN MAKE IT HAPPEN... I THINK IT'S TRUE.
YOU KNOW, A LOT OF PEOPLE CREDIT THAT KIND OF THINKING FOR THEIR SUCCESS, BUT I'M SURPRISED TO HEAR *YOU* SAY IT... WHAT HAVE YOU BEEN TRYING TO VISUALIZE?
PIG'S FAILURE.
IT REALLY WORKS!
7/24

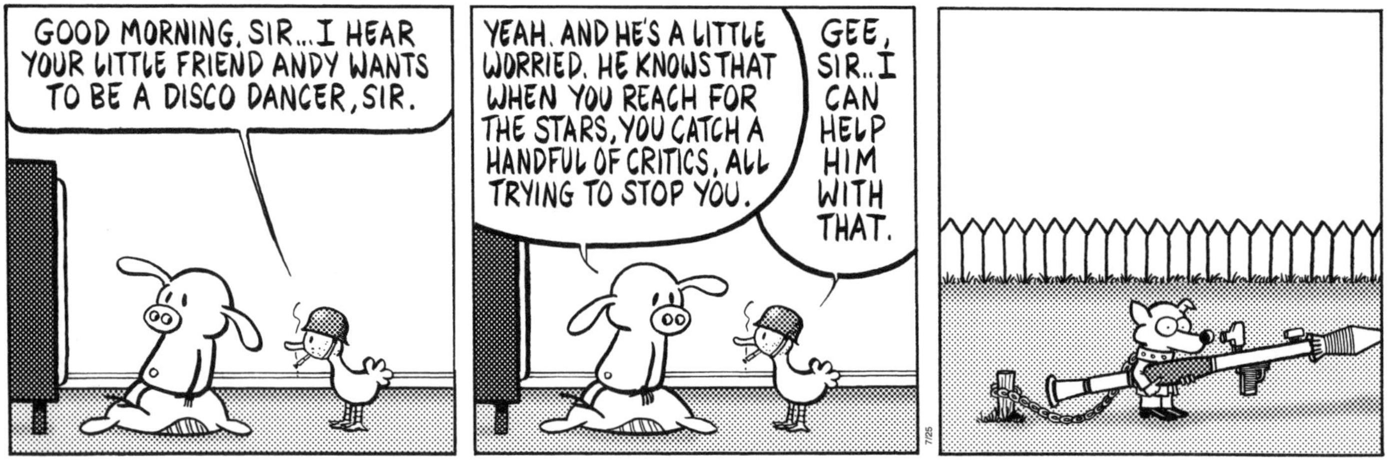
GOOD MORNING, SIR... I HEAR YOUR LITTLE FRIEND ANDY WANTS TO BE A DISCO DANCER, SIR.
YEAH. AND HE'S A LITTLE WORRIED. HE KNOWS THAT WHEN YOU REACH FOR THE STARS, YOU CATCH A HANDFUL OF CRITICS, ALL TRYING TO STOP YOU.
GEE, SIR.. I CAN HELP HIM WITH THAT.
7/25

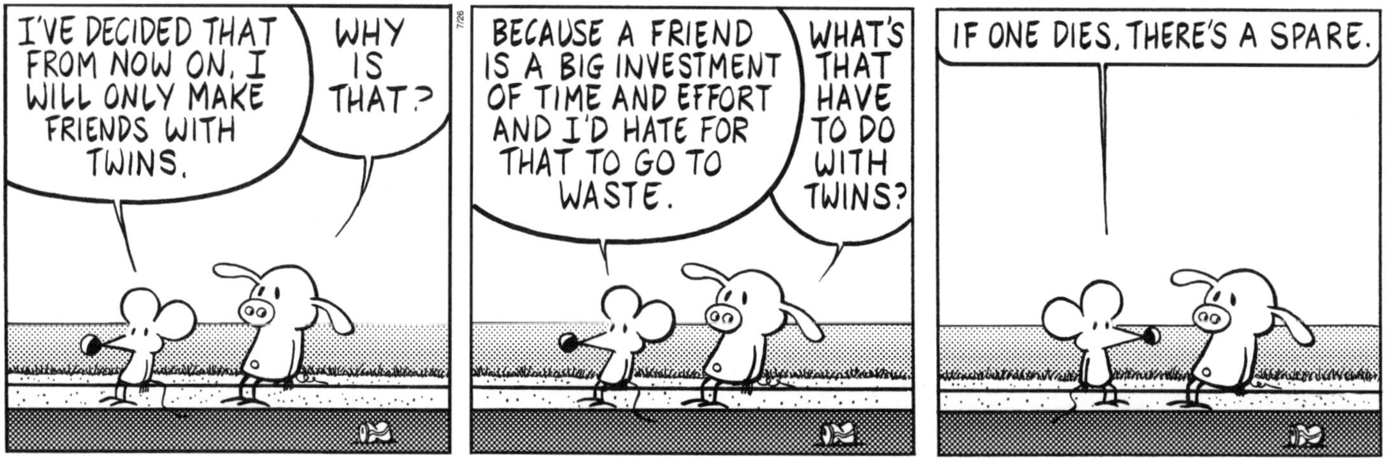
I'VE DECIDED THAT FROM NOW ON, I WILL ONLY MAKE FRIENDS WITH TWINS.
WHY IS THAT?
BECAUSE A FRIEND IS A BIG INVESTMENT OF TIME AND EFFORT AND I'D HATE FOR THAT TO GO TO WASTE.
WHAT'S THAT HAVE TO DO WITH TWINS?
IF ONE DIES, THERE'S A SPARE.
7/26

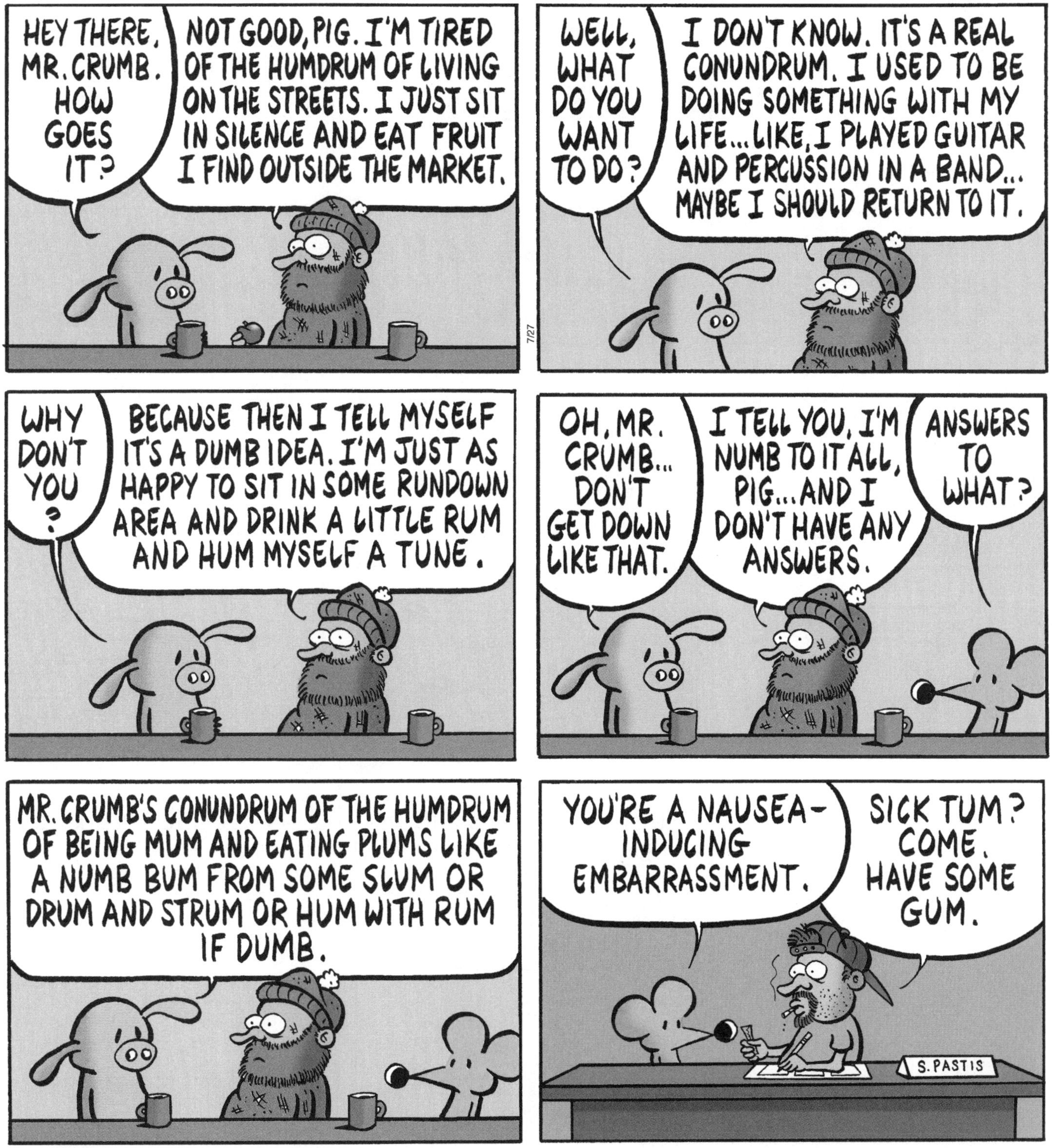
HEY THERE, MR. CRUMB. HOW GOES IT?
NOT GOOD, PIG. I'M TIRED OF THE HUMDRUM OF LIVING ON THE STREETS. I JUST SIT IN SILENCE AND EAT FRUIT I FIND OUTSIDE THE MARKET.
7/27
WELL, WHAT DO YOU WANT TO DO?
I DON'T KNOW. IT'S A REAL CONUNDRUM. I USED TO BE DOING SOMETHING WITH MY LIFE... LIKE, I PLAYED GUITAR AND PERCUSSION IN A BAND... MAYBE I SHOULD RETURN TO IT.
WHY DON'T YOU?
BECAUSE THEN I TELL MYSELF IT'S A DUMB IDEA. I'M JUST AS HAPPY TO SIT IN SOME RUNDOWN AREA AND DRINK A LITTLE RUM AND HUM MYSELF A TUNE.
OH, MR. CRUMB... DON'T GET DOWN LIKE THAT.
I TELL YOU, I'M NUMB TO IT ALL, PIG... AND I DON'T HAVE ANY ANSWERS.
ANSWERS TO WHAT?
MR. CRUMB'S CONUNDRUM OF THE HUMDRUM OF BEING MUM AND EATING PLUMS LIKE A NUMB BUM FROM SOME SLUM OR DRUM AND STRUM OR HUM WITH RUM IF DUMB.
YOU'RE A NAUSEA-INDUCING EMBARRASSMENT.
SICK TUM? COME. HAVE SOME GUM.
S. PASTIS

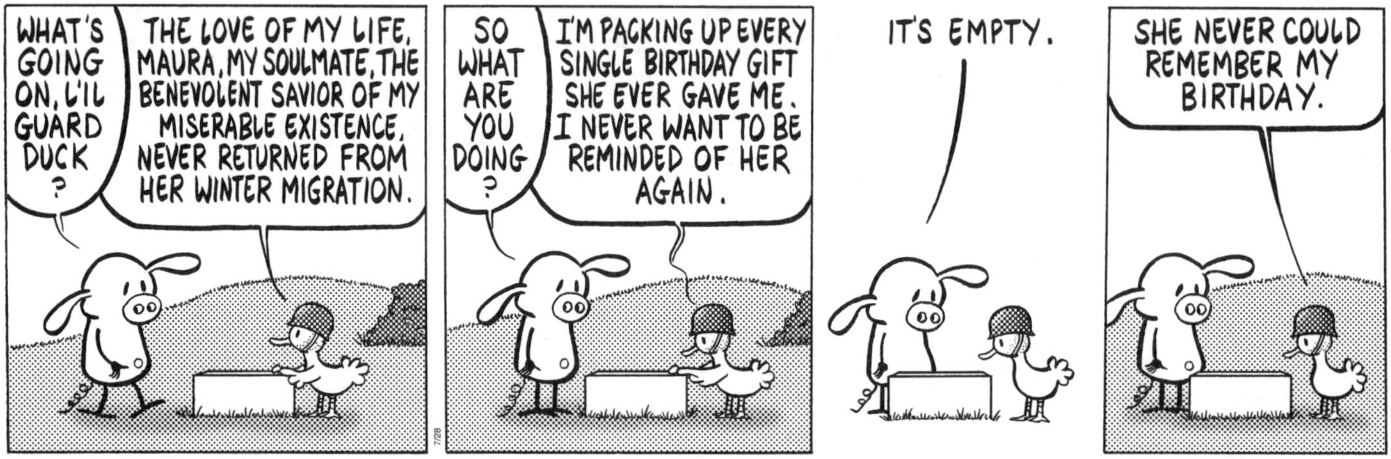
WHAT'S GOING ON, L'IL GUARD DUCK ?
THE LOVE OF MY LIFE, MAURA, MY SOULMATE, THE BENEVOLENT SAVIOR OF MY MISERABLE EXISTENCE, NEVER RETURNED FROM HER WINTER MIGRATION.
SO WHAT ARE YOU DOING ?
I'M PACKING UP EVERY SINGLE BIRTHDAY GIFT SHE EVER GAVE ME. I NEVER WANT TO BE REMINDED OF HER AGAIN.
IT'S EMPTY.
SHE NEVER COULD REMEMBER MY BIRTHDAY.
7/28

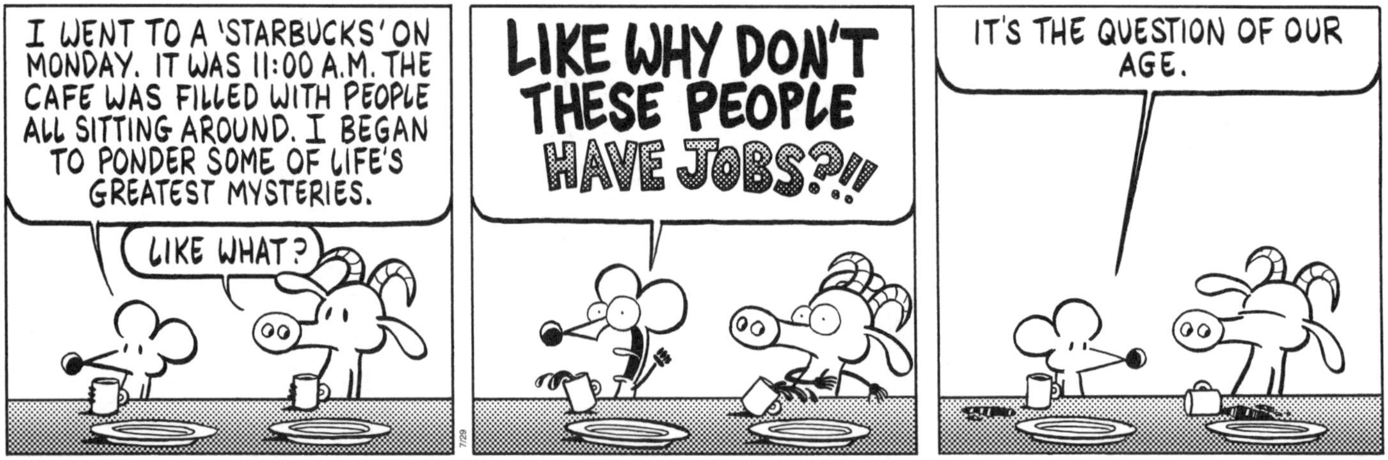
I WENT TO A 'STARBUCKS' ON MONDAY. IT WAS 11:00 A.M. THE CAFE WAS FILLED WITH PEOPLE ALL SITTING AROUND. I BEGAN TO PONDER SOME OF LIFE'S GREATEST MYSTERIES.
LIKE WHAT?
LIKE WHY DON'T THESE PEOPLE HAVE JOBS?!!
IT'S THE QUESTION OF OUR AGE.
7/29

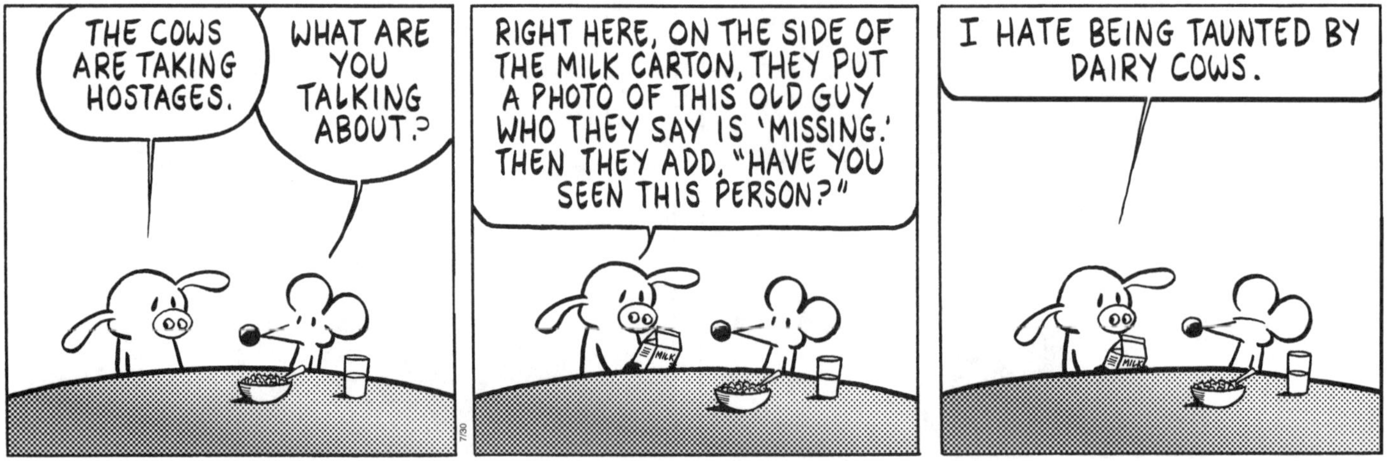
THE COWS ARE TAKING HOSTAGES.
WHAT ARE YOU TALKING ABOUT ?
RIGHT HERE, ON THE SIDE OF THE MILK CARTON, THEY PUT A PHOTO OF THIS OLD GUY WHO THEY SAY IS 'MISSING.' THEN THEY ADD, "HAVE YOU SEEN THIS PERSON?"
I HATE BEING TAUNTED BY DAIRY COWS.
MILK
7/30

Panel 1: WHAT'S THE MATTER, L'IL GUARD DUCK? — IT'S MAURA, SIR. SHE'S NEVER COMING BACK... I KNOW IT.

Crate O' Sadness

Panel 2: OH, L'IL GUARD DUCK. — I DON'T GET IT, SIR.. THEY SAY IF YOU LOVE SOMEONE, SET THEM FREE... WELL, I DID THAT, SIR, AND SHE NEVER CAME BACK... OHHH, SIR.. WHAT'S IT ALL MEAN? WHAT'S IT ALL MEAN?

Crate O' Sadness

Panel 3: IF YOU LOVE SOMEONE, CHAIN THEM TO A HEAVY KITCHEN APPLIANCE.? — WELL NOW THERE'S A SUGGESTION! — I WANT A GIRLFRIEND, SIR... NOT A HOSTAGE.

Crate O' Sadness

Panel 1: Dear Cell phone company, Last month I exceeded my monthly minutes while talking to my relatives and got charged extra.

Panel 2: While I admit making these calls to my relatives, I must ask for a refund for the following reason.

Panel 3: I did not enjoy their conversation.

Panel 4: HOPEFULLY, THEY KNOW MY RELATIVES.

Panel 1: Dear Me, Hi. You're nice. Will you be my pen-pal? If yes, please so indikate with a happy ☻ smiley face. ☺ (like this)

Panel 2: DUDE, IF I EVER FOUND OUT A FRIEND OF MINE WAS SUCH A LOSER THAT HE AGREED TO BECOME HIS OWN PEN PAL, I WOULD KICK HIS SAD LOSER BUTT FROM HERE TO THE POST OFFICE.

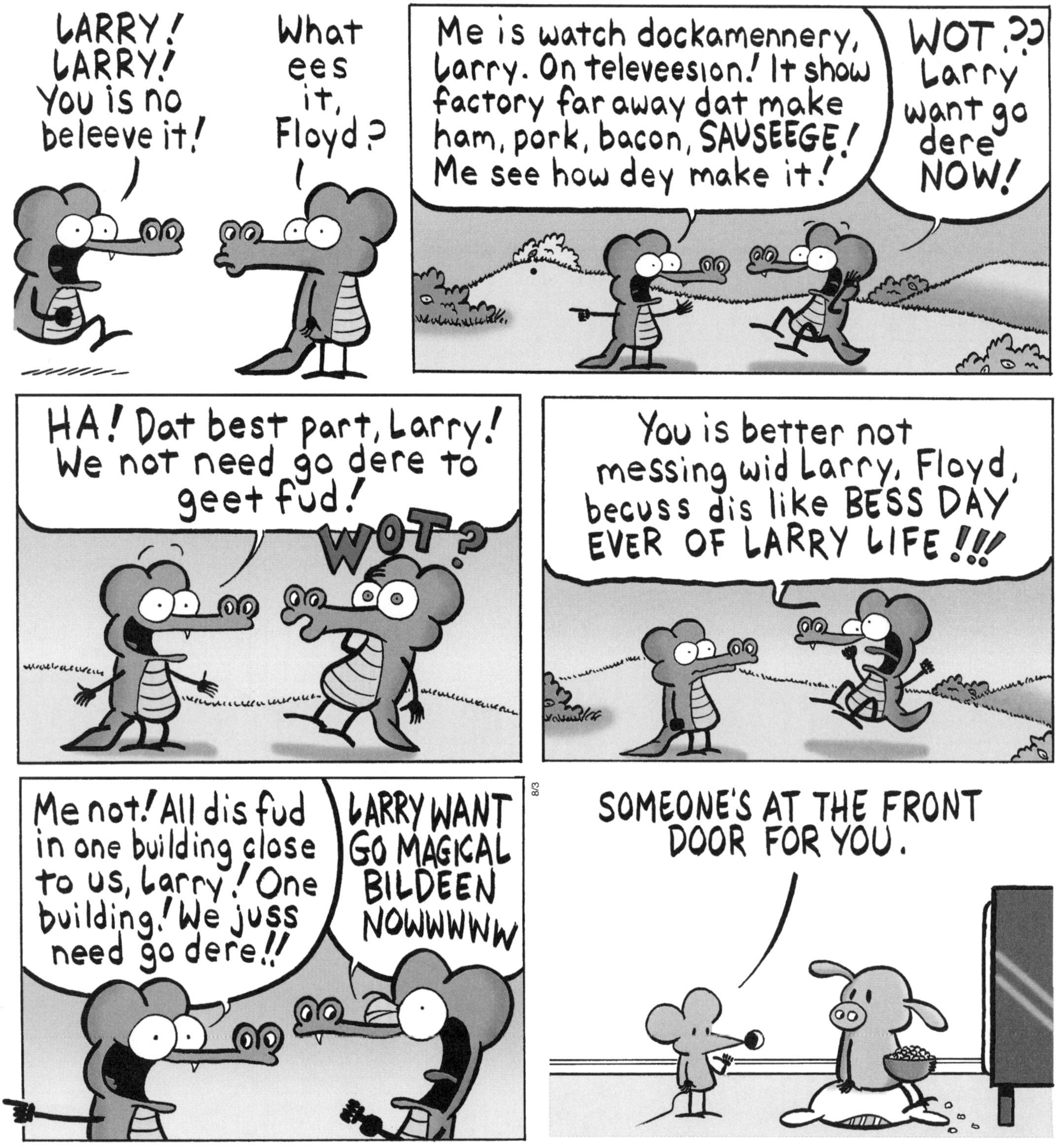
LARRY! LARRY! You is no beleeve it!
What ees it, Floyd?
Me is watch dockamennery, Larry. On televeesion! It show factory far away dat make ham, pork, bacon, SAUSEEGE! Me see how dey make it!
WOT?? Larry want go dere NOW!
HA! Dat best part, Larry! We not need go dere to geet fud!
WOT?
You is better not messing wid Larry, Floyd, becuss dis like BESS DAY EVER OF LARRY LIFE!!!
Me not! All dis fud in one building close to us, Larry! One building! We juss need go dere!!
LARRY WANT GO MAGICAL BILDEEN NOWWWWW
SOMEONE'S AT THE FRONT DOOR FOR YOU.

Panel 1:
DID I GET ANY MAIL? DID I GET ANY MAIL?

YOU DID, ACTUALLY. YOU BETTER NOT BE ACTING AS YOUR OWN PEN PAL AGAIN.

Panel 2:
I'M NOT. I GOT A REAL PEN PAL! SOMEONE WHO WRITES ALL THE TIME! SOMEONE WHO KEEPS INVITING ME TO HIS HOUSE! FINALLY, SOMEONE WHO NEEDS A FRIEND AS MUCH AS I DO! HE'S EVEN GIVEN ME A NICKNAME, STRANGE AS IT IS.

WHAT'S THE NICKNAME?

Panel 3:
Dear Bacon Butt

Panel 4:
Hullooooo leetle piggy... How you like play game? We call 'No Go Croc Mouf.'

OH, BOY! HOW'S IT WORK?

Panel 5:
You ees run toward croc mouf! Eef you avoid mouf, you WEEN!

I WIN? OH, BOY!! BUT WHAT IF I CAN'T AVOID IT?

Panel 6:
Uh. You lose.

NUTS.

Weening not everyting.

Panel 7:
I'M AFRAID OF THE FUTURE.

WHY?

Panel 8:
BECAUSE IT'S SO NEBULOUS.

WHAT DOES NEBULOUS MEAN?

Panel 9:
IT'S REALLY UNCLEAR.

THEN WHY USE THE WORD?

Panel 10:
I'M AFRAID YOU'RE AN IDIOT.

THAT'S PRETTY CLEAR.

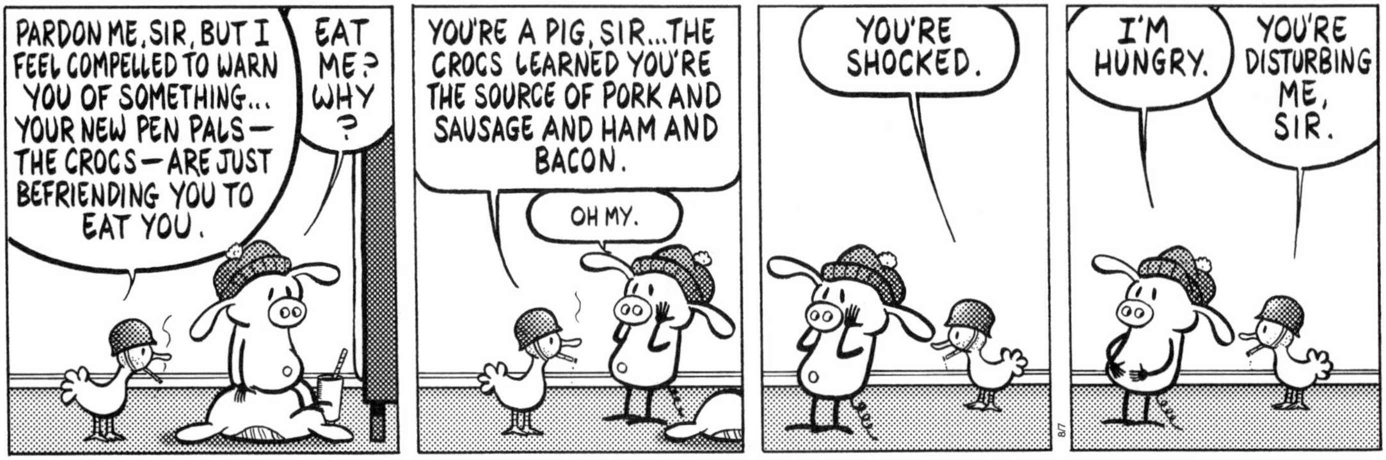
PARDON ME, SIR, BUT I FEEL COMPELLED TO WARN YOU OF SOMETHING... YOUR NEW PEN PALS—THE CROCS—ARE JUST BEFRIENDING YOU TO EAT YOU.
EAT ME? WHY?
YOU'RE A PIG, SIR...THE CROCS LEARNED YOU'RE THE SOURCE OF PORK AND SAUSAGE AND HAM AND BACON.
OH MY.
YOU'RE SHOCKED.
I'M HUNGRY.
YOU'RE DISTURBING ME, SIR.
8/7

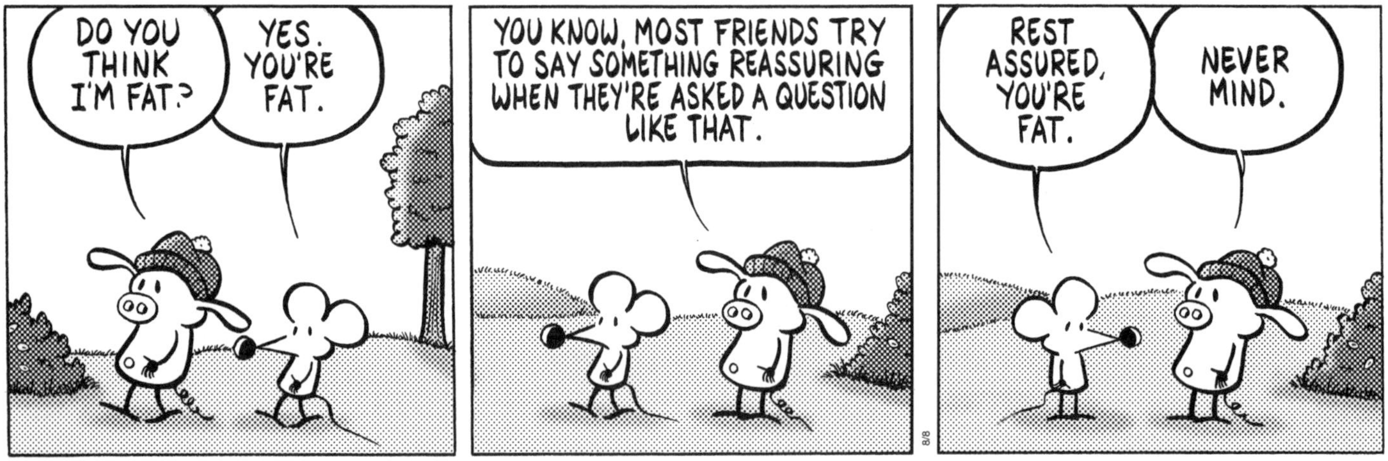
DO YOU THINK I'M FAT?
YES. YOU'RE FAT.
YOU KNOW, MOST FRIENDS TRY TO SAY SOMETHING REASSURING WHEN THEY'RE ASKED A QUESTION LIKE THAT.
REST ASSURED, YOU'RE FAT.
NEVER MIND.
8/8

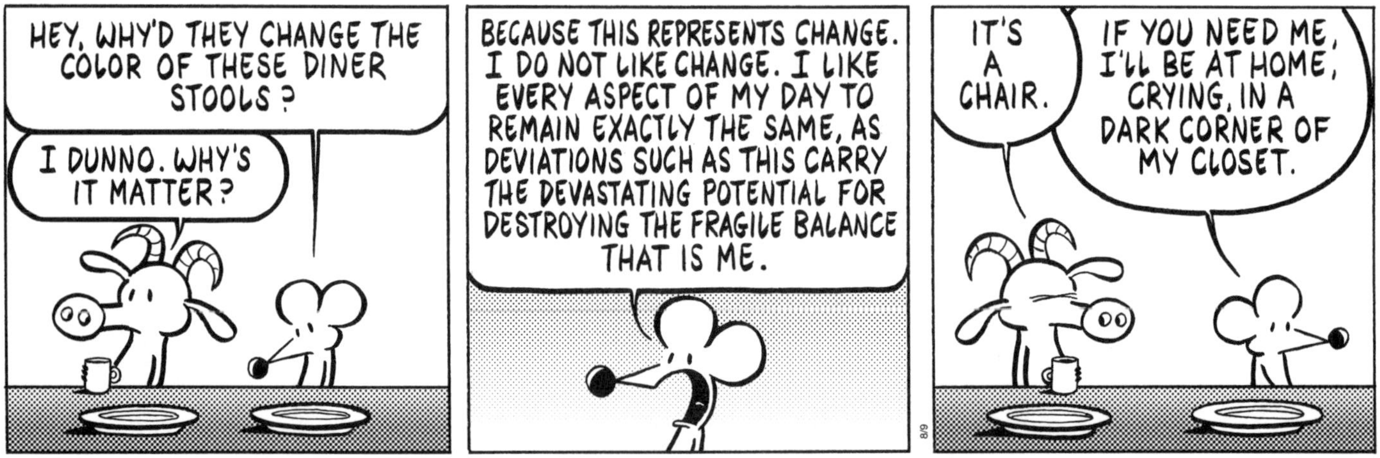
HEY, WHY'D THEY CHANGE THE COLOR OF THESE DINER STOOLS?
I DUNNO. WHY'S IT MATTER?
BECAUSE THIS REPRESENTS CHANGE. I DO NOT LIKE CHANGE. I LIKE EVERY ASPECT OF MY DAY TO REMAIN EXACTLY THE SAME, AS DEVIATIONS SUCH AS THIS CARRY THE DEVASTATING POTENTIAL FOR DESTROYING THE FRAGILE BALANCE THAT IS ME.
IT'S A CHAIR.
IF YOU NEED ME, I'LL BE AT HOME, CRYING, IN A DARK CORNER OF MY CLOSET.
8/9

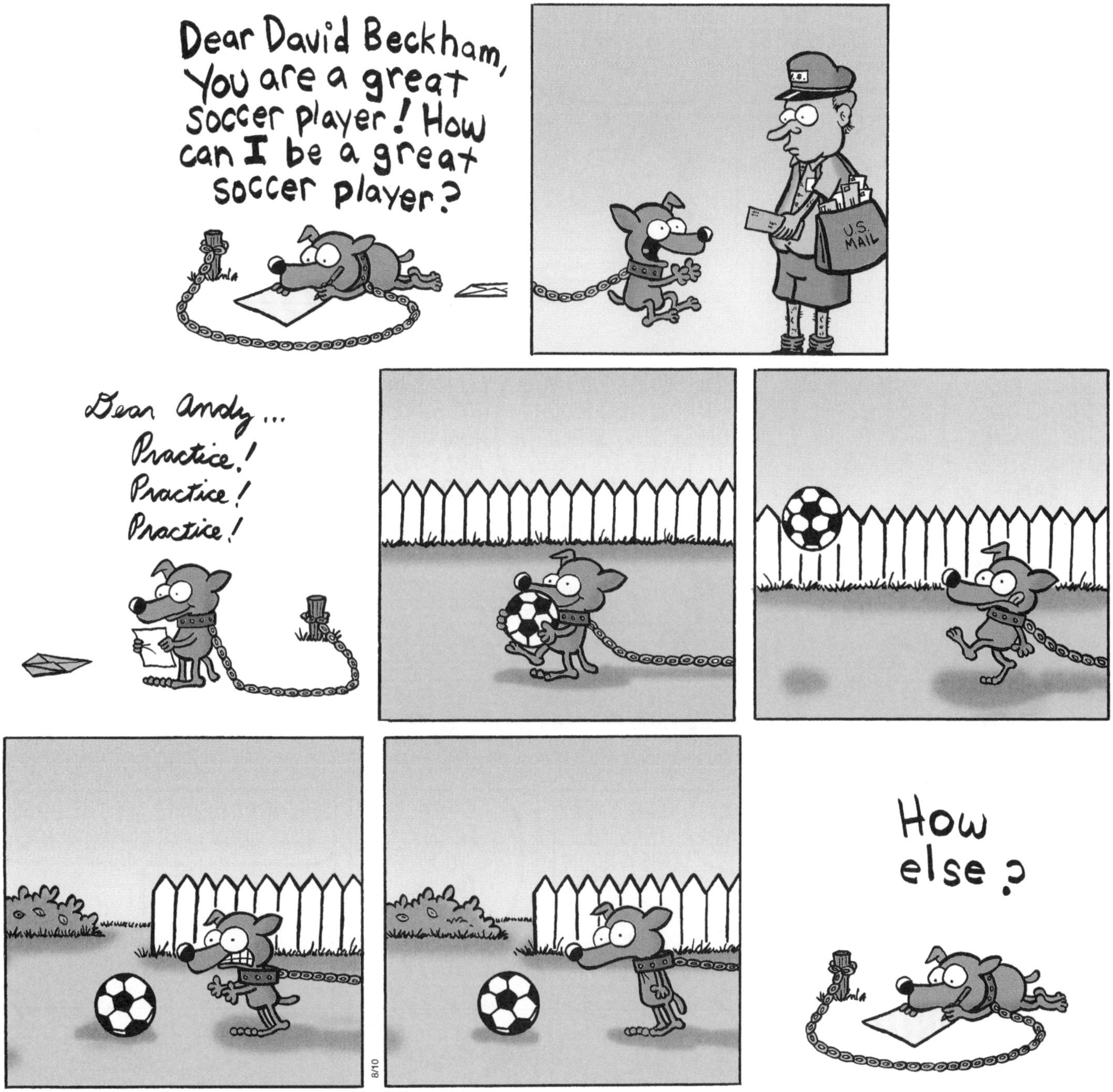
Dear David Beckham,
You are a great soccer player! How can I be a great soccer player?
U.S. MAIL
Dear Andy...
Practice!
Practice!
Practice!
8/10
How else?

Panel 1: PIG IS TAKING GYMNASTICS. HE WANTS TO ONE DAY BE ON THE U.S. OLYMPIC TEAM. CAN YOU IMAGINE ANYTHING MORE EFFEMINATE THAN THAT?

Panel 2: ARE YOU NUTS? THERE'S NOTHING EFFEMINATE ABOUT WANTING TO BE ON A GYMNASTICS TEAM.

THERE IS WHEN IT'S THE WOMEN'S GYMNASTICS TEAM.

Panel 3: CALL ME NADIA.

Panel 4: HOW'S PIG DOING ON THE WOMEN'S GYMNASTICS TEAM?

HE'S DOING THE RINGS.

Panel 5: THE RINGS? DO YOU KNOW HOW MUCH UPPER BODY STRENGTH IT TAKES TO HANG FROM THOSE THINGS?

YEAH. I'M NOT SURE HOW HE'S ABLE TO DO IT.

Panel 6:

Panel 7: MY GOAL IN LIFE IS TO LEAVE EVERY PLACE I VISIT A LITTLE BETTER THAN WHEN I ARRIVED.

I THINK YOU DO THAT.

Panel 8: YOU DO??

YEAH. EVERY TIME YOU LEAVE A ROOM, I SAY TO MYSELF, 'HEY, THE ROOM'S A LITTLE BETTER.'

Panel 9: OHH. THANK YOU!! THANK YOU!!

Panel 10: THE BEST INSULTS ARE THE ONES THAT LOOK LIKE COMPLIMENTS.

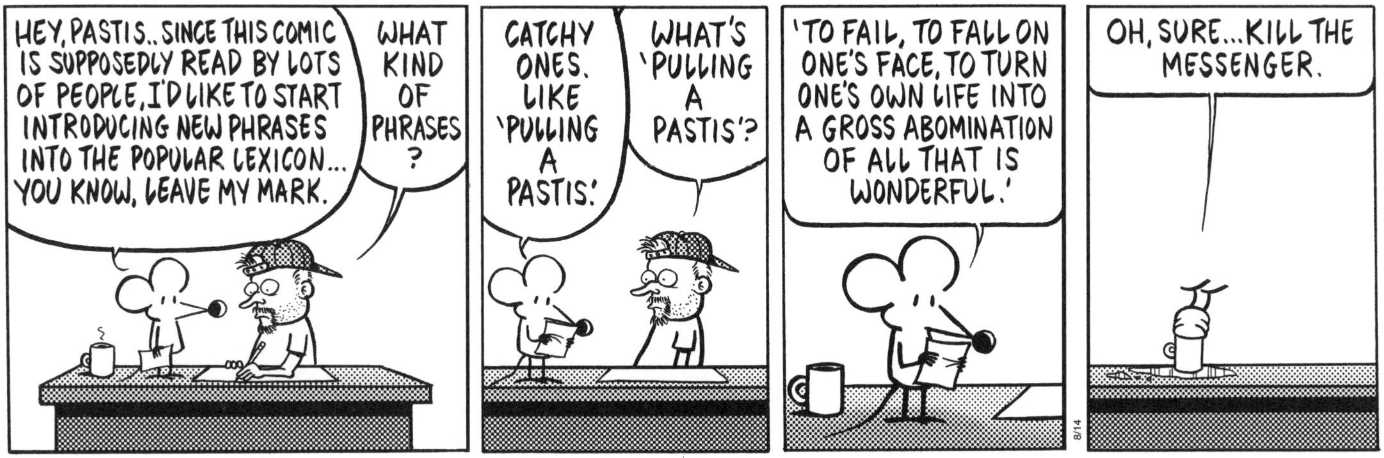
HEY, PASTIS.. SINCE THIS COMIC IS SUPPOSEDLY READ BY LOTS OF PEOPLE, I'D LIKE TO START INTRODUCING NEW PHRASES INTO THE POPULAR LEXICON... YOU KNOW, LEAVE MY MARK.
WHAT KIND OF PHRASES?
CATCHY ONES. LIKE 'PULLING A PASTIS.'
WHAT'S 'PULLING A PASTIS'?
'TO FAIL, TO FALL ON ONE'S FACE, TO TURN ONE'S OWN LIFE INTO A GROSS ABOMINATION OF ALL THAT IS WONDERFUL.'
OH, SURE... KILL THE MESSENGER.
8/14

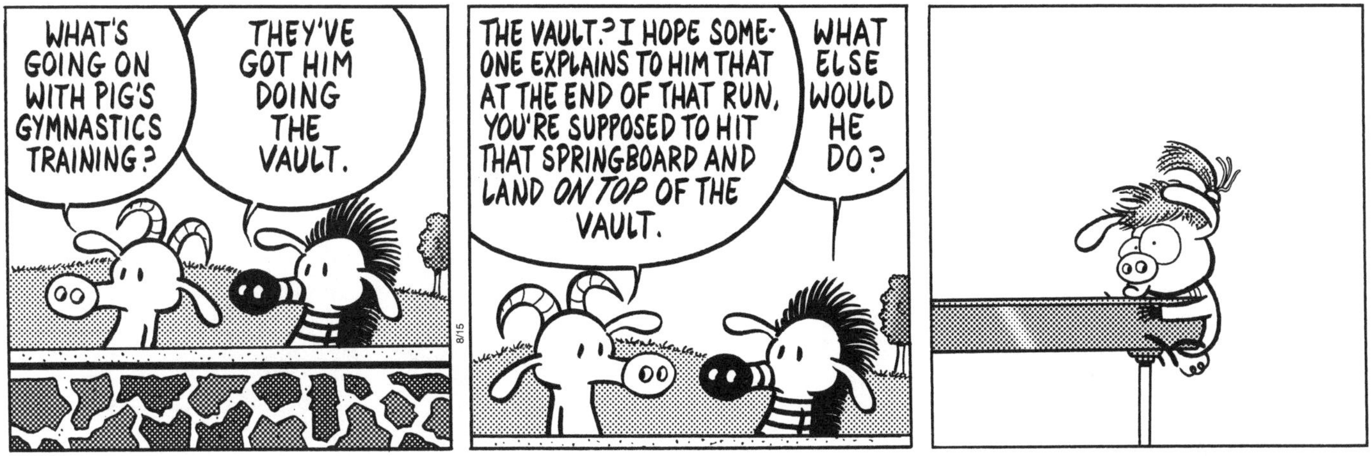
WHAT'S GOING ON WITH PIG'S GYMNASTICS TRAINING?
THEY'VE GOT HIM DOING THE VAULT.
8/15
THE VAULT? I HOPE SOMEONE EXPLAINS TO HIM THAT AT THE END OF THAT RUN, YOU'RE SUPPOSED TO HIT THAT SPRINGBOARD AND LAND *ON TOP* OF THE VAULT.
WHAT ELSE WOULD HE DO?

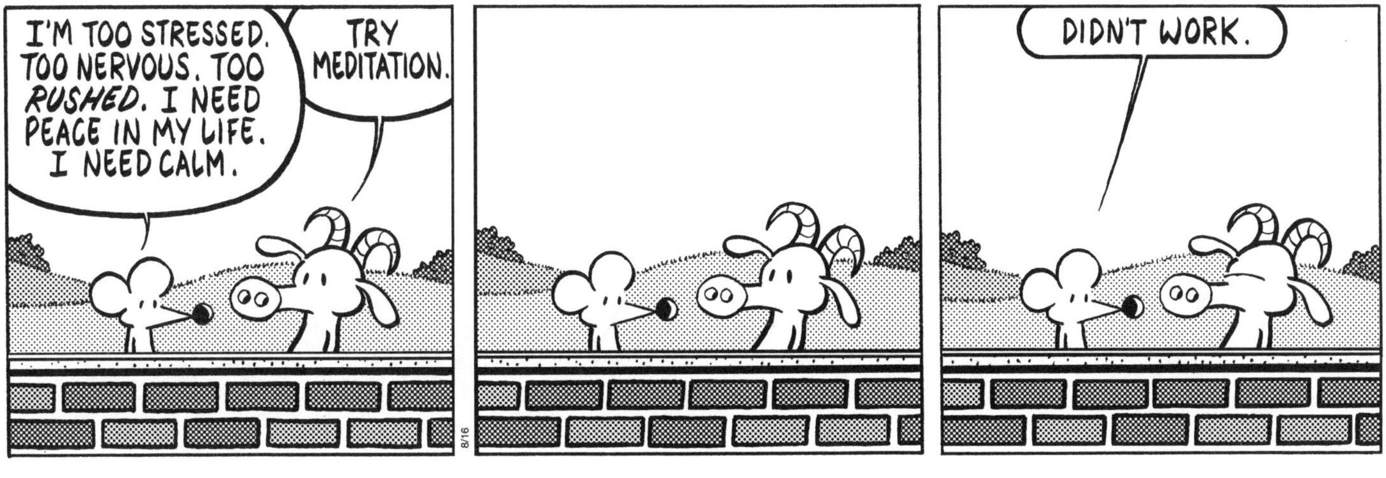
I'M TOO STRESSED. TOO NERVOUS. TOO *RUSHED*. I NEED PEACE IN MY LIFE. I NEED CALM.
TRY MEDITATION.
8/16
DIDN'T WORK.

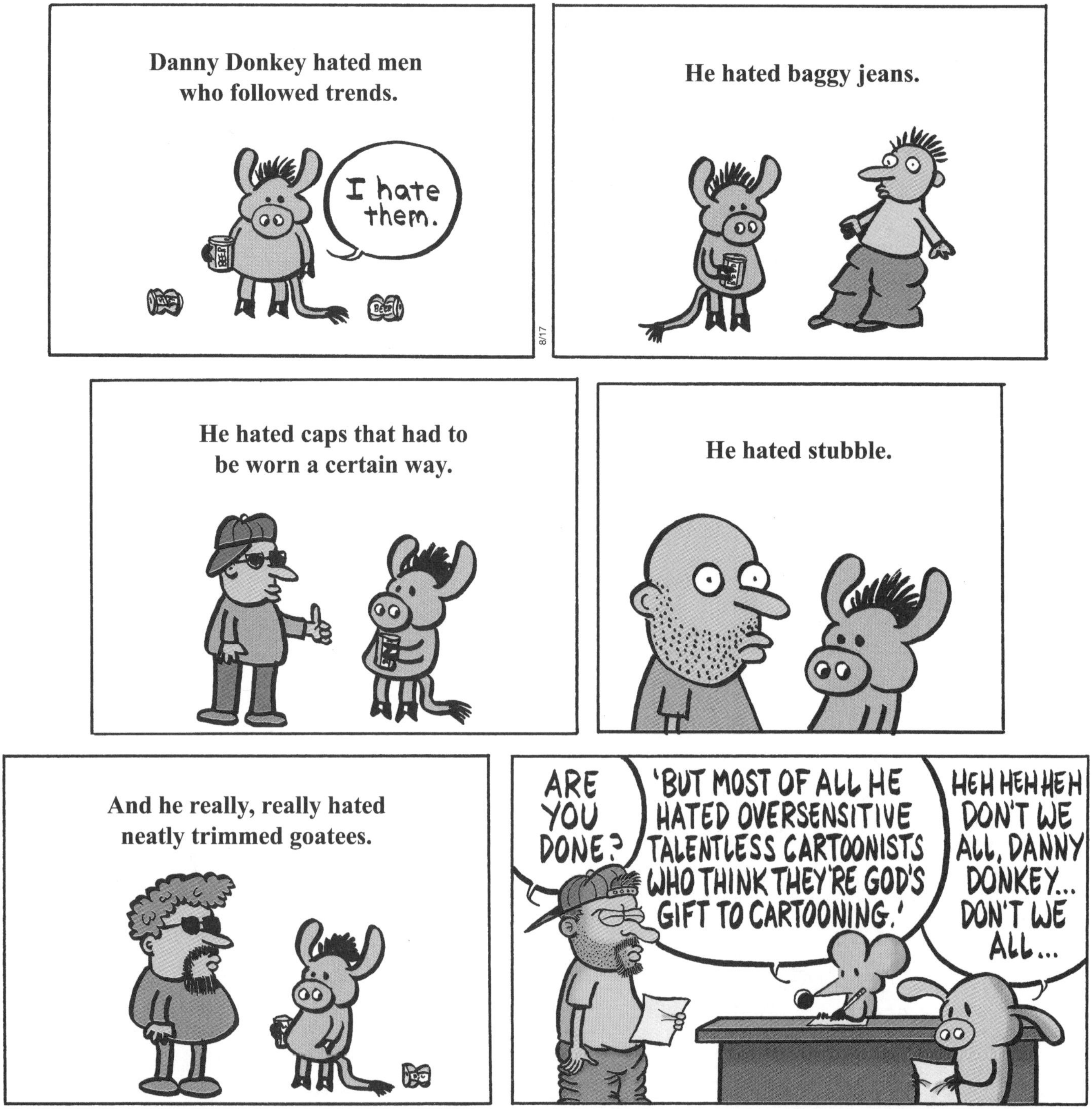
Danny Donkey hated men who followed trends.
I hate them.
He hated baggy jeans.
8/17
He hated caps that had to be worn a certain way.
He hated stubble.
And he really, really hated neatly trimmed goatees.
ARE YOU DONE?
'BUT MOST OF ALL HE HATED OVERSENSITIVE TALENTLESS CARTOONISTS WHO THINK THEY'RE GOD'S GIFT TO CARTOONING.'
HEH HEH HEH DON'T WE ALL, DANNY DONKEY... DON'T WE ALL...

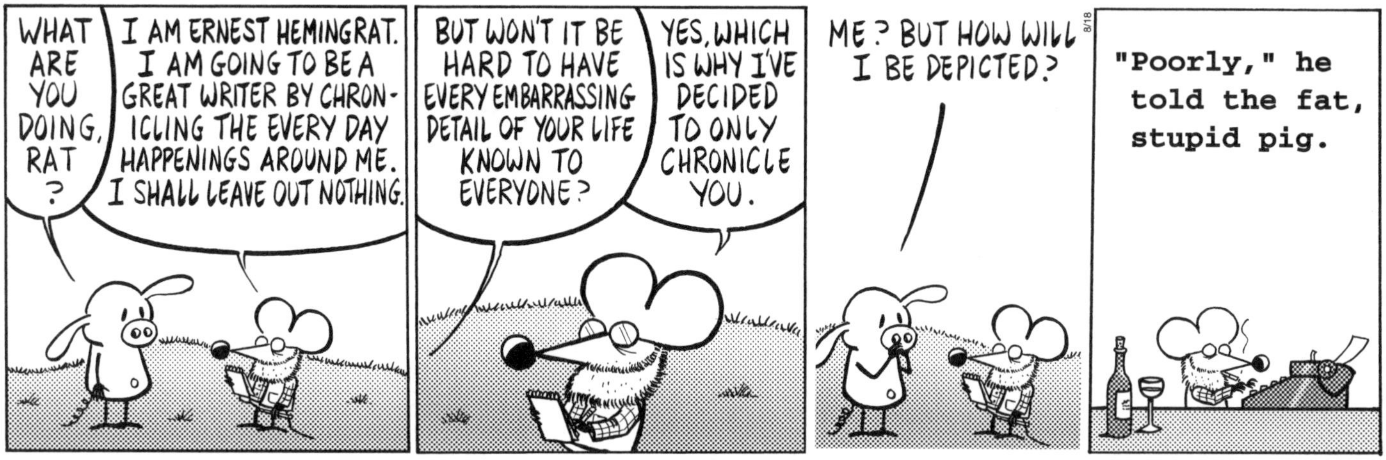
WHAT ARE YOU DOING, RAT?
I AM ERNEST HEMINGRAT. I AM GOING TO BE A GREAT WRITER BY CHRONICLING THE EVERY DAY HAPPENINGS AROUND ME. I SHALL LEAVE OUT NOTHING.
BUT WON'T IT BE HARD TO HAVE EVERY EMBARRASSING DETAIL OF YOUR LIFE KNOWN TO EVERYONE?
YES, WHICH IS WHY I'VE DECIDED TO ONLY CHRONICLE YOU.
ME? BUT HOW WILL I BE DEPICTED?
8/18
"Poorly," he told the fat, stupid pig.

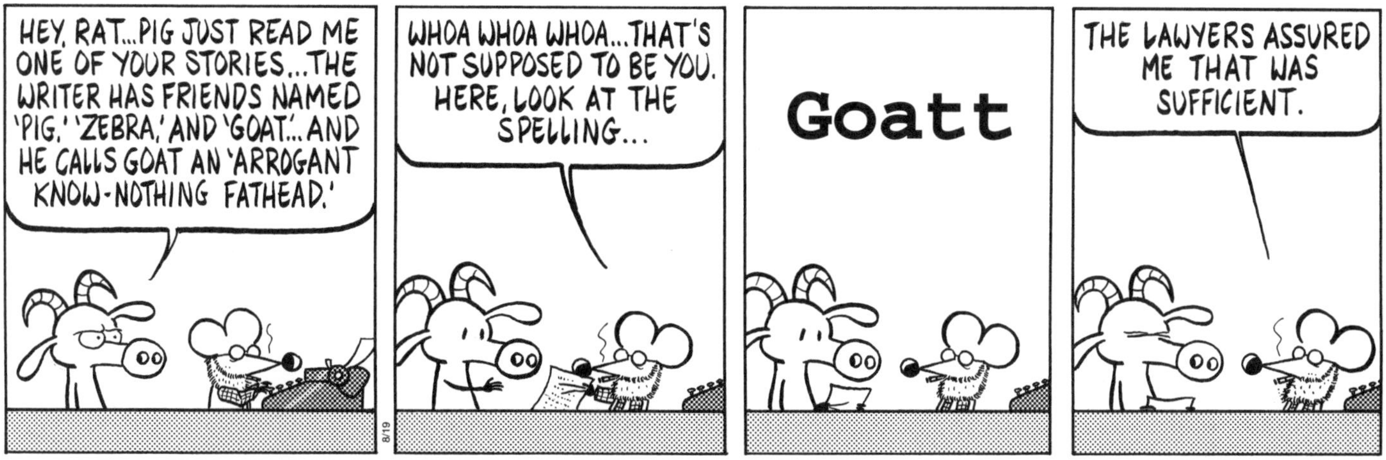
HEY, RAT...PIG JUST READ ME ONE OF YOUR STORIES...THE WRITER HAS FRIENDS NAMED 'PIG,' 'ZEBRA,' AND 'GOAT.'...AND HE CALLS GOAT AN 'ARROGANT KNOW-NOTHING FATHEAD.'
8/19
WHOA WHOA WHOA...THAT'S NOT SUPPOSED TO BE YOU. HERE, LOOK AT THE SPELLING...
Goatt
THE LAWYERS ASSURED ME THAT WAS SUFFICIENT.

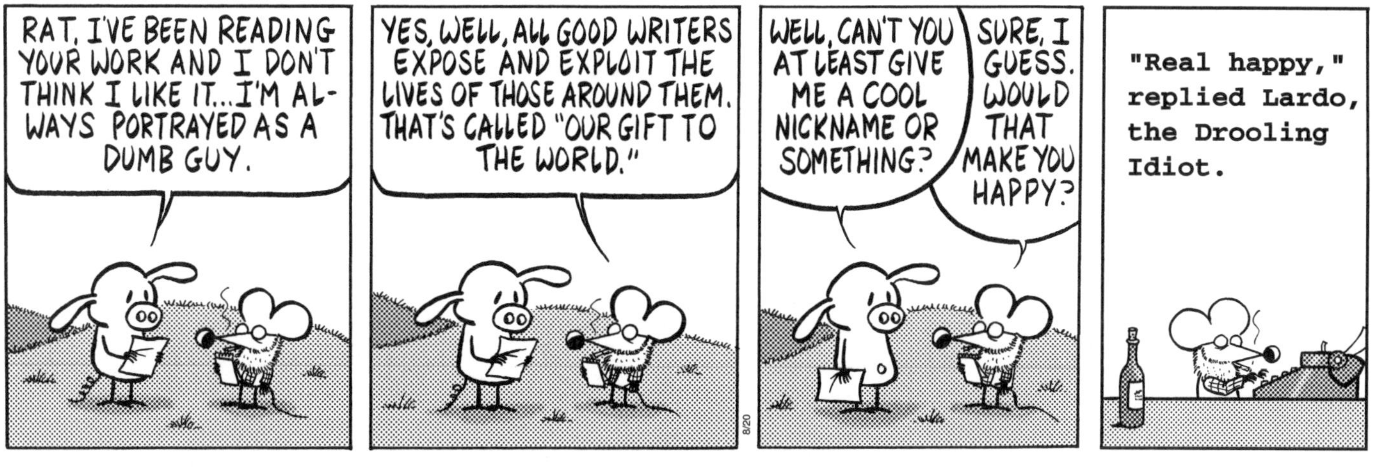
RAT, I'VE BEEN READING YOUR WORK AND I DON'T THINK I LIKE IT...I'M ALWAYS PORTRAYED AS A DUMB GUY.
YES, WELL, ALL GOOD WRITERS EXPOSE AND EXPLOIT THE LIVES OF THOSE AROUND THEM. THAT'S CALLED "OUR GIFT TO THE WORLD."
WELL, CAN'T YOU AT LEAST GIVE ME A COOL NICKNAME OR SOMETHING?
SURE, I GUESS. WOULD THAT MAKE YOU HAPPY?
8/20
"Real happy," replied Lardo, the Drooling Idiot.

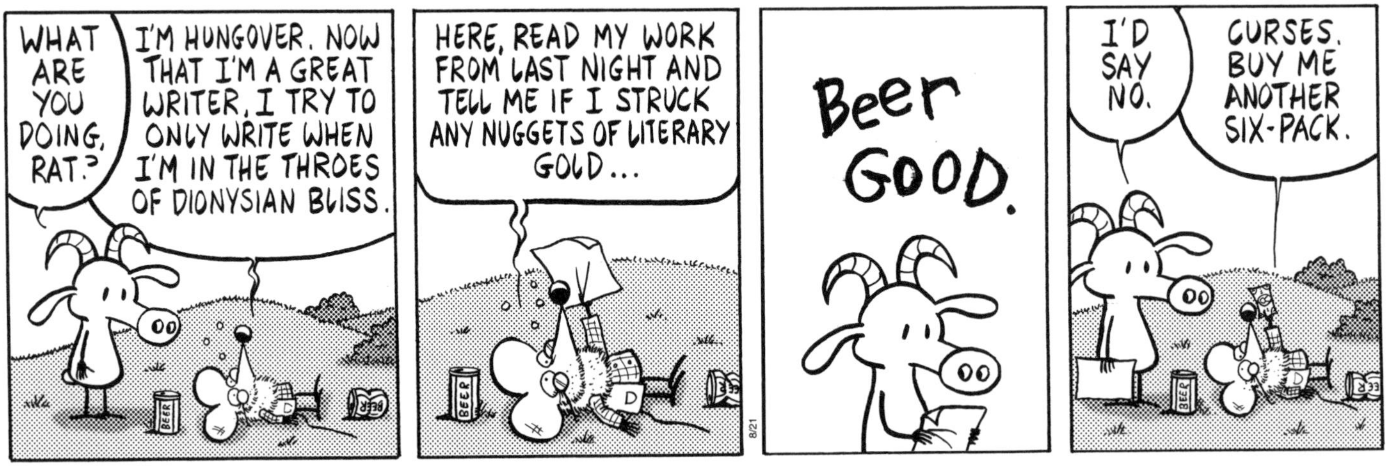
WHAT ARE YOU DOING, RAT?
I'M HUNGOVER. NOW THAT I'M A GREAT WRITER, I TRY TO ONLY WRITE WHEN I'M IN THE THROES OF DIONYSIAN BLISS.
BEER
HERE, READ MY WORK FROM LAST NIGHT AND TELL ME IF I STRUCK ANY NUGGETS OF LITERARY GOLD...
BEER
8/21
Beer GOOD.
I'D SAY NO.
CURSES. BUY ME ANOTHER SIX-PACK.
BEER

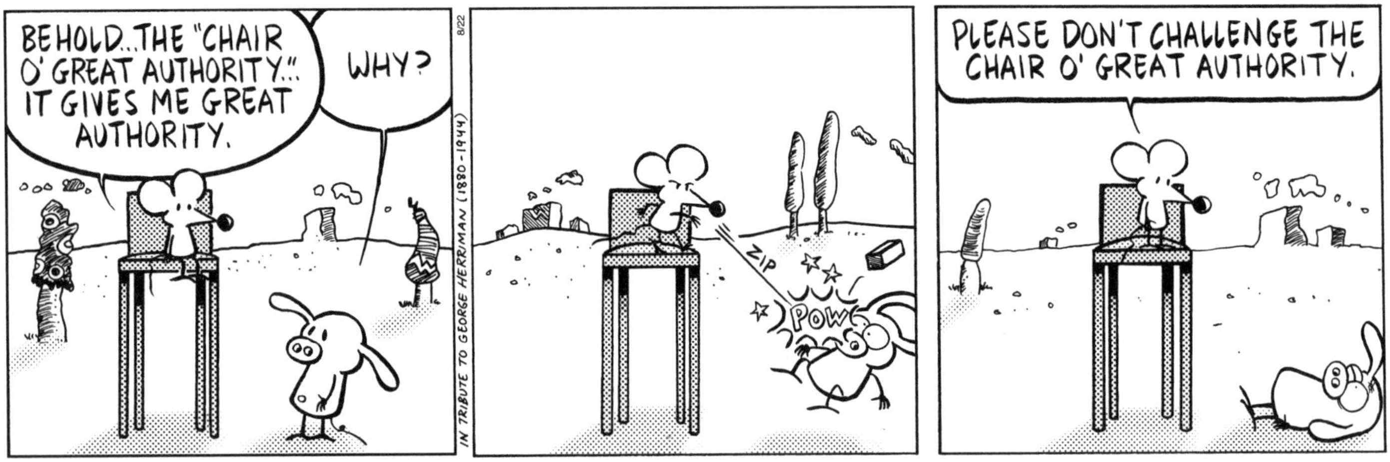
BEHOLD...THE "CHAIR O' GREAT AUTHORITY." IT GIVES ME GREAT AUTHORITY.
WHY?
8/22
IN TRIBUTE TO GEORGE HERRIMAN (1880-1944)
ZIP
POW
PLEASE DON'T CHALLENGE THE CHAIR O' GREAT AUTHORITY.

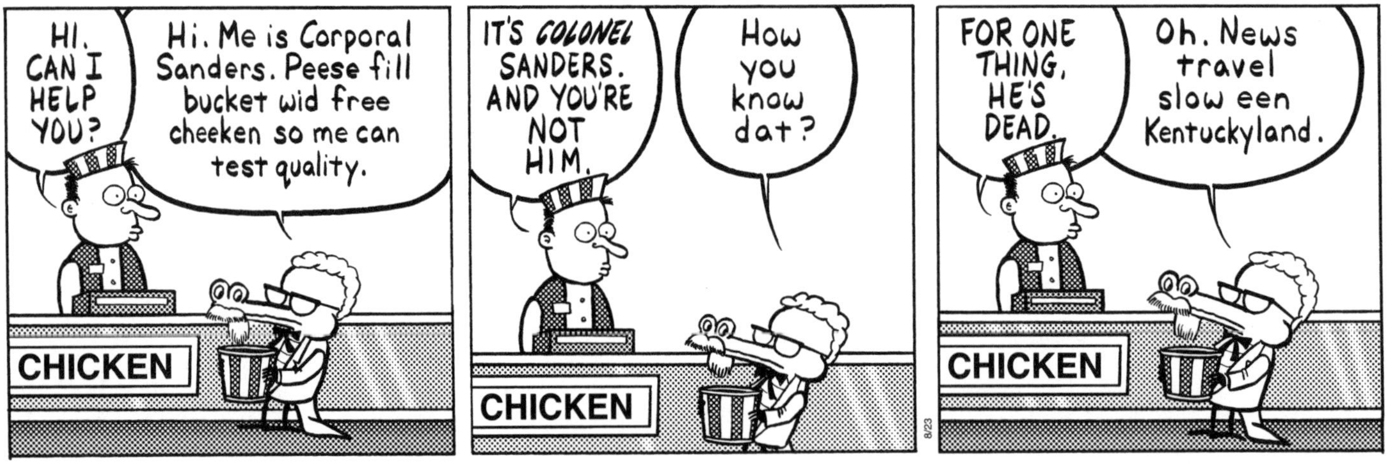
HI. CAN I HELP YOU?
Hi. Me is Corporal Sanders. Peese fill bucket wid free cheeken so me can test quality.
CHICKEN
IT'S COLONEL SANDERS. AND YOU'RE NOT HIM.
How you know dat?
CHICKEN
8/23
FOR ONE THING, HE'S DEAD.
Oh. News travel slow een Kentuckyland.
CHICKEN

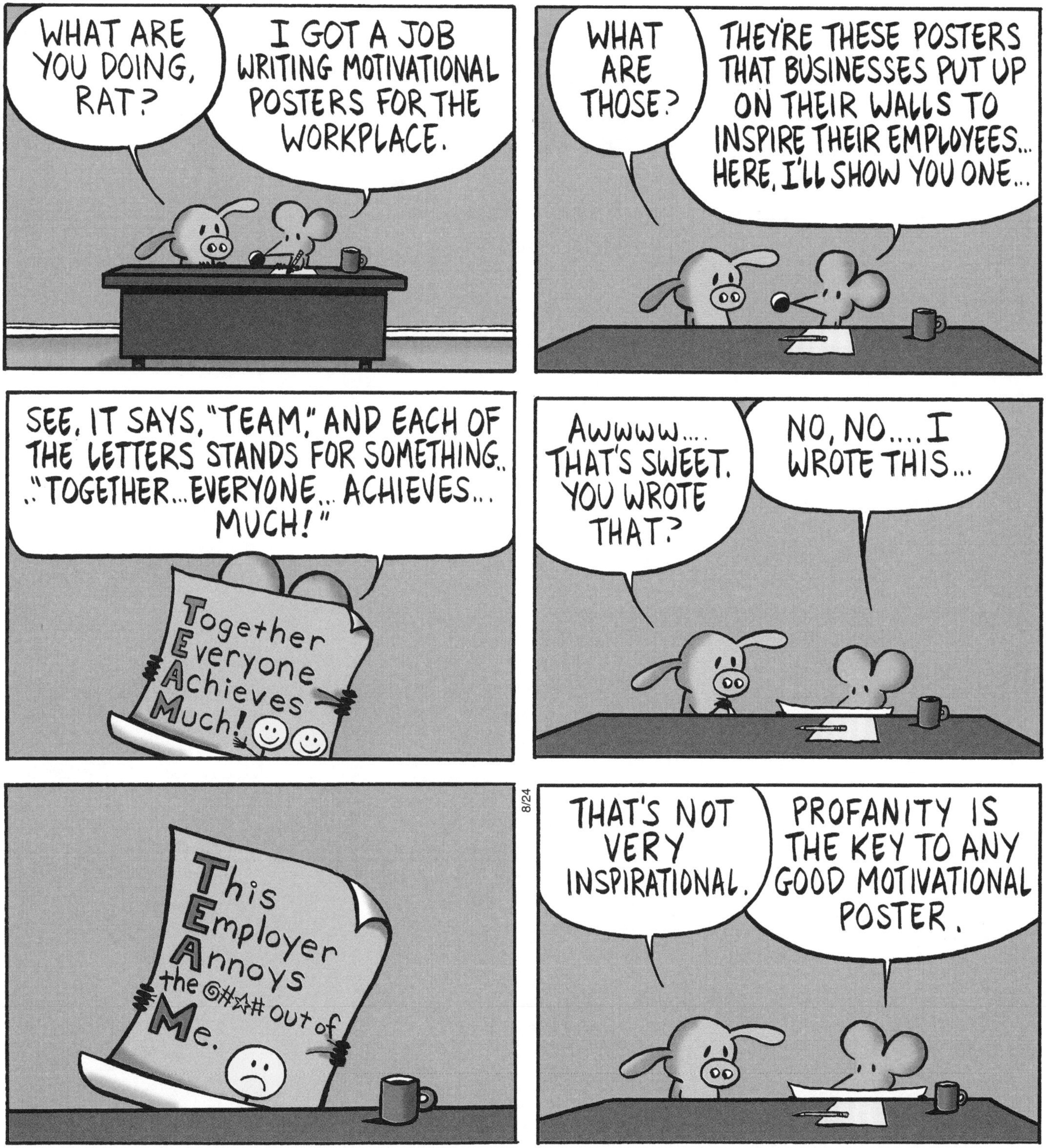
WHAT ARE YOU DOING, RAT?
I GOT A JOB WRITING MOTIVATIONAL POSTERS FOR THE WORKPLACE.
WHAT ARE THOSE?
THEY'RE THESE POSTERS THAT BUSINESSES PUT UP ON THEIR WALLS TO INSPIRE THEIR EMPLOYEES... HERE, I'LL SHOW YOU ONE...
SEE, IT SAYS, "TEAM," AND EACH OF THE LETTERS STANDS FOR SOMETHING.. .."TOGETHER...EVERYONE... ACHIEVES... MUCH!"
Together
Everyone
Achieves
Much!
AWWWW.... THAT'S SWEET. YOU WROTE THAT?
NO, NO.... I WROTE THIS...
This
Employer
Annoys
the @#☆# out of
Me.
8/24
THAT'S NOT VERY INSPIRATIONAL.
PROFANITY IS THE KEY TO ANY GOOD MOTIVATIONAL POSTER.

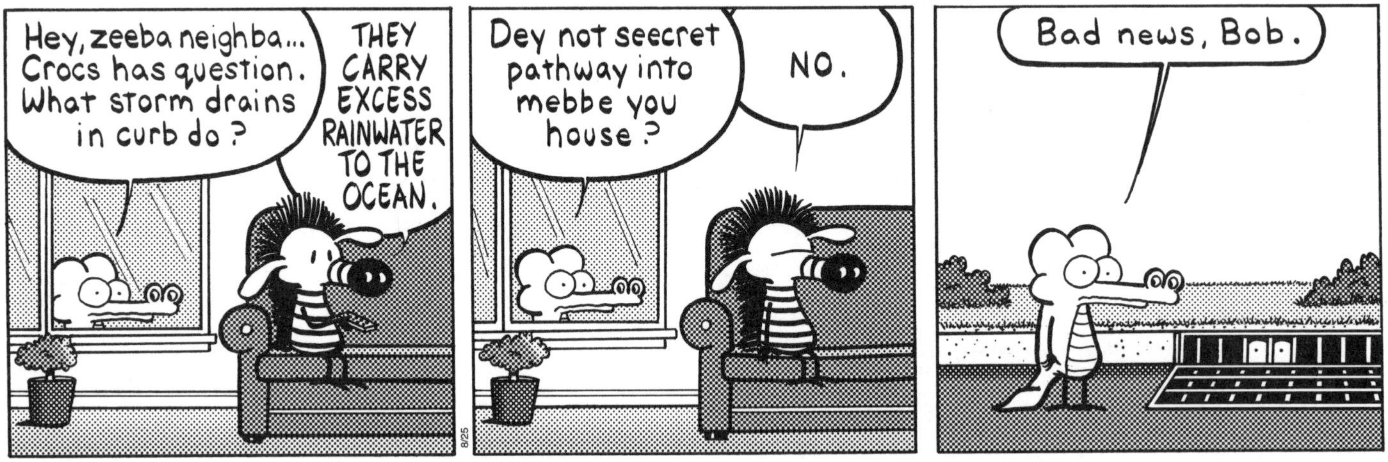
Hey, zeeba neighba... Crocs has question. What storm drains in curb do?
THEY CARRY EXCESS RAINWATER TO THE OCEAN.
Dey not seecret pathway into mebbe you house?
NO.
Bad news, Bob.

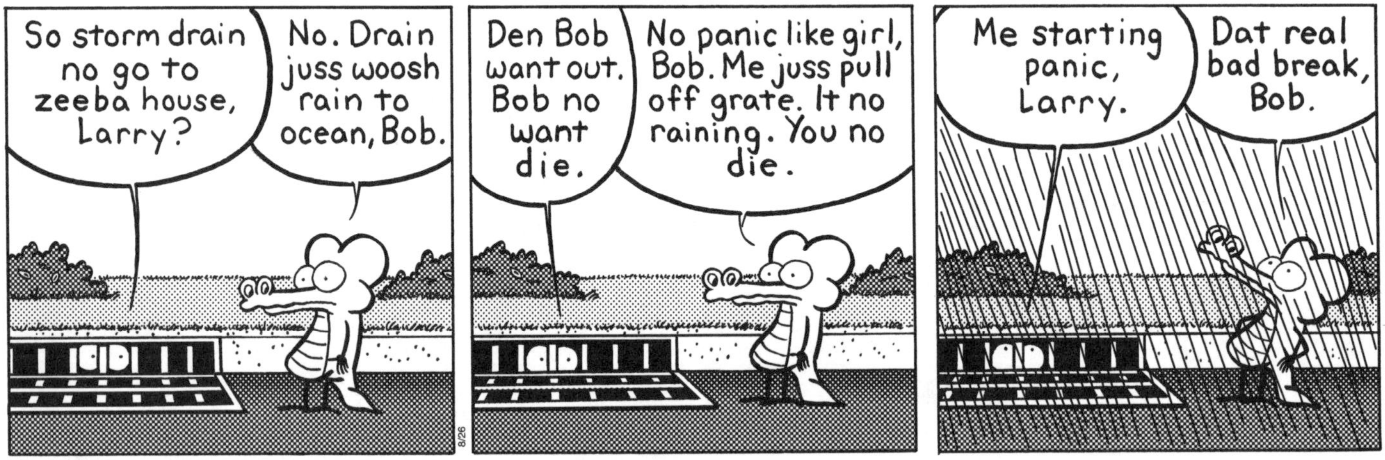
So storm drain no go to zeeba house, Larry?
No. Drain juss woosh rain to ocean, Bob.
Den Bob want out. Bob no want die.
No panic like girl, Bob. Me juss pull off grate. It no raining. You no die.
Me starting panic, Larry.
Dat real bad break, Bob.

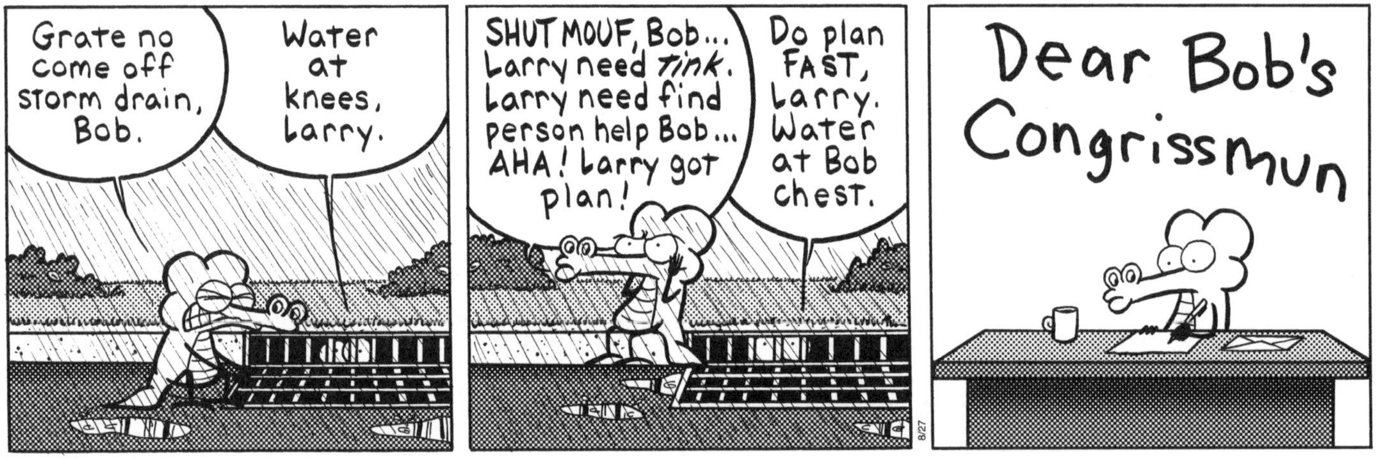
Grate no come off storm drain, Bob.
Water at knees, Larry.
SHUT MOUF, Bob... Larry need tink. Larry need find person help Bob... AHA! Larry got plan!
Do plan FAST, Larry. Water at Bob chest.
Dear Bob's Congrissmun

Panel 1: Bad news, brudder crocs...Brudder Bob drown een storm drain.

Why he een storm drain?

Panel 2: Crocs tink it lead to zeeba house. But no true. Ees **sewer system** dat lead eenside zeeba house.

How we get een dere?

Panel 3: Ees one small step for Larry... One giant leap for croc-kind.

Panel 4: THANKS FOR INVITING ME TO WATCH 'EXTRAS' WITH YOU, ZEBRA... HEY, DO YOU MIND IF I USE YOUR BATHROOM?

SURE, PIG.

Panel 6: I CAN HOLD IT.

Panel 7: I'M SORRY, MISTER CROC, BUT I REALLY NEED TO HAVE SOME ALONE BATHROOM TIME.

Too bad for you. Crocs on meeshun. No can be stopped.

Panel 8: FLUSHHHHH

Panel 9: NO ONE MESSES WITH MY ALONE BATHROOM TIME.

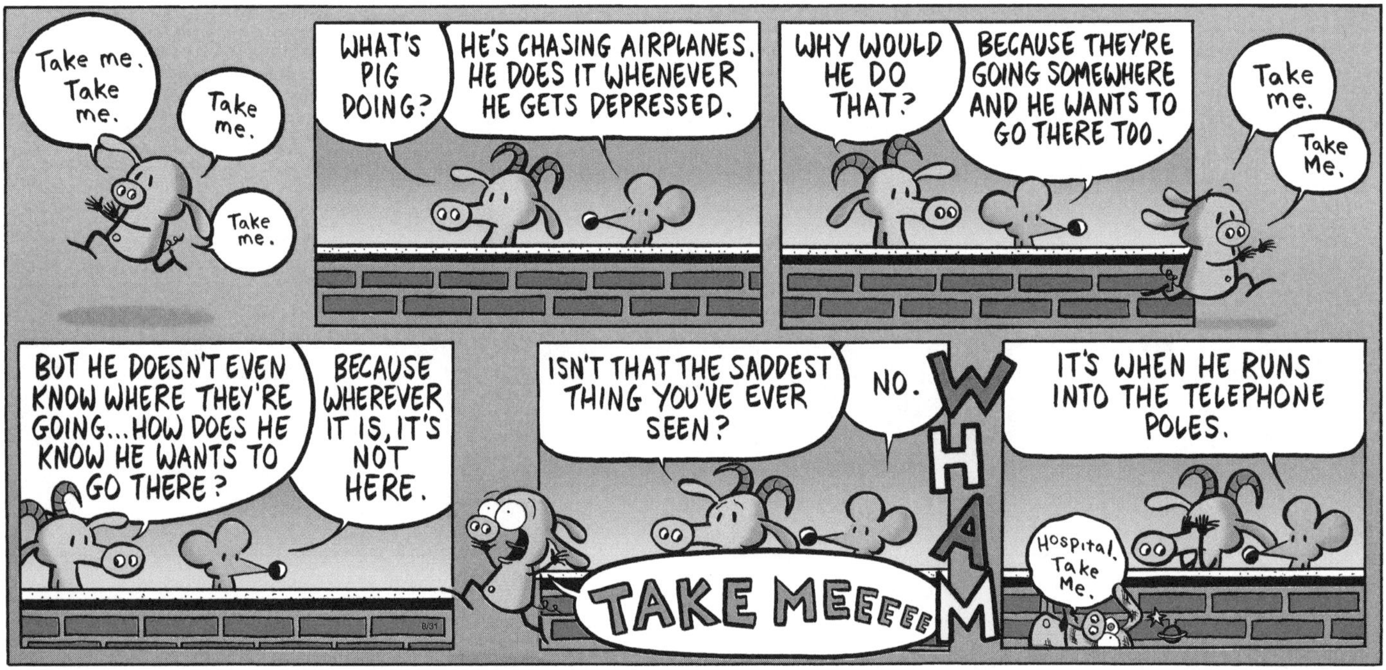
Take me. Take me.
Take me.
Take me.
WHAT'S PIG DOING?
HE'S CHASING AIRPLANES. HE DOES IT WHENEVER HE GETS DEPRESSED.
WHY WOULD HE DO THAT?
BECAUSE THEY'RE GOING SOMEWHERE AND HE WANTS TO GO THERE TOO.
Take me.
Take Me.
BUT HE DOESN'T EVEN KNOW WHERE THEY'RE GOING... HOW DOES HE KNOW HE WANTS TO GO THERE?
BECAUSE WHEREVER IT IS, IT'S NOT HERE.
ISN'T THAT THE SADDEST THING YOU'VE EVER SEEN?
NO.
TAKE MEEEEEE
WHAM
IT'S WHEN HE RUNS INTO THE TELEPHONE POLES.
Hospital. Take Me.

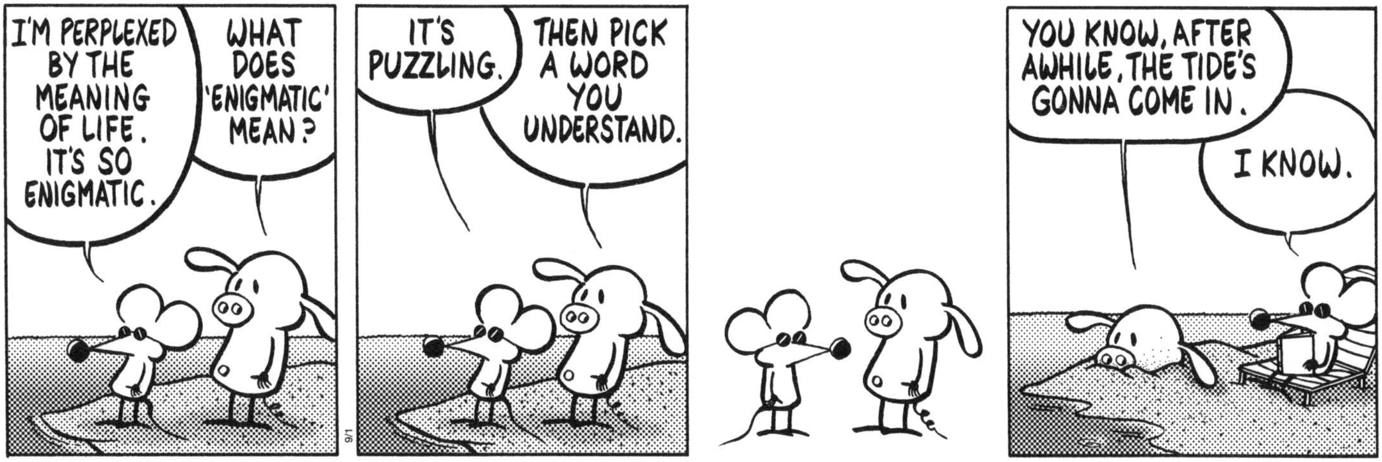
I'M PERPLEXED BY THE MEANING OF LIFE. IT'S SO ENIGMATIC.
WHAT DOES 'ENIGMATIC' MEAN?
IT'S PUZZLING.
THEN PICK A WORD YOU UNDERSTAND.
YOU KNOW, AFTER AWHILE, THE TIDE'S GONNA COME IN.
I KNOW.

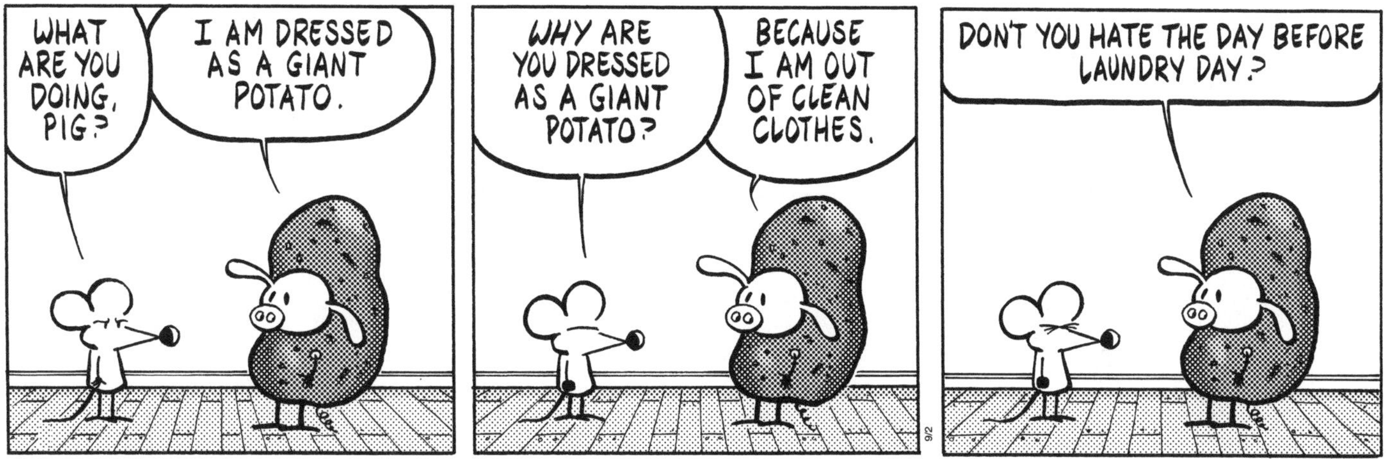
WHAT ARE YOU DOING, PIG?
I AM DRESSED AS A GIANT POTATO.
WHY ARE YOU DRESSED AS A GIANT POTATO?
BECAUSE I AM OUT OF CLEAN CLOTHES.
DON'T YOU HATE THE DAY BEFORE LAUNDRY DAY?

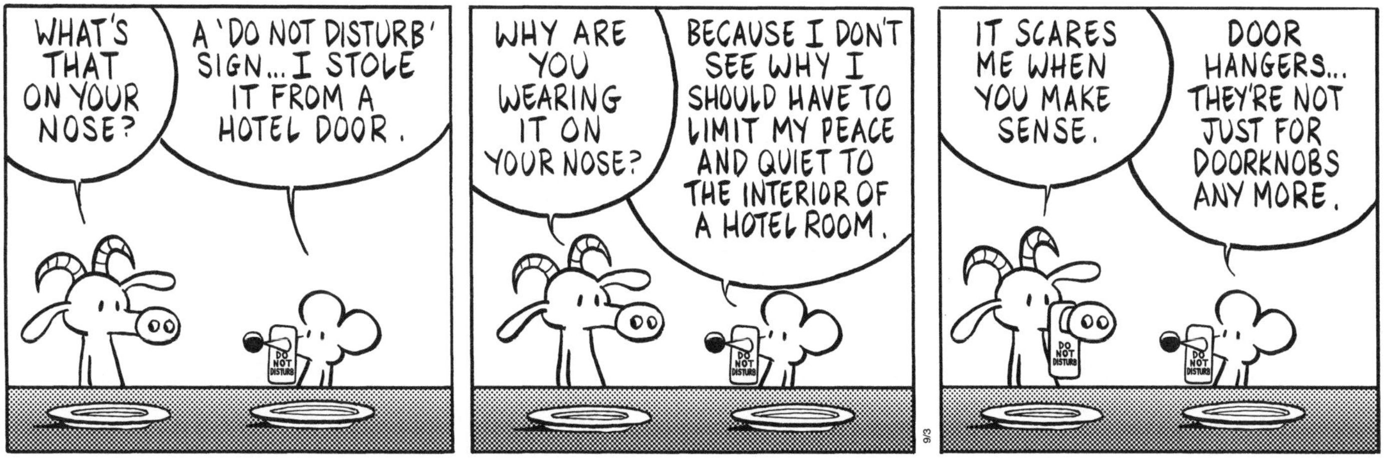
WHAT'S THAT ON YOUR NOSE?
A 'DO NOT DISTURB' SIGN... I STOLE IT FROM A HOTEL DOOR.
WHY ARE YOU WEARING IT ON YOUR NOSE?
BECAUSE I DON'T SEE WHY I SHOULD HAVE TO LIMIT MY PEACE AND QUIET TO THE INTERIOR OF A HOTEL ROOM.
IT SCARES ME WHEN YOU MAKE SENSE.
DOOR HANGERS... THEY'RE NOT JUST FOR DOORKNOBS ANY MORE.

Panel 1:

WHAT ARE YOU DOING, RAT?

I'VE STARTED SELLING STOCK IN YOU. TODAY'S THE INITIAL PUBLIC OFFERING... HOW MUCH WOULD YOU LIKE TO BUY?

BUY STOCK in PIG! Ticker Symbol: DUMB

Panel 2:

NONE. I'M A TOTAL FAILURE.

BUY STOCK in PIG! Ticker Symbol: DUMB

Panel 3:

THAT WILL NOT LOOK GOOD IN THE PROSPECTUS.

BUY STOCK in PIG! Ticker Symbol: DUMB

Panel 4:

WHATEVER HAPPENED TO MIKE, THAT FRIEND OF YOURS WHO WAS THE REAL ESTATE AGENT?

Panel 5:

HE DIED. HE WAS WAITING TO MEET A FRIEND ON THE CORNER OF MAIN AND THIRD AND A BUS HIT HIM. THE SAD PART WAS, THEY USUALLY MET AT A DIFFERENT SPOT.

Panel 6:

LOCATION. LOCATION. LOCATION.

Panel 7:

IN AN EFFORT TO PROMOTE WORLD PEACE, I AM PUTTING TOGETHER A LIST OF PEOPLE WHO ARE BAD AND IN NEED OF PHYSICAL SEPARATION FROM THE REST OF THE GENE POOL.

Panel 8:

SO WHAT HAVE YOU WRITTEN DOWN SO FAR? PEOPLE WHO START WARS? PEOPLE WHO HURT ANIMALS?

Panel 9:

"GUYS WHO WEAR SALMON-COLORED SHIRTS."

Panel 10:

THEY'RE SORT OF A PRIORITY.

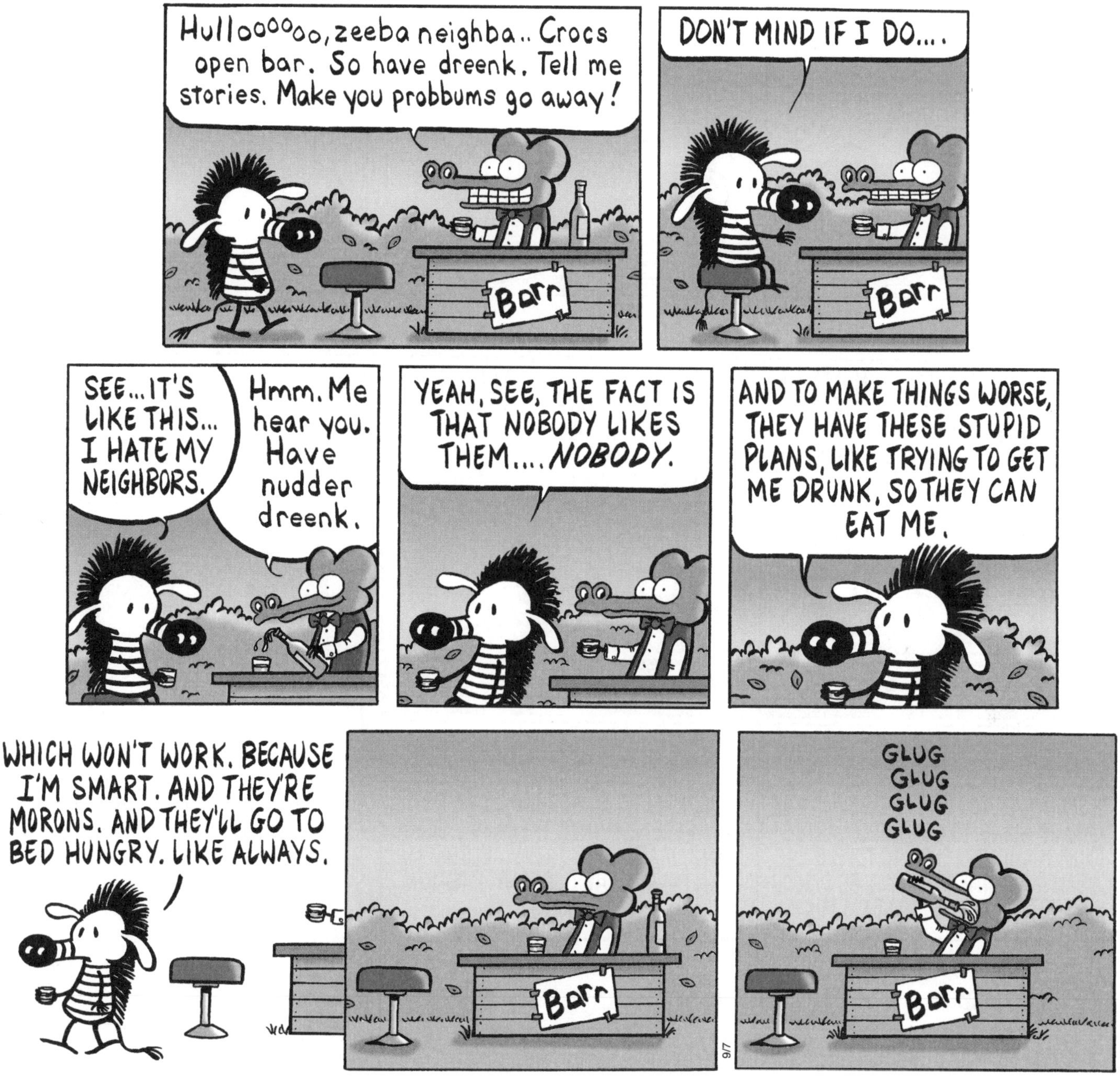
Hulloooooo, zeeba neighba.. Crocs open bar. So have dreenk. Tell me stories. Make you probbums go away!
DON'T MIND IF I DO....
Barr
SEE...IT'S LIKE THIS... I HATE MY NEIGHBORS.
Hmm. Me hear you. Have nudder dreenk.
YEAH, SEE, THE FACT IS THAT NOBODY LIKES THEM.....NOBODY.
AND TO MAKE THINGS WORSE, THEY HAVE THESE STUPID PLANS, LIKE TRYING TO GET ME DRUNK, SO THEY CAN EAT ME.
WHICH WON'T WORK. BECAUSE I'M SMART. AND THEY'RE MORONS. AND THEY'LL GO TO BED HUNGRY. LIKE ALWAYS.
Barr
GLUG
GLUG
GLUG
GLUG
Barr

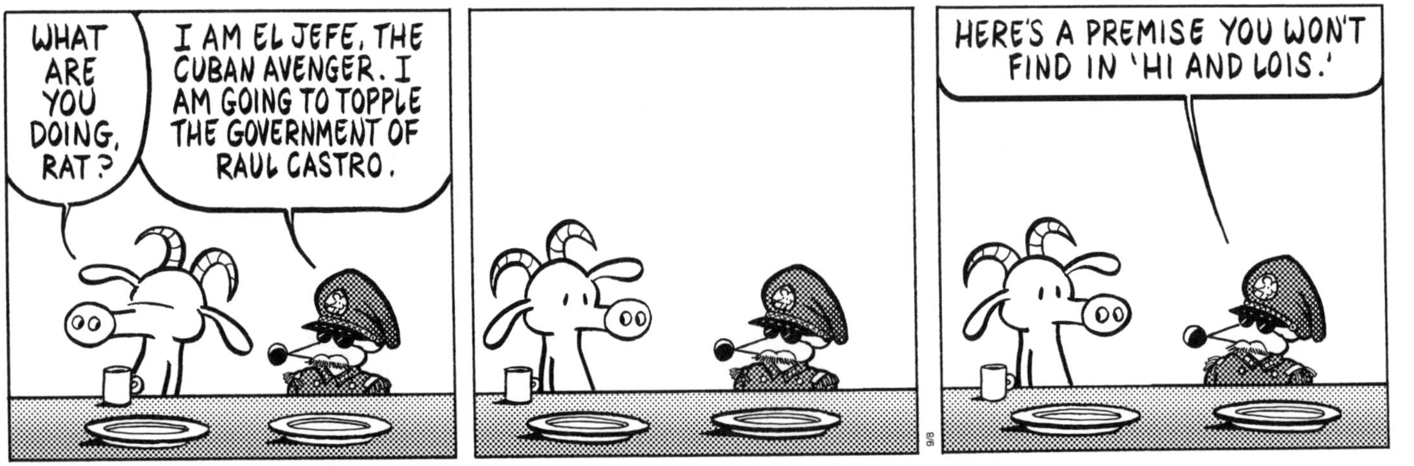
WHAT ARE YOU DOING, RAT?
I AM EL JEFE, THE CUBAN AVENGER. I AM GOING TO TOPPLE THE GOVERNMENT OF RAUL CASTRO.
HERE'S A PREMISE YOU WON'T FIND IN 'HI AND LOIS.'
9/8

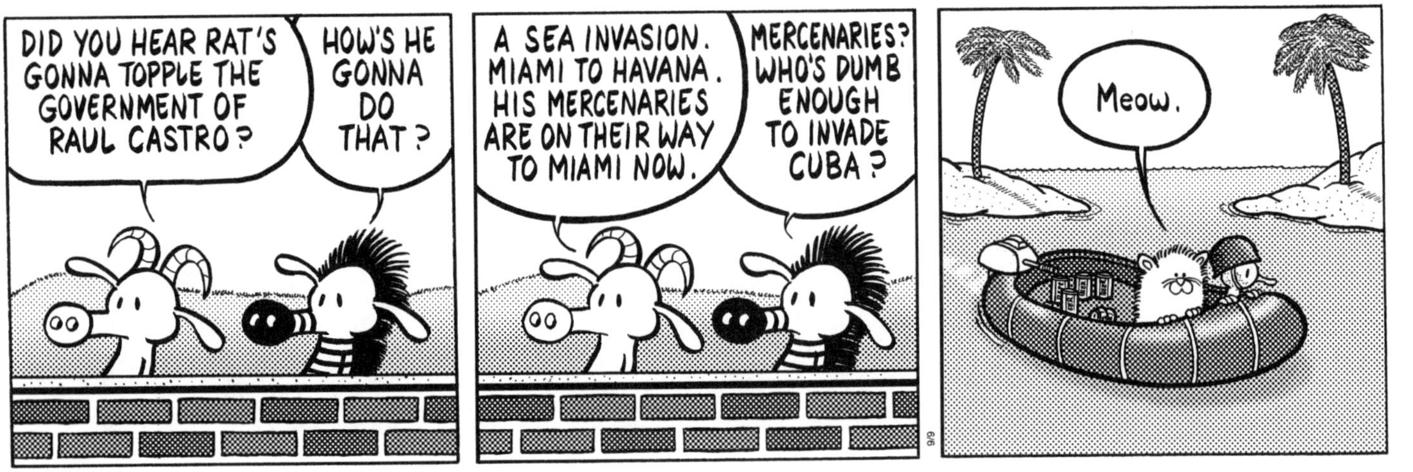
DID YOU HEAR RAT'S GONNA TOPPLE THE GOVERNMENT OF RAUL CASTRO?
HOW'S HE GONNA DO THAT?
A SEA INVASION. MIAMI TO HAVANA. HIS MERCENARIES ARE ON THEIR WAY TO MIAMI NOW.
MERCENARIES? WHO'S DUMB ENOUGH TO INVADE CUBA?
9/9
Meow.

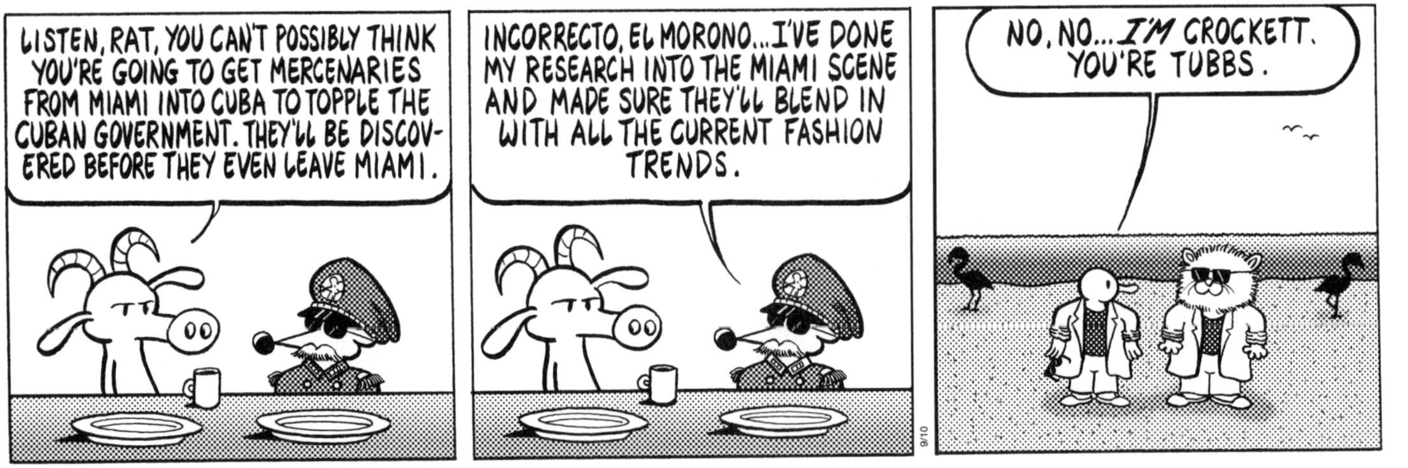
LISTEN, RAT, YOU CAN'T POSSIBLY THINK YOU'RE GOING TO GET MERCENARIES FROM MIAMI INTO CUBA TO TOPPLE THE CUBAN GOVERNMENT. THEY'LL BE DISCOVERED BEFORE THEY EVEN LEAVE MIAMI.
INCORRECTO, EL MORONO...I'VE DONE MY RESEARCH INTO THE MIAMI SCENE AND MADE SURE THEY'LL BLEND IN WITH ALL THE CURRENT FASHION TRENDS.
9/10
NO, NO...*I'M* CROCKETT. YOU'RE TUBBS.

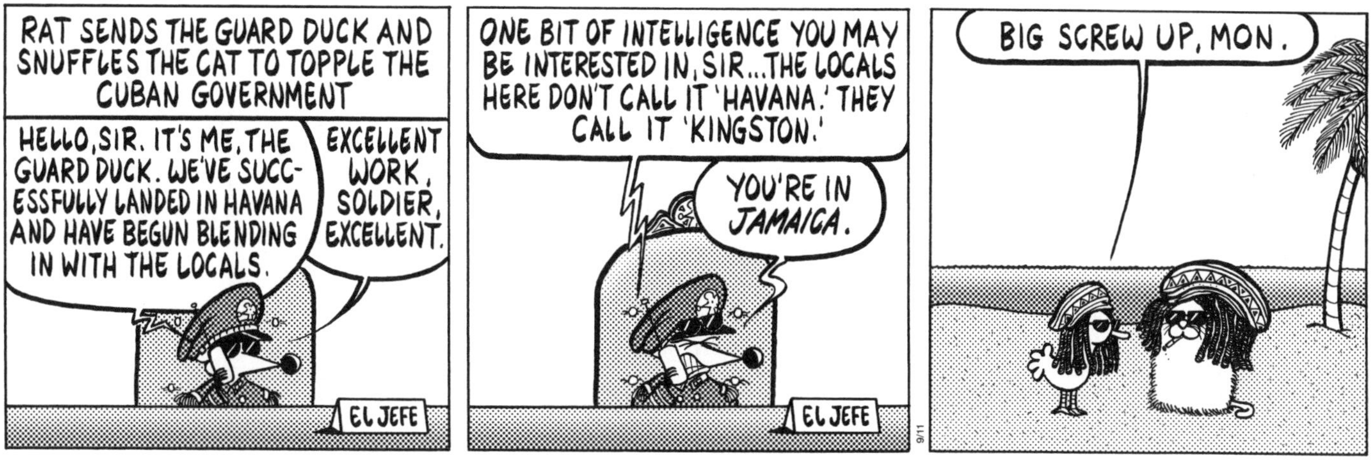
RAT SENDS THE GUARD DUCK AND SNUFFLES THE CAT TO TOPPLE THE CUBAN GOVERNMENT
HELLO, SIR. IT'S ME, THE GUARD DUCK. WE'VE SUCCESSFULLY LANDED IN HAVANA AND HAVE BEGUN BLENDING IN WITH THE LOCALS.
EXCELLENT WORK, SOLDIER, EXCELLENT.
EL JEFE
ONE BIT OF INTELLIGENCE YOU MAY BE INTERESTED IN, SIR...THE LOCALS HERE DON'T CALL IT 'HAVANA.' THEY CALL IT 'KINGSTON.'
YOU'RE IN *JAMAICA*.
EL JEFE
9/11
BIG SCREW UP, MON.

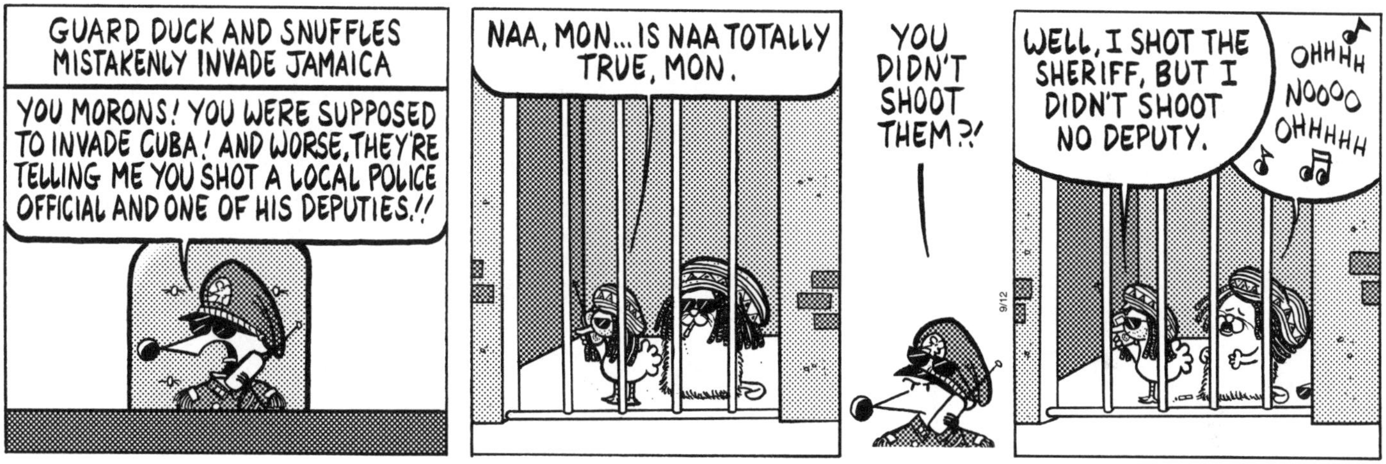
GUARD DUCK AND SNUFFLES MISTAKENLY INVADE JAMAICA
YOU MORONS! YOU WERE SUPPOSED TO INVADE CUBA! AND WORSE, THEY'RE TELLING ME YOU SHOT A LOCAL POLICE OFFICIAL AND ONE OF HIS DEPUTIES!!
NAA, MON... IS NAA TOTALLY TRUE, MON.
YOU DIDN'T SHOOT THEM?!
9/12
WELL, I SHOT THE SHERIFF, BUT I DIDN'T SHOOT NO DEPUTY.
OHHHH NOOOO OHHHHHH

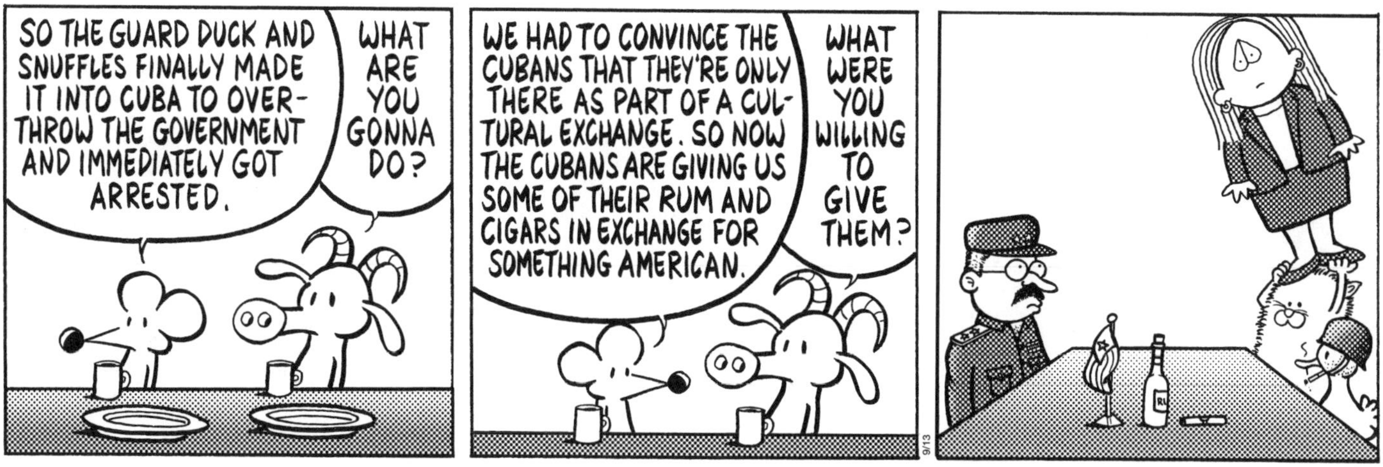
SO THE GUARD DUCK AND SNUFFLES FINALLY MADE IT INTO CUBA TO OVERTHROW THE GOVERNMENT AND IMMEDIATELY GOT ARRESTED.
WHAT ARE YOU GONNA DO?
WE HAD TO CONVINCE THE CUBANS THAT THEY'RE ONLY THERE AS PART OF A CULTURAL EXCHANGE. SO NOW THE CUBANS ARE GIVING US SOME OF THEIR RUM AND CIGARS IN EXCHANGE FOR SOMETHING AMERICAN.
WHAT WERE YOU WILLING TO GIVE THEM?
9/13

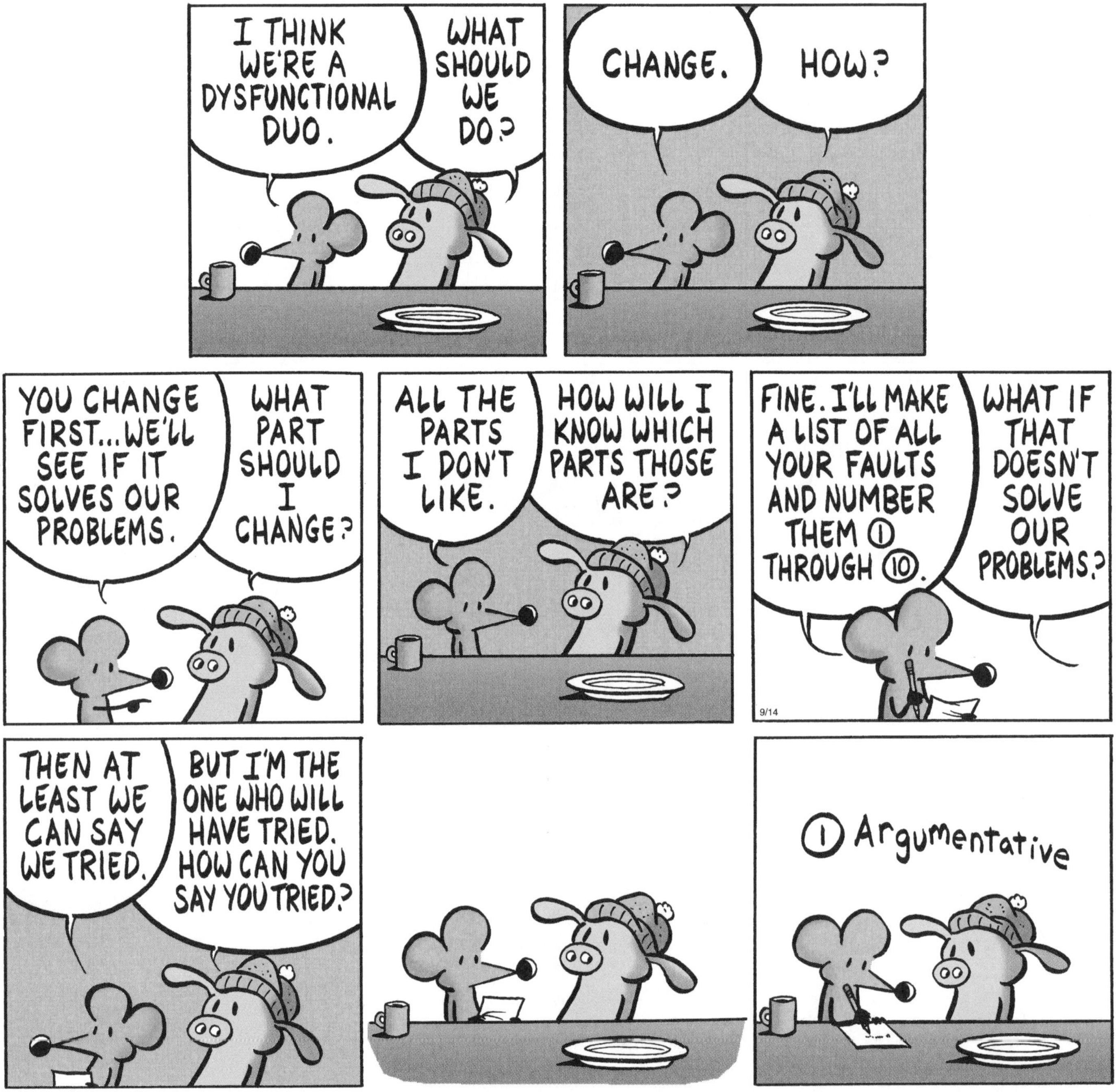
I THINK WE'RE A DYSFUNCTIONAL DUO.
WHAT SHOULD WE DO?
CHANGE.
HOW?
YOU CHANGE FIRST...WE'LL SEE IF IT SOLVES OUR PROBLEMS.
WHAT PART SHOULD I CHANGE?
ALL THE PARTS I DON'T LIKE.
HOW WILL I KNOW WHICH PARTS THOSE ARE?
FINE. I'LL MAKE A LIST OF ALL YOUR FAULTS AND NUMBER THEM ① THROUGH ⑩.
WHAT IF THAT DOESN'T SOLVE OUR PROBLEMS?
9/14
THEN AT LEAST WE CAN SAY WE TRIED.
BUT I'M THE ONE WHO WILL HAVE TRIED. HOW CAN YOU SAY YOU TRIED?
① Argumentative

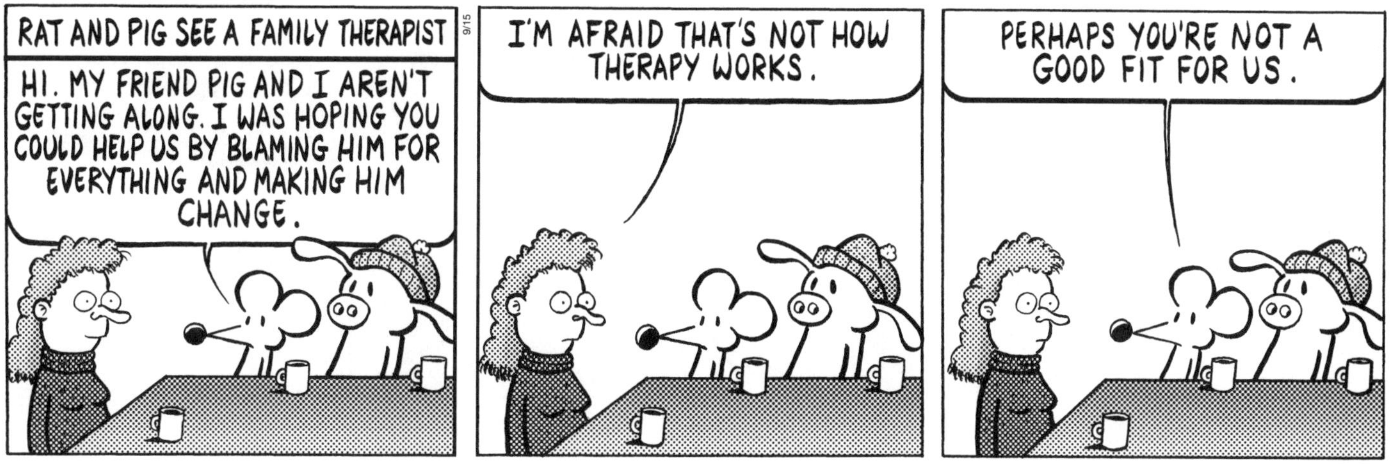
RAT AND PIG SEE A FAMILY THERAPIST
HI. MY FRIEND PIG AND I AREN'T GETTING ALONG. I WAS HOPING YOU COULD HELP US BY BLAMING HIM FOR EVERYTHING AND MAKING HIM CHANGE.
9/15
I'M AFRAID THAT'S NOT HOW THERAPY WORKS.
PERHAPS YOU'RE NOT A GOOD FIT FOR US.

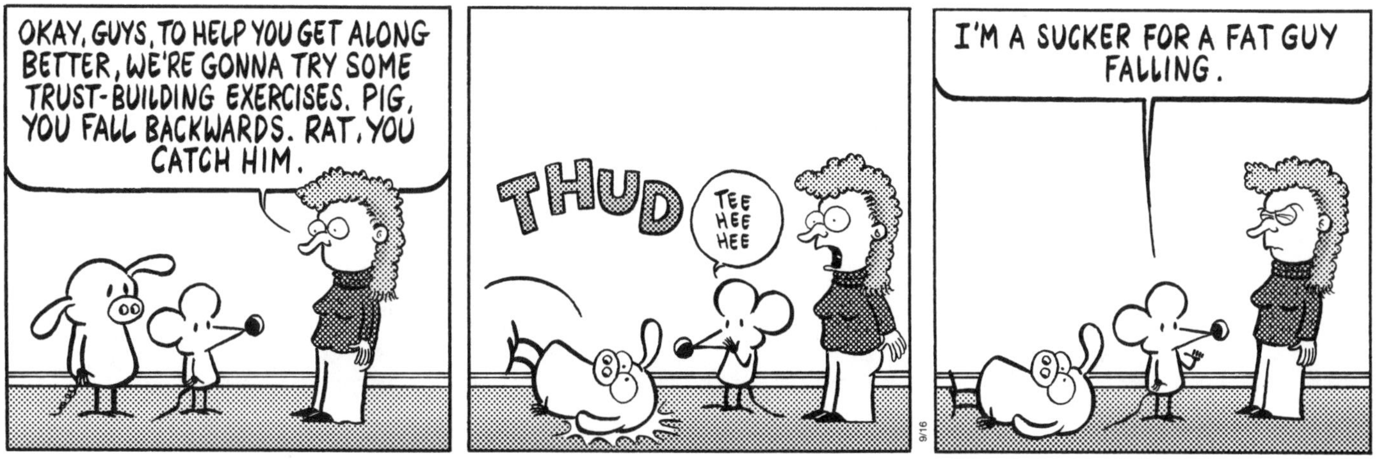
OKAY, GUYS, TO HELP YOU GET ALONG BETTER, WE'RE GONNA TRY SOME TRUST-BUILDING EXERCISES. PIG, YOU FALL BACKWARDS. RAT, YOU CATCH HIM.
THUD
TEE HEE HEE
9/16
I'M A SUCKER FOR A FAT GUY FALLING.

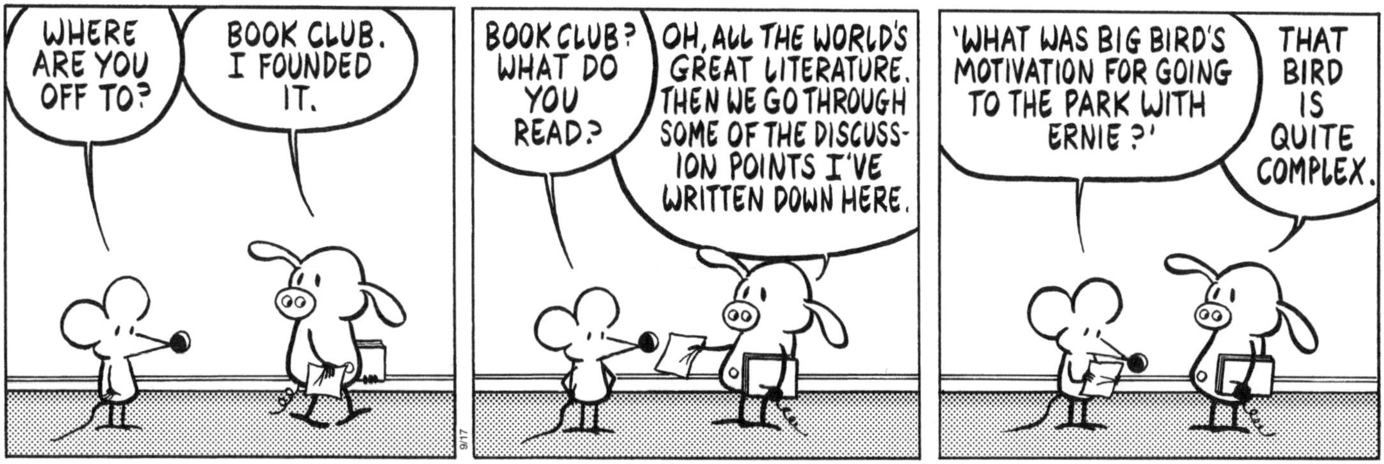
WHERE ARE YOU OFF TO?
BOOK CLUB. I FOUNDED IT.
9/17
BOOK CLUB? WHAT DO YOU READ?
OH, ALL THE WORLD'S GREAT LITERATURE. THEN WE GO THROUGH SOME OF THE DISCUSSION POINTS I'VE WRITTEN DOWN HERE.
'WHAT WAS BIG BIRD'S MOTIVATION FOR GOING TO THE PARK WITH ERNIE?'
THAT BIRD IS QUITE COMPLEX.

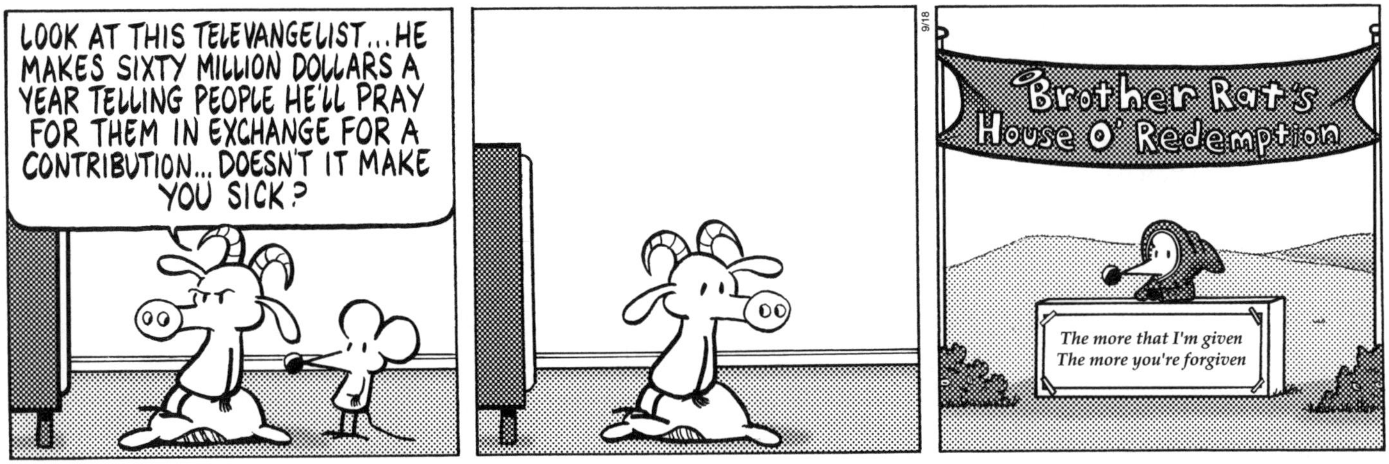
LOOK AT THIS TELEVANGELIST... HE MAKES SIXTY MILLION DOLLARS A YEAR TELLING PEOPLE HE'LL PRAY FOR THEM IN EXCHANGE FOR A CONTRIBUTION... DOESN'T IT MAKE YOU SICK?
9/18
Brother Rat's House O' Redemption
The more that I'm given
The more you're forgiven

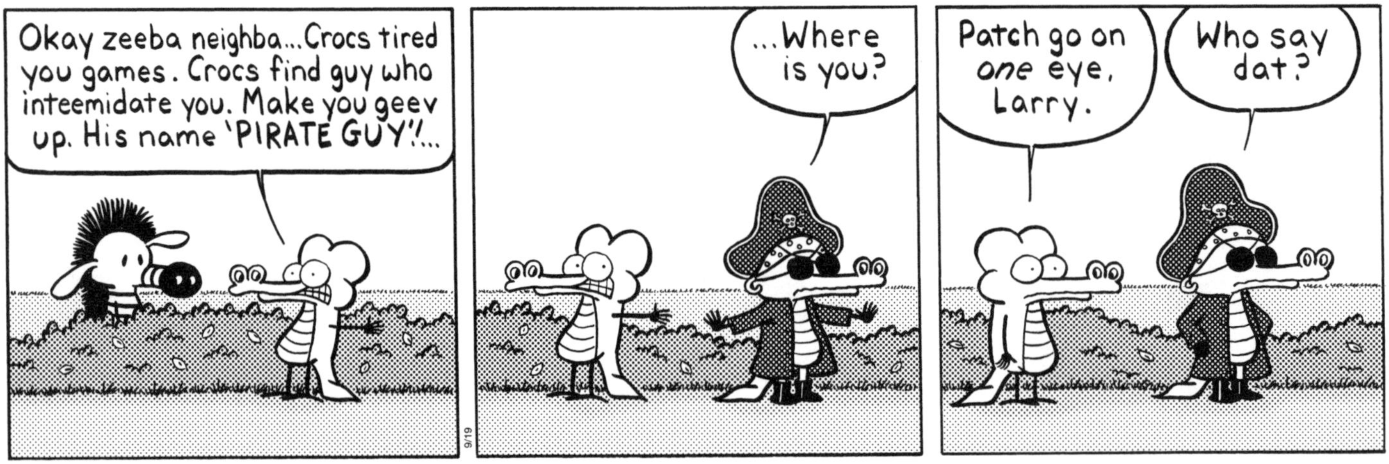
Okay zeeba neighba... Crocs tired you games. Crocs find guy who inteemidate you. Make you geev up. His name 'PIRATE GUY'!...
9/19
...Where is you?
Patch go on *one* eye, Larry.
Who say dat?

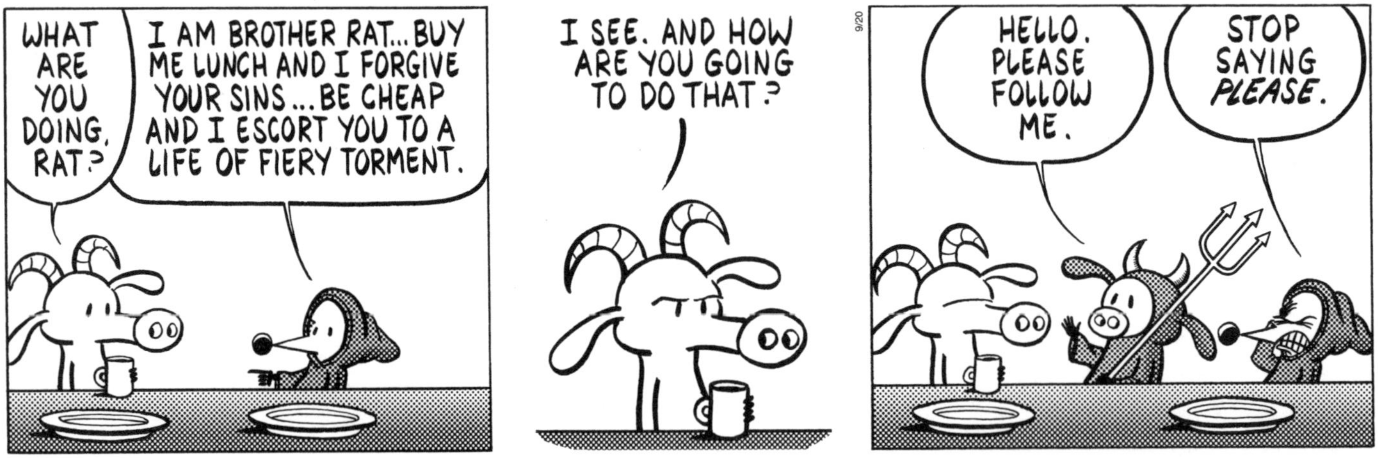
WHAT ARE YOU DOING, RAT?
I AM BROTHER RAT... BUY ME LUNCH AND I FORGIVE YOUR SINS... BE CHEAP AND I ESCORT YOU TO A LIFE OF FIERY TORMENT.
I SEE. AND HOW ARE YOU GOING TO DO THAT?
9/20
HELLO. PLEASE FOLLOW ME.
STOP SAYING *PLEASE*.

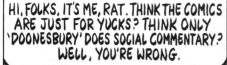

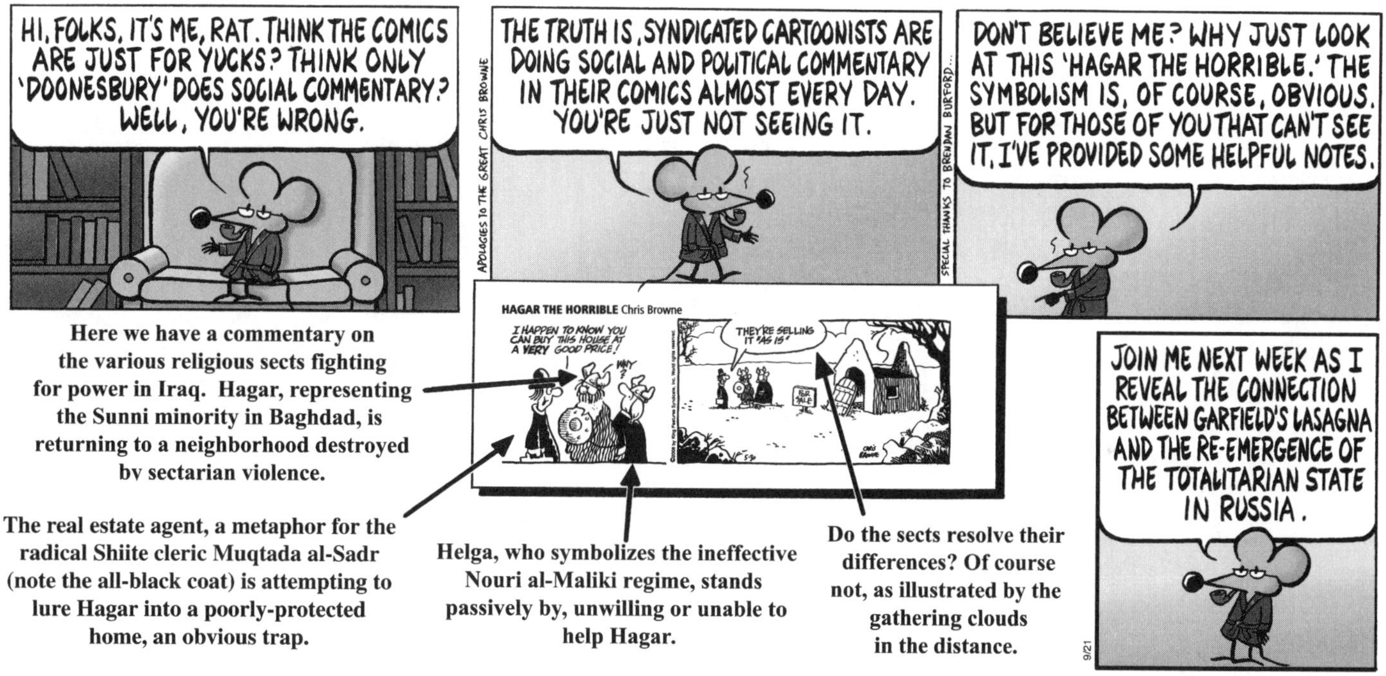

HI, FOLKS, IT'S ME, RAT. THINK THE COMICS ARE JUST FOR YUCKS? THINK ONLY 'DOONESBURY' DOES SOCIAL COMMENTARY? WELL, YOU'RE WRONG.
APOLOGIES TO THE GREAT CHRIS BROWNE
THE TRUTH IS, SYNDICATED CARTOONISTS ARE DOING SOCIAL AND POLITICAL COMMENTARY IN THEIR COMICS ALMOST EVERY DAY. YOU'RE JUST NOT SEEING IT.
SPECIAL THANKS TO BRENDAN BURFORD...
DON'T BELIEVE ME? WHY JUST LOOK AT THIS 'HAGAR THE HORRIBLE.' THE SYMBOLISM IS, OF COURSE, OBVIOUS. BUT FOR THOSE OF YOU THAT CAN'T SEE IT, I'VE PROVIDED SOME HELPFUL NOTES.
HAGAR THE HORRIBLE Chris Browne
I HAPPEN TO KNOW YOU CAN BUY THIS HOUSE AT A VERY GOOD PRICE!
WHY?
THEY'RE SELLING IT 'AS IS'
FOR SALE
Here we have a commentary on the various religious sects fighting for power in Iraq. Hagar, representing the Sunni minority in Baghdad, is returning to a neighborhood destroyed bv sectarian violence.
The real estate agent, a metaphor for the radical Shiite cleric Muqtada al-Sadr (note the all-black coat) is attempting to lure Hagar into a poorly-protected home, an obvious trap.
Helga, who symbolizes the ineffective Nouri al-Maliki regime, stands passively by, unwilling or unable to help Hagar.
Do the sects resolve their differences? Of course not, as illustrated by the gathering clouds in the distance.
JOIN ME NEXT WEEK AS I REVEAL THE CONNECTION BETWEEN GARFIELD'S LASAGNA AND THE RE-EMERGENCE OF THE TOTALITARIAN STATE IN RUSSIA.
9/21

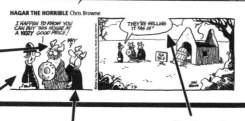

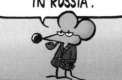

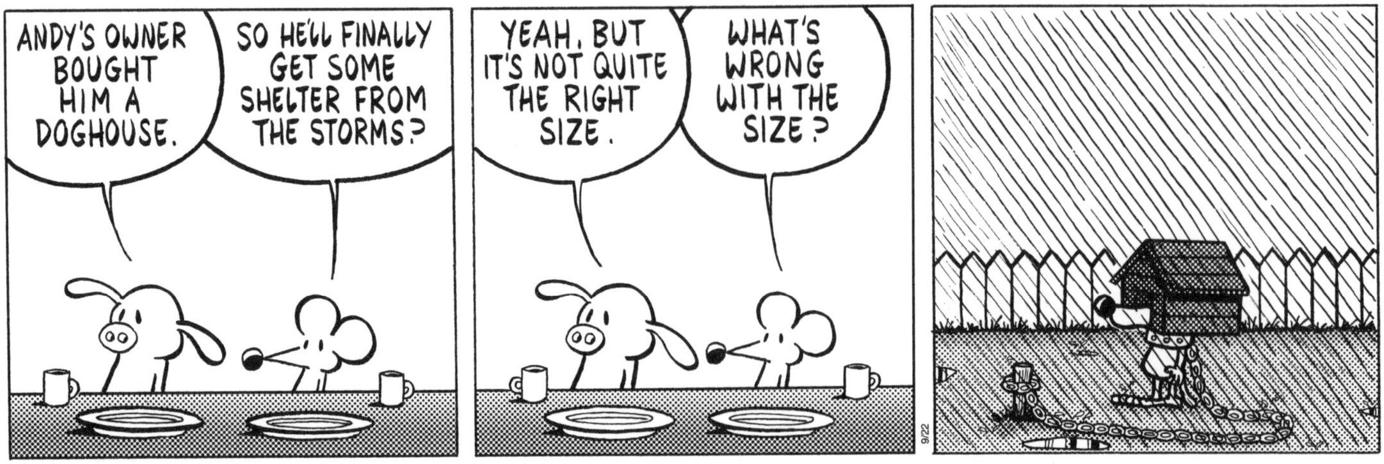
ANDY'S OWNER BOUGHT HIM A DOGHOUSE.
SO HE'LL FINALLY GET SOME SHELTER FROM THE STORMS?
YEAH, BUT IT'S NOT QUITE THE RIGHT SIZE.
WHAT'S WRONG WITH THE SIZE?

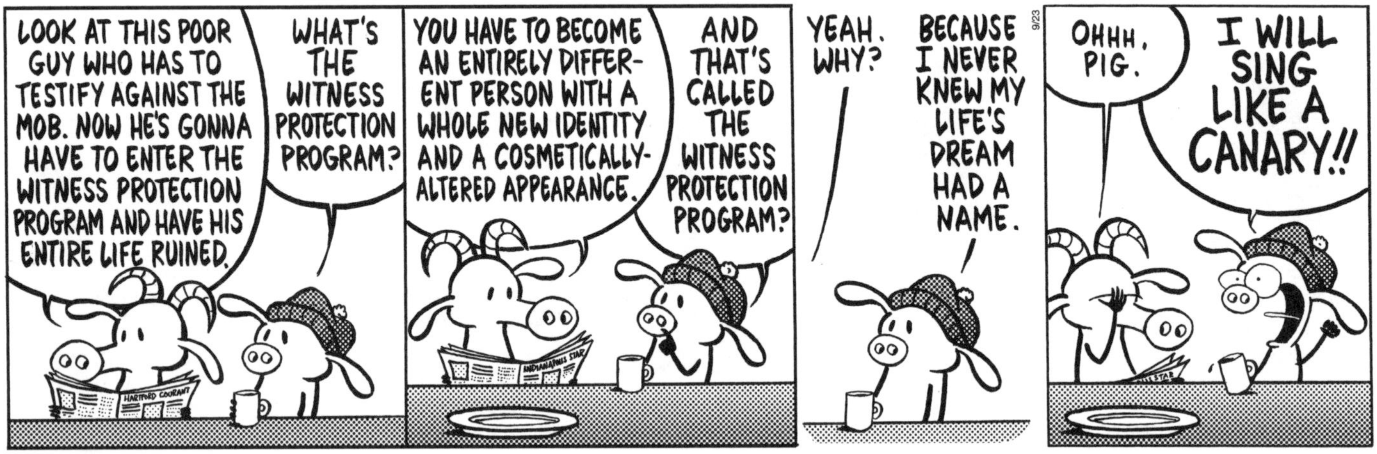
LOOK AT THIS POOR GUY WHO HAS TO TESTIFY AGAINST THE MOB. NOW HE'S GONNA HAVE TO ENTER THE WITNESS PROTECTION PROGRAM AND HAVE HIS ENTIRE LIFE RUINED.
WHAT'S THE WITNESS PROTECTION PROGRAM?
YOU HAVE TO BECOME AN ENTIRELY DIFFERENT PERSON WITH A WHOLE NEW IDENTITY AND A COSMETICALLY-ALTERED APPEARANCE.
AND THAT'S CALLED THE WITNESS PROTECTION PROGRAM?
YEAH. WHY?
BECAUSE I NEVER KNEW MY LIFE'S DREAM HAD A NAME.
OHHH, PIG.
I WILL SING LIKE A CANARY!!

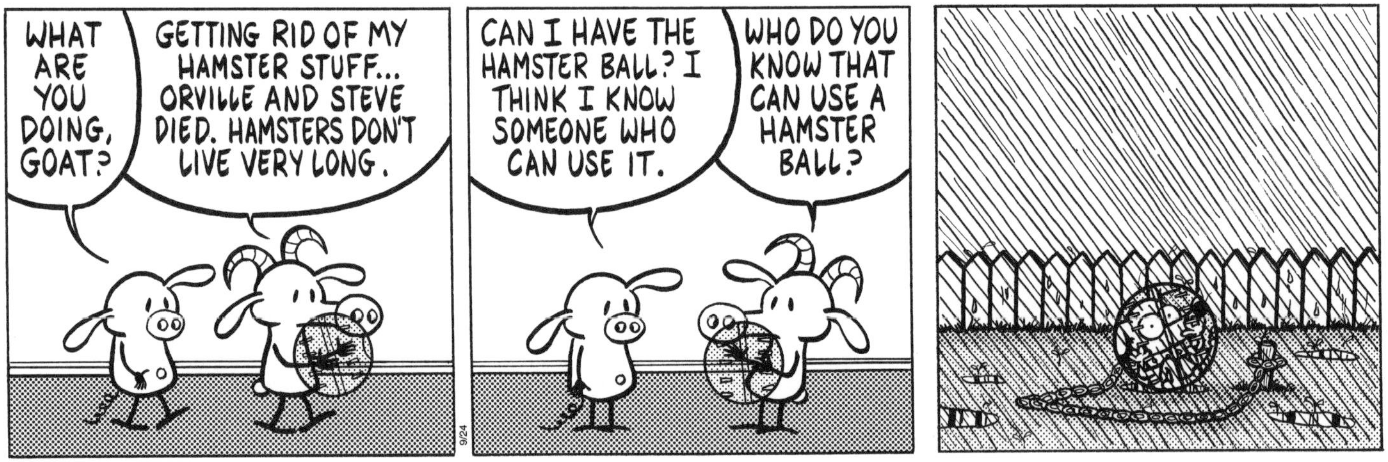
WHAT ARE YOU DOING, GOAT?
GETTING RID OF MY HAMSTER STUFF... ORVILLE AND STEVE DIED. HAMSTERS DON'T LIVE VERY LONG.
CAN I HAVE THE HAMSTER BALL? I THINK I KNOW SOMEONE WHO CAN USE IT.
WHO DO YOU KNOW THAT CAN USE A HAMSTER BALL?

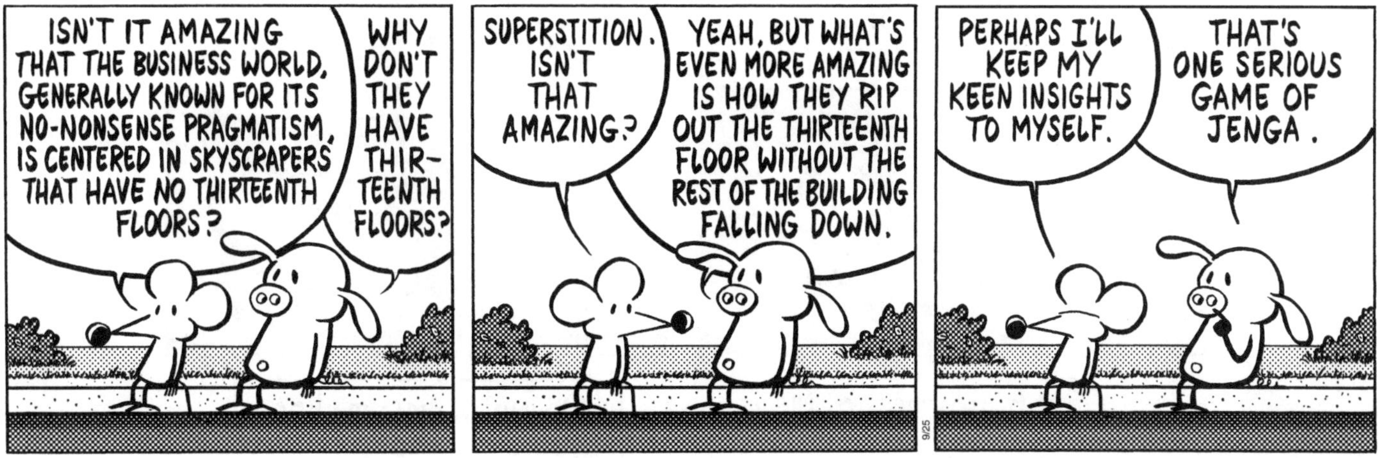
ISN'T IT AMAZING THAT THE BUSINESS WORLD, GENERALLY KNOWN FOR ITS NO-NONSENSE PRAGMATISM, IS CENTERED IN SKYSCRAPERS THAT HAVE NO THIRTEENTH FLOORS?
WHY DON'T THEY HAVE THIRTEENTH FLOORS?
SUPERSTITION. ISN'T THAT AMAZING?
YEAH, BUT WHAT'S EVEN MORE AMAZING IS HOW THEY RIP OUT THE THIRTEENTH FLOOR WITHOUT THE REST OF THE BUILDING FALLING DOWN.
PERHAPS I'LL KEEP MY KEEN INSIGHTS TO MYSELF.
THAT'S ONE SERIOUS GAME OF JENGA.
9/25

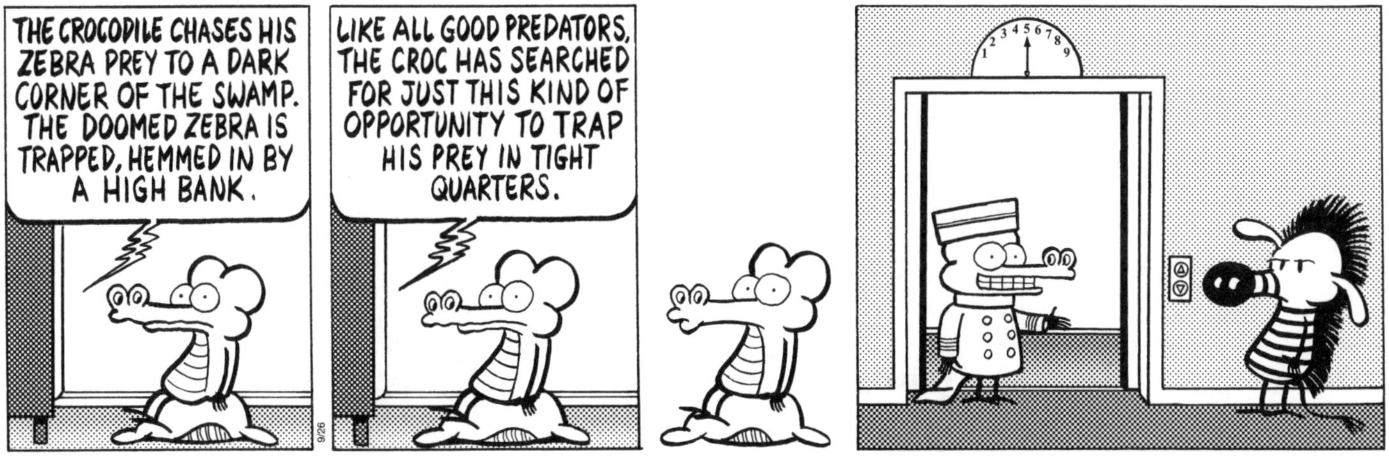
THE CROCODILE CHASES HIS ZEBRA PREY TO A DARK CORNER OF THE SWAMP. THE DOOMED ZEBRA IS TRAPPED, HEMMED IN BY A HIGH BANK.
LIKE ALL GOOD PREDATORS, THE CROC HAS SEARCHED FOR JUST THIS KIND OF OPPORTUNITY TO TRAP HIS PREY IN TIGHT QUARTERS.
9/26

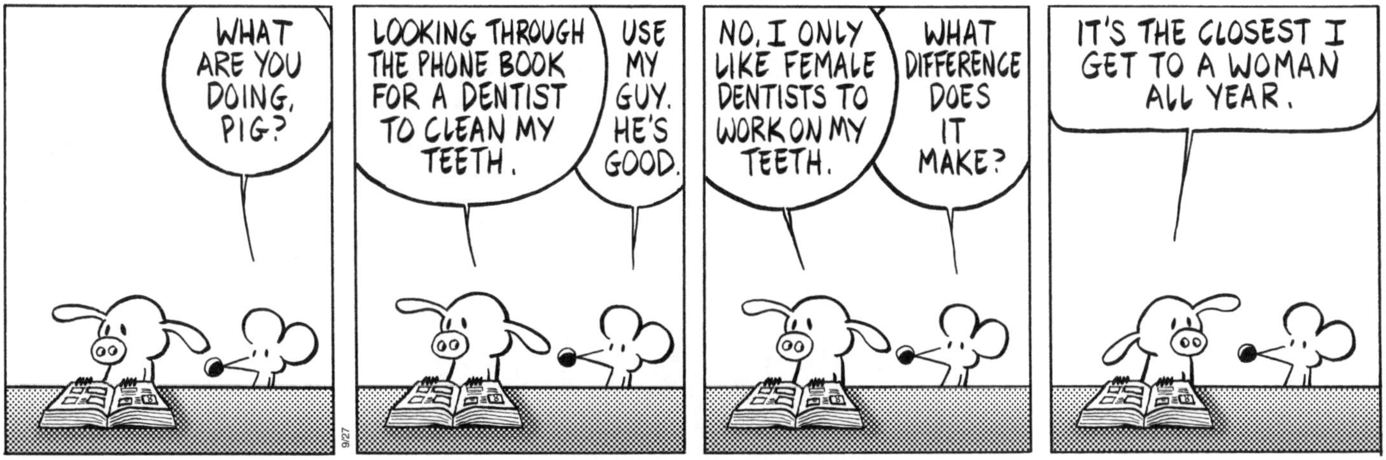
WHAT ARE YOU DOING, PIG?
LOOKING THROUGH THE PHONE BOOK FOR A DENTIST TO CLEAN MY TEETH.
USE MY GUY. HE'S GOOD.
NO, I ONLY LIKE FEMALE DENTISTS TO WORK ON MY TEETH.
WHAT DIFFERENCE DOES IT MAKE?
IT'S THE CLOSEST I GET TO A WOMAN ALL YEAR.
9/27

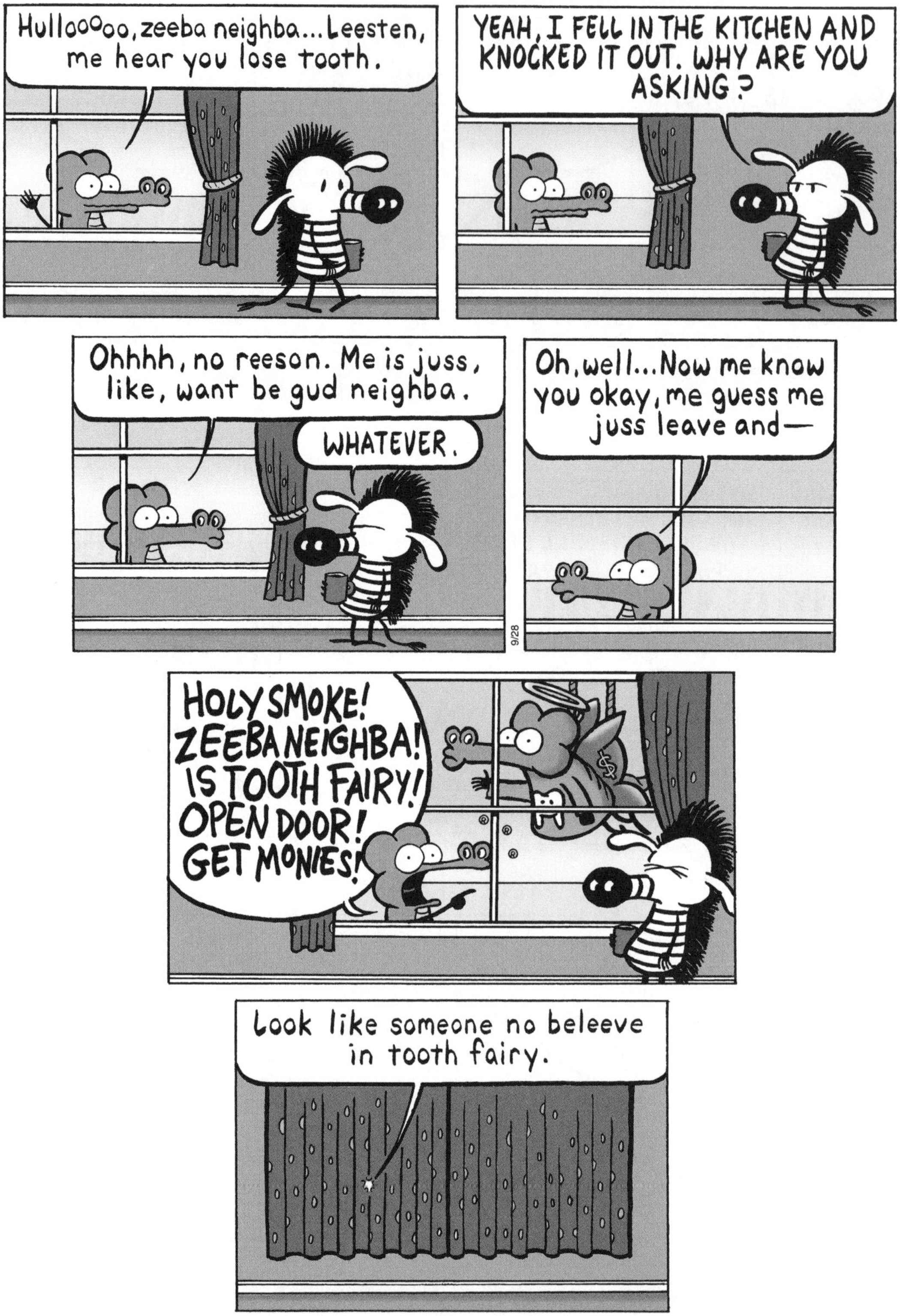
Hulloooo, zeeba neighba... Leesten, me hear you lose tooth.
YEAH, I FELL IN THE KITCHEN AND KNOCKED IT OUT. WHY ARE YOU ASKING?
Ohhhh, no reeson. Me is juss, like, want be gud neighba.
WHATEVER.
9/28
Oh, well... Now me know you okay, me guess me juss leave and—
HOLY SMOKE! ZEEBA NEIGHBA! IS TOOTH FAIRY! OPEN DOOR! GET MONIES!
Look like someone no beleeve in tooth fairy.

♪ Country Rooooads ♪ Take me hooooome To the plaaaace I belooooooong ♪ West Virginiaaa ♪ Mountain Mamaaa ♪ Take me hoooooome Country Rooooads ♪

WHAT ARE YOU DOING, RAT?

I'M PLANTING EARWORMS... AN EARWORM'S A SONG YOU HEAR ONCE AND CAN'T GET OUT OF YOUR HEAD FOR THE REST OF THE DAY.

Ha Ha Ha Ha THAT'S THE SILLIEST THING I'VE EVER— ♪ COUNTRY ROADS, ♪ TAKE ME HOOOME

GOOD LUCK.

YOU EVER WONDER WHAT THESE LITTLE HALF CIRCLES THEY PUT AROUND DOORS ARE FOR? I THINK THEY'RE 'MAGIC ZONES'! WHEN YOU STAND IN THEM, MAGIC HAPPENS!

SMACK

TA-DAAAAAAAAA.

GEE, LOOK AT ALL THESE DEBATES ON OUR DWINDLING OIL SUPPLIES AND OUR DWINDLING WATER SUPPLIES AND OUR DWINDLING FOOD SUPPLIES.

I'M NO EXPERT, BUT DO YOU SUPPOSE IT COULD MEAN WE HAVE...GOSH, I DON'T KNOW... MAYBE...

TOO MANY PEOPLE?!!

PAID FOR BY THE 'SOMEONE BETTER START POINTING OUT THE OBVIOUS' COMMITTEE FOR A BETTER PLANET.

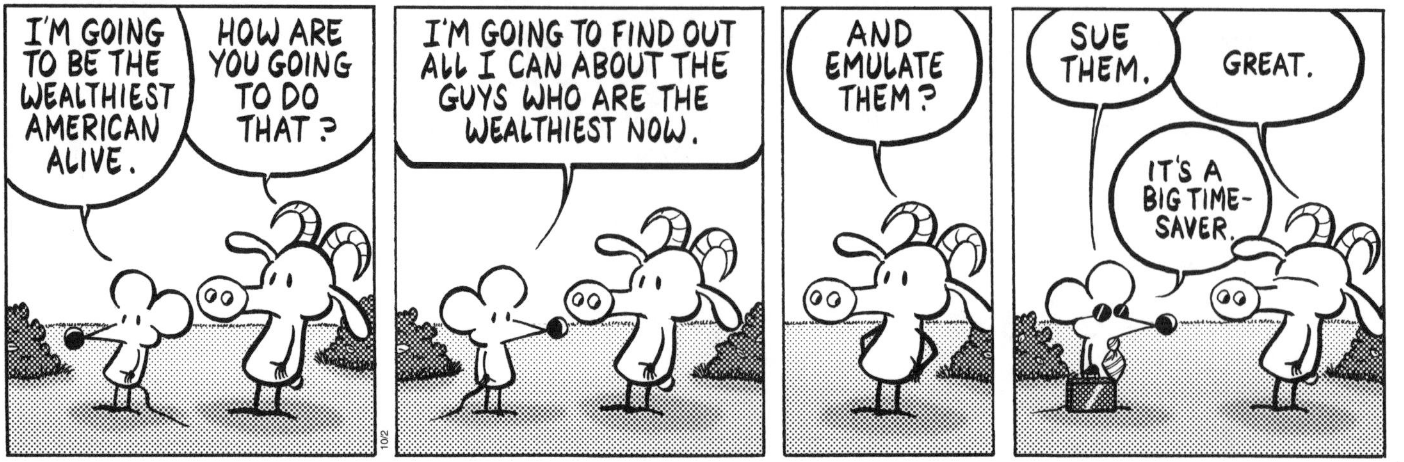
I'M GOING TO BE THE WEALTHIEST AMERICAN ALIVE.
HOW ARE YOU GOING TO DO THAT?
I'M GOING TO FIND OUT ALL I CAN ABOUT THE GUYS WHO ARE THE WEALTHIEST NOW.
AND EMULATE THEM?
SUE THEM.
GREAT.
IT'S A BIG TIME-SAVER.
10/2

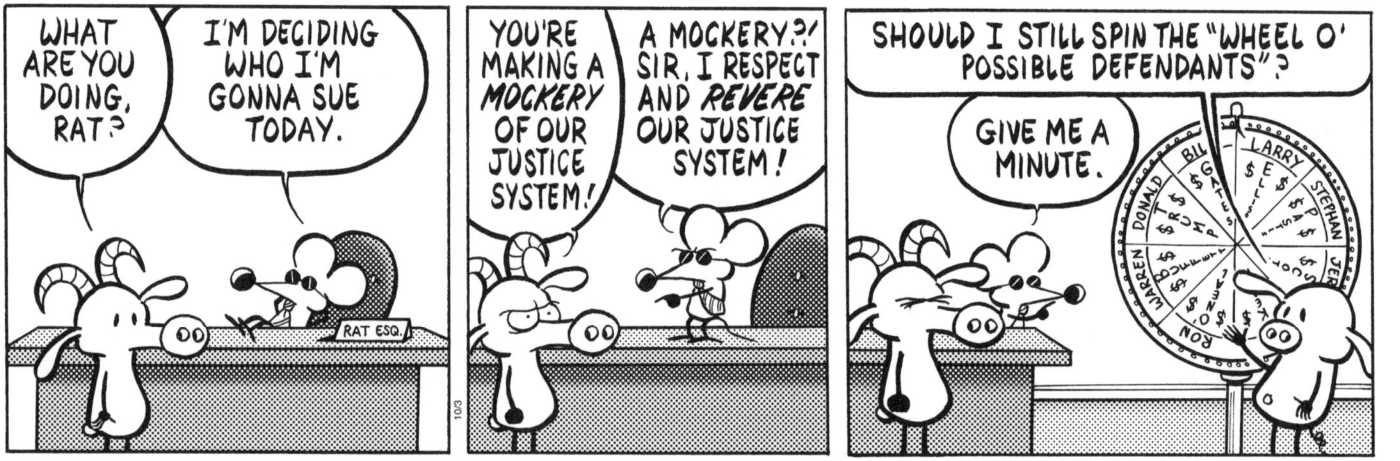
WHAT ARE YOU DOING, RAT?
I'M DECIDING WHO I'M GONNA SUE TODAY.
RAT ESQ.
YOU'RE MAKING A *MOCKERY* OF OUR JUSTICE SYSTEM!
A MOCKERY?! SIR, I RESPECT AND *REVERE* OUR JUSTICE SYSTEM!
SHOULD I STILL SPIN THE "WHEEL O' POSSIBLE DEFENDANTS"?
GIVE ME A MINUTE.
LARRY
STEPHAN
DONALD
WARREN
RON
10/3

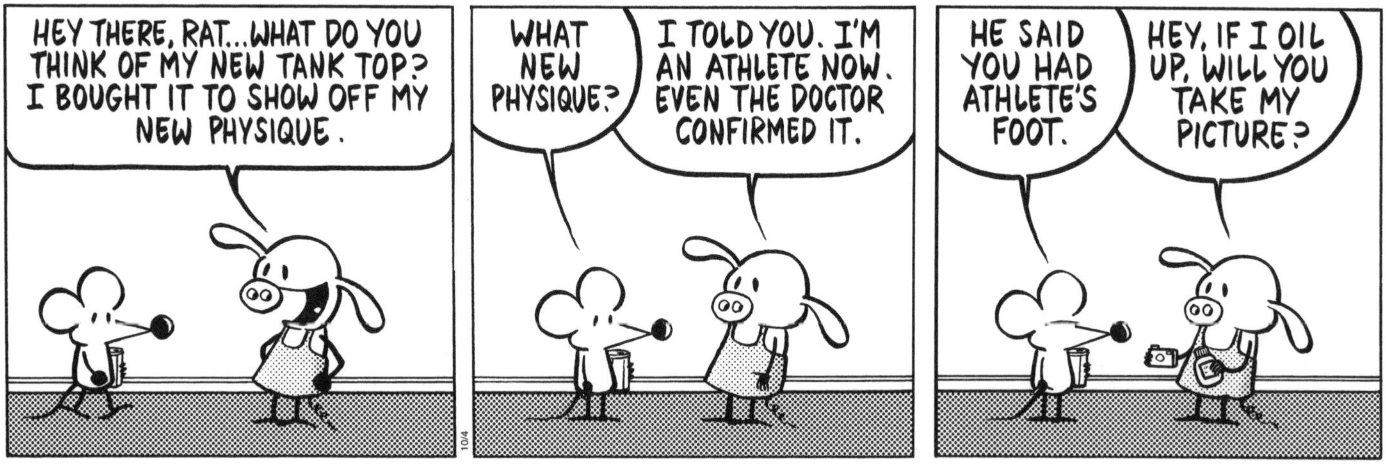
HEY THERE, RAT...WHAT DO YOU THINK OF MY NEW TANK TOP? I BOUGHT IT TO SHOW OFF MY NEW PHYSIQUE.
WHAT NEW PHYSIQUE?
I TOLD YOU. I'M AN ATHLETE NOW. EVEN THE DOCTOR CONFIRMED IT.
HE SAID YOU HAD ATHLETE'S FOOT.
HEY, IF I OIL UP, WILL YOU TAKE MY PICTURE?
10/4

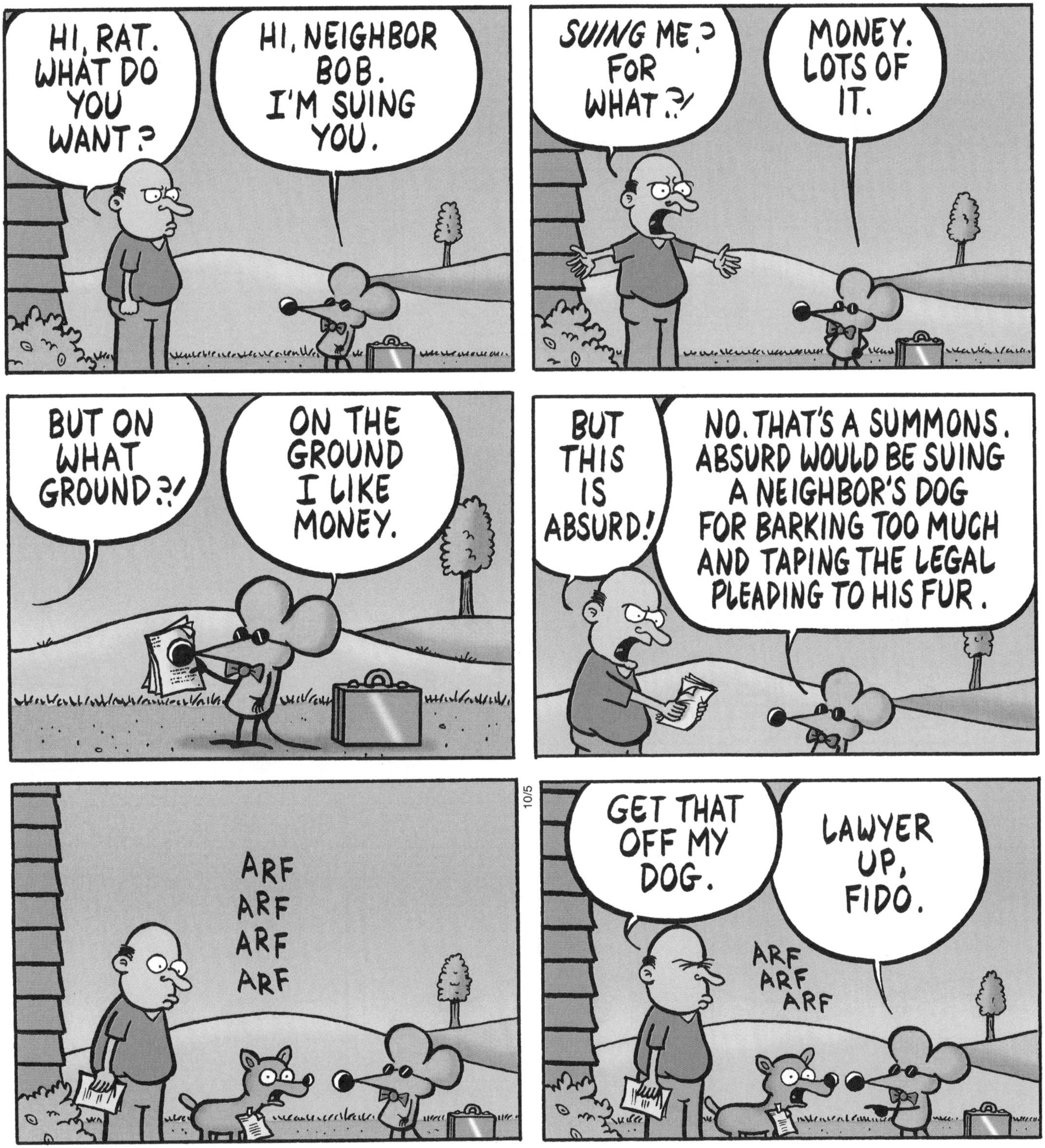
HI, RAT. WHAT DO YOU WANT?
HI, NEIGHBOR BOB. I'M SUING YOU.
SUING ME? FOR WHAT?!
MONEY. LOTS OF IT.
BUT ON WHAT GROUND?!
ON THE GROUND I LIKE MONEY.
BUT THIS IS ABSURD!
NO. THAT'S A SUMMONS. ABSURD WOULD BE SUING A NEIGHBOR'S DOG FOR BARKING TOO MUCH AND TAPING THE LEGAL PLEADING TO HIS FUR.
ARF ARF ARF ARF
10/5
GET THAT OFF MY DOG.
ARF ARF ARF
LAWYER UP, FIDO.

Panel 1:
WHAT ARE YOU WATCHING?

ANDERSON COOPER ON CNN. I LIKE HIM, BUT SOMETIMES THE OTHER ANCHORS MAKE HIM LAUGH AND THEN I HAVE TO—

Panel 2:
EH EH EH EH EH EH EH EH EH EH EH EH EH EH EH EH EH EH

Panel 3:
A MAN'S LAUGH SHOULD NOT SOUND LIKE A WEASEL DYING AT THE GATES OF HELL.

DID YOU SAY SOMETHING?

Panel 4:
WHAT ARE YOU DOING, RAT?

I'M STARTING A SOFTBALL TEAM. I WANT YOU TO PLAY CENTERFIELD.

Panel 5:
BUT THIS WHOLE SCENE IS A 'PEANUTS' RIP-OFF.

HEY, CAN'T OTHER COMICS PLAY A LITTLE BALL WITHOUT BEING ACCUSED OF RIPPING OFF 'PEANUTS'?

Panel 6:
POW!

Panel 7:
NO.

WOW. I DON'T EVEN WEAR CLOTHES.

Panel 8:
I DON'T WANT TO PLAY SOFTBALL ON YOUR TEAM, RAT. I HAVE POOR HAND-EYE COORDINATION AND VERY SLOW REACTION TIME.

I KNOW THAT, YOU DUMB PIG. THAT'S WHY I'M PUTTING YOU AT THIS POSITION.

Panel 9:
SMACK

Panel 10:
GOSH. MAYBE THIRD BASE ISN'T RIGHT FOR YOU AFTER ALL.

OHHHHHHHH MY OOMPA LOOMPAS.

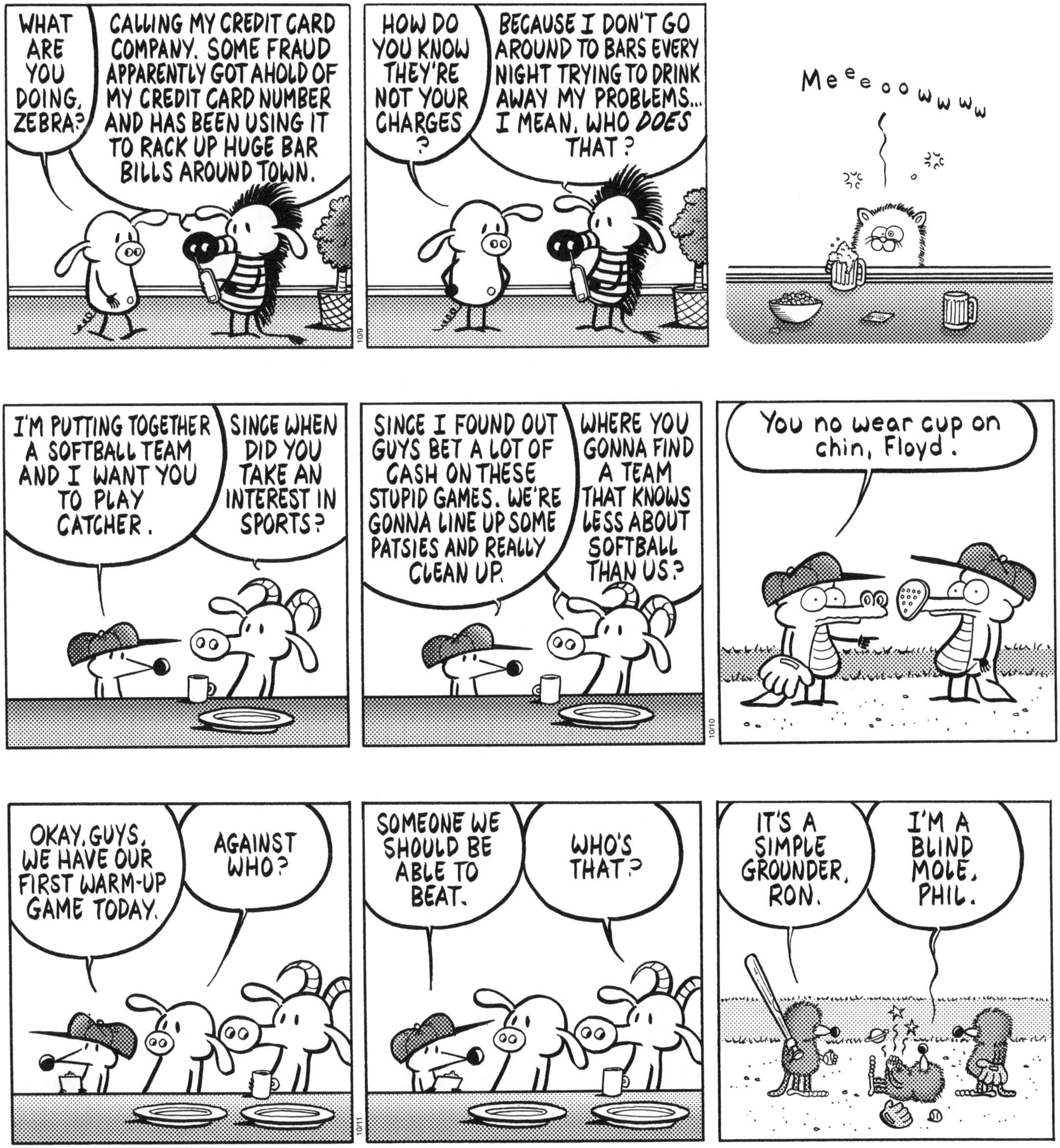
WHAT ARE YOU DOING, ZEBRA?
CALLING MY CREDIT CARD COMPANY. SOME FRAUD APPARENTLY GOT AHOLD OF MY CREDIT CARD NUMBER AND HAS BEEN USING IT TO RACK UP HUGE BAR BILLS AROUND TOWN.
HOW DO YOU KNOW THEY'RE NOT YOUR CHARGES?
BECAUSE I DON'T GO AROUND TO BARS EVERY NIGHT TRYING TO DRINK AWAY MY PROBLEMS... I MEAN, WHO *DOES* THAT?
Meeeoowwwww
10/9
I'M PUTTING TOGETHER A SOFTBALL TEAM AND I WANT YOU TO PLAY CATCHER.
SINCE WHEN DID YOU TAKE AN INTEREST IN SPORTS?
SINCE I FOUND OUT GUYS BET A LOT OF CASH ON THESE STUPID GAMES. WE'RE GONNA LINE UP SOME PATSIES AND REALLY CLEAN UP.
WHERE YOU GONNA FIND A TEAM THAT KNOWS LESS ABOUT SOFTBALL THAN US?
You no wear cup on chin, Floyd.
10/10
OKAY, GUYS, WE HAVE OUR FIRST WARM-UP GAME TODAY.
AGAINST WHO?
SOMEONE WE SHOULD BE ABLE TO BEAT.
WHO'S THAT?
IT'S A SIMPLE GROUNDER, RON.
I'M A BLIND MOLE, PHIL.
10/11

I SAW A DOCUMENTARY LAST NIGHT ON THESE NAVY GUYS WHO WORK ON SUBMARINES.

OH YEAH?

YEAH, IT WAS AMAZING. WHEN THE SUB SURFACED, THEY GOT OUT AND STOOD ON TOP OF IT.

WHY WAS THAT AMAZING?

BECAUSE THE POOR LITTLE SUB WAS ROCKING BACK AND FORTH AND THESE GUYS JUST STOOD ON TOP OF IT WITH THEIR HANDS BEHIND THEIR BACK, SO BALANCED, SO CONTROLLED.

10/12

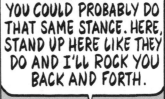

YOU COULD PROBABLY DO THAT SAME STANCE. HERE, STAND UP HERE LIKE THEY DO AND I'LL ROCK YOU BACK AND FORTH.

WELL, GEE, DO YOU REALLY THINK I COULD —

THERE YOU GO, PIG! YOU'RE DOING IT! YOU'RE DOING IT!

EXCUSE ME, BUT CAN I ASK WHAT'S GOING ON HERE?

HI, OFFICER! LOOK AT ME! I HAVE A CONTROLLED SUB STANCE!

※SIGH※

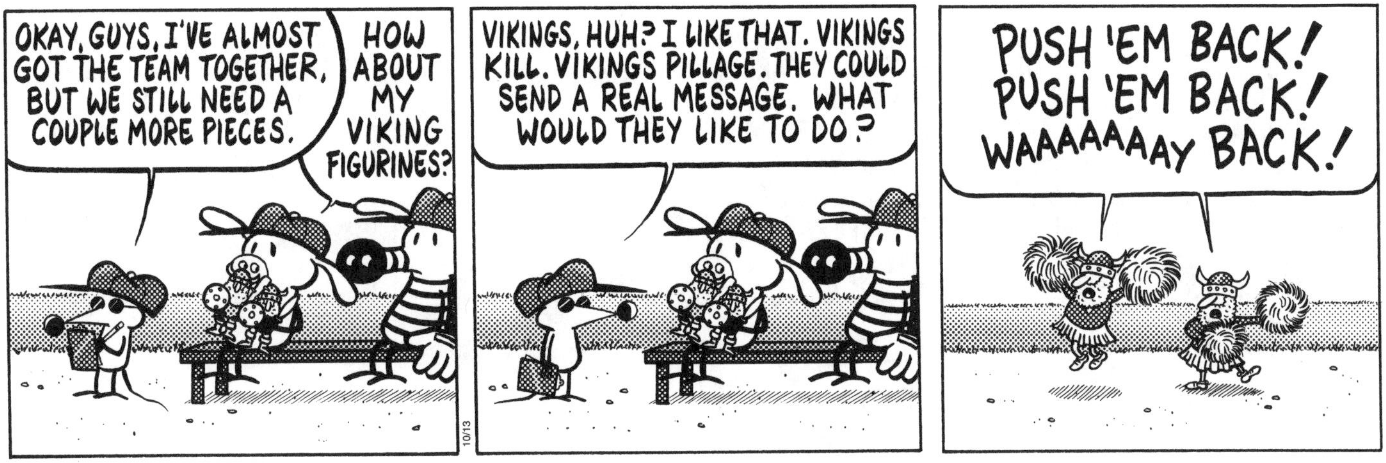
OKAY, GUYS, I'VE ALMOST GOT THE TEAM TOGETHER, BUT WE STILL NEED A COUPLE MORE PIECES.
HOW ABOUT MY VIKING FIGURINES?
10/13
VIKINGS, HUH? I LIKE THAT. VIKINGS KILL. VIKINGS PILLAGE. THEY COULD SEND A REAL MESSAGE. WHAT WOULD THEY LIKE TO DO?
PUSH 'EM BACK! PUSH 'EM BACK! WAAAAAAAY BACK!

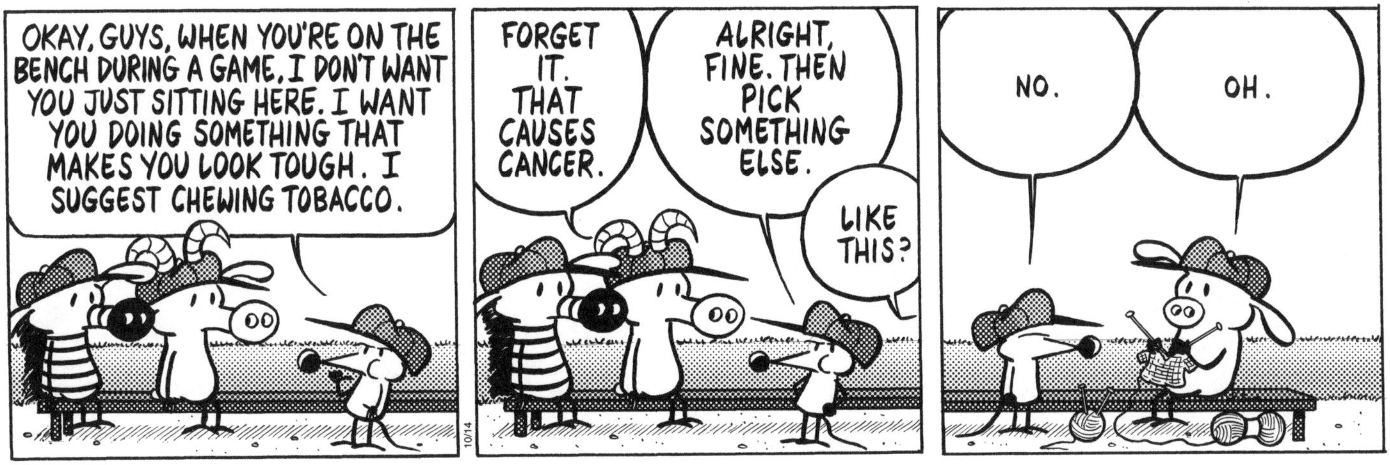
OKAY, GUYS, WHEN YOU'RE ON THE BENCH DURING A GAME, I DON'T WANT YOU JUST SITTING HERE. I WANT YOU DOING SOMETHING THAT MAKES YOU LOOK TOUGH. I SUGGEST CHEWING TOBACCO.
10/14
FORGET IT. THAT CAUSES CANCER.
ALRIGHT, FINE. THEN PICK SOMETHING ELSE.
LIKE THIS?
NO.
OH.

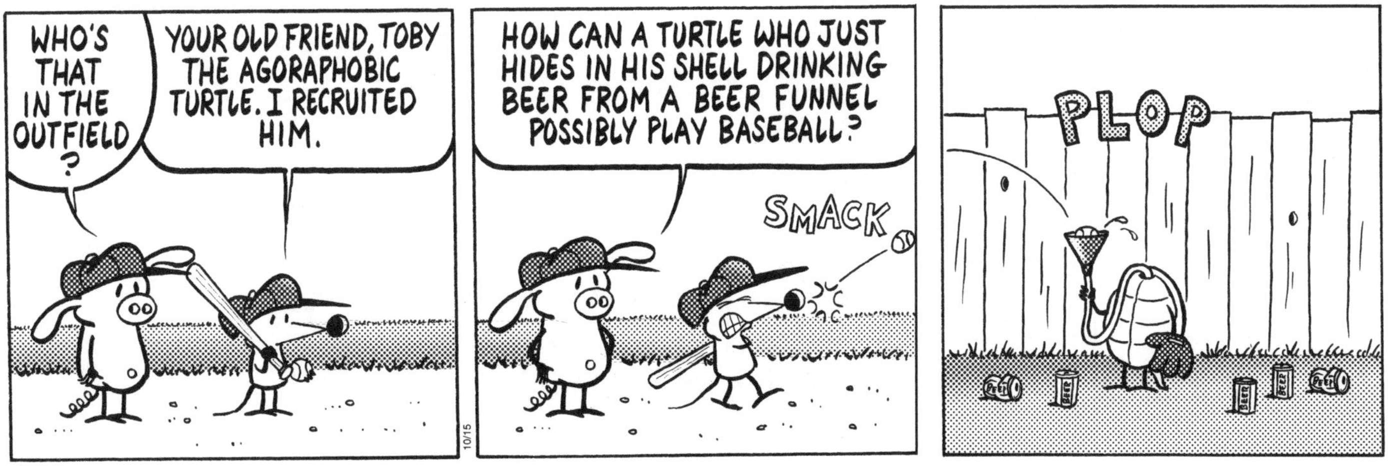
WHO'S THAT IN THE OUTFIELD?
YOUR OLD FRIEND, TOBY THE AGORAPHOBIC TURTLE. I RECRUITED HIM.
10/15
HOW CAN A TURTLE WHO JUST HIDES IN HIS SHELL DRINKING BEER FROM A BEER FUNNEL POSSIBLY PLAY BASEBALL?
SMACK
PLOP

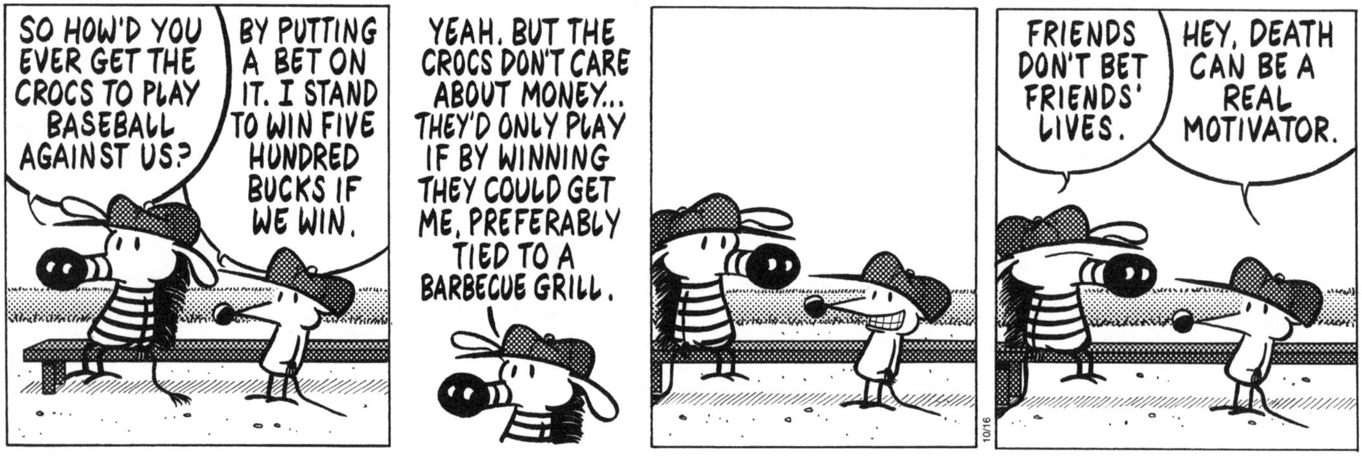
SO HOW'D YOU EVER GET THE CROCS TO PLAY BASEBALL AGAINST US?
BY PUTTING A BET ON IT. I STAND TO WIN FIVE HUNDRED BUCKS IF WE WIN.
YEAH. BUT THE CROCS DON'T CARE ABOUT MONEY... THEY'D ONLY PLAY IF BY WINNING THEY COULD GET ME, PREFERABLY TIED TO A BARBECUE GRILL.
FRIENDS DON'T BET FRIENDS' LIVES.
HEY, DEATH CAN BE A REAL MOTIVATOR.
10/16

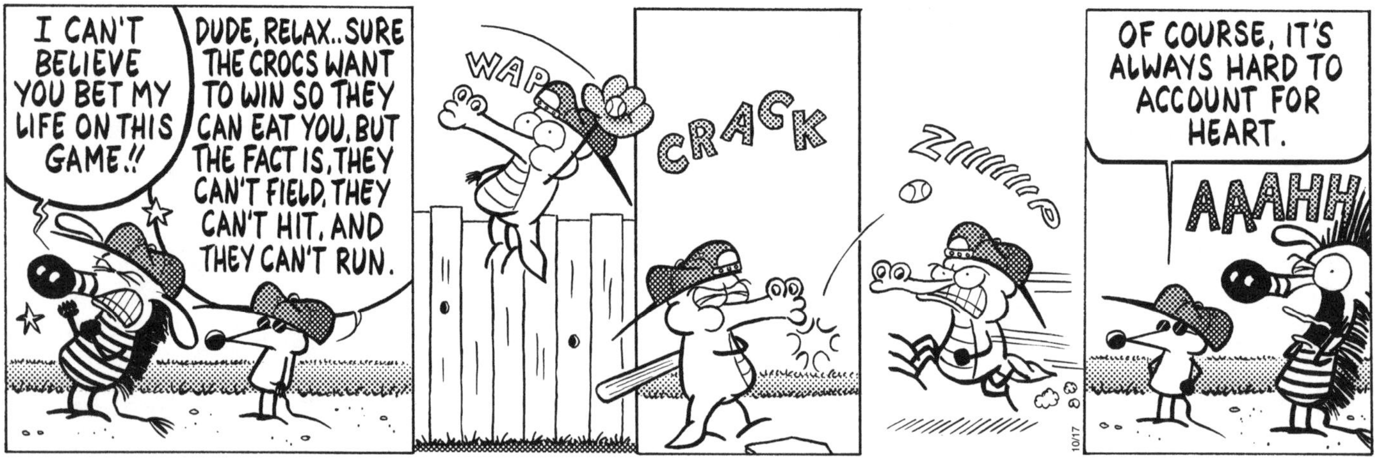
I CAN'T BELIEVE YOU BET MY LIFE ON THIS GAME!!
DUDE, RELAX..SURE THE CROCS WANT TO WIN SO THEY CAN EAT YOU, BUT THE FACT IS, THEY CAN'T FIELD, THEY CAN'T HIT, AND THEY CAN'T RUN.
WAP
CRACK
ZIIIIIIP
10/17
OF COURSE, IT'S ALWAYS HARD TO ACCOUNT FOR HEART.
AAAHH

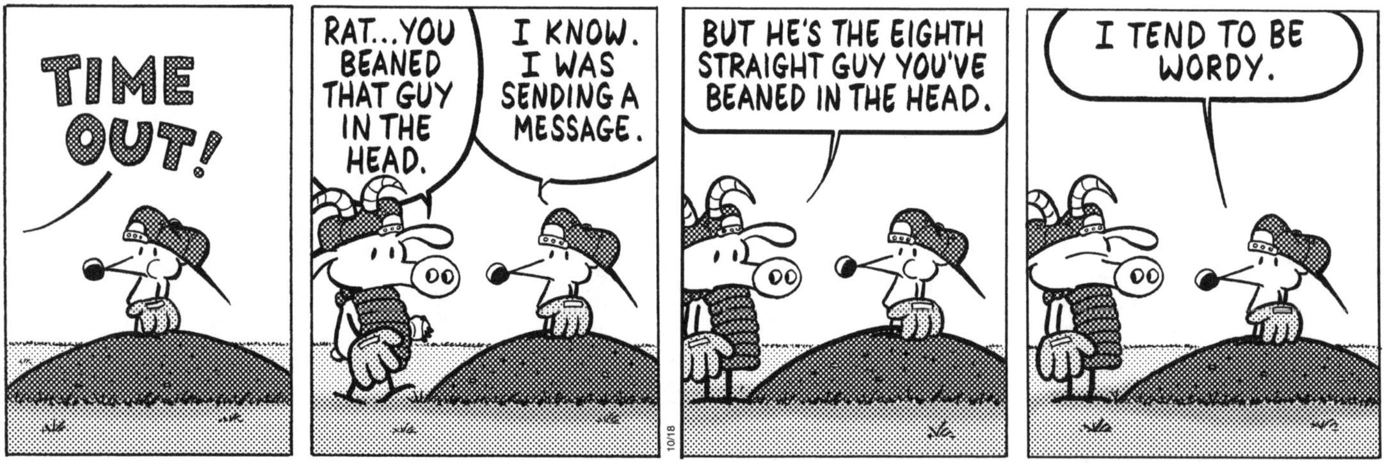
TIME OUT!
RAT...YOU BEANED THAT GUY IN THE HEAD.
I KNOW. I WAS SENDING A MESSAGE.
10/18
BUT HE'S THE EIGHTH STRAIGHT GUY YOU'VE BEANED IN THE HEAD.
I TEND TO BE WORDY.

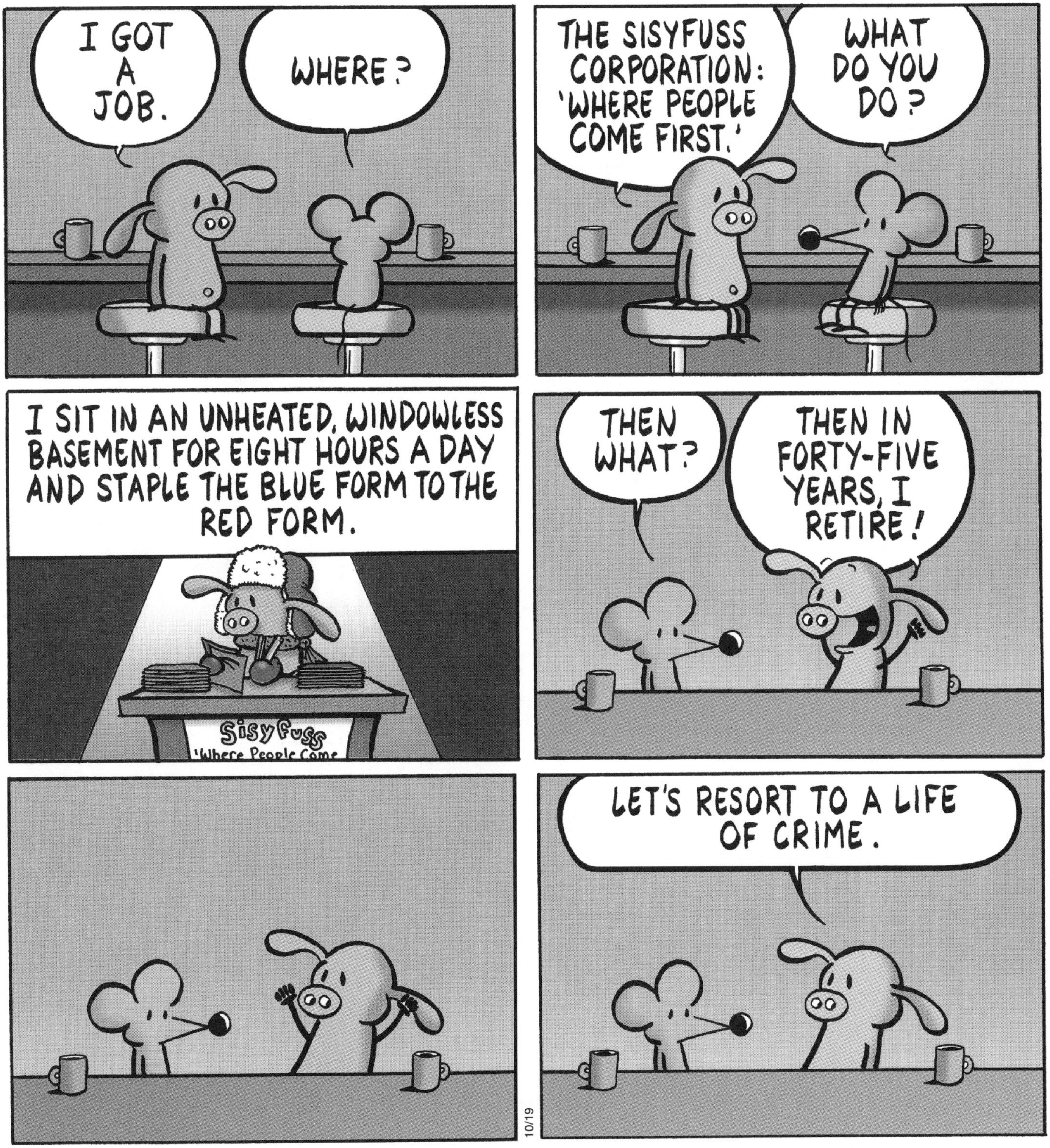
I GOT A JOB.
WHERE?
THE SISYFUSS CORPORATION: 'WHERE PEOPLE COME FIRST.'
WHAT DO YOU DO?
I SIT IN AN UNHEATED, WINDOWLESS BASEMENT FOR EIGHT HOURS A DAY AND STAPLE THE BLUE FORM TO THE RED FORM.
Sisyfuss
'Where People Come
THEN WHAT?
THEN IN FORTY-FIVE YEARS, I RETIRE!
LET'S RESORT TO A LIFE OF CRIME.
10/19

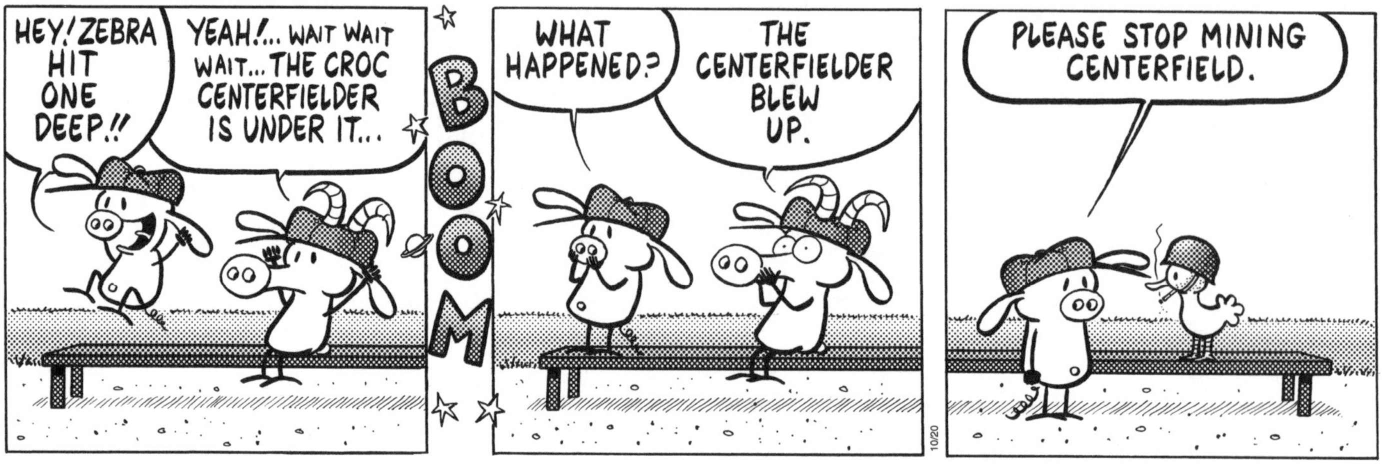
HEY! ZEBRA HIT ONE DEEP!!
YEAH!... WAIT WAIT WAIT... THE CROC CENTERFIELDER IS UNDER IT...
BOOM
WHAT HAPPENED?
THE CENTERFIELDER BLEW UP.
PLEASE STOP MINING CENTERFIELD.
10/20

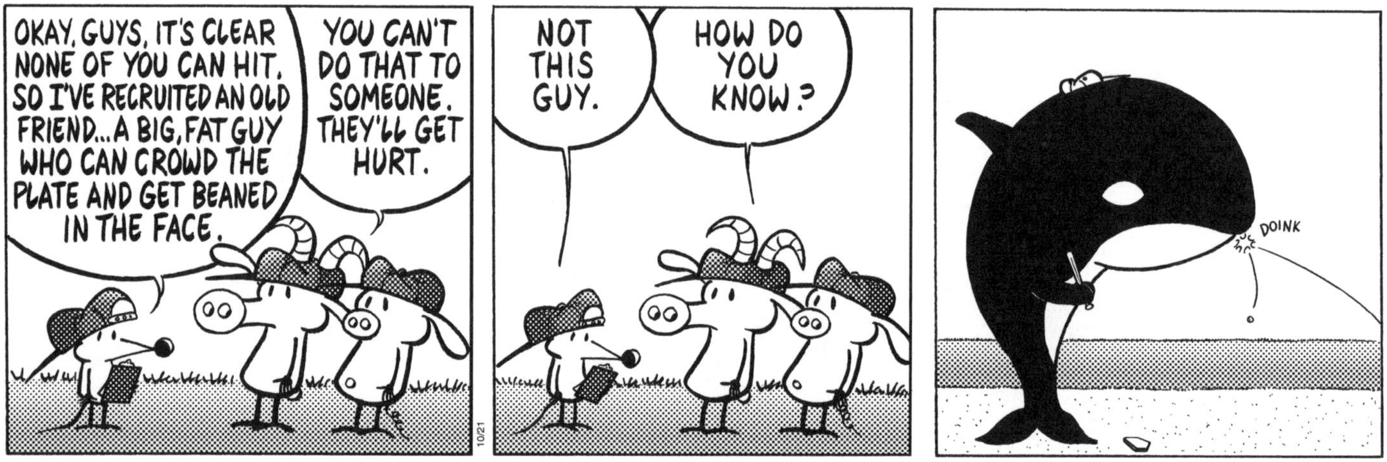
OKAY, GUYS, IT'S CLEAR NONE OF YOU CAN HIT, SO I'VE RECRUITED AN OLD FRIEND... A BIG, FAT GUY WHO CAN CROWD THE PLATE AND GET BEANED IN THE FACE.
YOU CAN'T DO THAT TO SOMEONE. THEY'LL GET HURT.
10/21
NOT THIS GUY.
HOW DO YOU KNOW?
DOINK

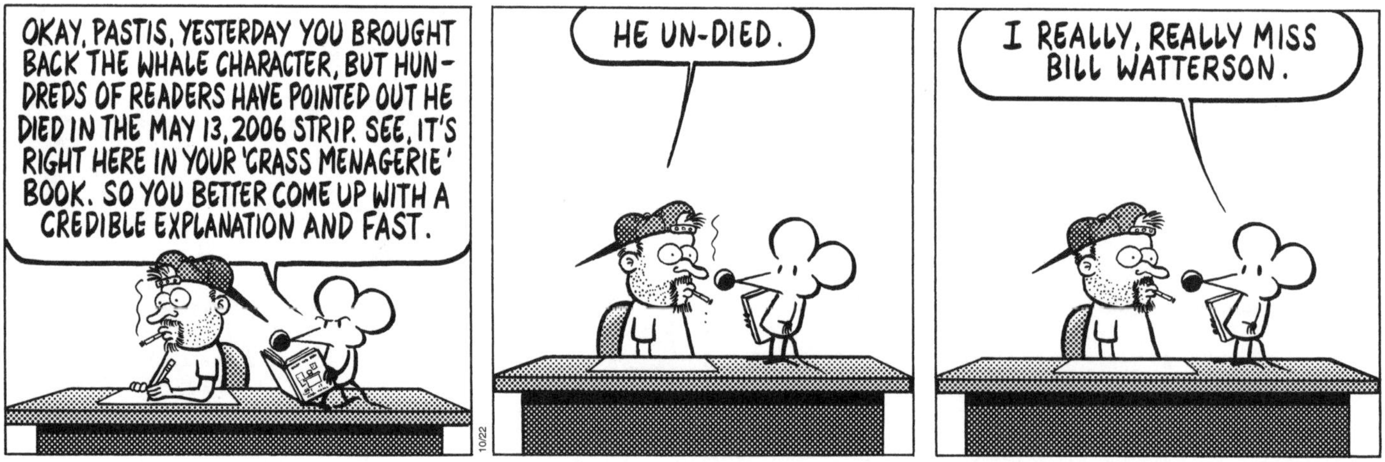
OKAY, PASTIS, YESTERDAY YOU BROUGHT BACK THE WHALE CHARACTER, BUT HUNDREDS OF READERS HAVE POINTED OUT HE DIED IN THE MAY 13, 2006 STRIP. SEE, IT'S RIGHT HERE IN YOUR 'CRASS MENAGERIE' BOOK. SO YOU BETTER COME UP WITH A CREDIBLE EXPLANATION AND FAST.
10/22
HE UN-DIED.
I REALLY, REALLY MISS BILL WATTERSON.

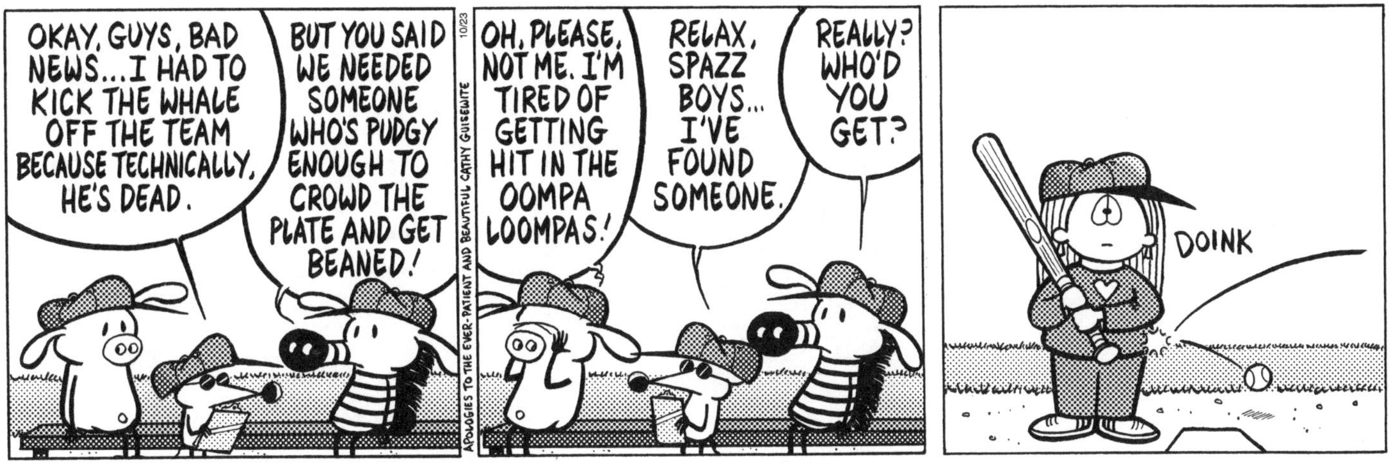
OKAY, GUYS, BAD NEWS...I HAD TO KICK THE WHALE OFF THE TEAM BECAUSE TECHNICALLY, HE'S DEAD.
BUT YOU SAID WE NEEDED SOMEONE WHO'S PUDGY ENOUGH TO CROWD THE PLATE AND GET BEANED!
10/23
APOLOGIES TO THE EVER-PATIENT AND BEAUTIFUL CATHY GUISEWITE
OH, PLEASE, NOT ME. I'M TIRED OF GETTING HIT IN THE OOMPA LOOMPAS!
RELAX, SPAZZ BOYS... I'VE FOUND SOMEONE.
REALLY? WHO'D YOU GET?
DOINK

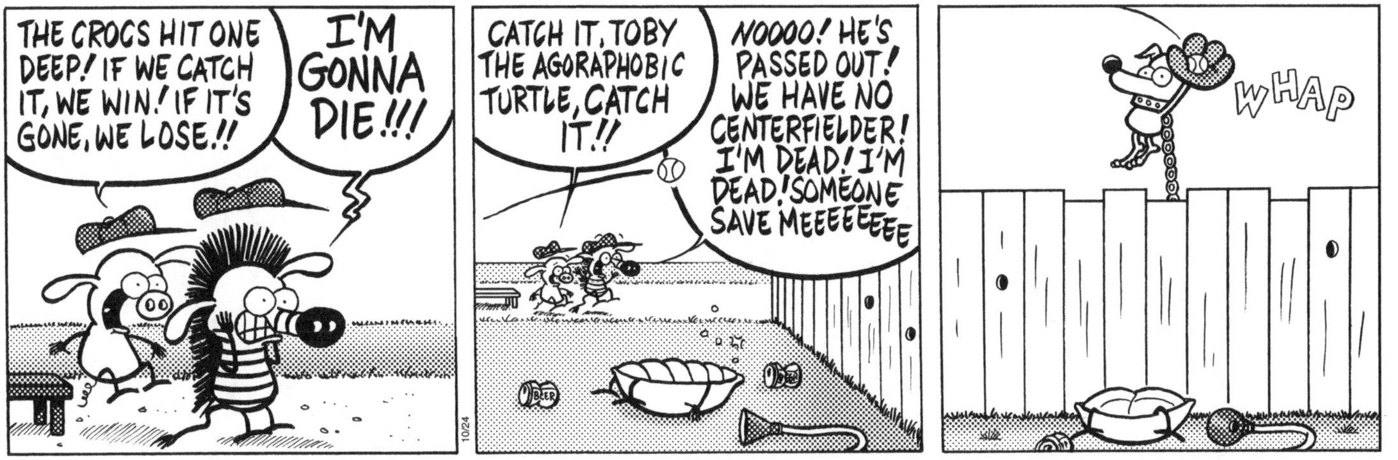
THE CROCS HIT ONE DEEP! IF WE CATCH IT, WE WIN! IF IT'S GONE, WE LOSE!!
I'M GONNA DIE!!!
10/24
CATCH IT, TOBY THE AGORAPHOBIC TURTLE, CATCH IT!!
NOOOO! HE'S PASSED OUT! WE HAVE NO CENTERFIELDER! I'M DEAD! I'M DEAD! SOMEONE SAVE MEEEEEEEEE
BEER
WHAP

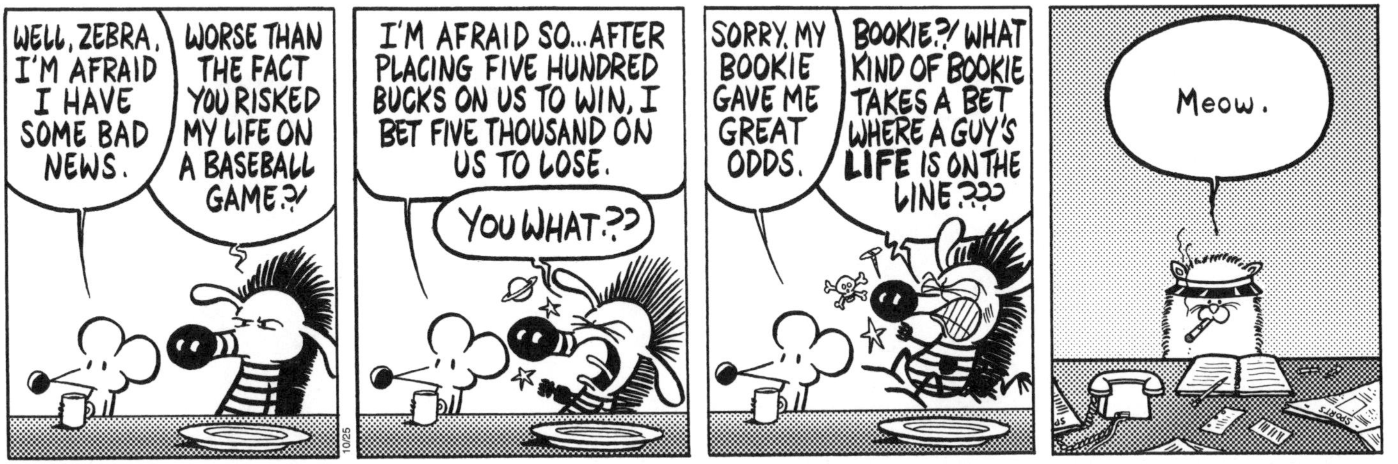
WELL, ZEBRA, I'M AFRAID I HAVE SOME BAD NEWS.
WORSE THAN THE FACT YOU RISKED MY LIFE ON A BASEBALL GAME?!
10/25
I'M AFRAID SO...AFTER PLACING FIVE HUNDRED BUCKS ON US TO WIN, I BET FIVE THOUSAND ON US TO LOSE.
YOU WHAT??
SORRY, MY BOOKIE GAVE ME GREAT ODDS.
BOOKIE?! WHAT KIND OF BOOKIE TAKES A BET WHERE A GUY'S LIFE IS ON THE LINE???
Meow.

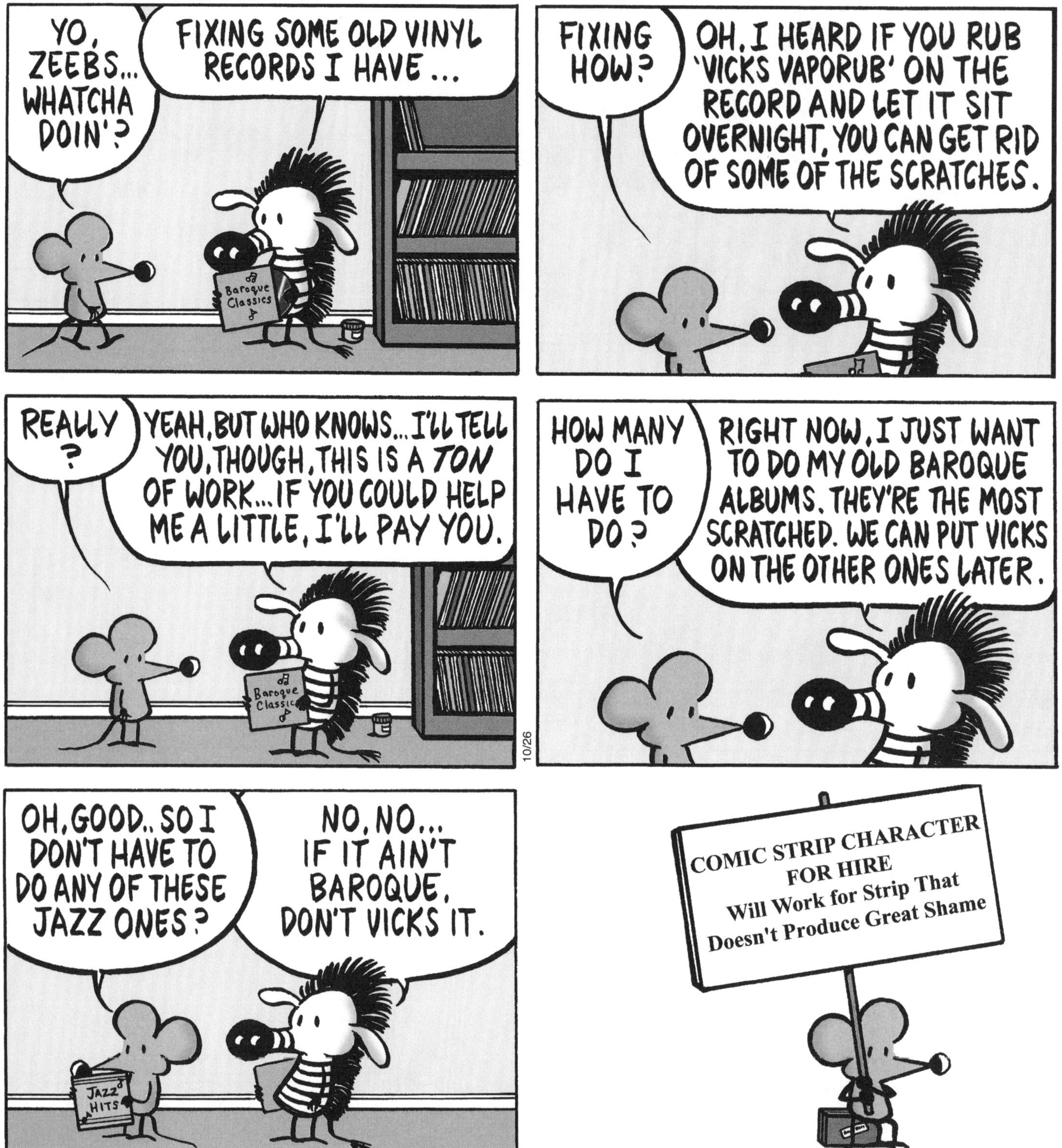
YO, ZEEBS... WHATCHA DOIN'?
FIXING SOME OLD VINYL RECORDS I HAVE...
Baroque Classics
FIXING HOW?
OH, I HEARD IF YOU RUB 'VICKS VAPORUB' ON THE RECORD AND LET IT SIT OVERNIGHT, YOU CAN GET RID OF SOME OF THE SCRATCHES.
REALLY?
YEAH, BUT WHO KNOWS... I'LL TELL YOU, THOUGH, THIS IS A *TON* OF WORK... IF YOU COULD HELP ME A LITTLE, I'LL PAY YOU.
Baroque Classic
10/26
HOW MANY DO I HAVE TO DO?
RIGHT NOW, I JUST WANT TO DO MY OLD BAROQUE ALBUMS. THEY'RE THE MOST SCRATCHED. WE CAN PUT VICKS ON THE OTHER ONES LATER.
OH, GOOD.. SO I DON'T HAVE TO DO ANY OF THESE JAZZ ONES?
NO, NO... IF IT AIN'T BAROQUE, DON'T VICKS IT.
JAZZ HITS
COMIC STRIP CHARACTER FOR HIRE
Will Work for Strip That Doesn't Produce Great Shame

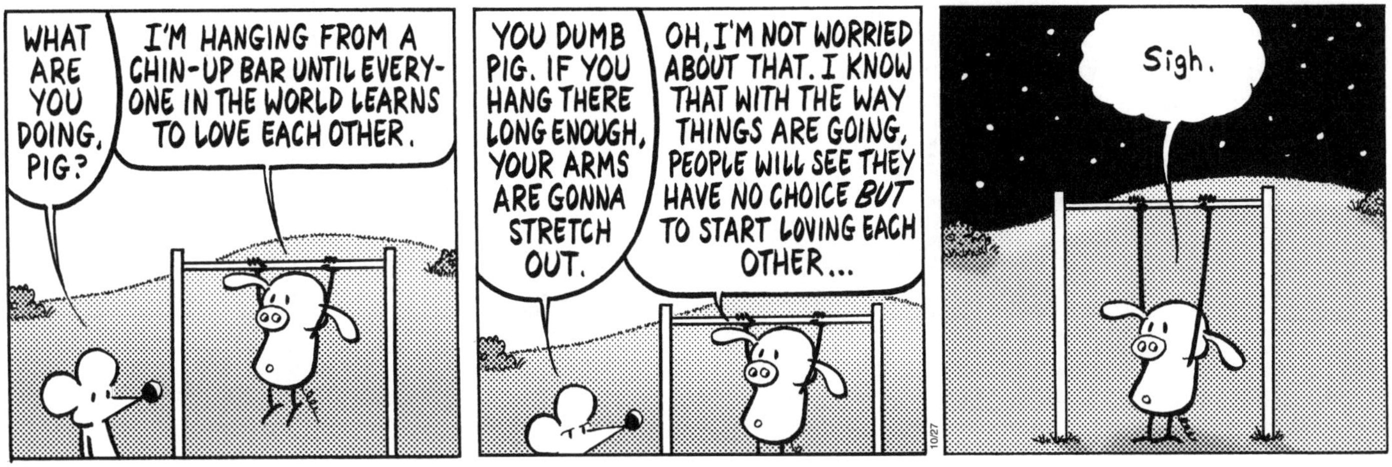
WHAT ARE YOU DOING, PIG?
I'M HANGING FROM A CHIN-UP BAR UNTIL EVERYONE IN THE WORLD LEARNS TO LOVE EACH OTHER.
YOU DUMB PIG. IF YOU HANG THERE LONG ENOUGH, YOUR ARMS ARE GONNA STRETCH OUT.
OH, I'M NOT WORRIED ABOUT THAT. I KNOW THAT WITH THE WAY THINGS ARE GOING, PEOPLE WILL SEE THEY HAVE NO CHOICE *BUT* TO START LOVING EACH OTHER...
10/27
Sigh.

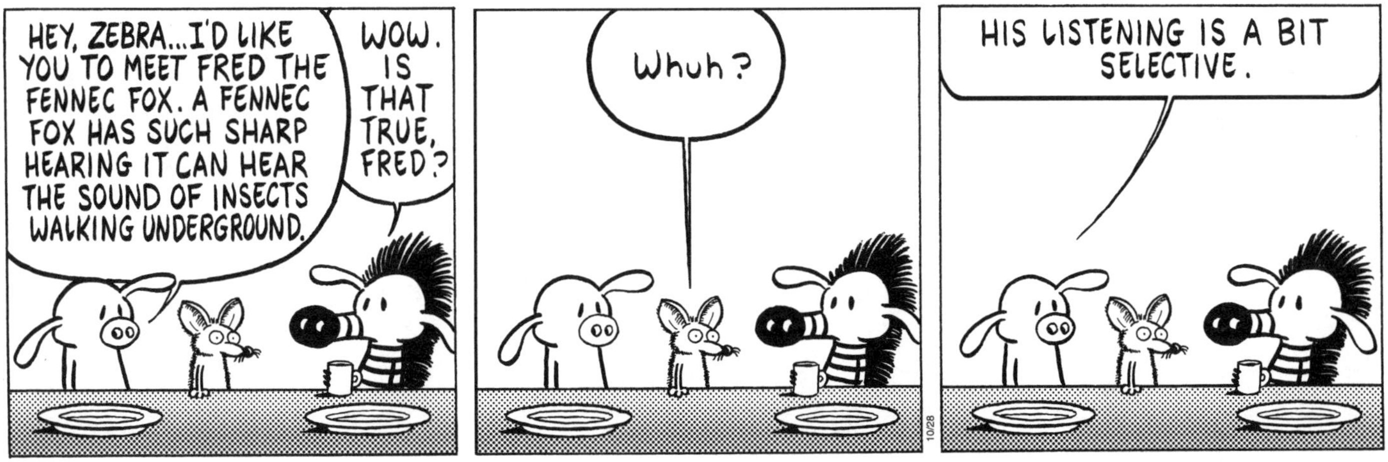
HEY, ZEBRA...I'D LIKE YOU TO MEET FRED THE FENNEC FOX. A FENNEC FOX HAS SUCH SHARP HEARING IT CAN HEAR THE SOUND OF INSECTS WALKING UNDERGROUND.
WOW. IS THAT TRUE, FRED?
Whuh?
10/28
HIS LISTENING IS A BIT SELECTIVE.

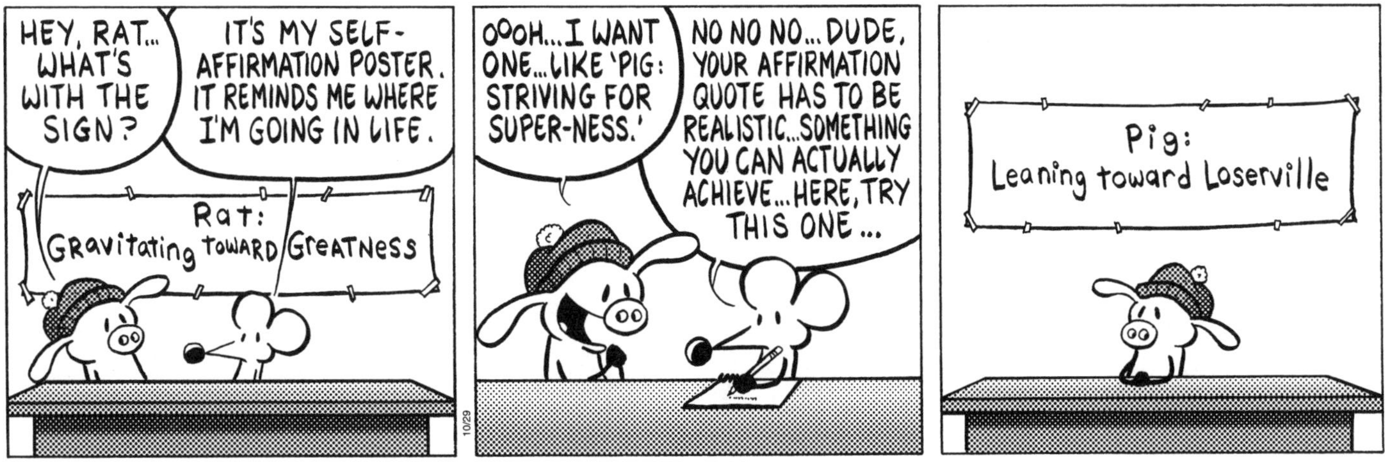
HEY, RAT... WHAT'S WITH THE SIGN?
IT'S MY SELF-AFFIRMATION POSTER. IT REMINDS ME WHERE I'M GOING IN LIFE.
Rat:
Gravitating toward Greatness
10/29
OOOH...I WANT ONE...LIKE 'PIG: STRIVING FOR SUPER-NESS.'
NO NO NO...DUDE, YOUR AFFIRMATION QUOTE HAS TO BE REALISTIC...SOMETHING YOU CAN ACTUALLY ACHIEVE...HERE, TRY THIS ONE...
Pig:
Leaning toward Loserville

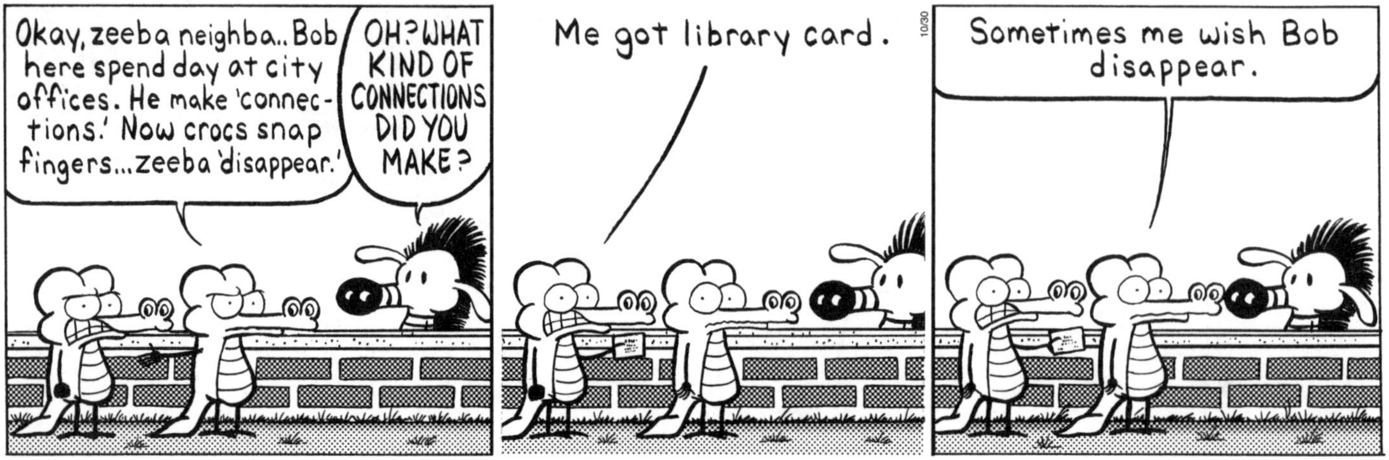
Okay, zeeba neighba.. Bob here spend day at city offices. He make 'connections.' Now crocs snap fingers...zeeba 'disappear.'
OH? WHAT KIND OF CONNECTIONS DID YOU MAKE?
Me got library card.
Sometimes me wish Bob disappear.
10/30

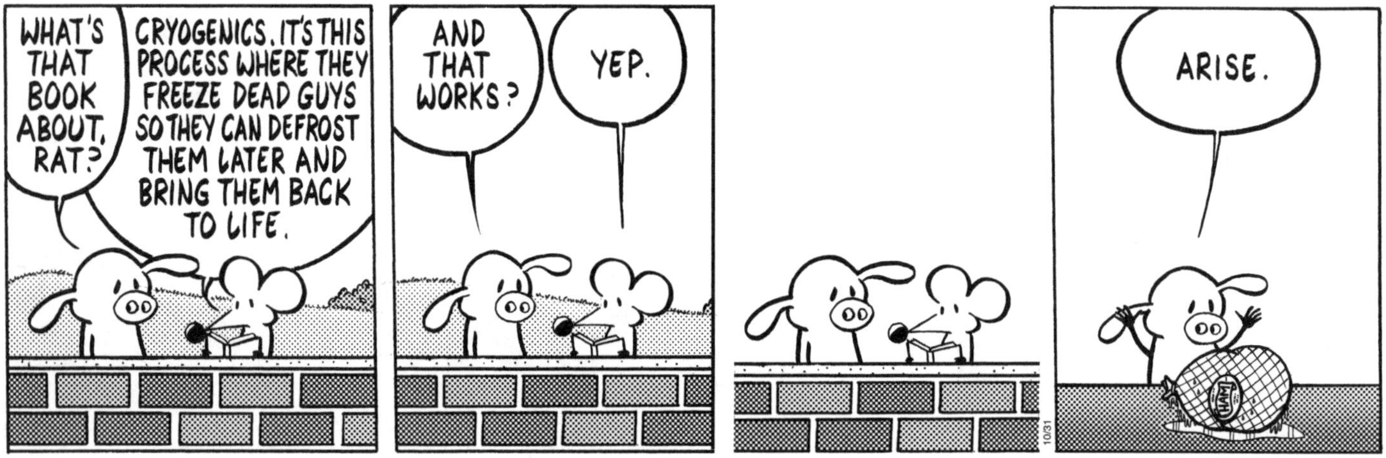
WHAT'S THAT BOOK ABOUT, RAT?
CRYOGENICS. IT'S THIS PROCESS WHERE THEY FREEZE DEAD GUYS SO THEY CAN DEFROST THEM LATER AND BRING THEM BACK TO LIFE.
AND THAT WORKS?
YEP.
10/31
ARISE.
HAM

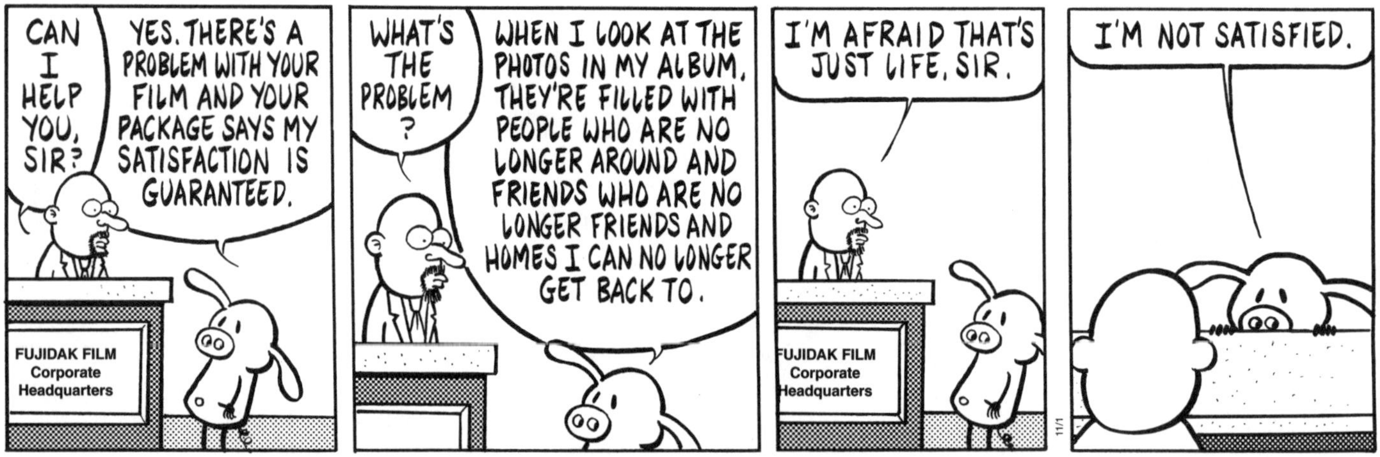
CAN I HELP YOU, SIR?
YES. THERE'S A PROBLEM WITH YOUR FILM AND YOUR PACKAGE SAYS MY SATISFACTION IS GUARANTEED.
FUJIDAK FILM
Corporate
Headquarters
WHAT'S THE PROBLEM?
WHEN I LOOK AT THE PHOTOS IN MY ALBUM, THEY'RE FILLED WITH PEOPLE WHO ARE NO LONGER AROUND AND FRIENDS WHO ARE NO LONGER FRIENDS AND HOMES I CAN NO LONGER GET BACK TO.
I'M AFRAID THAT'S JUST LIFE, SIR.
FUJIDAK FILM
Corporate
Headquarters
11/1
I'M NOT SATISFIED.

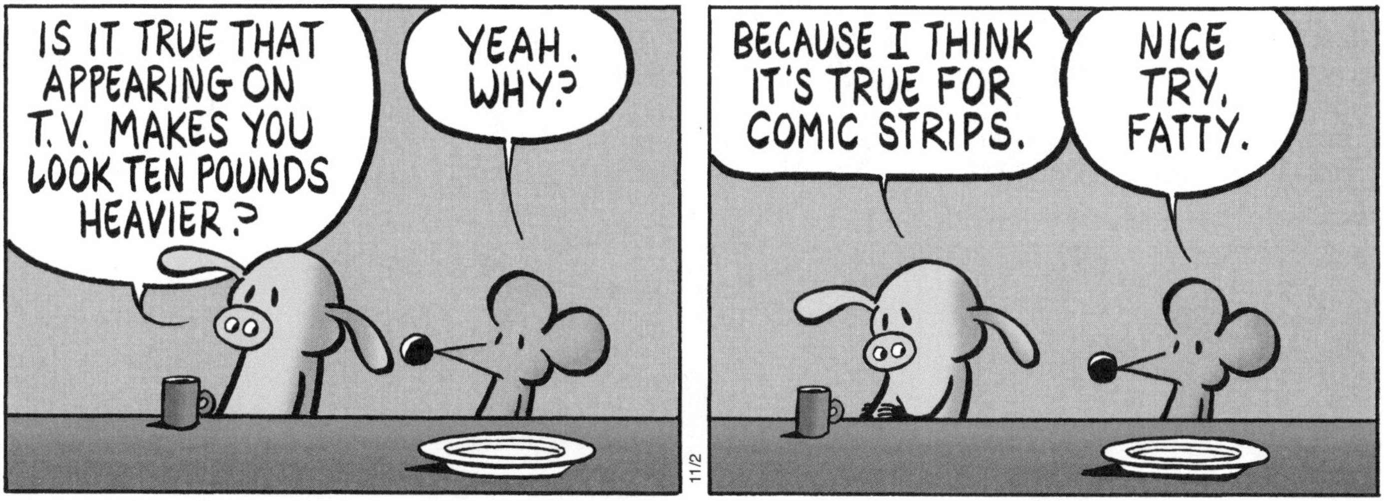

IS IT TRUE THAT APPEARING ON T.V. MAKES YOU LOOK TEN POUNDS HEAVIER?
YEAH. WHY?
BECAUSE I THINK IT'S TRUE FOR COMIC STRIPS.
NICE TRY, FATTY.
11/2

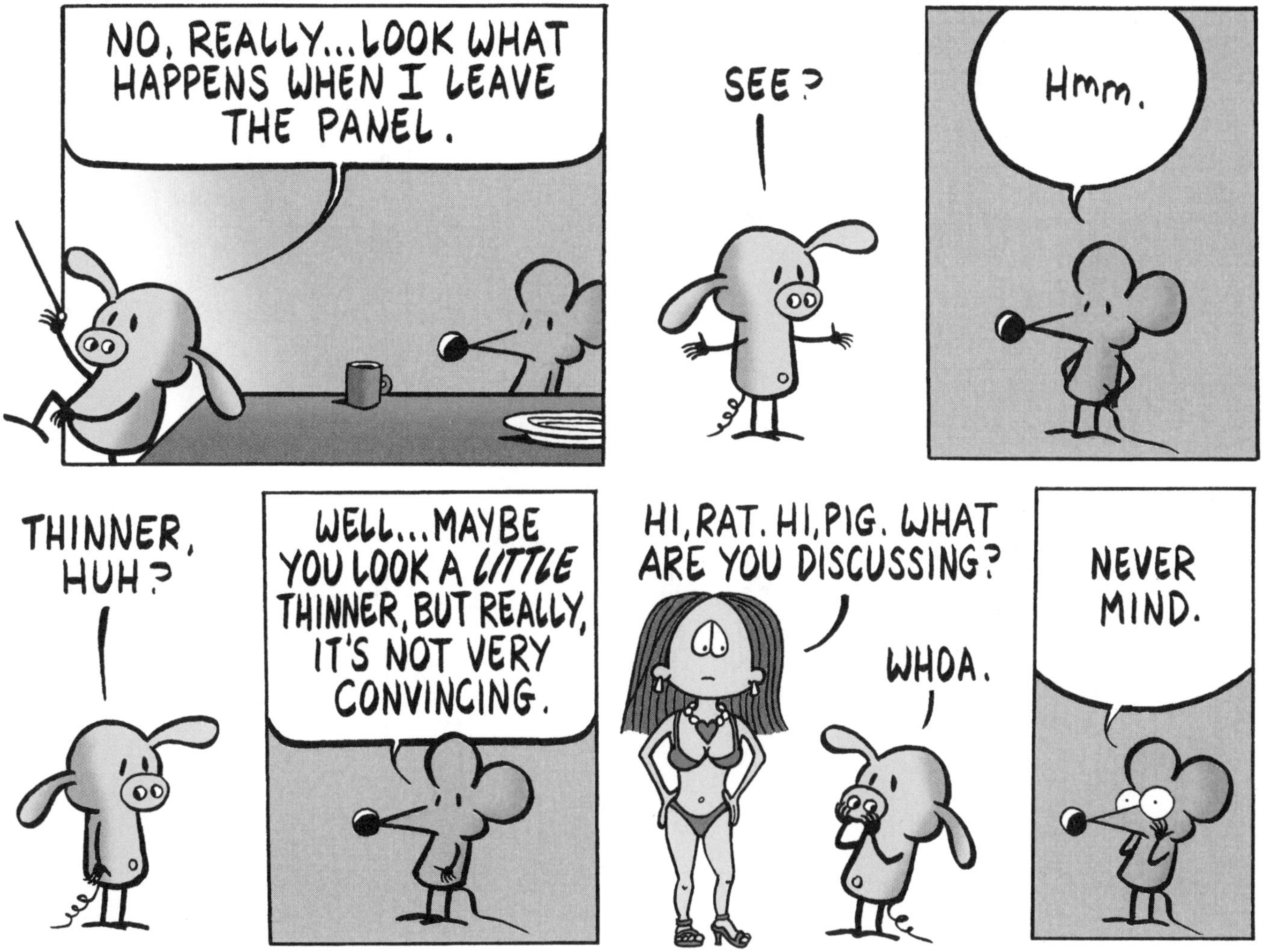

NO, REALLY... LOOK WHAT HAPPENS WHEN I LEAVE THE PANEL.
SEE?
Hmm.
THINNER, HUH?
WELL... MAYBE YOU LOOK A *LITTLE* THINNER, BUT REALLY, IT'S NOT VERY CONVINCING.
HI, RAT. HI, PIG. WHAT ARE YOU DISCUSSING?
WHOA.
NEVER MIND.

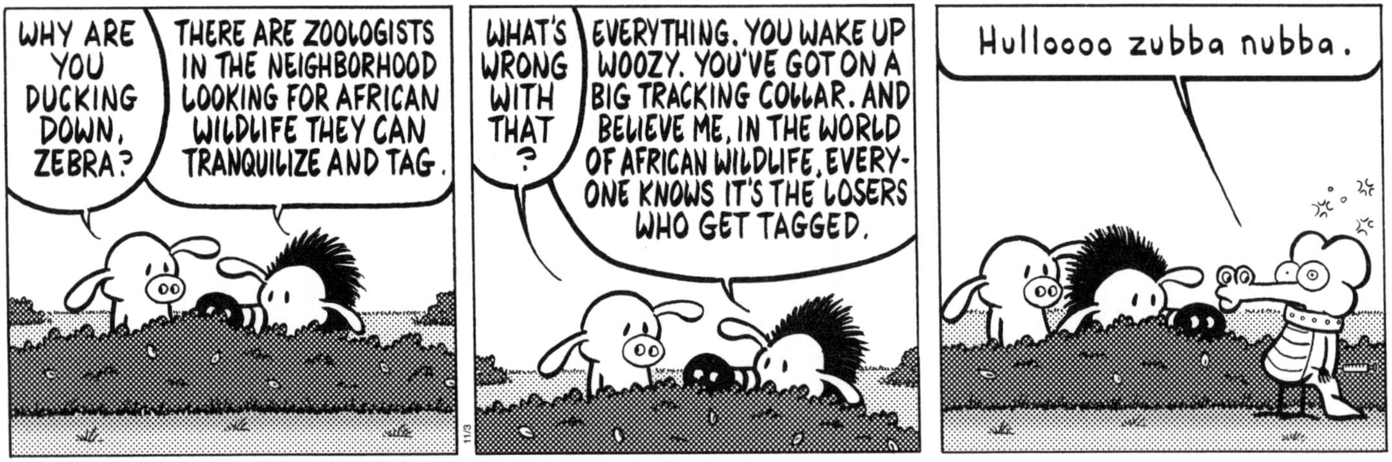
WHY ARE YOU DUCKING DOWN, ZEBRA?
THERE ARE ZOOLOGISTS IN THE NEIGHBORHOOD LOOKING FOR AFRICAN WILDLIFE THEY CAN TRANQUILIZE AND TAG.
WHAT'S WRONG WITH THAT?
EVERYTHING. YOU WAKE UP WOOZY. YOU'VE GOT ON A BIG TRACKING COLLAR. AND BELIEVE ME, IN THE WORLD OF AFRICAN WILDLIFE, EVERYONE KNOWS IT'S THE LOSERS WHO GET TAGGED.
Hulloooo zubba nubba.
11/3

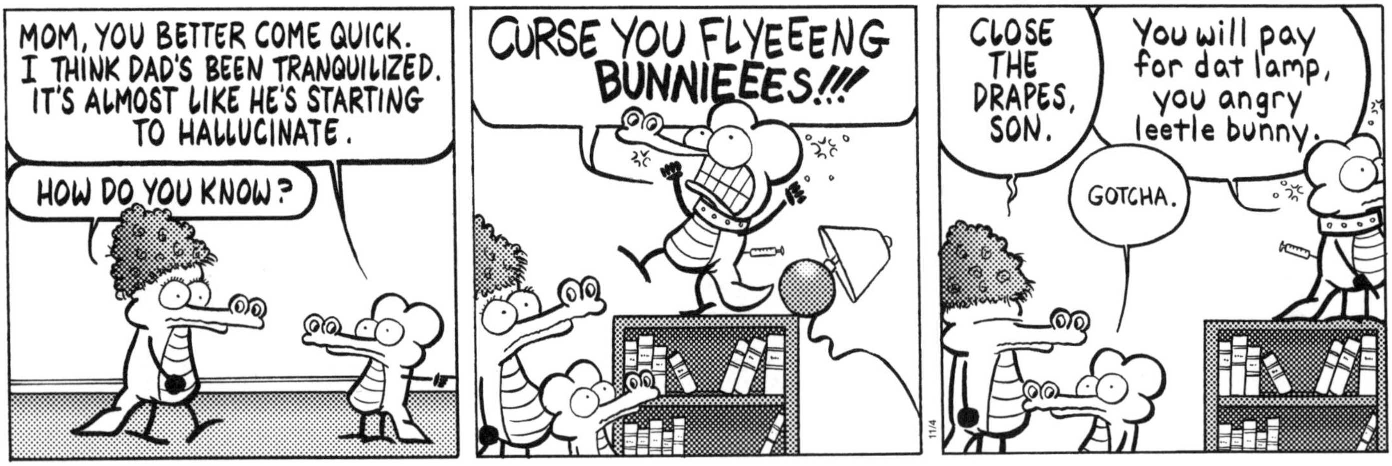
MOM, YOU BETTER COME QUICK. I THINK DAD'S BEEN TRANQUILIZED. IT'S ALMOST LIKE HE'S STARTING TO HALLUCINATE.
HOW DO YOU KNOW?
CURSE YOU FLYEEENG BUNNIEEES!!!
CLOSE THE DRAPES, SON.
You will pay for dat lamp, you angry leetle bunny.
GOTCHA.
11/4

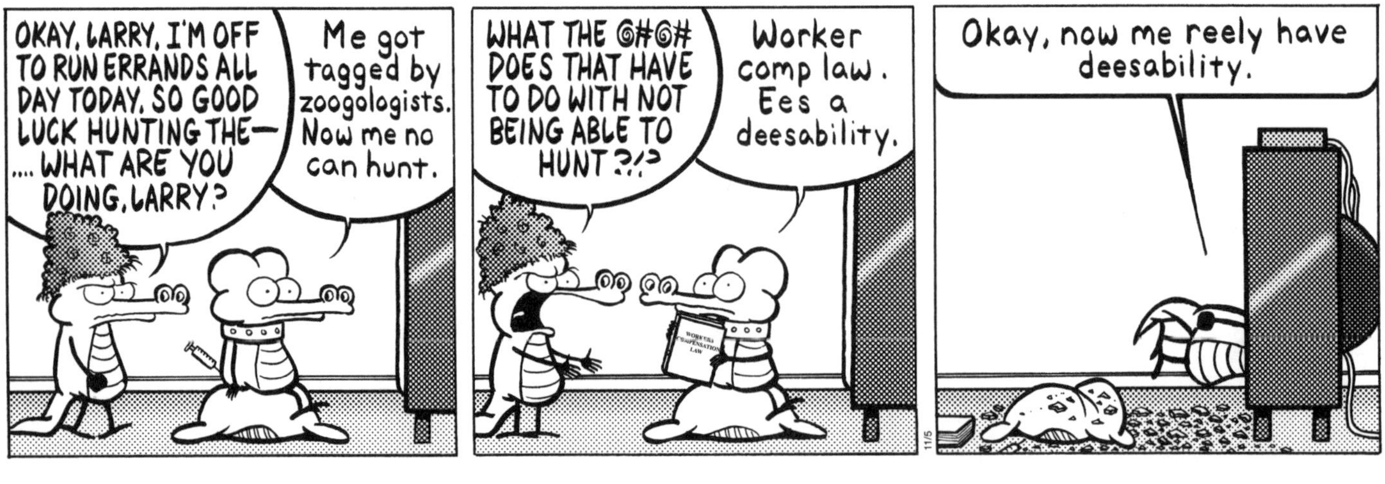
OKAY, LARRY, I'M OFF TO RUN ERRANDS ALL DAY TODAY, SO GOOD LUCK HUNTING THE— .... WHAT ARE YOU DOING, LARRY?
Me got tagged by zoogologists. Now me no can hunt.
WHAT THE @#@# DOES THAT HAVE TO DO WITH NOT BEING ABLE TO HUNT?!?
Worker comp law. Ees a deesability.
Okay, now me reely have deesability.
11/5

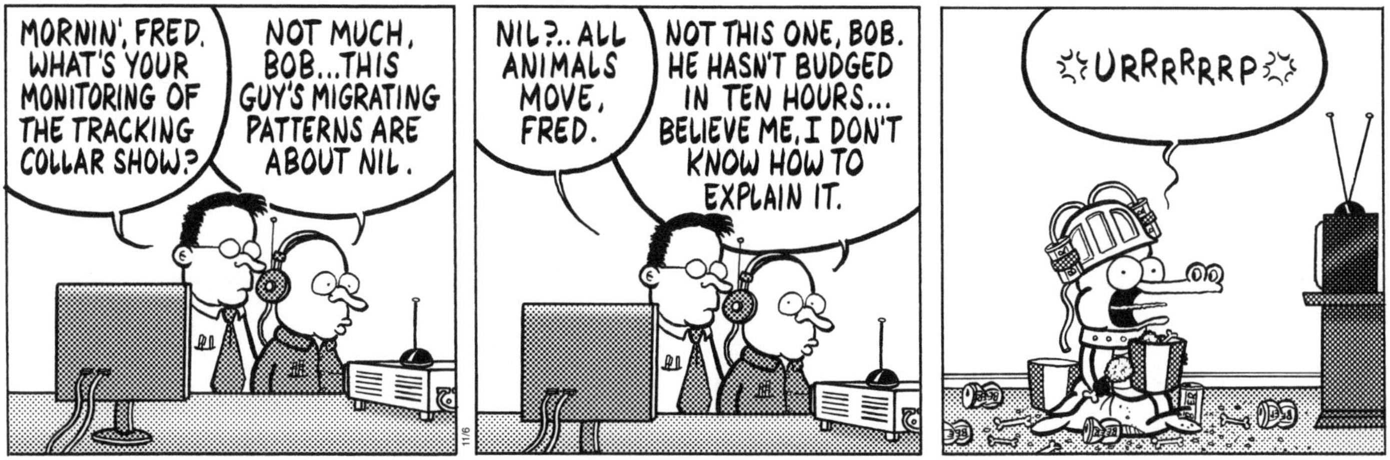
MORNIN', FRED. WHAT'S YOUR MONITORING OF THE TRACKING COLLAR SHOW?
NOT MUCH, BOB...THIS GUY'S MIGRATING PATTERNS ARE ABOUT NIL.
NIL?.. ALL ANIMALS MOVE, FRED.
NOT THIS ONE, BOB. HE HASN'T BUDGED IN TEN HOURS... BELIEVE ME, I DON'T KNOW HOW TO EXPLAIN IT.
URRRRRRP
11/6

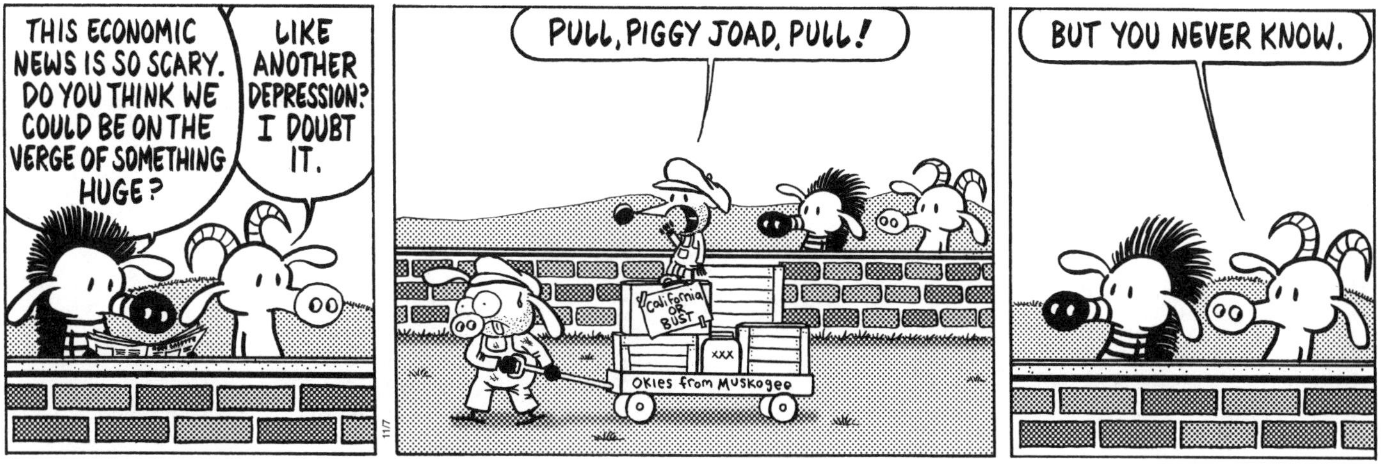
THIS ECONOMIC NEWS IS SO SCARY. DO YOU THINK WE COULD BE ON THE VERGE OF SOMETHING HUGE?
LIKE ANOTHER DEPRESSION? I DOUBT IT.
PULL, PIGGY JOAD, PULL!
California OR BUST
XXX
Okies from Muskogee
BUT YOU NEVER KNOW.
11/7

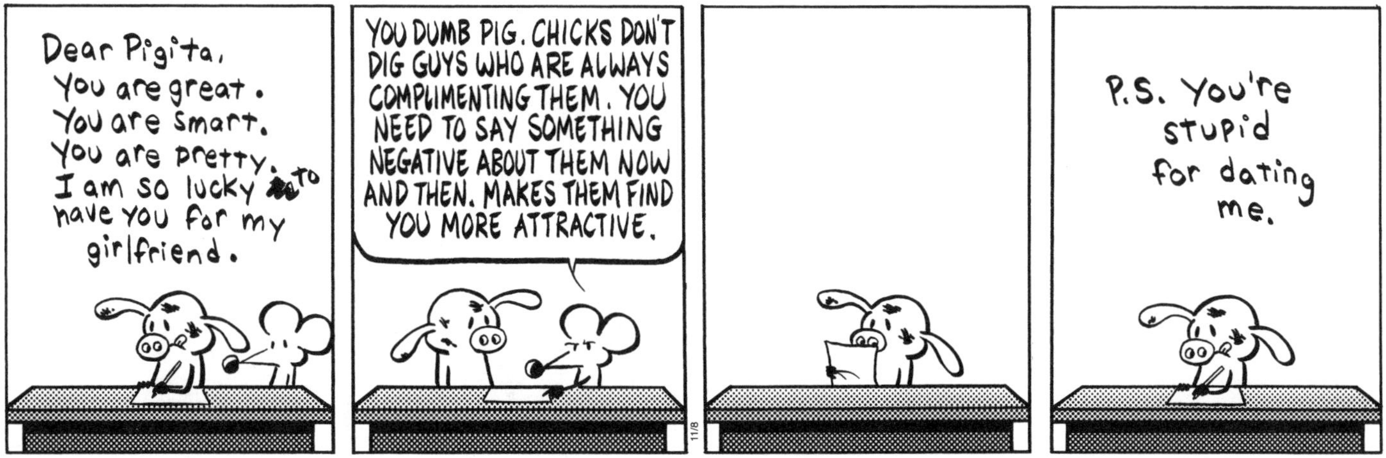
Dear Pigita,
You are great.
You are smart.
You are pretty.
I am so lucky to have you for my girlfriend.
YOU DUMB PIG. CHICKS DON'T DIG GUYS WHO ARE ALWAYS COMPLIMENTING THEM. YOU NEED TO SAY SOMETHING NEGATIVE ABOUT THEM NOW AND THEN. MAKES THEM FIND YOU MORE ATTRACTIVE.
P.S. You're stupid for dating me.
11/8

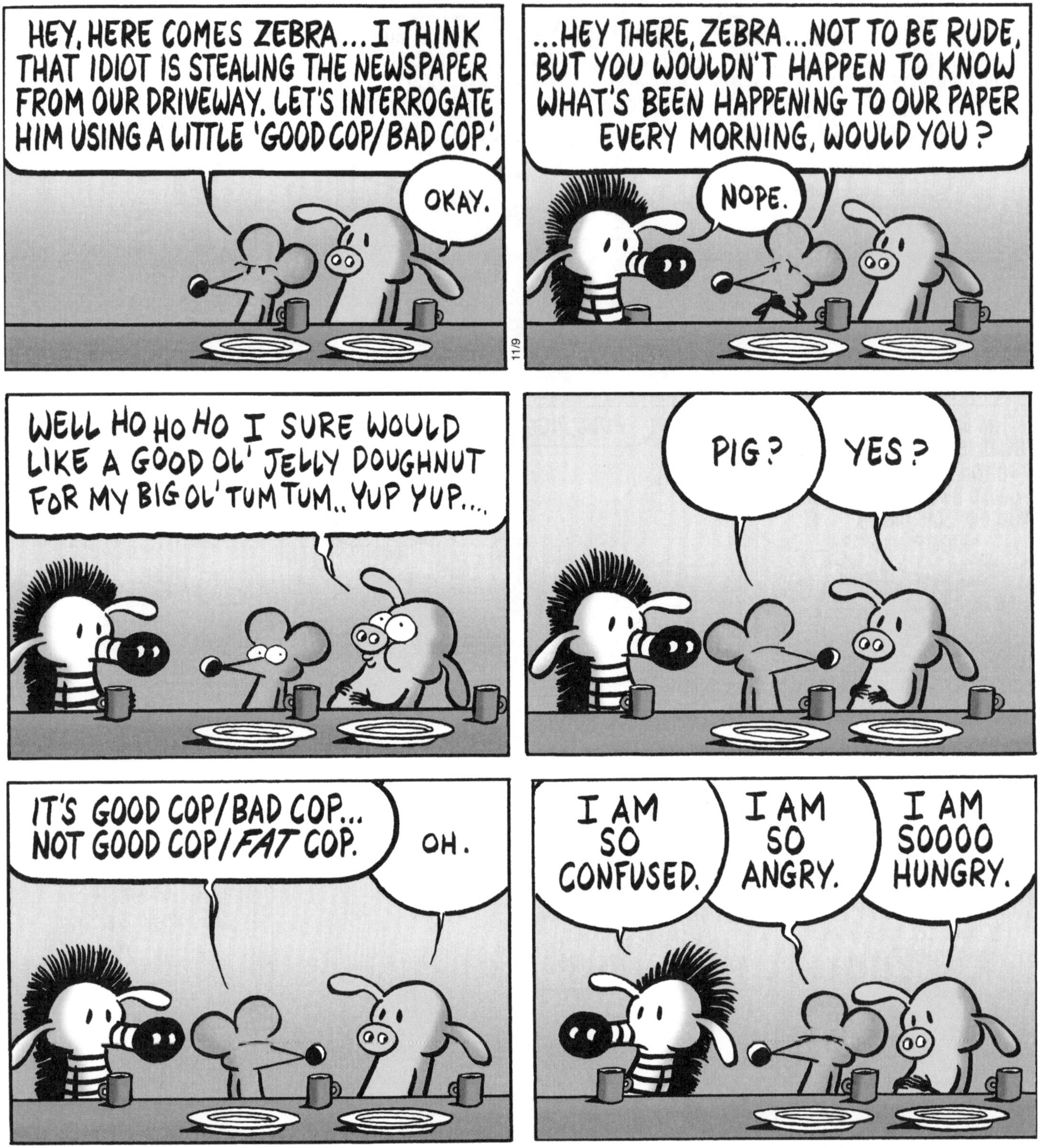
HEY, HERE COMES ZEBRA...I THINK THAT IDIOT IS STEALING THE NEWSPAPER FROM OUR DRIVEWAY. LET'S INTERROGATE HIM USING A LITTLE 'GOOD COP/BAD COP.'
OKAY.
...HEY THERE, ZEBRA...NOT TO BE RUDE, BUT YOU WOULDN'T HAPPEN TO KNOW WHAT'S BEEN HAPPENING TO OUR PAPER EVERY MORNING, WOULD YOU?
NOPE.
WELL HO HO HO I SURE WOULD LIKE A GOOD OL' JELLY DOUGHNUT FOR MY BIG OL' TUM TUM.. YUP YUP....
PIG?
YES?
IT'S GOOD COP/BAD COP... NOT GOOD COP/*FAT* COP.
OH.
I AM SO CONFUSED.
I AM SO ANGRY.
I AM SOOOO HUNGRY.
11/9

WELL, IT LOOKS LIKE I'M GONNA HAVE TO FIND A NEW MORNING COFFEE PLACE.

WHY?

BECAUSE THE PLACE I GO TO HIRED BACK AN OLD EMPLOYEE I CAN'T STAND.

HOW BIG A DIFFERENCE CAN ONE EMPLOYEE MAKE?

YOU'LL GET YOUR CHANGE IF I *SAY* YOU'LL GET YOUR CHANGE.

Joe's ROASTERY

HI. GIMME A DECAF NONFAT 200 DEGREE NO FOAM MOCHA.

REMEMBER THAT OLD 'BURGER KING' AD WHERE THOSE HAPPY EMPLOYEES SING, "SPECIAL ORDERS DON'T UPSET US"?

Joe's ROASTERY

YEAH.

WELL, THEY UPSET THE @#☆# OUT OF ME.

Joe's ROASTERY

GIVE ME YOUR MANAGER.

AND UPSET HIM TOO? NO THANK YOU.

Joe's ROASTERY

I JUST DID MY FINANCES AND FIGURED OUT THAT EVERY DAY I GO TO WORK, I LOSE MONEY.

HOW CAN THAT BE?

THE PRICE OF GAS. IT COSTS ME MORE TO GO TO AND FROM WORK THAN WORK ACTUALLY PAYS ME.

SO THE KEY TO FINANCIAL SECURITY IS NOW..

UNEMPLOYMENT!!

THE DREAM HAS COME TRUE.

WE WERE SO AHEAD OF OUR TIME.

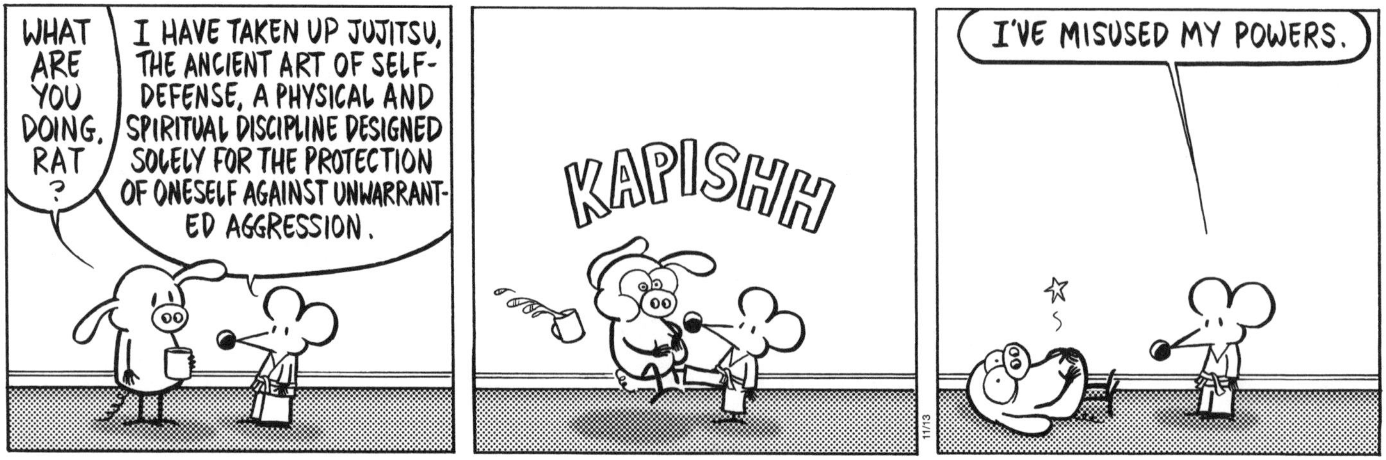
WHAT ARE YOU DOING, RAT?
I HAVE TAKEN UP JUJITSU, THE ANCIENT ART OF SELF-DEFENSE, A PHYSICAL AND SPIRITUAL DISCIPLINE DESIGNED SOLELY FOR THE PROTECTION OF ONESELF AGAINST UNWARRANTED AGGRESSION.
KAPISHH
I'VE MISUSED MY POWERS.
11/13

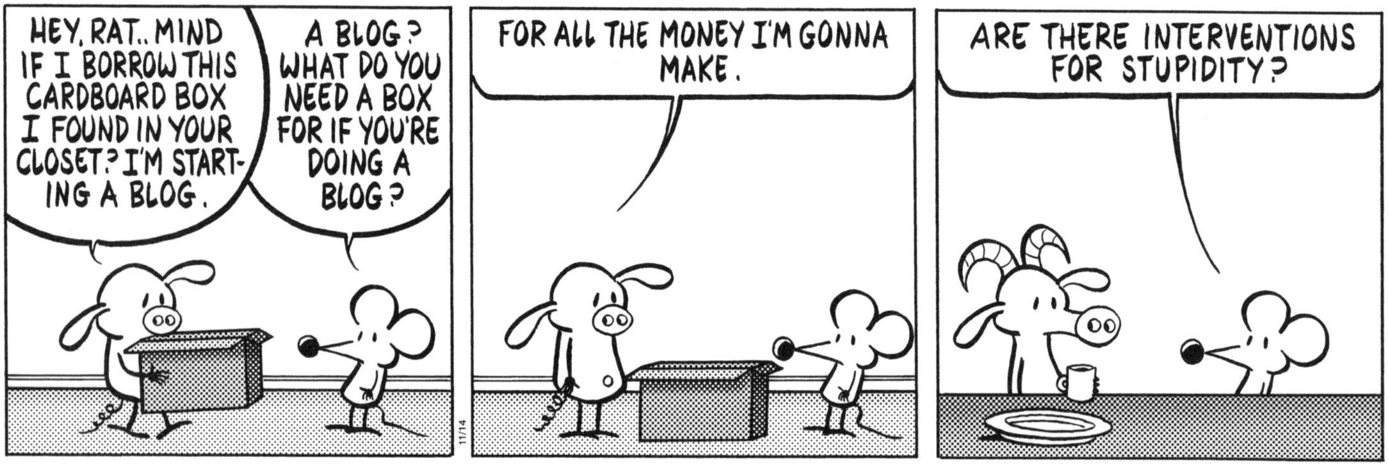
HEY, RAT.. MIND IF I BORROW THIS CARDBOARD BOX I FOUND IN YOUR CLOSET? I'M STARTING A BLOG.
A BLOG? WHAT DO YOU NEED A BOX FOR IF YOU'RE DOING A BLOG?
11/14
FOR ALL THE MONEY I'M GONNA MAKE.
ARE THERE INTERVENTIONS FOR STUPIDITY?

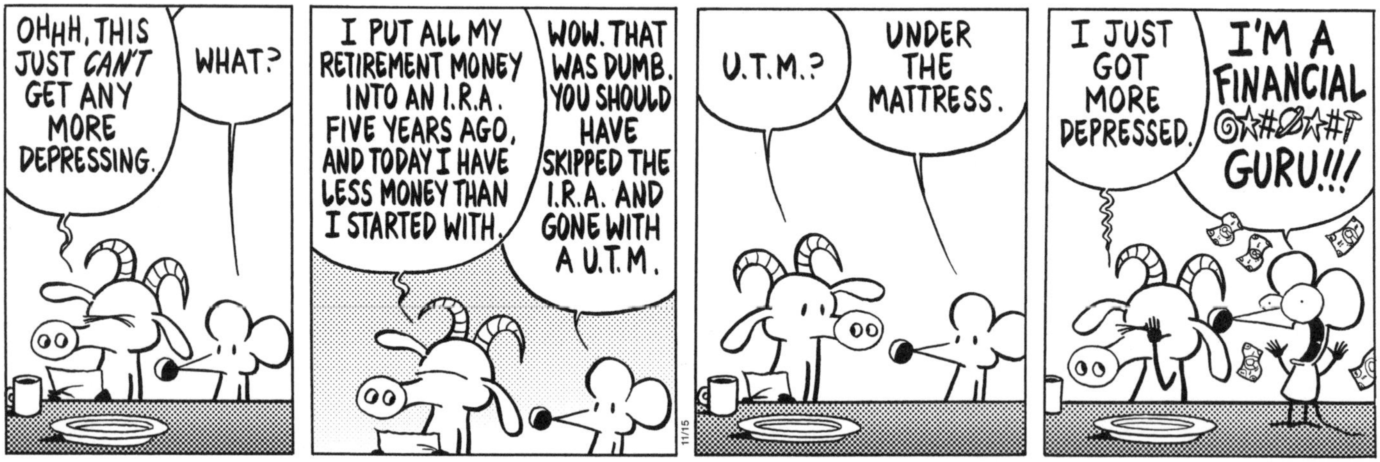
OHHH, THIS JUST *CAN'T* GET ANY MORE DEPRESSING.
WHAT?
I PUT ALL MY RETIREMENT MONEY INTO AN I.R.A. FIVE YEARS AGO, AND TODAY I HAVE LESS MONEY THAN I STARTED WITH.
WOW. THAT WAS DUMB. YOU SHOULD HAVE SKIPPED THE I.R.A. AND GONE WITH A U.T.M.
11/15
U.T.M.?
UNDER THE MATTRESS.
I JUST GOT MORE DEPRESSED.
I'M A FINANCIAL
GURU!!!

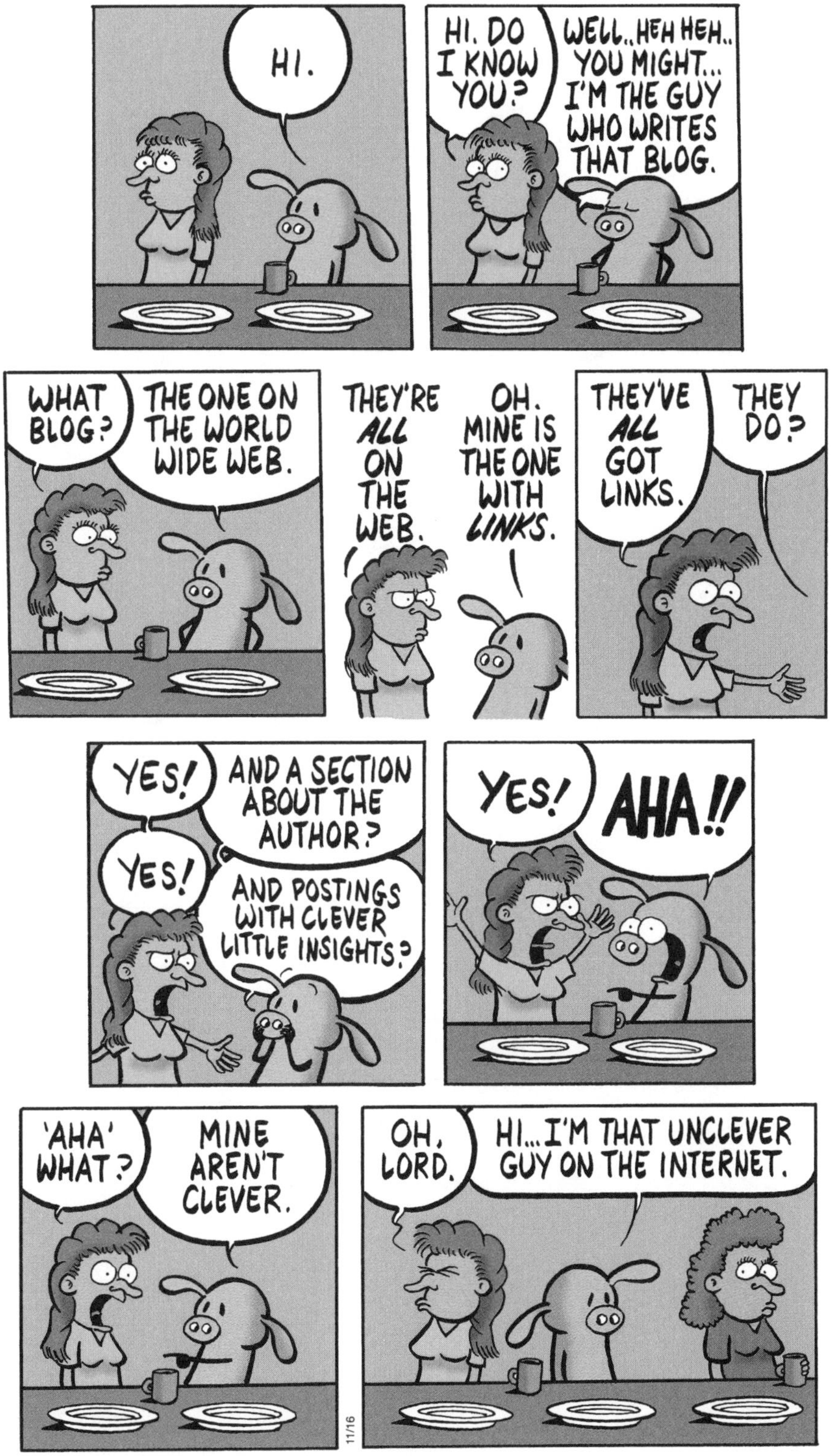
HI.
HI. DO I KNOW YOU?
WELL.. HEH HEH.. YOU MIGHT... I'M THE GUY WHO WRITES THAT BLOG.
WHAT BLOG?
THE ONE ON THE WORLD WIDE WEB.
THEY'RE ALL ON THE WEB.
OH. MINE IS THE ONE WITH LINKS.
THEY'VE ALL GOT LINKS.
THEY DO?
YES!
AND A SECTION ABOUT THE AUTHOR?
YES!
AND POSTINGS WITH CLEVER LITTLE INSIGHTS?
YES!
AHA!!
'AHA' WHAT?
MINE AREN'T CLEVER.
11/16
OH, LORD.
HI... I'M THAT UNCLEVER GUY ON THE INTERNET.